CARING *for* Souls

COUNSELING UNDER
THE AUTHORITY OF SCRIPTURE

Harry Shields
A N D
Gary Bredfeldt

Library of Congress Cataloging-in-Publication Data

Shields, Harry, 1946–
    Caring for souls: counseling under the authority of scripture /
    Harry Shields and Gary Bredfeldt. p. cm.
    Includes biographical references and index.
    ISBN 0-8024-3741-9
    1. Pastoral psychology 2. Pastoral counseling 3. Counseling—
Religious aspects—Christianity. I. Bredfeldt, Gary J. II. Title.

BV4012 .S48 2001
253.5'2—dc21
                                                           00-064741

1 3 5 7 9 10 8 6 4 2
Printed in the United States of America

For the glory of our Lord and Savior, Jesus Christ,
and
to Carol, my wife, my friend, and one whose wisdom I value greatly.

—Harry

To my parents,
Lois and John Bredfeldt,
who have taught me, both in word and deed,
the meaning of genuine Christian love
as they consistently live out their faith in Jesus Christ.

—Gary

CONTENTS

ACKNOWLEDGMENTS

While teaching a graduate school course in pastoral care and counseling, I was struck by the selectivity that students employed when describing their ministries. They used glowing terms to portray the joy they experienced when preparing and delivering weekly sermons. They spoke with a certain degree of confidence when they talked about their successes in crafting mission statements, creating programs, and leading the church into new dimensions of change and growth. But when those same students talked about the work of pastoral care and counseling, they expressed obvious apprehension. When I asked them to elaborate on the reasons for their reluctance to engage in the work of soul care, the majority said that they simply did not know what to do with people who were depressed, fearful, anxiety-ridden, or in conflict with spouses and children. Obviously they were taking a class in caregiving, but they admitted they would rather refer "people-problems" to other counselors.

I am not a professional counselor by training. However, I am convinced that pastors have been all too willing to surrender their role as spiritual counselors. I affirm the contribution that professional counseling can have in the community at large. But the apostle Peter's exhortation for pastoral leaders to shepherd God's flock still stands. Pastors will want to continue to prepare biblically sound messages and manage church tasks as effectively as possible.

However, these same pastors must also be concerned about spiritual counsel that enables every believer to live a Christ-centered life that is shaped by the truths of God's Word.

I am grateful to my friend and colleague, Gary Bredfeldt, for agreeing to coauthor a book on spiritual counsel. We had several lively discussions regarding the role of psychological theory in the care and cure of souls. But both of us agree that the Bible must be preeminent in all aspects of the caregiving process.

I am especially grateful to Greg Thornton, Jim Bell, and the staff at Moody Press for believing in the importance of a book that discusses both the theory and the practice of pastoral care. Cheryl Dunlop has been a very special ally in putting together a final product. Her attention to detail and her probing questions have forced me to think clearly about ideas that I have sometimes taken for granted. Cheryl, I have been greatly blessed by your editorial skills.

I also want to acknowledge my gratitude to Dr. Robert Woodburn and the Faculty Development Committee of the Moody Bible Institute. Their willingness to grant me a sabbatical during the fall semester of 1999 greatly aided me in meeting publishing deadlines. Likewise, John Koessler and Dwight Perry shouldered additional academic responsibilities so that I could devote more time to writing.

Special thanks go to my wife, Carol. She has always encouraged me to put my ideas in print, believing that I had something worth saying. She took time to read the manuscript and offered several helpful suggestions. She is my best friend and my most cherished confidant.

Harry E. Shields

$\mathcal{A}$s a child growing up in the Chicago area, I always enjoyed playing baseball. Before every game, one of my favorite baseball coaches often told us, "Baseball is a team sport. It takes nine players to win a ball game." His goal was to help us all remember that we were important in the game regardless of the position we played on the field. Like baseball, writing is a collaborative effort. Books are not the result of one or two persons' labors, but are the product of a team of individuals. This book is no exception. Although two names are listed as the authors, many could be included as contributing members of this writing team.

I am grateful to my teaching colleague and friend, Harry Shields, who coauthored this book. When he shared his vision for this book and asked me to take part in its writing, I was honored. Harry is a wonderful communicator and a competent pastoral counselor. Harry is one of those people who encourages, prods, challenges, and commends. Harry, thanks. You are a blessing in my life.

Some team members are less visible, but were still essential to the work. To the Moody Press editorial staff, my sincere thanks for your ministry. It was again a joy to work with Cheryl Dunlop as she meticulously edited the text, sent e-mails with suggestions for changes, and kept the project on schedule. I am grateful to Greg Thornton and Jim Bell, who bring leadership to Moody Press. Gentlemen, thank you for your confidence and clear sense of mission at MP. Thank you as well to Rachel Powell, who read some of the manuscript, offering suggestions and editorial changes. Joy Wilfong also assisted in typing the "Works Cited and Consulted" section.

My appreciation goes to the administration of the Moody Bible Institute, especially Dr. Robert Woodburn, who provided a sabbatical leave to work on this book. Thanks as well to Marta Alvarado and Wayne Widder, who helped to cover many of my administrative responsibilities while I was on sabbatical.

Finally, I offer a special thank-you to my wife and children. Marlene, my devoted wife, thank you for your encouragement to keep on writing in those days when I grew weary. Lynne, Stephen, Michael, and Amy, thank you for allowing Dad so much of your time to write. Each of you encouraged me in this project.

Heavenly Father, may You be honored and pleased.

Gary Bredfeldt

$\mathcal{I}$NTRODUCTION

$\mathcal{W}$e are not theorists. We are doers—practitioners of pastoral ministry. But after several years of doing pastoral ministry and responding to the needs of our parishioners, we have both turned to the role of professor. Now we train a new generation of practitioners. As such, we want to connect theory with practice. While we are trained in, knowledgeable of, and teachers of counseling and personality theory, we are, by nature, praxis people (*praxis:* the point where theory meets practice). This book is a praxis book.

Most recently, for more than twenty-five years of combined ministry, we have served as professors at the Moody Bible Institute in Chicago, Illinois. One of us (Dr. Gary Bredfeldt) is the chair of the Educational Ministries Department and the other (Dr. Harry Shields) is the chair of the Pastoral Studies Department. We mention this not to promote this book, or ourselves, but to establish our unreserved commitment to the Bible and to ministry. This book grows out of these two commitments. Our goal has been to produce a theoretically sound and yet highly practical work for use in pastoral care and counseling ministry. It is important to us that it be rooted in the authoritative bedrock of Scripture.

We have envisioned two types of readers. The first is the student preparing for a pastoral ministry role. The second is the person, lay or professional, who is engaged in pastoral care in the local church or a church-related agency. But we hope others will find the book informative and personally helpful as well.

As we surveyed the landscape of Christian counseling resources, it became apparent to us that most of the books in the field could be fit into a few categories. Some offer highly technical summaries of major counseling and personality theories. Others offer practical counseling techniques but many times without an adequate focus on the theoretical and theological foundations behind those techniques. Still other books in the field focus on the debate over the use of psychological theory in Christian counseling ministry and seek to sway their readers to a particular position on that issue. Although we have written a book that has a theoretical component, offers practical advice, and weighs in on the psychology/theology debate, our intent is different. Our goal is to equip for ministry. It is to prepare spiritual counselors or directors who are able to offer meaningful help to fellow believers. It is a book designed to equip readers to do the work of ministry.

This is an introductory text on what we call "Spiritual Counseling." You will find that this book is divided into two sections. The first section establishes "The Foundations of Spiritual Counsel" (chapters 1–8). The second section equips the reader with tools for engaging in "The Practice of Spiritual Counsel" (chapters 9–16). In chapters 1 through 3 we seek to establish biblical and theological boundaries to guide the reader's evaluation of counseling and personality theories. In chapters 4 through 8 we present and evaluate those theories in what we hope is a simple, accurate, and illustrative manner. Then in chapters 9 through 16 we seek to show the reader how those theories can be used in the real world of ministry in order to care for people.

Throughout this text we use stories and case studies to illustrate many of the concepts we present. Of course, we have changed names in these accounts to protect the identity and privacy of individuals. We use stories because they speak with power and illustrate cold, factual information with a real-life quality.

It is our sincere prayer that this book will contribute to your effectiveness in counseling ministry. We offer it as a contribution to the always challenging task of spiritual counsel and pastoral care.

— *Part One* —

THE FOUNDATIONS
OF SPIRITUAL
DIRECTION

BIBLICAL AND THEOLOGICAL FOUNDATIONS OF HUMAN PERSONALITY

— *Chapter 1* —

SOLA SCRIPTURA:
The Matter of Biblical Authority

The teacher's appraisal read with a clarity that Kathy and John Carpenter could not ignore.

> Matthew fails to give attention to details and makes careless mistakes. He fidgets and squirms excessively in his seat. Matthew often blurts out answers before questions have been completed. He has a problem of talking excessively and he often loses things necessary for daily tasks. Matthew often leaves his seat when remaining in his seat is expected, has difficulty waiting his turn, and sometimes bullies others.

The assessment went on to recommend testing for ADD or *Attention Deficit Disorder*. Matthew's teacher explained to Kathy and John that no medical tests exist for ADD, but various diagnostic guidelines have been established. She showed them the guidelines. Comparing Matthew's behavior to those guidelines, it seemed to Kathy and John that their son might have ADD. In order to find out, the teacher encouraged them to visit the school psychologist. But the Carpenters remained unsure how to proceed. They were aware that a debate over ADD was raging—a debate over its existence, diagnosis, and treatment. Given the generic nature of the guidelines for determining ADD, they were concerned that their son could be misdiagnosed and wrongly labeled.

They were concerned also about the treatment that Matthew would receive. Ritalin is a drug used to treat children and adults with ADD. Although they knew that Ritalin enables individuals to focus their attention, they also had read of its side effects that alter mood and temperament. Not knowing the long-term effects of the drug, they were uncertain that they wanted to pursue a personality-altering remedy.

As evangelical Christians, they had another concern, the use of a secular school psychologist and psychological treatment. Would their acceptance of Matthew's diagnosis and the use of Ritalin be consistent with their stance that Christ and His Word are sufficient, or would they be compromising with the world by accepting a secular solution to Matthew's problems? How exactly should Christians relate to the research, findings, theories, and treatments of psychology? These questions motivated the Carpenters to contact their pastor. With a sincere longing for answers, the Carpenters sought his advice. Unfortunately, the conversation that followed left them even more confused.

After hearing their concerns, he turned in his Bible to 2 Peter 1:3–4, where he read,

> His divine power has given us everything we need for life and godliness through our knowledge of him who called us by his own glory and goodness. Through these he has given us his very great and precious promises, so that through them you may participate in the divine nature and escape the corruption in the world caused by evil desires.

He then asked, "Kathy and John, I know you believe God's Word and seek to follow it. Let me ask you, do you believe that when God said 'everything' in this passage He meant *everything*?" John and Kathy nodded in agreement. He proceeded to tell them that they "should not pollute the pure stream of God's Word with the impure stream of secular psychological ideas." Instead, he told them, they should find the work of Christ and His Word sufficient for their son's scholastic problems. Finally, he said, "Matthew's behavior is a problem of disobedience to authority and a lack of self-discipline." He then gave them a book on child discipline that he said advocated a biblical approach to their son's problems.

At first his words sounded logical. Certainly, Christ is the sufficient answer to all human need. What Christian could or would question that? And, of course, they believed the Bible was relevant to their lives. Still they could not avoid a deep sense that his comments were overly simplistic and had a pat-answer tone to them. Furthermore, something was lacking in his reasoning and in the consistency of his actions. On the one hand, he advised them not to take the counsel of the secular school psychologist, yet, only moments before, they had watched him take a drug called dihydroergotamine (DHE) used in the treatment of migraine headaches. Sure, the tablet of DHE was only for a headache, but was not his use of this pain reliever similar to their son's potential use of Ritalin? Both drugs help to maintain concentration in order to deal with daily tasks.

As they glanced around the room, another inconsistency struck them. They noted that one of their pastor's bookcases stored several books on management, communication theory, and sermon delivery. Nearby, in another bookcase, were books dealing with group dynamics and interpersonal relationships. They wondered how he could justify his use of "secular psychological theorists" when it came to managing the church, leading a small group Bible study, or delivering his weekly message. How could he use these practical applications of psychological research while claiming that *everything* he needed for his life is contained in the pages of Scripture? Didn't he just say that everything meant everything? How did he deal with this contradiction? Surely, he could not deny that truth is found outside the Bible, for he was employing extrabiblical truth in his own life and ministry. Maybe he just wasn't aware of the inconsistencies between his actions and his position when it came to the matter of psychology and its use by Christians.

Although names have been changed in this story, it is true. And it is a good illustration of the confusion brought out by questions of psychology and counseling in the church.

As another example of how theories play out in the real world, meet Carl Hartman, lone pastor at a Midwestern church of one hundred and fifty attendees located on the edge of one of the largest communities in his state. While joined by many laypersons in the work of the ministry, Carl still finds that serving as a pastor is stretching. As solo pastor, Carl must wear several hats—teacher, preacher, leader, administrator, and counselor to name a few. Preaching demands that he be a Bible scholar and communicator. Teaching ministry requires that he be both a student of the Bible and capable facilitator of learning. Administrative tasks and organizational leadership duties necessitate effective management skills. In each of these areas, Carl has gained some measure of confidence and competence. But it is his role as counselor that presents the greatest challenge.

There are simply more human struggles and tales of tragedy than Carl feels equipped to address. He hears of so many needs and broken lives, so many stressed marriages and shattered families, so many neglected children and wayward adolescents that his heart is burdened daily. He wonders how to help—how to bring counsel to those whom he serves. How will he give the spiritual counsel they require to reorder their chaotic and sorrowful lives? Of course there is one thing of which Carl is certain: The truth that gives sure direction is found in the pages of his Bible. He is equally certain of his commitment to the authority of the Bible in his ministry of providing spiritual counsel.

In an effort to more effectively care for his congregation, Carl read several books on counseling. Some offered helpful insights into the pastoral care of people. But others concerned him. One book in particular caused him to contemplate. In it, the author questioned the validity of using the tools and theories of psychology in counseling ministry. Although Carl recognized that this author was advocating an extreme position, he did raise an important issue—the appropriate use of the social science field of psychology in caring for people. From his reading, Carl came to understand that several views exist on this topic. Some writers advocated an almost indiscriminate use of psychology within a counseling ministry. Others proposed a more moderate view in which psychological theories and treatments are selected within the parameters of biblical teaching. Still others entirely opposed any use of psychology in the emotional and spiritual healing of people. For them, only the Bible is to be used.

As a pastor dedicated to the goal of being thoroughly biblical in his ministry, what viewpoint should he adopt? He is committed to serve Christ and His church and to faithfully submit his ministry to the authority of God's Word, so how should he proceed? Should he take the "antipsychology" view of the so-called "biblical counseling" apologists, which, on the surface, appears to be the least risky position because of its Bible-only stance? Or should he adopt the "integrationist" position of the "Christian counseling" authors with its wide array of people-helping techniques and practical methods, many of which are drawn from the research of secular psychologists?

THE ISSUE OF BIBLICAL AUTHORITY

The case studies of Matthew Carpenter and Carl Hartman raise some important questions. What exactly does it mean to live one's life under the authority of Scripture? Does it mean that we are to find all truth for life in the Bible alone? What does it mean to embrace the doctrine of biblical authority? How is a commitment to biblical authority relevant to the ministry of counseling? Does it mean that the Bible alone is our basis for counseling? Could there be some other understanding of biblical authority that would lead to greater consistency in daily living and counseling ministry? Is there a way to tap the many sources of human knowledge and use those understandings in ministry while, at the same time, remaining true to God's Word? These are among the foundational questions that those who seek to provide spiritual counsel to others must consider.

The debate over how to address human needs and how to counsel people in a way that is consistent with Scripture is not simply a theoretical matter. It is a human issue. We must first recognize that real people with real problems come to pastoral or lay counselors seeking spiritual counsel, biblical wisdom, and practical solutions to life's many hurts and stresses. What may seem simply an interesting debate in an Internet chat room or an "Introduction to Counseling" course at a Christian seminary is, in reality, a highly practical and people-impacting concern.

We offer this book as a practical resource for those who seek to help and counsel others. We begin with a chapter on the authority of the Bible because, first and foremost, we are committed to the authority of Scripture. In fact, we have subtitled this book *Counseling Under the Authority of Scripture* because of the supreme place we give to God's Word in doing the work of ministry. What we offer in this chapter is a review of the doctrine of biblical authority and practical help in applying that doctrine in the care of God's people. We believe that this is the correct starting point for those of us who desire to give spiritual counsel to the men and women who attend our churches. By beginning with the subject of biblical authority, clearly defined and illustrated, the lines of demarcation necessary for the evaluation, selection, and employment of various approaches to counseling and treatment can be established. To do this with accuracy will require a brief but enlightening look into history.

A Historic Debate: The Compatibility of Human Reason and Divine Revelation

As strange as it may seem, we will find the clearest direction for our thinking regarding the matter of psychology and its use in counseling ministry not in books written in the field of counseling, but in church history and theology textbooks. This is because, while the debate over the use of modern psychological theory and therapy methods in counseling God's people is a contemporary issue, the fundamental questions behind that debate are actually centuries old. We would frame these questions as follows:.

- How should knowledge gained through human reasoning be related to the truths communicated in the sacred Scriptures?

- What measure of authority should be granted to knowledge derived from such extrabiblical sources as philosophy, the church, personal experience, science, or, in our day, the social sciences?
- How should such knowledge be used in ministry?

A brief survey of church history reveals that these questions have troubled Christians in other times as well. Since the very early years of the church, Christians have had to wrestle with the issue of how human reason relates to matters of faith. Is there a place for human reasoning in addressing human problems, or are the only true answers found in the realm of faith and the pages of the Bible? Can we rely on human reason, or is it deceptive, leading only to a devilish wisdom and to corrupt misunderstandings? Three perspectives have been proposed.

Reason Corrupts Faith

Some have held that human reasoning and learning are the polar opposites of divine knowledge and faith. They would suggest that human reasoning corrupts a pure faith. Speaking specifically of the relationship of secular philosophical thought to Christian theological understanding, Tertullian (160–230) expressed a view that no relationship could exist between Christianity and Greek philosophy. He wrote:

> What is there in common between Athens and Jerusalem?
> What between the Academy and the Church?
> What between heretics and Christians? (7)

For Tertullian, human reasoning and learning, as expressed in philosophy, had nothing to contribute to Christianity and the Christian life. It was plain to him that the Christian should completely avoid dialogue with the philosopher. Christian theology was seen as heavenly and full of truth, whereas philosophy was deemed to be worldly and empty of truth. To use secular thinking in any form was to pollute the pure message of Scripture and to cavort with paganism (Erickson 40).

Trained in speaking and law, Tertullian was a great apologist for the early Western church. From his pen came passionate defenses of the persecuted Christians. Probably his most famous observation was with regard to the ineffectiveness of the martyrdom of Christians by the Romans. Tertullian wrote "the blood of the martyrs is the seed of the church." But it is also true that Tertullian often wrote with what one author calls "a fiery and fighting spirit" that sometimes skewed his thinking toward intolerance. At times he took a militant separationist approach to the world and to those with whom he disagreed (Cairns 22, 117).

Later the *reason corrupts faith* position was reaffirmed, albeit with more grace, in the theology of Kuyper (1837–1920), Berkouwer (1903–1996), and Van Til (1895–1987), all of whom believed that sinful man was incapable of any knowledge, spiritual or scientific, and that the only facts that exist are "theistic facts." They held that human reasoning leads nowhere but to error. Facts derived from the natural world are isolated and futile. Because of the human tendencies toward self-centeredness, self-worship, and corruption, such facts merely generate a human wisdom—the antithesis of divine truth. So men, professing to be wise, become as fools (Rom. 1:22). Only divine revelation, made known specifically in the pages of Scripture, could be trusted to give valid understanding. Human reasoning is, from this viewpoint, hopelessly distorted and erroneous. On this basis, Christians should have nothing to do with the world's wisdom and claims to truth (Demarest 135–56).

Reason Supports Faith

Some have argued that reason can serve to support faith and that a place exists for human learning apart from the study of the Bible alone. This view, while recognizing the primacy of special revelation, also recognized a valid place for knowledge gained through natural revelation. Aurelius Augustine, bishop of Hippo (354–430), espoused this alternative to Tertullian's antagonistic understanding of the relationship of human reason to divine revelation.

Augustine acknowledged the presence of considerable truth in Greek philosophy. He believed truth was present there because of the universal disclosure of God through general revelation or things that are made. For Augustine, human reasoning served to elucidate and support Christian theological understandings. Augustine considered human intellect to be a divine gift that could be used to better understand the Christian faith. For Augustine, reason is an essential support to genuine faith, but it is faith that is foundational to ultimate understanding. To put it another way, "thinking is prior to believing" and "believing prior to understanding." Augustine saw an interrelationship between reason and faith. Both were to play an essential role. Reason leads to faith and faith completes reason by granting understanding (Demarest 34–42).

Augustine coined the now famous phrase "All truth is God's truth," meaning that truth, wherever it is discovered and whoever discovers it, has its origins in God. Augustine differentiated between two kinds of truths, termed *sapienta* (wisdom) and *scientia* (knowledge). The first is eternal and changeless, while the second is temporal and changing. Augustine held that the revealed truth of God's Word was sapienta truth and the discoveries of human reason were scientia truths (*NPNF* 3:161–68). Because of the crippling effects of sin, humans are unable to intuit the eternal and changeless truths apart from divine illumination. Humans can, however, discover truths in the temporal realm. Although such knowledge is still distorted by the limitations of sin and the darkness of the natural mind, the gift of common grace (not a term used by Augustine) and the image of God in human beings enables people to come to a partial understanding of eternal truth. Of course, Augustine would stress, any human understanding must be completed by the divine revelation of Scripture (Demarest 27).

Augustine held that human reasoning does not create truth but, instead, discovers it (*LCC*, 6:261). God is the creator of all truth, and men and women are merely discoverers of that truth—His truth. Although recognizing the possibility of human beings reasoning to truthful understandings through general revelation, Augustine held firmly to the complete dependability of the Bible as God's final authority. According to Augustine, God is not known in a personal and intimate way through the induction of truth from the finite world and sense perception. God is known by faith in Christ as presented in the revealed written Word of God (Cairns 156–61).

Reason Establishes Faith

The third view of the role of human reasoning in the Christian faith was that of Thomas Aquinas (1225–1274) who held that, through reason alone, one could establish the existence of God and His divine attributes. Furthermore, Aquinas believed Christianity to be a reasonable faith that could be established by use of rational inductive thinking without direct reference to the Bible. Aquinas is best known for his rational arguments for the existence of God. Aquinas argued that, because of an untarnished *imago Dei* (image of God) in man, both non-Christians and Christians were capable of reasoning from the empirical data of nature to the God of the Bible. Using the principle of cause and effect, Aquinas established five arguments for God's existence. He argued that God is the first mover of all that is in motion, that God is the first cause of all effects, that God is the first being of all beings, that God is the perfect source of all morality, and that God is the intelligent designer behind the order and harmony of nature (Demarest 34–42).

Working from an Aristotelian philosophic framework, Aquinas argued that reality was divided into a hierarchy of two orders. The higher order was the supernatural realm, the lower order the natural realm. Aquinas considered the human mind to be the passageway between those worlds, and reason the key to the door that opened that passage. Aquinas spoke of a "twofold truth of divine things" (Demarest 34). The first he was referring to was truth communicated directly from God through Scripture and the second, truth reasoned by natural man through the study of what God has made and human logic. Thus, Aquinas divided truth into knowledge that is revealed and knowledge that is natural. Aquinas believed that human beings could reason, through rational inductive processes, from what has been made and from the effects of God's actions, to empirical knowledge of God, but that reasoning would not lead to a saving knowledge of Christ. Salvation knowledge, Aquinas held, came through the specific revelation of the Scriptures authoritatively interpreted by the Roman Catholic Church (Demarest 35).

Aquinas attempted to harmonize the knowledge of the natural realm with knowledge of the realm of revelation. He believed that this was possible because the knowledge from both realms is from God and all truth fits into a single totality. In this way Aquinas was an early integrationist. But in the final analysis, Aquinas's emphasis on knowledge gained in two separate realms through two different methods led to a separation of knowledge into two compartments, the sacred and the secular. Later a final divorce would occur in the thinking of many, one that continues to the present. It is a divorce not intended by Aquinas, but one to which he ultimately contributed. That was a divorce of faith from reason, a compartmentalization into scientific truth and theological truth instead of understanding both to be parts of a whole that is unified by God, the Author of all that is true (Cairns 251–60).

Although Aquinas should be commended for stressing the rationality of the Christian faith, he must be criticized for his inflated view of the power of human reason. He failed to recognize that not only has the Fall affected the spiritual status of men and women before God, but it also depreciated human cognitive abilities. We do not understand clearly because fallen man is cognitively crippled. We miss the true God and fabricate gods of our own making, ending up worshiping the creature rather than the Creator (Rom. 1:25).

In summary, the pre-Reformation church espoused three primary views regarding the role of human reason in the life of the believer. One view (Tertullian) called for an absolute separation from worldly wisdom and embraced a very low view of the worth of human intellectual inquiry. The second was a more moderate position (Augustine) that placed Scripture as the final authority over all knowledge gained from human study and reasoning. The Bible was not the only source of knowledge, but it was the norm by which such knowledge is judged. The third view (Aquinas) magnified human reasoning powers. The Bible was depreciated in its authoritative role, sharing its authority with philosophy and human reasoning. From this third position a full-fledged divorce

TABLE 1-1
Faith and Reason: Three Historic Perspectives

	Reason Corrupts Faith	Reason Supports Faith	Reason Establishes Faith
Proponents	Tertullian (160–230 A.D.)	Augustine (354–430 A.D.)	Aquinas (1225–1274 A.D.)
Key Concepts	Human reasoning is hopelessly distorted by sin and leads to corrupted ideas. Two types of wisdom exist, heavenly and worldly. Christian theology is heavenly wisdom, whereas Greek philosophy is worldly wisdom. Human reasoning will always lead one to errant views of life. Human wisdom is, therefore, the antithesis of divine truth. Facts derived from the natural world are isolated and futile. The only truths that can be used in daily living are "theistic facts." The Bible alone is truthful. Only the Bible should be used to discover truth.	Human reason can secure genuine and truthful understandings of the world because of God's general revelation in His creation. All truth is God's truth, whether found in Scripture or in the created order. There is only one source of truth, God. Human reasoning can serve to support the Christian faith and is not inherently in conflict with the truths of the Bible. There are two kinds of truth, *sapienta* (wisdom) and *scientia* (knowledge). The first type of truth can only be discovered in the pages of the Bible. Believers and unbelievers, through the use of inductive thinking, can discover the second type.	Rational inductive thinking processes can be used to establish the Christian faith. Through the use of apologetics, without direct reference to the Bible, one can come to an empirical knowledge of God. Through a study of visible effects, one can reason backward to discover their cause. This reasoning process leads to an understanding of the first cause, God Himself. The human mind is a passageway between two worlds, the natural and the supernatural (secular and sacred). Careful application of the rules of logic can overcome the limitation of sin and free the mind to think about truth accurately.
Implications	Christians should have nothing to do with philosophy and cannot trust human reason. Human reasoning pollutes the pure stream of scriptural truth. Incorporation of human reasoning into the Christian faith will produce a false wisdom and will, in fact, lead to foolishness. Christians should reject all aspects of philosophy rather than risk the corruption of their faith.	Christians can pursue truth in all domains of human learning including philosophical study. Truth and error come to us as a mixture; therefore, Scripture must be used as the final authority in evaluating truth claims. Saving faith can only be known through the truths revealed in the Bible. One cannot reason his way to God. That knowledge comes through the Word of God.	Human reason is exalted and the impact of the Fall on human thinking minimized. One need not be a Christian to come to the knowledge of the truth, provided careful, logical, inductive reasoning is employed. Two kinds of knowledge are possible, scientific and theological. While both find their source in God, one need not study theology to understand science or science to understand theology.

between faith and reason developed, leading to a compartmentalization of truth into secular and sacred categories. In these three basic views, we have the essence of the debate over the place of human reason and theory in the practice of ministry. But we must now turn the page of our historic review to the period of the Protestant Reformation where the matter was crystallized.

It is plain from our brief discussion of Tertullian, Augustine, and Aquinas that the issue of the use of human reason, human discovery, and extrabiblical authorities is not new. Three views were identified. Although these early followers of Christ debated the place of philosophy and its authority in Christian thought and life, others who came later debated the authority of the Roman church. In doing so, these church reformers sought to return the church to its earlier commitment to the Bible as the ultimate standard for all matters of faith and practice. Proclaiming God's Word to be the means by which all other authorities are finally judged, the Reformers proclaimed the doctrine of "Sola Scriptura" (Cairns 333).

What did the Reformers mean by "Sola Scriptura" or "Scripture alone"? Did they mean that the Bible was the sole source of truth and that all truth claims that were derived from a reasoned study of the natural world were corrupt? Did they mean, alternatively, that the Bible alone is the authoritative standard by which all matters of faith and practice are ultimately judged? Did the Reformers seek to return to the more narrow separationist understanding of Tertullian or the more moderate view of Augustine? The answers to these questions are essential in establishing how Christians in ministry are to deal with concepts addressed by extrabiblical sources, including the ministry of counseling and the field of psychology.

"Sola Scriptura" was one of the basic tenets of the Reformation. Rejecting both the exaltation of reason and the Roman Church, the distinguishing conviction of the Reformers was their belief that the Scriptures alone were the ultimate and final authority in matters of faith and practice. They rejected the priority given by Aquinas to human reason and the church authorities in determining what it is true. Instead, they called for a return to the Bible as final authority (Demarest 43–60). Such central figures of Protestantism as Martin Luther, John Calvin, Huldrych Zwingli, Menno Simons (Mennonites), and Jacob Amman (Amish) agreed that only the Scriptures could be given the place of infallible authority against which the opinions of men, the church, and society were to be confirmed and conformed. Although each of these reformers recognized the immeasurable importance of "Sola Scriptura," they could not agree as to its application. Luther and Calvin represented one view of Sola Scriptura; Zwingli, Simons, and Ammann another.

Luther and Calvin

Drawing heavily on the writings of Augustine, both Martin Luther (1483–1546) and John Calvin (1509–1564) held that "Sola Scriptura" meant that the Bible was to be a measuring stick, a standard or norm, against which human thoughts and ideals were to be compared. They advocated a return to the views of Augustine regarding the place of human reason and the use of extrabiblical knowledge. They allowed for a twofold knowledge base, one drawn from the general revelation of God in the natural world, the other from God's special revelation in Christ and His written Word. Luther described this knowledge as "left-handed" and "right-handed" knowledge. Left-handed knowledge was the knowledge of the philosopher. It contained truth, but was incomplete and vague and could not save. Right-handed knowledge, by contrast, was evangelical in nature, gained from God's self-disclosure in the Bible and in Christ, and led to salvation. To Luther and Calvin, both were legitimate pursuits so long as the limitations of the first were acknowledged (Demarest 44, 51).

Luther argued against a proud reason and philosophic speculation that sought to dethrone God. He described *natural reason* as a gift from God appropriate to its appointed domain. He saw this reasoning ability as a quality that distinguished human beings from God's created beasts. It was this natural reasoning that enabled men and women to manage households, build cities, govern in civil affairs, invent, create, and discover. *Regenerate reason* is found in the Spirit-filled person. The Spirit enables the believer to interpret the Scriptures and sanctifies the believer's mind for heavenly service. *Arrogant reason* attempts to usurp God as authority. It seeks alternatives to the God of the Bible. It is driven by man's fallen nature and no longer seeks God as God. Thus, for Luther it is possible that through natural reason men could discover divine truths consistent with the Scripture. Those same persons can then distort that truth in an effort to deny God and seek, in pride and spiritual blindness, to enthrone some other god in the true God's place (Demarest 47).

When it came to Christian living, both Calvin and Luther allowed for Christians to integrate into their Christian practice what the Bible did not expressly prohibit. In other words, if the Bible did not speak against something or if something were not in opposition to a direct teaching of Scripture, it was deemed permissible.

In Calvin's view, the creation serves as a mirror in which the invisible attributes of God are reflected. God's handiwork, the precision and orderliness of His created world, and His providential care all point to God's existence and qualities. Because of the message of general revelation, nature is an open book that all persons, Christian or non-Christian, can read. It tells of God's existence, His eternal power, and His divine attributes. Calvin also recognized God's revelation in the detail and structure of the human body. Calvin believed that in the study of the human frame—particularly in its utility, functionality, and beauty—God's nature could be recognized. Calvin held that the evidences of the Godhead are so many in the structure of man that people need not go beyond their own bodies to discover the hand of God. But to Calvin, the knowledge gained through the study of the world or the body does not bring salvation or piety. Instead, because of sin's cloud, it merely condemns because humans reject the knowledge of God it bestows. Only Scripture can grant knowledge that leads to salvation. Nature merely offers human inquirers information, but the Word of God offers redemption (Cairns 334–40).

Zwingli, Simons, and Amman

While Calvin and Luther sought to establish the Scriptures as the final authority through the doctrine of "Sola Scriptura," other

TABLE 1–2
Sola Scriptura: Reformation Perspectives on Biblical Authority

Integrationists	Separationists		
Luther (1483–1546) and Calvin (1509–1564)	Zwingli (1484–1531)	Simons (1496–1561)	Amman (1644–1729)
Influenced by the writings of Augustine.	Influenced by the writings of Tertullian. Sought to reconstitute the first-century church by rejecting all authority except Scripture.		
Sola Scriptura understood to mean that the Bible is a measuring stick or norm against which all truth claims are judged.	Sola Scriptura understood to mean that the Bible is the only source of truth that one can reliably accept. All other claims to truth should be considered risky links to a secular world system. Divided truth into sacred and secular. Secular was to be rejected in favor of the sacred. Extreme distrust for philosophical and scientific study.		
Encouraged education, study in all fields of human inquiry, and the development of an integrative Christian worldview based upon the authority of the Bible.	Embraced a form of anti-intellectualism but did not forbid continued education. Biblical study was considered preferable to advanced studies in "secular" fields, however.	Simons and Amman were especially skeptical of any form of advanced education. Amman forbad study beyond the eighth grade. Rejected the concept of formal training of the clergy in favor of learning in the context of community and everyday living.	
Recognized a twofold basis for gaining knowledge of the truth, through general revelation and through special revelation.	Discouraged study of general revelation in favor of the study of special revelation (the Bible). Sought to be the people of the Book. Dualistic approach divided life and learning into godly and worldly categories.		
Promoted the concept of discernment. Scripture is seen as a standard to use in discerning truth from error in various fields of study. Taught also that reason only takes a person so far. Human reason fails to bring one to salvation. Special revelation is needed to come to a saving knowledge of God.	Promoted the rejection of study in fields deemed to be secular in order to avoid the polluting influence of human wisdom. Promoted knowledge of the Bible as antidote to worldly wisdom.		
If the Bible does not prohibit a practice or speak against an idea, it is permissible, though not always profitable.	If the Bible does not permit a practice or explicitly teach an idea, such practice or teaching is prohibited.		
Separation is a matter of personal conscience. Christian liberty is the norm. The principle of the weaker brother should be observed when in doubt.	Separation from the world is essential to godly living but does not extend as far as technological advancements. Separation includes avoidance of worldly values and lifestyles, but does not include a complete rejection of advanced education or the practice of shunning.		Separation is essential to maintaining a distinct people of God. Separation extends to education, technology, customs, and lifestyle. Shunning is used to keep people from too close of a worldly association.

reformers called for a return to the strict separationist position of Tertullian and, in their view, the position of the first-century church. In the northern, German-speaking regions of Switzerland, Zwingli held to the absolute authority of the Bible and permitted nothing in religion that could not be proven explicitly by the Scriptures. For example, Zwingli, early in his ministry, argued against infant baptism because he could find no biblical warrant for the practice. For Zwingli this view of Sola Scriptura also meant that an organ should not be used in a worship service since organs were not prescribed in the Bible or used by the first-century church. In essence then, whereas Luther and Calvin allowed for the practice of those things the Bible did not expressly prohibit, Zwingli prohibited what the Bible did not specifically prescribe (Cairns 331–33).

Some, such as Menno Simons and Jacob Amman, felt even Zwingli did not go far enough in applying Sola Scriptura. In their view, the doctrine of Sola Scriptura demanded an absolute separation from the world and a distinct people of the Holy Book. Their goal was not the reformation of the church (Roman Catholic), but the reconstitution of the first-century church with no authority but Scripture alone. These Anabaptist leaders (called "Anabaptists" because of their belief in adult baptism of believers only—thus rebaptizing those who had been baptized as infants) were far more radical than Zwingli and, as a result, were marginalized by society and often persecuted (Cairns 334).

As the horse-drawn buggy approached them over the hilltop, Jim Shellborn applied his brakes so the family could all take a look. His wife, Karen, spoke first. "Look at the Amish farmer, children. See how different Amish people live. They still live like people did before we had cars and electricity." She went on to explain to the children that many Amish communities seek to maintain a separated existence that demands distinctive dress and very simple lifestyles. It seemed an oddity to see a small black and gray buggy, drawn by an old plow horse, negotiating a modern highway. Jim thought how different life must be for this Amish family. Jim's world is filled with laptop computers, digital phones, e-mail communication, and instant stock market trades. He benefits daily from scientific and technological advancements occurring at a truly amazing rate. So his mind questioned, Why would some of God's people choose lives marked by such a plain and basic existence when so many modern conveniences are available? Jim did not realize it, but these quaint buggies and the lifestyle they represent are rooted in a particular view of scriptural authority. They are the practical outworking of a radical understanding of "Sola Scriptura."

Although their application of "Sola Scriptura" is far less radical than that of the Amish, modern "antipsychology" folk follow a similar line of theological reasoning. Like their Anabaptist forerunners, "biblical counselors" understand Sola Scriptura to mean that the Bible alone is to be used in counseling and that counselors should maintain a complete separation from "worldly" psychological theory. But this is not what the Reformers meant by "Sola Scriptura." Upholding Sola Scriptura does not require that we rule out the incorporation of findings from psychology and its many subfields simply because we do not find them specifically expressed in Scripture. The Reformation understanding of Sola Scriptura requires that we be more discerning than that. We are to "test the spirits to see whether they are from God' (1 John 4:1) or as Paul put it, to "Test everything. Hold on to the good" (1 Thess. 5:21).

We would suggest that the doctrine of Sola Scriptura is more accurately understood when aligned with the views of Augustine, Luther, and Calvin than it is with those of Tertullian, Zwingli, and the Anabaptists. Like the apostle Paul, we are open to employing truth discovered outside the Bible in pursuit of changed lives, but only under the authoritative parameters of a biblical understanding of God and human beings. In Acts 17 we read of Paul's use of the philosophic thought of his day when he spoke in the city of Athens. After surveying the city and its many idols, Paul was distressed. But he drew on his understanding of Greek culture and prepared a message focused on his audience. When he had opportunity to present Christ, Paul appealed to the philosophic base of the Athenians with these words:

Paul then stood up in the meeting of the Areopagus and said: "Men of Athens! I see that in every way you are very religious. For as I walked around and looked carefully at your objects of worship, I even found an altar with this inscription: TO AN UNKNOWN GOD. Now what you worship as something unknown I am going to proclaim to you.

"The God who made the world and everything in it is the Lord of heaven and earth and does not live in temples built by hands. And he is not served by human hands, as if he needed anything, because he himself gives all men life and breath and everything else. From one man he made every nation of men, that they should inhabit the whole earth; and he determined the times set for them and the exact places where they should live. God did this so that men would seek him and perhaps reach out for him and find him, though he is not far from each one of us. 'For in him we live and move and have our being.' As some of your own poets have said, 'We are his offspring.'

"Therefore since we are God's offspring, we should not think that the divine being is like gold or silver or stone—an image made by man's design and skill. In the past God overlooked such ignorance, but now he commands all people everywhere to repent. For he has set a day when he will judge the world with justice by the man he has appointed. He has given proof of this to all men by raising him from the dead." (Acts 17:22–31)

It is interesting to note that Paul, although distressed at his observations of idol worship, did not present a message condemning their idolatry. From this scriptural record we can see that Paul was comfortable in using and even crediting the secular poets of Athens to strengthen his point. He recognized that even these who worship false gods also had discovered some truth about man and his relationship with God, and so he built upon their correct yet distorted understandings. Like Paul, we believe that non-Christians can discover truth, but that truth must be sifted by the authoritative sieve of Scripture to filter out the "arrogant reasoning" and inaccurate conclusions of fallen man.

In many regards, when we speak of the Bible as our authority for matters of faith and practice, we mean that the Bible serves as a kind of map. In the same way that a map gives direction and provides a point of reference for the traveler in making judgments and decisions, so also does the written Word of God for the Christian pilgrim on his journey. A map is not the only source of information a traveler employs. Along the way are many travelers' aids and information centers. People seek to give direction. Some fellow travelers have already traversed the land and seek to offer guidance to the pilgrim. And, of course, the traveler can make his own observations. Each traveler, through the use of the senses and reasoning skills, can make judgments about the direction to proceed. By study not just of maps but of the terrain, the direction of the sun, or the position of the stars in the night sky, the traveler can make reasonable assertions about the direction that his journey should take.

The wise traveler knows that the map offers the greatest authority for the journey. He trusts it. It alone serves as the standard by which he can judge the accuracy of his observations or the quality of the directions or advice from fellow travelers. It alone can serve as the ultimate authority for deciding which way is the true way to the planned destination. In much the same manner, the Bible serves as our map through this dark world. It judges the opinion and "truths" of men. By it we gain essential information about God and godly living that we could know through no other means. And it is that information that rightly orders all of life. It is that information that comes from God as a special revelation that unlocks the truths found in the natural revelation of God. It is the Word, rightly interpreted, that enables us to fashion a view of the world consistent with the nature and will of our Maker.

Our plane touched down a little before three o'clock in the afternoon. It was a sunny and warm October day in San Francisco, and we had until late in the evening before our conference was to begin. After gathering our bags and checking into our hotel, we had several hours free to explore the city. Alone in San Francisco with good friends watching our children, Marlene and I (Gary) ventured off to the heart of the city. We had time to take a trolley ride and get dinner at Fisherman's Wharf. Our map was a small city guide that showed the major expressways and a few key city arteries. It seemed adequate to get us to our destination and back to our hotel, but little did we know how inadequate our pocket map was for the day that lay before us. You see, at 5:07 P.M. on October 17, 1989, San Francisco was shaken by a devastating earthquake.

For a while we did not realize the extent of the disaster. We did not know of the persons trapped under tons of concrete due to the collapse of the Embarcadero Freeway. We knew nothing of the failure of the Oakland Bay Bridge. All we observed were some new cracks in the sidewalk. At first we thought the city had experienced a minor, non-life-threatening trembler. But in a few minutes we became aware of the power of the earthquake as stunned citizens gathered in the streets to observe smoke rising from the Marina District. For an hour or so we watched as firefighters sought to control the blazes caused by broken gas pipes. Then came the aftershocks. Slowly it began to dawn on us. This was no small event. This was a catastrophe.

As the evening grew later, a man standing near us asked if we were from the area. We told him we were tourists and had just arrived from Toronto. He then made a comment that got our full attention. "Well, if I were you, I would get myself out of here before it gets dark. I'm a shop owner downtown and I'm heading back to get my shotgun and stand watch for looters. Once it gets dark, who knows what could happen next!"

It seemed to us that he might be on to something. Taking his advice, we returned to our rental car parked nearby, and we began our drive back to our hotel located near the airport. It was then that we discovered just how worthless our little map was. Our map could guide us to Fisherman's Wharf well enough, but now, with all of San Francisco's major expressways closed, it was of minimal value. We turned on the radio in the car and listened to the only radio station that was still operational. News reports streamed in describing the devastation. We now began to grasp our own situation. Here we were in a major city, by this time enveloped in the darkness of a moonless night, the only lights visible being those of cars and fires. No stoplights, no streetlights, and no clue how to get to our destination. We were without an adequate map to deal with the darkness of our world. We had no sure authority on which to make crucial decisions at the many crossroads we would face. It was a night of high adrenaline to say the least. At one point we passed a lumberyard totally in flames and for a moment our way was lit. But generally we drove in the dark, making what we hoped were the correct turns.

Eventually, four-and-one-half hours later, we made it to our hotel. What had taken only twenty-five minutes earlier in the day became a nearly insurmountable journey in the dark. Life's journey has a much less encouraging ending without the authoritative map of the Word of God. The Bible is our map. Our guide. Our norm for all matters of faith and practice. Sola Scriptura—the Scripture alone is our measure, our light, and our standard in this present darkness. It is our one sure criterion by which we can judge truth claims and truth contributions from other sources. That is what the Reformers meant by "Sola Scriptura." They did not mean that the Bible was the only stream from which truth could be drawn, but that it was the only pure stream against which claims to truth could be judged.

THE PRACTICE OF SOLA SCRIPTURA

Consider these two statements.

Statement one: *The Bible alone is completely true and reliable as our standard of truth.*

Statement two: *The Bible alone is true and is our one source of truth.*

Which of these statements is true? If you answered that the first is true and the second is false, give yourself 100 percent on this quiz. You are right. The Bible is entirely true and, as such, it stands as our rule or standard to determine the truthfulness of all human ideas. The second statement falls short. It is not accurate because there are indeed truths to be gleaned from extrabiblical sources. Take, for example, the growing data on brain functioning and activity. From this research, Alzheimer's patients can find an increasing sense of promise that a cure may one day be found. The Bible does not tell us in which parts of the brain our memories or emotions reside. Neurological research does. What the Bible does tell us is that those memories are important to defining who we are as people and that to forget the works of God on our behalf is to risk the shipwrecking of our spiritual lives.

Although the Bible does not give us all the data that we might use in daily living or in ministry with others, it does provide salvation truth we can know in no other way and it functions as the final authority over all truth claims. It does this by providing a worldview. By this we mean that it establishes the parameters for accurately understanding reality. One of the challenges of Christian living and ministry is to live all of our lives under the authority of the Word of God. We must actually practice Sola Scriptura, not just embrace it. Let us consider how we might do that with regards to the use of the social sciences.

An Example: Management Under the Authority of Scripture

Keith Martin is heading a search committee that is seeking an assistant pastor for his church of four hundred–plus persons. Keith was selected to head the committee for two major reasons. The first is his Christian life and character. Keith is a godly man who seeks to live for Christ in all aspects of his life. From his family life to his business life, from his church life to his community service, Keith is noted for his integrity and consistency. Keith is a person the church leadership trusts and who is able to infuse a solidly biblical perspective into the search for a pastoral candidate.

The second reason that Keith was chosen for the search committee is that he is the director of the human resources department of a major company in his city. Because of his work role, Keith has a good understanding of the recruitment, interviewing, and hiring processes. Keith's knowledge is helpful to the search committee. Keith will be able to bring that knowledge to the effort as his church seeks the best possible candidate for the position now open on its pastoral staff. But still, the Bible must remain the authority in such an endeavor. The Bible must provide the parameters as it establishes the character qualifications for those who would occupy the position of assistant pastor. The Bible must give guidance to the committee as to what kind of person to select, how that person should be treated by the congregation, and, in a broad sense, the role that the person should take as a pastor of the church. In this way, the Bible remains the authority in the search process. Practicing Sola Scriptura in this situation demands that Keith and his search committee use the Bible as a kind of map. It should show them the boundaries into which their decision and selection process must fit.

When we speak of the Bible as our ultimate authority and our rule for matters of faith and practice, we do not mean that the Bible is the only source of information valuable to those who serve Christ. The Bible is true, but there is truth outside of the Bible as well. When we speak of the Bible as our authority, we mean that the teachings of the Bible should serve as a sieve through which ideas from extrabiblical sources are sifted. Biblical authority demands that the thinking Christian know and understand the Bible in a systematic way in order to discern the correctness and failings of ideas derived from human reason and study in the various fields or disciplines of human knowledge.

Should we use secular theories and studies of management in ordering and operating the church? How about in managing our personal lives? Some would say, "Absolutely not!" They would suggest that the Bible should be our only source of information for managing the church. Others would offer a more qualified caution. "We can use knowledge from management theory just so long as we do not violate the clear teachings of the Word of God as to how the church should be run or how people should be treated." This is a more moderate and realistic position.

Most local churches employ knowledge gained from the world of business management in running at least some of the affairs of the church. The Bible does not give details on these issues. Knowledge of accounting, as an example, would be helpful to the one appointed to the post of church treasurer. Likewise, organizational skills taught in a school of management could help a Sunday school superintendent lead in the process of organizing the Sunday school program. On a personal level, most people have found benefit in the use of personal information management systems, such as daily planners and filing systems.

None of the above tools of management are derived directly from the pages of the Bible, although many of the principles they use are biblical. The best-selling book *The Seven Habits of Highly Effective People*, written by Stephen Covey, is another example. Many a Christian leader has benefited from Covey's work and has found principles in the pages of his book that are often parallel with the teachings of the Bible. Covey is a Mormon, yet that does not keep him from discovering truths that, when applied to the lives of Christian leaders, bring greater effectiveness. But his work, valuable as it may be, must be critiqued by the teachings of the Word of God. Concepts that violate the clear teaching of the Bible must be rejected as errant, no matter how eloquently or effectively presented. This is what is meant by practicing Sola Scriptura.

Management theory, whether used in running an organization or running an individual life, is a clear example of the concept of what we mean by practicing the authority of the Scriptures. Management theory is actually applied psychology. What management writers do is to take the findings from the realm of individual and group psychology and show readers how to apply them in practical ways in managing a group of people or an individual life. When Christians use these ideas in their daily lives or in the corporate life of the church, they may not realize it, but they are, in reality, applying and integrating psychology into life and ministry. Furthermore, the integration of psychological theory into our lives and ministry is probably inevitable. For this reason the issue does not become one of whether to incorporate psychological research findings and truth claims in our lives, but of how to do so while remaining under the authority of Scripture. Do we integrate in a haphazard and an uninformed way, or do we do so with a discerning eye and spirit?

The Views: Counseling Under the Authority of Scripture

In the previous section we tried to show how, by allowing the Bible to establish the boundaries or grid through which truth claims from outside the Bible are judged, we can practice Sola Scriptura. But now we must ask, "What about psychology?" Are Christians to use psychology in ministry? How shall we practice Sola Scriptura in this arena of human learning? To answer these questions, we must pause for a moment to understand how Christians have dealt with studies in psychology.

The Bible-Only Approach

Some have contended that the practice of Sola Scripture demands that only the Bible is to be used in ministry and that psychology has no valid place in providing spiritual direction and counsel. This position is really a revisiting of the separationist perspectives of Tertullian, Zwingli, and the Anabaptists. For those who hold this view, psychology is seen to be an enemy of Christianity and the Bible. *Psychology* is a term used as a synonym for "man's wisdom." Thus Christians who use psychology in counseling others or in their personal walk have been seduced. Like Tertullian, those who hold this view contend that such use of human reasoning and theorizing can only corrupt true faith. This leads those who embrace this position to reject any use of psychology as dangerous, unwise, and unfounded.

Probably the most vocal and the most representative element of this viewpoint is the "nouthetic counseling" contingent. Jay Adams (heavily influenced by the theology of Cornelius Van Til), Martin and Deidre Bodgan, and Ed Bulkley are examples of those who advocate this orientation. The term "nouthetic" is taken from Paul's use of the Greek word *nouthesia* in Colossians 1:28 that is translated "admonish" in many English texts. The term describes the confrontational methodology and basic elements of the nouthetic counseling approach. Because this approach is presented as the "biblical" view and its adherents claim to have the stamp of Scripture on its technique, it is sometimes presented in a tenacious and combative way. Its advocates are found doing battle with fellow believers whom they believe to be seduced by theories of psychology and guilty of compromising the truth of Scripture through the integration of psychological findings in the ministry of counseling. It is an approach reminiscent of the radical Anabaptist separationist leanings (Hurding 277–90).

The sign was located next to the elevator in the main classroom building and in most of the dorms. Its purpose was to inform the students attending a major Bible college of a counseling seminar sponsored by a local church. The seminar's subject matter was unmistakable in its boldface title—"Biblical Counseling vs. Psychological Counseling . . . What's the difference?" An interesting choice of terms and tone, isn't it? The word *versus*, against, is most often employed between sporting competitors or litigating parties. Its purpose is to set a combative or at least corrective tone, appropriate for a battle or a debate. Terms like "Biblical Counseling" and "Psychological Counseling" were chosen to convey a message of orthodoxy on the one hand and a perceived secularism on the other hand. From the title of the seminar, one might be led to think that some form of a debate between a Bible-believing, conservative Christian counselor and a God-denying secular therapist was about to occur. But this was not the case. Two authors of recently published books would speak. No, they did not represent opposing views. This was not going to be a debate. The advertisement made it clear that both were from the "biblical counseling" camp seeking to speak against the use of psychology in Christian ministry. Strangely, the other side was no godless, secular social scientist, but fellow Christians who are considered errant in their use of psychology in people-helping ministries.

Ironically, the carrot by which the Bible students would be drawn to the seminar was proclaimed not once, but eight times, in giant-sized print—"Free Pizza, Free Pizza, Free Pizza." Little did the seminar organizers realize it, but in their quest to motivate seminar attendance, they had practiced the integration of behaviorist psychology in their promotional materials. Apparently they felt that Bible college students are akin to Pavlov's famous salivating dogs. While their judgment may well be correct, it demonstrates the simple fact that one cannot entirely avoid the integration of faith and learning.

Nouthetic counselors seek to be biblical in all aspects of their counseling, and for this they should be commended. The problem, however, arises with this group's understanding and practice of Sola Scriptura. Taking an extreme dualistic, two-kingdom perspective that divides all reality into Christian and non-Christian, this view reduces all knowledge to that of divine or devilish. The knowledge revealed in Scripture and expressed in theology is divine. All other knowledge is devilish and misleading. Additionally, this view is excessively simplistic in that it categorizes all human problems as the result of demonic activity, personal sin, or physical malfunction. It allows for no middle ground, no mental illness or abnormal psychological development and thus, no value in research connected with such disorders (Adams, *Christian Counselor's* 72; Adams *Theology* 4). While its contribution to the ministry of counseling has been enormously valuable, because of its polarized view of reality this view fails to provide an adequate model for the consistent practice of Sola Scriptura in ministry.

The Bible-and Approach

At the other end of the continuum of views with regards to the use of psychology in people-healing ministry, we find what we might term "The Bible-*and* Approach." It is an approach similar to that of Aquinas. This viewpoint elevates studies in psychology to a level that is on par with the Scriptures so that the Bible and psychology are given an equal or nearly equal place in counseling ministry. Three variations on this approach are often observed. The first involves an intentional compartmentalization of theology and psychology. This approach contends that theological study is distinct from study in psychology. It holds that theology and psychology use their own terms that describe reality from radically different vantage points. Each effort is valid, but each is distinct and is best kept separated. Among Christians, this position has been termed a "perspectivist" view, meaning that theology and psychology describe men and women from differing perspectives and therefore, any attempt to integrate their conceptualizations distorts both fields of study. The *and* in this view is seen in that both theology and psychology can coexist without necessitating any attempt at integration so long as both remain in their appropriate compartments.

The second variation of the Bible-*and* psychology approach also compartmentalizes psychology and theology. In this case, compartmentalization is done for more pragmatic reasons rather than for intentional ones. This is the classic separation of sacred and secular. One finds this approach among many average parishioners. Here thinking is divided into different compartments. Faith, the Bible, and theology are kept in a compartment that is opened most typically on Sunday at church. The rest of life, including psychology, is placed in a compartment that is entered Monday through Saturday. Whether it is the study of mathematics, physics, law, or psychology, the truths of theology and the Bible are thought to have little direct bearing. For many, this compartmentalized attitude allows for a comfortable segmentation of life into the sacred and the secular, thus allowing for the use of a non-Christian psychoanalyst in addressing life's problems. People's beliefs are considered to be irrelevant unless they are seeking a position on the church board. Upholding a separation of theological and nontheological truths in this way allows for the Bible and psychology to work separately in people's lives.

The third variation of the Bible-*and* approach takes a far different path from the first two that we have discussed. Rather than compartmentalizing, this approach welcomes psychology and seeks to incorporate its concepts freely and directly into Christian thinking and practice. Whenever possible, theological and psychological concepts are equated. For example, Robert Schuller has done this with his incorporating of self-esteem and positive-thinking literature of the humanistic branch of psychology into his preaching ministry. Blending the message of Maslow with that of Matthew and Mark is the ultimate result. Many pastors and church leaders practice this approach in ministry. They incorporate the findings of psychology into the counsel and care of people without first doing the hard work of evaluating those ideas in light of the clear teachings of the Bible.

The Bible-Over Approach

The Reformers used words like norm, standard, rule, and measure to describe their understanding of the role of the Bible in the life of the church and the believer. They chose those terms for a reason. For them, all claims to truth and authority, whether from philosophy, science, or church leadership, were to be placed

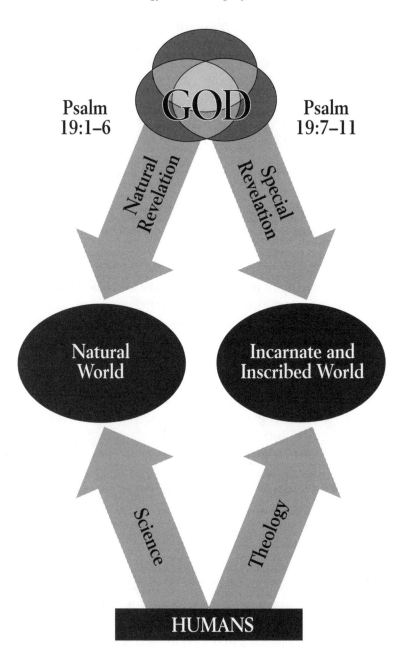

FIGURE 1–1
Science and Theology: Human Inquiry into God's Revelation

against the Bible. Luther and Calvin sought not to deny the value of human reason, nor to exalt it either. They did not deny the church had authority, but they did deny that the church's authority should be held above that of the Word of God. They also granted that in the natural world truth is revealed that both Christians and non-Christians can discover, but they were clear that such truth could never lead to salvation and ultimate spiritual healing. They understood the limits both of natural revelation and the mind of man to comprehend it, but they did not deny it. They demanded that the Bible be placed in authority over all truth, all practice, and all matters of faith and worship. It is this view of Sola Scriptura that we believe can be most effectively practiced by those who seek to provide spiritual direction and counsel to others.

Figure 1-1 depicts this understanding of divine revelation. God has made Himself known in two primary ways—through the world He made and all of its creatures, including human beings, and through His Word, both incarnate in Jesus and inscribed in the Bible. Human beings inquire into those two revelatory realms. Through use of reason, humans inquire into the natural order through a process of study that may be termed "science." Through reason and illumination of the Spirit, humans delve into special revelation doing what may be termed "theology." Although discovery of truth is possible in either domain, theological study in the Word must be given greatest authority because by it we can determine the parameters of an accurate worldview and the means to a right relationship with God. Theology can tell us what ought to be; science can only tell us what is. This is not to say that in specific details science might not serve to inform one's theology, but in those issues that deal with the nature of man, the nature of God, or God's purposes in this world, only the Word can make these truths known. For example, science may tell us how to clone a person, but it is only the Bible and the truths of theology that can give us any hope of knowing whether or not we should create such a clone.

TABLE 1–3
Contemporary Approaches to the Relationship of Psychology and the Bible

	The Bible-*Only* Approach	The Bible-*Over* Approach	The Bible-*And* Approach
Brief Summary	The Bible is the only valid source of truth to be used in counseling ministry. Psychology is "man's wisdom." Those who use psychological findings in ministry have been seduced by lies of the devil. The pure stream of Scripture must not be polluted with the impure stream of psychology.	The Bible is the norm or standard against which all claims of truth must be judged. Because of natural revelation, the study of psychology has a place, but Scripture must be given authority over psychological findings. As authority over psychology, the Bible is central to all learning.	Psychology is given equal role with the Scriptures in counseling ministry. Through an equal but compartmentalized approach to faith and reason, or through a total interweaving of the two, this approach magnifies the role of psychology while lessening the role of the Bible.
Earliest Historical Roots	Tertullian	Augustine	Aquinas
Reformation Roots	Zwingli, Simons, Amman	Luther, Calvin	Post-Reformation modernist and postmodernist thought.
Orientation to Truth	Separationist Approach (truth vs. error)	Integrationist Approach (discern truth amidst error)	Compartmentalist Approach (categories of truth)
Contemporary Proponents	Nouthetic counselors (sometimes call themselves "biblical counselors")	Most Christian counselors	Some Christian and some non-Christian counselors

The Principles: Practical Guidance in the Practice of Sola Scriptura

How shall we actually go about evaluating truth claims from sources outside of the Bible? In this final section we will identify some principles that we believe will guide those who seek to counsel under the authority of Scripture. We will develop this matter further in the book, but here are five principles we believe are helpful in considering ideas drawn from the field of psychology.

Is the proposed psychological concept or conclusion . . .

1. *Directly Supported by Scripture?*

Some claims to truth derived from extrabiblical sources are also explicitly taught in the Bible.

2. Theologically Consistent with Scripture?

Some claims to truth derived from the field of psychology are consistent with a scriptural understanding of human nature. Although these concepts are not taught explicitly in the Bible, they are in keeping with biblical concepts and are found implicitly in the overall teachings of God's Word.

3. Addressed by Scripture?

It is possible that a particular concept or issue is not directly addressed in the Bible. In this case, assuming that valid scientific findings are involved, believers can carefully integrate the concept into their ministry or personal life. Of course one must be cautious to observe two fundamental principles in this process. These are the principle of profitable benefit and the principle of the weaker brother. By "profitable benefit" we mean that although an act, concept, method, or technique may be lawful for the believer to practice, it may not be to that person's spiritual benefit (1 Cor. 6:12; 10:23). By "weaker brother" we are referring to Paul's teaching that our actions should not make another believer stumble in his faith (Rom. 14:13–21; 1 Cor. 8:13).

4. Explicitly Denied by Scripture?

Some concepts taught or practiced by psychologists may be in direct conflict with the teachings of the Bible. These should be rejected and not practiced or supported by the Christian.

5. Doubtfully Consistent with Scripture?

At times there is a sense that something just does not stack up with the Bible. It is possible that the teaching rests on faulty premises or results in actions inconsistent with godly character. In these times of doubt it is wise for the believer to bypass the idea or action in favor of prudence.

— A Final Thought —

*O*ur goal is to be thoroughly biblical caregivers. If that goal is to be attained, we must always keep the Word of God as the sole norm or authority in matters of faith and practice. That is the message of the Reformers. The Word must guide us in judging all claims of truth and ideas of men. That is the means by which we can discern truth and error. For without that sure Word as our standard and rule, we would be lost on a sea of modern thought, scientific claims, and theoretical proliferation. But with the Word of God central in our thinking, we can appropriately incorporate truth from all potential sources in the day-to-day demands of ministry. This is the meaning of Sola Scriptura.

We must now consider the biblical dimensions of human personality. We will, in the next two chapters, seek to establish a biblical anthropology, one that can serve as a sieve to sift and separate truth and error in various personality theories. In doing so, we will establish an authoritative foundation for the development of our counseling ministry.

NOTES

Adams, Jay E. *The Christian Counselor's Manual.* Grand Rapids: Zondervan, 1973.

————. *A Theology of Christian Counseling.* Grand Rapids: Zondervan, 1979.

Augustine, Aurelius. *Augustine: Earlier Writings.* Trans. J. H. S. Burleigh. Philadelphia: Westminster, 1953. Vol. 6 of *Library of Christian Classics (LCC)*.

————. *A Select Library of the Nicene and Post-Nicene Fathers of the Christian Church (NPNF)*. Ed. P. Schaff. 1st series. 8 vols. Grand Rapids: Eerdmans, 1956.

Cairns, Earle E. *Christianity Through the Centuries.* Rev. ed. Grand Rapids: Zondervan, 1974.

Demarest, Bruce A. *General Revelation: Historical Views and Contemporary Issues.* Grand Rapids: Zondervan, 1982.

Erickson, Millard J. *Christian Theology.* Grand Rapids: Baker, 1990.

Hurding, Roger F. *The Tree of Healing: Psychological and Biblical Foundations for Counseling and Pastoral Care.* Grand Rapids: Zondervan, 1985.

Tertullian. *De praescriptione haereticorum.* 24 July 2000 <http://www.tertullian.org/works/de_praescriptione_haereticorum.htm>.

— Chapter 2 —

WONDERFULLY CREATED:
The Biblical Dimensions of Personality
(Part One)

*B*oundaries are important. Norm Cline discovered that when he installed his new aboveground pool. As a homeowner, Norm did a few odd jobs around the house, saving him the sometimes costly expense of professional home repair assistance. But when the family decided on a pool for the yard instead of an annual family vacation, Norm went beyond his amateur home improvement skills and knowledge.

Norm read the materials handed to him by the pool salesman. It seemed easy enough. Take up the sod, level the ground with sand, and assemble the pool. He could do this, he thought, and so he did. Actually, he did a great job handling the project and saved the five-hundred-dollar installation charge. He was proud of his workmanship. Everything, including the new filtering system, worked like a charm. That is, until the city inspector stopped by.

"Mr. Cline, I am afraid you have a bit of a problem," the inspector said. "It seems that your pool did not have a construction permit," he continued. The inspector explained that a drawing was required that showed the boundary lines of Norm's property, the location of all underground utilities, the placement of his home, and the proposed placement of his pool. The inspector understood Norm's failure to comply with the city laws, but he told Norm he would have to submit the drawing and pay a fine. The next day Norm set out to comply with the inspector's request. Much to Norm's surprise, he discovered the pool was located right over underground electrical cables and about six inches over his property line. A pool with thousands of gallons of water had to be relocated. It was a handyman's nightmare. What was to be a money-saving, do-it-yourself project, turned out to be an expensive lesson in the importance of knowing one's limits and one's boundaries.

Boundaries are important. Take a family budget, for example. By setting out spending limits, a family can make good decisions about what it should buy and what it should resist buying. Many a new product, entertainment experience, or modern convenience has sought to seduce the consumer to buy now and pay later. The ease of credit availability has made the wisdom of budgetary controls even more beneficial.

In much the same way as a budget aids a family in controlling spending or a carefully marked-out drawing helps a homeowner when installing a pool, staking out theological boundaries for our discussion of human personality and the counseling care of people is a wise action. This is the first step in counseling under the authority of Scripture. By identifying the boundaries of a biblical anthropology, we can create a means by which various psychological findings and theories, with their related assumptions, conclusions, and applications, can be evaluated. We begin then with an understanding of the various biblical dimensions of human personality—the "lot lines" of a scriptural description of human beings. Three such boundaries are presented in the Bible. By establishing these boundaries, our understanding of human personality will be more accurately biblical and our assessment of extrabiblical descriptions of human personality, much more discerning.

BOUNDARY 1: HUMANS ARE CREATED BEINGS

When surveyors take up the task of establishing the property lines of a parcel of land, they look first for a reference point. Typically this is a stake driven just below the surface of the ground in one of the corners of the lot. From that point of reference it is possible to survey clear lines of demarcation that establish the legal limits of the property.

In many ways, the matter of human origins is that reference point. If we start with some other point of reference, our survey of the land will be incorrect. So it is essential to begin to clearly define biblical boundary lines of human personality with the issue of human origins.

Scripture affirms a creation view of human origins. Believers might debate whether the days of creation were six literal days or whether the Genesis account allows for lengthy periods of time. Likewise, fellow believers can disagree over whether or not micro-evolutionary development (small changes within a kind or species) was a tool that God used to make the first human. Believers too can dispute whether the creation of Adam was a direct act of God or the result of theistic control over natural processes. In all of these debates, believers on both sides are within the bounds of biblical orthodoxy. But one cannot embrace a naturalistic evolutionary understanding of human origins and remain biblical in one's viewpoint. Although the details of the creation/evolution debate and the merits of the various views of creation (e.g., fiat, theistic evolution, progressive creation, etc.) are beyond the scope and purpose of this book, the implications of a creation perspective cannot be overstated.

Scripture is plain. "In the beginning God created . . ." (Gen. 1:1). "The LORD God formed the man from the dust of the ground and breathed into his nostrils the breath of life, and the man became a living being" (Gen. 2:7). Human beings are created beings. This is a boundary line necessary in the consideration of various theories of human psychology. Although it does not rule out the potential contributions of those theorists who disagree with a creation perspective, those who seek to counsel under the authority of Scripture must cautiously approach such theories seeking to discern where naturalistic assumptions skew findings and conclusions. Let us now consider the important implications of a belief in the creation of human beings by the one true God.

Dependent, Not Independent

The fact that humans are created beings means that they depend on their Creator for their existence. Humans are not indispensable, nor are they accidental. Human beings were made by the Creator God to serve His purposes. This gives humans both dignity and a destiny. Our life comes from God, and we enjoy life because of His provision and care. Although we may claim independence from God and we may conduct our daily lives as if we are independent of our Maker, such an understanding is wrongheaded. It does not alter the reality that God is God and we are His creatures. Our existence is contingent on His will and His good pleasure. We should not think that we could ever live a fully satisfying life apart from being dependent on God and in sync with His divine purposes. No counsel, however helpful in the immediate, will serve man well if it moves a person toward an independence from God rather than a dependence on God.

Finite, Not Infinite

Humans have limitations. It has always been that way, even prior to the Fall. Limitations, in themselves, are not sin, for God looked on His creation, including man, and pronounced it "very good" (Gen. 1:31). Our finiteness means that we are creatures, not God. It is when we come to accept our own finiteness that we can hope to develop a balanced life and become aware of our need for the infinite God. This principle has enormous importance when it comes to issues of emotional health and spiritual well-being. At least three specific applications can be drawn.

First, our finiteness explains why we cannot control all events. Some are simply beyond us, but not beyond God. Events sometimes come into our lives that we cannot handle apart from God's grace. The unexpected loss of a loved one, the failure of a business, or a natural disaster can be negotiated, not on our own, but with the strength of God and the support of friends. Recognizing our finite nature will aid us when these out-of-control moments occur. We cannot manage life to avoid all pain or predict all contingencies. Situations will occur that push us beyond our ability to control them. In the process we can become stressed and frustrated, but it is helpful to recall that no one but God Himself can control everything.

Second, our finite nature means that there are practical limitations on our achievements. In our finiteness we can discover that we need not fear failure. We come to understand that we must expect some measure of failure as a predictable result of trying. By this, we are not speaking of moral failure, although that too is predictable because of our sin nature. We are referring to our many human tasks, pursuits, and pioneering endeavors. Since failure is human, we will at times fail. But such failure need not be viewed as a reason for shame. As finite creatures we know that only God can be credited with never making a mistake.

Third, our finite nature tells us that we cannot attain all knowledge and that our understanding will always be incomplete and subject to error. Our finiteness tells us that we should humbly acknowledge that we will not always be right. We cannot know everything correctly, nor must we. We can learn from others. This encourages us to retain a measure of humility, teachability, and tolerance in our personal lives and our counseling ministry. It is important to remember that those we counsel will never fully understand or always make the right judgments either.

Recognizing our finiteness has one more benefit. It helps us to understand that we will never create a perfect world or a totally secure existence. One of the chief goals of human beings is to create a life of security. Numerous hours go into planning for a secure retirement. Significant dollars are spent on insurance premiums so that our homes, cars, health, and lives are secure. We put deadbolt locks on our doors, alarms on our windows, and "fire walls" on our computers, all in the name of security. Prudence may indeed make all of these actions appropriate to a point, but believers know that there is no true freedom in a totally secure environment. Eventually we become the prisoners of our own efforts to achieve security and our own insecurities. In a real sense, our work to build a secure existence leads to further insecurity, for the more we have, the more we have at risk. It is only in a right relationship with God (specifically through the work of His Son, Jesus Christ) that we discover genuine security. This is not to say that nothing painful will befall a believer or that believers are not subject to loss. It means that we do not find our security in preventing pain or loss. We find it in a confidence in the God who created us.

Different, Not Unique

Human beings are a part of God's creation. In a real sense we have a kinship with the created order and with every other created being. God made this world as a sequence of creative events. Although humans were the final act of that creative drama, like everything around us, we too were created. As a matter of fact, we shared the same creation day with the land animals (day six). A gap exists between man and the animal kingdom, but not so great a gap as between God and creation. We are not unique in that we are totally distinct from animals. We share many common qualities. We depend on the same environment, we have breath and we have life, we eat and we sleep, we are born and we die, like all of God's other creatures except angels. As the final beings created by God, God called us to exercise dominion over His created order, but not a dominion of careless, wasteful indulgence. Rather we are to be stewards exercising a distinct role while sharing a common creatureliness.

It is also true that we are different from one another, not unique. We like to speak of each person as a unique creation of God. There is a sense in which that is true, of course. But it may be better to focus first on our commonalities that make us very much alike and then on our differences that distinguish us from one another. Humans grow in similar ways. This enables developmental researchers to predict, with a high degree of accuracy, the stages of growth and change that are common to children and adults. As fellow humans, we share many of the same goals and desires. Whether we are born in Moscow or Minneapolis, human beings face many of the same trials, exhibit many of the same needs, long for many of the same things, and enjoy many of the same pleasures. We share emotions, attitudes, talents, and tendencies. But we are different as well. Different languages, values, customs, and cultures—all differences that matter and that define the wide variety of human experiences. We have different upbringings and different genetic roots. We differ in our likes and dislikes. We differ too in our temperaments and our individual gifts. These are differences that those who seek to counsel others must recognize and reckon with. These are differences we must appreciate and accept.

Valuable, Not Supreme

As the peak and pinnacle of divine creation, human beings have an enormous value and a special place in God's created order. When we earlier said that humans are different, but not unique, we were not intending to communicate that humans are part of the animal kingdom—far from it! Human beings are God's last word of creation. When, in Genesis 1:26, after God had finished His wonderful creation, we read, "Then God said, 'Let us make man,'" we have the final act of creation, an action God proclaims to be "very good." As God's final creative act, humans are not restricted to a creature status. We are more than instincts and drives. We possess intellect and reason, emotion and will, creativity and talent. Theologians sometimes say we "share in the communicable attributes of God." Because of this we exist at a level that is higher than a purely animalistic existence.

As we work with those we counsel and as we analyze various counseling theories and techniques, we must be certain that we do not dehumanize people in the process. We will expand on this point later in this chapter, but we must be cautious never to reduce people to trainable animals or treat people as valueless or worthless sinners. We must always maintain a clear recognition of the enormous value that all humans possess and their worth before God as the highest of all creatures in His good work of creation.

We are valuable, but we are not supreme. God alone is the highest of all beings. Our value is derived from God. He is the higher value, the One of ultimate glory. Man is not the center of the universe. The goal of man is not his own glory or advancement or pleasure. The goal of man must be God's glory and God's pleasure. Humans exist only because God exists, and so our value must be kept in perspective. We cannot accept the self-centeredness of most modern psychological theories. This is not to say that such theories are devoid of truth, but on this point it is clear, the goal in life is not "self-actualization" (Maslow) but God-glorification.

Purposeful, Not Meaningless

Speaking at a college graduation, film actor and director Woody Allen began an address with these words:

> More than at any other time in history, mankind faces a crossroads. One path leads to despair and utter hopelessness. The other, to total extinction. Let us pray we have the wisdom to choose correctly. I speak, by the way, not with any sense of futility, but with a panicky conviction of the absolute meaninglessness of existence that could easily be misinterpreted as pessimism. It is not. It is merely a healthy concern for the predicament of modern man. (75)

In one sense, Allen has a point. There is a great sense of meaninglessness in modern society. It is said that President John F. Kennedy once commented, "Modern American youth have everything—except a reason to live." Apart from a Creator who has fashioned us we might well ask, "Why life?" Are we really all just the product of random events and evolutionary processes? Are we nothing more than highly developed animals? Is the purpose of life to "eat and drink, for tomorrow we die" (a philosophy summarized in 1 Cor. 15:32)? Can wealth and fame bring happiness? Is life just pain, sorrow, and suffering with an occasional small joy interspersed?

Apart from a Creator, meaning cannot exist. Meaning by its very nature cannot come from within a person. It must be external, and it must be universal. If everyone creates his or her own meaning, then in reality, life is meaningless. The fact that God is our Maker gives purpose to life. By understanding that God made us, we have the foundation for establishing why we exist. Apart from the God of the Bible and specifically the work of God's Son, Jesus Christ, science can only lead us back to an evolutionary cesspool of meaningless happenstance. Science doesn't deal with ultimate things. Philosophy can only lead us back to an existential vacuum and personal emptiness. Psychology can only lead us back to self-focused hedonism. But if we start with a Creator God, we can begin to establish purposefulness to our existence.

Accountable, Not Autonomous

The year 1998 was a year of scandal. We were inundated with stories of immorality, perjury, and obstruction of justice at the very highest level of American government, the White House. William Jefferson Clinton became only the second president in United States history to be impeached by the House of Representatives. In 1999 his trial went to the Senate, where the two-thirds vote to remove him from office could not be mustered. The real issue at stake was one of accountability. To whom was Bill Clinton accountable for his actions? To the Congress? To the American people? To the voters who elected him? To his family alone? In the end, in some measure, he is accountable to all of these. But most significantly, like all human beings, he is finally accountable to God.

As God's creation, all persons are ultimately accountable to the Creator. We may think we are autonomous and may, at times, function in ways that ignore God, but in the end, the Creator will judge the creature. Our lives are His by virtue of our origin and His ownership. We are here because an intelligent being put us here with a purpose. That fact makes us accountable, but it also gives us a sense of identity. Our identity is a matter of fulfilling that divine purpose or plan in a way that honors God. As we consider the various theories of psychology and the methods of healing human emotions, we must recognize that only a right relationship with the Creator can ever produce the meaning we humans strive for or address the accountability that God demands.

BOUNDARY 2: HUMANS ARE DIVINE IMAGE-BEARERS

There is something wonderfully special about people. All people. Even those we have the hardest time loving or understanding. It is a quality of human nature that distinguishes human beings from all other life forms. Theologians call it the *imago Dei*, the image of God. We have already described persons as created. This immediately puts a biblical perspective of human nature in opposition to the evolutionary assumptions of many social scientists. We widen that gap still further when we proclaim persons to be divine image-bearers. For those who seek to counsel under the authority of Scripture, humans must be thought of as more than simply complex organisms or highly intelligent animals. They are, in some sense, like their Maker. Genesis 1:26 says, "Let us make man in our image, in our likeness." In some special way, human nature reflects something of the nature of God. To understand this biblical truth we must ask, "What is God like?" and "How are people like God?" The Genesis account of creation is our best hint as to the meaning of this important proclamation.

What Is God Like?

It is wise that we look to the nature of God first to determine the nature of humans. It is we who carry His image, and so we are wise to understand what God instilled in humans that mirrors His qualities. A simple appraisal of the Genesis account of creation reveals much of God's nature and parallel qualities in persons. These qualities may well constitute the divine image in us.

God Is Creator

It is immediately obvious that God created in Genesis 1 and 2. That is the point of the passage. God is the Maker of the heavens and earth, the Author of life, the One who fashioned the universe and everything in it.

God Has Dominion

God is the sovereign ruler over all He has made. He is the

King of kings and Lord of lords. He is the Almighty, the One who exercises complete dominion over His creatures and creation.

God Is Plural, Yet One

The use of the pronoun "us" in Genesis 1:26 is remarkable. Although it is not an explicit reference to the Trinitarian nature of God, it is clearly a plural pronoun allowing for the later revelation of the Trinity in the pages of the Bible. God is by nature three-in-one. He has a plural personage. We speak of Father, Son, and Spirit as three persons sharing one divine nature or essence— a tri-unity. The Trinity is not comprised of three different gods. He is the one true God expressed in three persons, each distinct in function.

God Is Volitional

God acted as a result of His divine will. He chose to act to create the heavens and earth. It was His will to make the fish of the sea and the birds of the air. It was His desire to create the stars, the sun, and the moon. By His free will He acted to make all that we see around us and to sustain everything by the graciousness of His good pleasure.

God Is Rational

God's creation shows logic and order. It demonstrated a plan and design. It followed a process. Day by day, step by step, God made the universe and eventually the man and the woman. He spoke the world into existence. We have no idea what language God used, but we do know that He communicated in words. Later we discover that God communicated with Adam and Eve in words, words they could comprehend. Order, structure, design, process, language, speech, and communication are all indicators of a rational, communicative God.

God Is Moral

God is without sin. He is pure and holy. God is just and righteous. He is without flaw in character. And this is how God created man. Although humans do not share in all of God's attributes—

we are not omniscient, omnipresent, or omnipotent—God did create Adam and Eve without sin, capable of making morally significant choices, participants in His moral goodness.

How Are People Like God?

Adam and Eve were, in a way, representatives of God. To look on Adam and Eve in their unfallen condition was to see something of the divine. They were not gods, but they were wonderful reflections of the image of God. Their nature served as a mirror of His nature. The reflection was not the true God, but a limited likeness of the invisible God. Not a physical image, but a spiritual one. So how are people like God? How do we reflect the nature of God in our nature?

Human Beings Are Creative

It is interesting to note that in a lesser sense, as God is creative, so we too are creative. We go beyond life actions that are done merely for the sake of survival or out of instinct. We create! Humans produce art, music, literature, and poetry. They design, devise, develop, and decorate. They measure time, make tools, and manufacture technologies. Humans are creative by nature. No, we do not create as God did just by the word of His mouth. But we do possess enormous creativity, and that dramatic creative ability serves to distinguish people from lesser life-forms. In our creative nature we are fashioned after the image of our Creator.

Human Beings Have Dominion

We said that God has absolute dominion over His creation. In creating Adam and Eve after His image, He chose to give the man and woman a role to play, a role of dominion as well. We read "and let them rule over the fish of the sea and the birds of the air, over the livestock, over all the earth, and over all the creatures that move along the ground"(Gen. 1:26). This stewardship is not given to the other creatures, only to humans. Ruling may well be a part of the image of God in man.

Humans Were Created Male and Female

In keeping with the plural nature of God's person, he made not one human, but two—the man and the woman. In their sexuality and personality differences is an illustration of God's nature. God is relational. So too, man and woman were created for a relationship. God is one, and so too the man was to be one with his wife. The relational bonds of husband and wife are partially reflective of the image of God in human beings.

Humans Have Volition

God gave human beings a will. Like God, people have the ability to act by choice. We are not programmed to act on instinct, pure survival, or simply animal needs—we have the ability to make choices. Without that ability, we would not reflect God's nature. It is that ability that made sin possible, yet it is that ability that makes us divine image-bearers. That ability, like all of these, has been limited by the Fall—we no longer have completely free will but are largely enslaved by sin. But we are not determined or limited to instinctual actions.

Humans Are Rational Beings

Clearly, humans possess a rational ability that goes far beyond anything we observe in the animal kingdom. We can speak of whales and dolphins as intelligent and even capable of communicating with one another. We can teach apes to use sign language, but such rational capacities are a far cry from the reasoning and communication ability we see in humans. We do not see dolphin libraries or orangutan space shuttles. We do not see animals establishing research facilities or building hospitals to treat the sick. Any attempt to equate animal rationality to human rational ability is a little like equating a spiderweb to the World Wide Web. Although there may be similarities, we are talking about entirely different levels of complexity, design, and rational ability in their construction. Humans share something of the nature of God in their rationality that is likely an aspect of the image of God in us.

Humans Are Moral Beings

It is true that in our fallenness we have become hideously immoral, but we still retain something of the moral nature of God. In their creation, Adam and Eve were without sin. They were innocent and blameless. They were given moral boundaries for the exercise of their will and eventually chose to violate those moral constraints. In that action sin entered the human race and their moral nature was marred. But even in their sinfulness they retained something of the pure conscience they once possessed.

The *imago Dei*—it makes humans something like God in that they reflect His nature. It gives humans immense value as well. When we work with persons in a counseling role we must always keep in mind that we are dealing with divine image-bearers. This fact gives each person dignity, value, and worth. We cannot depreciate persons through the methods we use or through the attitudes we convey. God's image is to be respected in others. James recognizes this principle in James 3:9–10 with reference to the use of the tongue. "With the tongue we praise our Lord and Father, and with it we curse men, who have been made in God's likeness. Out of the same mouth come praise and cursing. My brothers, this should not be." So the image of God is a basis for respect and right treatment of persons. It grants a special status to those we serve.

That image is marred by sin. It is not eradicated, but it is damaged. Like the distorted image in a carnival mirror, God's image in humans is refracted. It no longer presents a true view of the divine nature, but instead reflects an image that is skewed. Humans retain their distinct position as image-bearers, but the image is no longer pure.

BOUNDARY 3: HUMANS ARE MULTIFACETED BEINGS

In order that we might counsel under the authority of Scripture and accurately assess the validity of ideas about human personality from extrabiblical sources, a third biblical boundary must be constructed. This boundary speaks to the constitutional makeup of human beings. In this section, two faulty understandings of human nature will be identified and then a third view, which we believe to be more consistent with the teachings of Scripture, will be considered.

Dichotomist and Trichotomist Views

The mourners took encouragement from the clergyman's comments. "This body that is before us was just a vehicle that Edna used to travel this earth," he said. "Edna used this vehicle for some seventy-eight years, but now she is free of the limits of this weak body, a body that was wracked with illness. Her soul is free now and lives forever in eternity." After that the family paid their last respects and Edna's coffin was closed.

The most common understanding of the constitutional nature of human beings involves a two- or sometimes three-part conceptualization. We use such terms as *body and soul* or *body, soul, and spirit* to discuss the dimensions of human existence. We talk of the material and the immaterial aspects of human personality. And we take comfort in our loss to think that the "real person" is not the flesh and blood body that we place in the grave, but the inner person who continues on in an immortal existence. While comforting, such a view of people is influenced more by Platonic Greek dualism than by a biblical perspective of people.

Plato viewed reality as composed of two parts—the material realm and the spiritual realm. The material realm was considered to be an imperfect, temporal shadow of the perfect, permanent, and real realm of the spiritual. Plato considered the spiritual realm to be superior to the material realm. The mind, for Plato, is the bridge by which these realms are connected. It is against the backdrop of this Platonic, Hellenistic thought that the early church fashioned much of its understanding of human beings. Taking most of its theology of human personality from Paul, the early church leadership interpreted Paul's writings through a Hellenistic lens of duality—material and immaterial.

Trichotomistic or Tripartite Approach

Trichotomistic understandings of human nature identify three parts that comprise persons—usually the *body*, the *soul*, and the *spirit*. Drawn as a parallel with Greek philosophy, adherents of this view taught that the spirit of man *(pneuma)* was immortal and the body *(soma)* was mortal and carnal. An intermediate aspect or substance was required to enable these two elements to relate to one another. Their conclusion was that this was the function of the soul *(psuche)*. Those who held the tripartite position supported their view by claiming that man's nature is an illustration of the triune God in whose image humans are fashioned. It is interesting to note that one modern trichotomist equates the *soul (psuche)* of man with the *mind* (Bulkley 338–41), a nearly exact reaffirmation of Platonic thinking, and supports his view using the Trinitarian argument.

Trichotomists regard the physical body as something that humans share in common with animals and plants. They believe the physical difference between plants, animals, and people is not one of kind but of complexity. The soul is thought to be the psychological element of persons where thought, reason, learning, emotions, social interactions, and personality traits reside. Plants do not possess a soul, but animals are thought to possess a rudimentary soul and, thus, can show some humanlike qualities. The soul of man is more advanced than that of animals, but again is not different in kind. It is the third element within humans, that is, the spirit, that distinguishes humans from animals and plants. The spirit enables human beings to respond to God, who is spirit and gives all persons an inclination toward religiosity.

Scriptural support for the trichotomist position is gleaned from five key passages of Scripture. The first is 1 Thessalonians 5:23 where Paul wrote, "May God himself, the God of peace, sanctify you through and through. May your whole spirit *[pneuma]*, soul *[psuche]* and body *[soma]* be kept blameless at the coming of our Lord Jesus Christ." The second passage that is often used as support for the trichotomist view is Hebrews 4:12. Here the writer describes the probing power of the Word of God. We read that the Word of God is "living and active. Sharper than any double-edged sword, it penetrates even to dividing soul *[psuche]* and spirit *[pneuma]*, joints and marrow; it judges the thoughts and attitudes of the heart." A third passage used to support the trichotomist view of human nature is 1 Corinthians 2:14–3:4. In this passage Paul distinguishes between three kinds of people, one characterized by the flesh *(sarx)*, one characterized by the soul *(psuche)*, and one characterized by the spirit *(pneuma)*. The fourth reference to a three-fold division of man is 1 Corinthians 15:44, where Paul distinguishes between the "natural body" *(psuche*—"soulish body")* and a "spiritual body" *(pneuma)*. The fifth passage that is sometimes used to support a trichotomist view is Mark 12:33 where Christ's disciples are instructed to love God "with all your heart [spirit], with all your understanding [soul] and with all your strength [body]."

The trichotomist view is popular among many evangelicals, especially those who seek to incorporate psychological concepts into ministry. By identifying a third entity to the nature of man that is equated with human personality, propsychology counselors are able to create a three-part compartmentalized ministry. They are able to recognize the place of medical treatment for the body, pastoral care for the spirit, and psychological care for the soul. The simplicity of trichotomy is inviting. It explains how people are both similar to and different from animals, and it allows for an explanation of personality traits and abnormalities apart from purely spiritual or physical causation. Unfortunately, such an approach falls short of a unified understanding of truth and ministry. Likewise, it does not adequately take into account the various anthropological terms used in the Bible.

Dichotomistic or Bipartite Approach

Dichotomism, in one form or another, is the most widely held view throughout the historic record of the church. Dichotomists hold that human beings are composed of two parts—the material and the immaterial. All references to the spirit, soul, mind, heart, or other "inner person" terms are synonymous because such words are used interchangeably in the Bible.

It is interesting to note that both liberal theologians and conservative theologians have embraced dichotomism, but with differing understandings of the concept. Liberals distinguish between body and soul in a way that makes the soul and body of radically different substances. The spirit/soul is thought of as inhabiting and acting on the body, which is viewed as weak and burdensome. For the liberal, personality can exist apart from the body, for the body is merely a shell in which the real person temporally resides. The body is not considered to be essential; it is temporal, and people can function quite well without it. Death is the death of the body, not the separation of body and soul. The spirit is thought to live on, freed from the limitations of the mortal body. There is no future resurrection in the liberal view, but resurrection is believed to be an accommodation of the biblical writers to their culture (Fosdick 99–100).

Conservative dichotomists believe in the separate elements of body and soul and believe that the soul can survive death in a disembodied state, but they look forward to the resurrection of the body as well. Conservative dichotomists distinguish between the material and the immaterial aspects of human beings. In this way they compartmentalize the treatment of people into spiritual issues and physical issues. One of the tasks of the counselor is to determine which element of the person—the body, the soul, or both—must be treated. Doctors treat the body while pastors treat the spirit/soul. There is no place in this perspective for the psychologist or psychiatrist, for there is no third entity. All human struggles are physical or spiritual, for that is all there is to persons— material and immaterial (Welch 29–31).

Often the arguments in favor of a dichotomist position are actually arguments against the trichotomist viewpoint and, as such, they presuppose a distinction between immaterial and material rather than prove it. As a result, the question becomes one of how many parts comprise the immaterial part of human beings, not whether or not persons are indeed bipartite in nature.

Dichotomists would argue that if passages like 1 Thessalonians 5:23 and Hebrews 4:12 describe separate entities comprising human nature, then difficulties are encountered when other texts are considered. For example, Jesus tells His followers in Luke 10:27, "Love the Lord your God with all your heart and with all your soul and with all your strength and with all your mind." In this case four entities are identified that do not match those mentioned in 1 Thessalonians 5:23 or Hebrews 4:12. It is clear that Jesus was speaking of observable dimensions of the total person, not separate entities or components. Further, dichotomists would argue that the terms *spirit* and *soul* are used interchangeably or in a parallel manner in the New Testament (e.g., Luke 1:46–47; John 12:27 and 13:21). Additionally, dichotomists reference Jesus' warning in Matthew 10:28 where He states, "Do not be afraid of those who kill the body but cannot kill the soul. Rather, be afraid of the One who can destroy both soul and body in hell." Finally, dichotomists point to Paul's duality of thought as he speaks of being "away from the body and at home with the Lord" (2 Cor. 5:8). We would agree that these are all potent arguments, but other passages as well must guide our view as we seek to survey the theological lot lines of human personality. If we only recognize a dualism of the material and immaterial, we do not embrace the whole teaching of the Bible, as we will see later.

Monist Views

For all of the debate, it is important to note that trichotomists and dichotomists have more in common in their understandings of human nature than they have in dispute. Both agree that humans are compound in nature and that humans have an immaterial aspect to their nature that continues to exist after death. But an entirely different concept of persons exists among those who might be best termed *monists*. Monism is the belief that humans have only one aspect to their being. People are a whole, not parts, and the terms *body, soul, spirit, heart,* and *mind* are simply differing ways to speak of that whole, just different functions of the whole person.

Humans are, from the monist view, indivisible in nature. Such a view is gaining prominence in our day in three circles. First, it is gaining popularity among those who embrace a spiritual monism where the only true reality is the spiritual in nature. This view is found among those influenced by Eastern mystic religions. Hindus, for example, hold that there is a single reality that is of a "divine substance." Thus, from this viewpoint all persons, objects, and sources of energy together comprise the essence of God. Radical environmentalists and New Age religious adherents often espouse this perspective. A second monistic view is found in the scientific community. Based on materialistic assumptions about the nature of reality, there is no room for the supernatural and, accordingly, no place for an immaterial aspect to human beings. Finally, a monistic view is embraced among theists of two different theological orientations—those neo-orthodox in theological perspective (Robinson) and some Evangelicals who seek to harmonize the findings of neuropsychology with the teachings of Scripture (Jeeves; MacKay). We will address each of these perspectives.

Spiritual Monists

We live in an era in which Eastern mystic thinking is shaping Western culture. Spiritual monism is at the heart of this Eastern orientation. Spiritual monism teaches that all persons are part of a whole, of a single substance, namely "the Divine." This viewpoint understands God not as a transcendent being distinct from His creation, but enmeshed in and of the same essence as creation. Spiritual monists believe that, because God cannot be separated from His creation, He is found within the created order of things. Humans are part of that one single substance of the universe. Songs such as "The Circle of Life" and "We Are the World" are somewhat recent expressions of this philosophy. God is in "every rock, every creature, every thing" as the theme song from the movie *Pocahontas* proclaims. Authors like Shirley MacLaine (*Out on a Limb*), Larry Dossey (*Healing Words*), Betty J. Eadie (*Embraced by the Light*), and James Redfield (*Celestine Prophecy*) call readers to worship not the God of the Bible but "the Divine Within."

Such a view of God and of human beings is in direct contradiction to biblical Christianity, where God is separate and above His creation. We are called to worship only the one true God who created us along with everything in the world (Acts 17:24). Symbolized by the circle, spiritual monism stands in contrast to the linear, historic message of the Bible. The Bible is plain in teaching a duality of the Creator and the creation. They are separate. Although it is true that we can see in God's creation evidence of the Creator in a way that is similar to observing the painting and then drawing conclusions about the artist, creation is distinct from the Creator in substance, as the artist is distinct from his painting (Rom. 1:19–22).

Materialistic Monists

Those who embrace a materialistic monism also say that there is but one substance that comprises reality. But for them it is not an immaterial spirit, but the phenomenological world of matter. This form of materialism is not the desire to possess things, as we use the term in popular speech (although that is an outgrowth of a materialistic worldview). Philosophical materialism is a worldview that denies the possibility of the supernatural and embraces the material world as the only genuine reality. As a word of caution at this point, we must agree with Berkhof that "a great deal of present day psychology is definitely moving in the direction of materialism" (96).

Materialism is one of the foundational assumptions of modern science and is most clearly evident in B. F. Skinner's behaviorism in the social sciences. Behaviorism's denials of the soul, human worth and dignity, the mind, and human consciousness are all contrary to the teachings of historic biblical Christianity. Thus, we are right to be guarded in any attempt to apply, in a wholesale way, behaviorist techniques in ministry.

The modern materialistic understanding of human personality sees people as the result of the chance processes of evolution. Humans are viewed as advanced organisms or complex machines. In this view, humans are soulless animals responding to their environment within the limits and potential of their genetic code. What is commonly described as a soul, a mind, intelligence, human consciousness, or an inner person is attributed to neurons, axons, dendrites, synapse connections, neurochemical transmitters, and the neurological firing of this cognitive chemistry and hardware. For modern-day cognitive scientists, the relationship of the immaterial to the material is simple—mind equals brain. All behaviors, thoughts, dispositions, and personality traits can be causally linked to various brain-states. The brain is considered to be an adequate explanation of the immaterial aspects of human beings. It is thought that because of the billions of interrelated components of the brain and its enormous complexity, these "inner person" sensations emerge.

Foundational to their thinking is a concept called *supervenience*. Supervenience is a hierarchical understanding of people that rests on the assumption that all differences in cognition or personality between people can ultimately be explained as physical differences in the brain and brain chemistry. It is held that human intelligence and behavior are the results of neurophysiology, which rests upon molecular biology, which in turn rests on atomic physics, which in turn rests on elementary particle physics. Given this understanding, the goal of the material monist is to find the lowest level explanation for human behavior and thought.

In response to materialistic monism we must first recognize that this is a philosophical position, not a scientific one. If a person assumes that all that is real is material in nature, then it is highly unlikely that that person would recognize the immaterial or the supernatural even if shown evidence. To begin by denying the possibility of the supernatural or the immaterial predetermines the range of potential answers to all questions regarding the nature of the mind, none of which can include notions of an inner person. Further, to assume that the complexity of the brain is an adequate explanation for the mind, intelligence, and conscious awareness is a step of faith. It is precisely because the brain is so complex that no one actually knows what is going on in the brain. Although there is indeed a causal relationship between our brain's activity and our behavior, it is limited to the simplest levels of behavior. As soon as one moves to the higher levels of attitudes, goals, intentions, and hopes, cognitive scientists quickly give up any claim to understanding human beings from a neurological level. Instead they must turn by faith to their assumed concepts of supervenience and the emergence of mind from brain complexity.

And so, it is clear that materialistic monism is a philosophical position that begins with a denial of God, the spirit within man, and the supernatural. Needless to say, such a position cannot be reconciled with the teachings of Scripture. The scriptural counselor must acknowledge some alternative that allows for the immaterial and the supernatural.

Semimaterialistic Monists

Two theological camps have embraced a monist position that we would term "semimaterialistic" in nature. We use this term because, in both cases, adherents acknowledge the God of the Bible while denying the existence of an immaterial and immortal spirit in humans ontologically distinct from the material body. Both groups would argue that a Hebraic (Hebrew) or Old Testament understanding of human personality, rather than a Hellenistic (Greek) perspective, should be used to interpret the New Testament writings about human nature.

Neo-orthodox theologians have argued for a radical unity in human nature. In their view, the words *body*, *soul*, and *spirit* are simply synonymous with the concept of "self." They would argue the following points:

1. The Old Testament view of man is unitary in nature. No distinction is made between the human body and a separate soul. In fact, in the Hebrew language there is not a word for the body. Such a distinction is a New Testament understanding that came into the New Testament because of the influence of Greek culture.
2. The body and soul references of the New Testament are descriptions of the total human personality, not the component parts of man.
3. Man is a unity. To refer to a "person" as a disembodied spirit is to alter the normal usage of the term. Likewise, to speak of "death" as the separation of soul and body is, again, to alter the term's normal usage.
4. Human consciousness depends on the physical organism, specifically the brain.

Some Evangelicals who seek to develop an integrated view of man hold a second version of the semimaterialistic view. They believe that when the Bible speaks of souls or spirits, it is simply using prescientific terminology for human consciousness, which, they contend, emerges from the complex physiology of the brain. The spirit is a derivative of the body (brain), not a resident within the body. Donald MacKay and Malcolm Jeeves are two examples of writers who hold to a semimaterialistic monism. They do not quarrel with the cognitive scientists in their supervenient understanding of human beings except that they would recognize the existence of God and man's responsibility to God. They would also recognize the work of Christ on behalf of those who believe. At this point they would move away from historic orthodoxy to embrace an annihilationist view of unsaved man. Since there is no distinction between the soul and the body, semimaterialistic monists conclude that the eternal punishment of hell cannot be conscious. Instead, they would contend that unsaved persons are annihilated at death.

The problem with the semimaterialist view is threefold. First, it reinterprets theology in light of neuropsychology. Assuming the validity of supervenience, MacKay and Jeeves conclude that the spirit is derived from the complexity of the brain. Clearly, this is an accommodation to the materialistic, supervenient assumptions of science, which are neither indisputable conclusions of scientific inquiry, nor justified by the direct teachings of Scripture.

Second, this view leads to an inevitable annihilationist position and a "conditional immortality." Annihilationists who take this perspective teach that man is mortal and that immortality is a gift of God granted to those who believe. The person who does not accept Christ will lose all consciousness at death and be annihilated. Such a position cannot be reconciled with the clarity of Christ's words in Matthew 25:46 where we read, "Then they will go away to eternal punishment, but the righteous to eternal life." Other passages such as Matthew 10:15; 11:21–24; 16:27; Luke 12:47–48; Hebrews 10:29; and Revelation 20:11–15; 22:12 speak not simply of an eternal death, but of conscious punishment, of fire, and of eternal torment.

The third difficulty with this view is that it fails to adequately account for the passages of Scripture that indicate that an intermediate state exists between the physical death of a believer and the resurrection that entails a conscious relationship with Christ. Jesus had no difficulty telling the thief on the cross that "today you will be with me in paradise" (Luke 23:43). Neither did He struggle with telling the story of the rich man and the poor man, Lazarus (Luke 16:19–31). He said that the rich man went to Hades to great torment in the flames, while Lazarus was taken to Abraham's bosom. Both were a conscious existence after death. It is difficult to imagine that Jesus would intentionally mislead His hearers on this subject simply because of cultural understandings or pre-scientific knowledge. Paul too believed that to be "away from the body" was to be "at home with the Lord" (2 Cor. 5:8).

Essential Unity View

Water is remarkable in its properties. Consider, for example, its density. The density of water is greatest at 39.2°F (4°C). Like other liquids, water becomes less dense as it warms. But more important, unlike other liquids, it also becomes less dense as it freezes. If this were not the case, ice would sink, causing ponds to freeze from the bottom up, killing all life below the surface. Instead, ice on the top of a body of water acts as an insulator that slows down the freezing process and allows some of the water to remain in a liquid form.

A second special property of water is its role as the universal solvent. It has the ability to dissolve many other substances. Water molecules are polar molecules, meaning that they have a strong positive charge on one end and a strong negative charge on the other. Since opposite charges attract each other, these charges attract the charges of other substances. *Adhesion* is the term used to describe this attraction. It is water's strong adhesion characteristic that allows many substances to dissolve in it easily.

A third distinctive property of water is its cohesion. This is the attraction of molecules of the same substance to each other. Again the result of the polar charges of the water molecule, cohesion binds water molecules together. Cohesion produces a surface tension that allows water to have a sheeting action. It also allows water to form drops and bubbles, and it establishes a film on tops of lakes, ponds, and rivers. Many organisms live just above or just below this surface film.

You might well be wondering by now why we would be itemizing water's properties. The goal is to illustrate the fourth view of the constitutional nature of human beings. Imagine trying to explain the properties of water by describing its component parts—hydrogen and oxygen. Neither hydrogen nor oxygen has these properties independently. Both elements have distinct properties of their own, but it is only when they are understood together as H_2O that the properties of water and its uniqueness can be comprehended. Similarly, human beings are best understood as an "essential unity." It is only when spirits and bodies are united together that humanness in its truest sense can be described. Humans are a compound of the immaterial and the material; they are both spiritual and physical. And although it is true that this compound of human nature can be dissolved, to do so is the essence of death. It is in this essential unified state that the authentic qualities of the human being can be recognized.

It is interesting that, according to Genesis 2:7, God created man from the dust of the ground (material) and then breathed into him the breath of life (immaterial) and he became a living being (soul). Men and women were created from the beginning to be both material and immaterial simultaneously. Humans were not created as disembodied spirits seeking physical bodies to possess. Nor were they simply material beings. It is God's design that humans possess this unity of material and immaterial. Yes, for a period, we will indeed be "away from the body and at home with the Lord" (2 Cor. 5:8). But it is more than just an interesting fact that one day we will receive new bodies, glorified bodies, transformed and resurrected bodies that we will have for eternity (Phil. 3:20–21; 1 Thess. 4:16–17). And why is that? It is because a body is an essential component of the creation of God we term "human." God has not forgotten that fact and will reunite body and spirit into an immortal, inseparable, glorified compound that is the redeemed human being.

Scripture is not reductionistic. It does not seek to simplify human nature or reduce humans to our most basic parts. Furthermore, it does not seek to precisely describe each component part. Rather, the Word of God uses a wide array of terms to describe the multifaceted properties of human nature. The image painted by these multiple terms is more like a brilliant, carefully cut diamond with many sides or facets than a simple mixture of substances. The practical reality is that people must always be thought of and related to as a complex unity. Any effort to describe persons in a compartmentalized way is simply an accommodation to our limited reasoning abilities. Although we may speak of people in terms of their physical, cognitive, or psychosocial aspects for the purpose of discussion or research, no absolute division of human beings is evident in the text of Scripture. The scriptural perspective is of a multifaceted creature of enormous complexity rather than a compartmentalized being. Although compartmental divisions may make the study of human beings less complex and easier to process, they inherently destroy an accurate understanding of the total person.

The Bible uses several words to describe human personality. Each of these provides a rich perspective on the complex and multifaceted being that God has created. In the Old Testament, humans are viewed in a unified way. The Old Testament word *nephesh* is used for the total person. It is translated "soul," but is most accurately understood as the total being, body and spirit, united. *Nephesh* is used as we might use the word "soul" in describing a disaster at sea—"seventy *souls* were lost when the ship sank." It is best understood to be the life principle that animates human beings.

Although the Old Testament does not have a word for the human body as an organism, it does distinguish between a lower, earthly and weaker element and a higher, heavenly and divine element. The Old Testament primarily uses the word *basar* to speak of human flesh, but several other words are used as well—"dust," "bones," "house of clay"—to denote a physical element in humans.

A third term is used of humans in the Old Testament, the word *ruach*, meaning "spirit." It is the word used to describe the life of God, breathed into the dust of the ground to make Adam a living soul (Gen. 2:7). It is used elsewhere in the Old Testament to encompass a whole range of personality qualities including the emotional, social, and volitional aspects of persons.

In the New Testament, several Greek terms are employed to describe persons. First among these is the term *psuche* or *soul.* It is the word from which we get our word *psychology*. Paul uses the word *psuche* (soul) of the total person. For example, Paul wrote in Philippians 2:30 that Epaphroditus risked his life for Paul's *psuche*. By this he meant that Epaphroditus nearly lost his life for the sake of Paul's life. He was referring to his personal well-being, not his immortal soul. Most frequently in Paul's writings the term refers to the total person as a thinking, feeling, functioning being. But the term is used as well in the New Testament for an aspect or entity in humans that stands against the body, is capable of salvation, and can continue to exist apart from the body (Matt. 10:28; James 1:21; 1 Peter 1:9; Rev. 6:9; 20:4). So what then should we conclude is the meaning of the word *psuche*? It is best to think of this term as a description of man's essential self. It is the broadest term, widely applicable to the many facets of human personality.

A narrower term used to describe human beings is the word *pneuma*, translated *spirit*. *Pneuma* is the word from which we get our English word *pneumonia*. It literally means "wind" or "breath." The word is used in the Bible as a designation for God's Spirit but is also used to describe the inner dimensions of man as contrasted with the physical body. Romans 8:10–11 is a prime example of this contrast. "But if Christ is in you, your body is dead because of sin, yet your spirit is alive because of righteousness. And if the Spirit of him who raised Jesus from the dead is living in you, he who raised Christ from the dead will also give life to your mortal bodies through his Spirit, who lives in you." All persons possess this human *pneuma* (1 Cor. 2:11). It is not received as a result of salvation, as the semimaterialistic monists would contend. Rather, the true inner person becomes capable of enjoying fellowship with God's Spirit and, in fact, is renewed by the Spirit of God as a result of salvation (Col. 3:9–10). Paul described the human spirit as dead, that is, unable to enjoy fellowship with God, until God's Spirit quickens it, enabling the believer to enter into a living fellowship with God.

A third New Testament word used to describe human beings is the term *soma*, meaning *body*. Soma generally denotes the physical dimension of human beings. But it can also refer to the entire person in a way similar to *psuche* (soul). For example, Paul calls believers to offer their bodies as a living sacrifice (Rom. 12:1) to God. Here he was speaking of one's total self, not just one's physical body. When Paul spoke of giving the body to be burned (1 Cor. 13:3), of subduing the body (1 Cor. 9:27), or of magnifying Christ in his body (Phil. 1:20), he was referring to his entire person, not just his physical body. In other contexts the term refers to the outer person, which is wasting away and ultimately succumbs to death (2 Cor. 4:16). It is important to examine the immediate literary context to understand how *soma* is being used.

A fourth term used in the New Testament to describe human beings is the term *sarx*, or *flesh*. This is a very difficult word to translate because its usage is complex. At times it is used to refer to bodily tissue (1 Cor. 15:39). In other contexts it refers to the entire human body (1 Cor. 5:3). The term can refer to one's kinship with others, such as Paul's usage of his relationship to fellow Jews (Rom. 9:3). Another use of the term is to describe a human viewpoint as compared to a divine perspective (2 Cor. 5:16). A common use of the word *sarx* is in an ethical sense to contrast actions done in a sinful way with those done in the power of God's Spirit (Rom. 8:8–9; Gal. 2:20). Finally, the word is used to describe unregenerate human nature (Gal. 5:19–26).

Another New Testament term used to describe human beings includes *kardia* (heart), from which we get our word *cardiac*. This term refers to the inner person and is descriptive of the seat of emotions and the will (Rom. 8:27). Other terms include *syneidesis* (conscience) and *nous* (mind). The conscience is seen as a universally possessed faculty that enables moral judgment (Rom. 2:15). The mind is man's cognitive capacity making him a knowing, thinking, reasoning, and judging creature (1 Cor. 14:14). Each of these terms offers an opportunity to the Bible student for fruitful study in understanding God's perspective on human beings.

What shall we make of all of this? How shall we understand the biblical perspective on the constitutional nature of human beings? We would conclude that people are complex, multifaceted beings, unlike any other creature God has made. The biblical data indicate an essential unity to humans. The normal and intended nature of man is to be a materialized, unified being in intimate fellowship with his Creator. The body is not inherently evil and the spirit pure. No, the effects of sin have damaged the total person. Death involves the decay of the body, but also the separation of the material and the immaterial. For those who are redeemed, even while the material decays, there is an intermediate state in which fellowship with God can be enjoyed in a conscious way. Finally, at the resurrection, the material and the immaterial will reunite in some sort of a new body that has some points of continuity with the old body.

The implications of this view of human nature are significant for those who seek to counsel under the authority of Scripture. First, we must treat people as a unity. We cannot deal with people in a compartmentalized way. In ministry, we must seek to care for the total person and recognize the interrelatedness of the physical and spiritual. Second, we must recognize the complexity of persons. No single theory of human development or human behavior could ever serve to fully explain people. We must be careful of reductionistic approaches to counseling, whether proposed or practiced by Christians or non-Christians. Counseling models that offer a single answer or a single "biblical" technique for every issue or every person are likely to be excessively simplistic. Third, we must not depreciate any aspect of human nature. We cannot minimize human emotion, the human body, or the human intellect. All are interwoven aspects of a total being. We cannot divide issues into physical on the one hand and spiritual on the other hand. Such an approach to people is doomed to frustration and failure. Fourth, true spiritual growth and Christlikeness are not found in subjugating one aspect of human nature to another. There is no single, specific aspect of human nature that is evil. Depravity infects the whole person. Likewise, sanctification involves the entire person as well. And fifth, we must help people live in light of eternity, not simply the material world of the immediate, despite the pressure of society and science.

— *Within These Boundaries* —

We have established three major boundaries to help us understand human nature from a biblical perspective. The sinful nature is also fundamental to a biblical psychology of human beings. We are indeed bent away from the Creator by that devastating principle. But we will tackle that matter in the next chapter as we consider the factors that create the need for spiritual direction and personal counsel. Personal sin is clearly a major factor damaging people's lives, although we do not believe it is the only one.

Our analysis of various theories of the development of human personality must be considered within the boundaries we have established. We must carefully examine the assumptions that form the foundation of each theory under review. Does the theory embrace a creative view of people, or does it view people from an evolutionary perspective? Does the theory recognize the divine image in persons, or does it reduce people to organisms without dignity or worth? Does the theory recognize the multifaceted nature of persons, or does it treat people in a reductionistic way, overly simplifying human struggles and problems? Likewise, we will need to see if the conclusions reached by the various personality theorists, and writers who seek to apply those theories, fall within these boundaries.

How shall we respond if we find that the assumptions or conclusions of a given theory are outside of these boundaries? Should we reject the theory outright? Should we attack the theory as an opposing gospel? Should we ignore all aspects of the theory for fear that its errors will take us captive? Or is there a more productive approach? We would suggest that with a clear sense of the biblical and theological weaknesses of a psychological theory or treatment in view, we can evaluate and discern the contributions the theory makes to our ministry efforts. We may well find that a researcher has faulty assumptions and even biased conclusions and yet that elements of his research are valid and true discoveries have been made by the common grace of God. In this situation, we believe it is possible to adopt the aspects and applications of the theory that are harmonious with a biblical viewpoint.

NOTES

Allen, Woody. "My Speech to the Graduates." *Side Effects.* New York: Ballantine Books, 1980.

Berkhof, L. *Systematic Theology.* 4th & rev. ed. Grand Rapids: Eerdmans, 1949.

Bulkley, Ed. *Why Christians Can't Trust Psychology.* Eugene, Ore.: Harvest House, 1993.

Fosdick, Harry E. *The Modern Use of the Bible.* New York: Macmillan, 1933.

Welch, Edward T. "Who Are We? Needs, Longings and the Image of God in Man." *Journal of Biblical Counseling* 13.1 (Fall 1994): 25–38

— Chapter 3 —

BROKEN AND HURTING:
The Biblical Dimensions of Personality
(Part Two)

The news of Karen's death hit her college campus as if an emotional hand grenade had been lobbed into the women's dormitory. Unexpectedly, she slipped into a coma, and in just a matter of hours she was gone. The word spread through the student body. Karen had been diagnosed with anorexia nervosa and bulimia. She was not unlike many college-age women whose self-induced vomiting, use of laxatives, and obsessive exercise combine with extreme dieting and an intense fear of weight gain to create a potentially deadly result. In hindsight, the symptoms of starvation were clear: sleep disturbance, cessation of menstruation, insensitivity to pain, loss of hair, low blood pressure, reduced body temperature, and a skeletally thin body. But, despite the warnings, despite the caring friends and family, Karen suffered cardiovascular dysfunction and eventual heart failure. In fact, Karen had taken her own life, not in a single violent act, but gradually. Slowly she became more and more emaciated until she simply was physically unable to wake to another day.

How do we explain Karen's behavior? How do we interpret

such events? How do we understand why human beings have problems, inner struggles, and failings? If Karen were not a believer, or if believers were immune to such disorders, it would be much easier. But Karen was a Christian and by all accounts a strong, growing, and dedicated one. Did she fail to trust God enough? Was it because of unconfessed and unaddressed sin in her life that she died? Was God punishing Karen? Was this the direct result of personal sin? Or were there other factors—social, emotional, and cognitive—at work that led to Karen's premature death? This was not an accident where we can step back and say, "God had His reasons for taking Karen." No, this was predictable and even preventable. Although God was clearly at work, superintending the events of Karen's life, and He was not surprised by Karen's death, certain factors surely contributed to Karen's disorder that need to be understood so that other, future Karens might be helped and healed.

EXPLAINING HUMAN STRUGGLES: THE STARTING POINT—ONE'S WORLDVIEW

Several possible means of explaining Karen's self-destructive behavior and the events that led to her youthful death could be proposed. These explanations follow four different paths of thought, each governed by a different way of seeing the world. Let us briefly explore these perspectives.

Mythological Explanations

Some would explain Karen's behavior through the use of modern myth. In many cultures, including ancient Greece and modern America, human behavior and the events that shape human life have been understood in terms of forces, powers, or gods whose ways are mysterious and can only be submitted to or appeased. Probably the most common current example of a mythological explanation of human behavior is that of horoscopes. Each day people across the country open the pages of their newspaper to find out their horoscope. They hope that they might align life's choices with the position of stars and planets. But horoscopes are not the only example. With its crystals, pyramids, and powers, the New Age movement also stands as an example of a mythological approach to life.

Mythological perspectives can also be used by Christians to explain life, suffering, pain, and problems. Like those disciples who came to Jesus inquiring about a man blind from birth, some Christians may ask, "Rabbi, who sinned, this man or his parents, that he was born blind?" (John 9:2). Their assumption is a simplistic one. They assume that sin is the cause of all pain, suffering, and human need, and that suffering, pain, and death are the just rewards for that personal sin. But Jesus was quick to point out that such a false chain of logic cannot answer every situation. He replied, "Neither this man nor his parents sinned . . . but this happened so that the work of God might be displayed in his life" (v. 3). His point is important. There are reasons other than simple cause-and-effect answers to human sorrows and sufferings. To make such a leap is to believe a myth that if God is offended, people will suffer. A similar approach contends that if God is pleased, He will bless. It is reasoned that if I just go to church, give more in the offering plate, or make some personal sacrifice, God will be moved to respond in my favor. "I must have done something right today," we say when our stock goes up or we get that parking space close to the grocery store entrance.

Such mythological thinking shows itself in the false guilt felt by many who face a loss on the magnitude that Karen's parents experienced. "God must be punishing us" or "We just did not have enough faith that she would be healed" are not uncommon thoughts to those left behind. When we need to find a reason for all of life's problems in the suffering person's relationship with God, we reflect a mythological understanding of God, not a biblical understanding of human beings.

Philosophical Explanations

A more logical approach to explain Karen's failed battle with anorexia nervosa follows a philosophic line of thinking. This approach might reason that all human beings have needs and Karen's were unmet. Or that human suffering happens to the good and the bad alike, and that no one is immune to its impact. Again, philosophic reasoning may conclude that Karen's sufferings were the result of Karen's own decisions or the consequence of some missed cue by those around her. Regardless of the rationale proposed, philosophic explanations seek a reasonable answer to a problem or situation, not with reference to hard data, but through individual opinions and philosophic outlooks. This is the stuff on which both gossip and talk radio shows depend—an opinion without a factually proven basis.

Differing philosophic explanations of human behavior can serve to commend or to condemn the same choices. For example, some might reason that the right to privacy should allow a woman to have an abortion on demand, whereas others would argue that the right to life should prevail, prohibiting abortions as a matter of individual will. The arguments for or against abortion are philosophical in nature. Proponents of both positions could be logical in their defense, passionate in their argumentation, and intellectually honest in their debate of the issue. But in both cases it is a philosophic path that has been taken to explain life—its options and its pains.

Although a philosophic approach to understanding human behavior and human suffering offers a firmer footing than does a mythological approach, it too fails to provide an adequate basis for ministry. Depending on the rational starting point and working assumptions, a number of reasonable explanations could be derived for almost any event or problem. And so the discussion continues. Which seems right? Who has the best argument? Whose position makes the most sense? And so we debate and debate but never come to a knowledge of the truth. Philosophic reasoning about human suffering, hurt, and need is well and good, but it seldom leads to any clear answers or certainty as to how we might assist those in need.

Scientific Explanations

Moving beyond mythological superstition and philosophical logic, some would seek to understand Karen's anorexia scientifically. We live in a scientific age in which humans are being studied through more objective means. As with all scientific inquiry, the goal is to establish a hypothesis that explains human behavior and then test that hypothesis through rigorously controlled experiments and other research methods. In doing so, we hope that patterns of human behavior will emerge and with those patterns, predictors can be identified and treatments devised. Of course, the challenge is the complexity of persons and the difficulties of studying human beings as we would other research subjects.

Through the use of the scientific method, factors that are correlated with or that influence the causation of various human problems can be identified. These factors can give counselors insights into a variety of disorders and into which personality types are most likely to develop the given disorder. Likewise, the scientific study of human beings can establish commonalities of human development. By understanding, for example, the typical behaviors of the adolescent period, scientists can help parents, teachers, and youth workers predict the issues that adolescents will face in their teen years. In Karen's case, scientific data, if monitored and understood, could have readily predicted that she was an "at risk" individual for the devastating impact of anorexia nervosa. Appropriate treatment may have enabled Karen to cope with and eventually overcome her eating disorder. Such treatment, though not universally effective, would be tested and evaluated using scientific research standards. A scientific understanding of Karen's case could have better helped counselors to assist her than would simply working from their philosophic opinions, no matter how well reasoned.

Scientific explanations of human behavior have inherent limitations, however. First, scientific approaches presuppose that there is a natural explanation for everything. This presupposition is known as naturalism. Naturalism is the belief that the natural world is the full extent of reality and that the supernatural world is either a mythological creation of prescientific persons or is unknowable since it cannot be studied scientifically. As we explained in chapter 2, this naturalistic bias eliminates the possibility of supernatural intervention.

Second, scientific efforts can be hamstrung by a commitment to *logical positivism*. Logical positivism holds that only those statements open to some means of empirical verification have meaning and are worthy of scientific scrutiny. All other statements are held to be statements of faith, speculation, or conjecture. For example, the statement "Wood floats" has meaning to the scientist because it can be tested or verified in some manner. As a result, it can be discussed and the nature of wood understood. In this way, scientists seek to come to agreements about the mechanisms behind how the real world functions.

Take the statement "Humans are made in the image of God." Such a statement cannot be verified empirically so it is, from a scientific perspective, a statement of personal faith and not a matter of scientific pursuit. But consider the problem modern science faces because of its commitment to logical positivism. Look again at that foundational scientific premise we stated earlier. "Only those statements open to some means of empirical verification have meaning and are worthy of scientific scrutiny." Can that statement be verified empirically? Clearly it cannot. It is, in fact, a self-denying concept. One of the foundational premises of science is actually, by its own definition, a faith statement that is not worthy of scientific inquiry. So science is limited by its own assumptions, assumptions that may well overlook the important truths that set men and women free.

Third, science is unable to answer the major issues of life. It cannot tell us the meaning of life. It cannot tell us what it means to be a moral person. Science cannot tell us whether there is life after death. Science cannot tell us the values by which we are to govern our lives or manage human societies. Science cannot tell us what ought to be. It can only tell us what is and, with some degree of certainty, attempt to tell us how it got that way. We call this the "Is-Ought" problem. Science cannot tell us the "ought" because it is limited to the domain of natural revelation, what can be observed. It is only through God's special revelation in Scripture and in Jesus Christ that we can understand the "oughts" of life. God tells us what ought to be and how to achieve it through His revealed Word.

Science has limits but also makes contributions. As we will see later in this book, science can offer counselors tools and insights for the care and development of human beings. But it cannot give us what we need to deal with the entire matter of human pain, hurt, and suffering. For this we must understand the inner person, the immaterial as well as the material. We need a theological understanding of human beings to adequately explain human behavior.

Theological Explanations

Those who embrace theological explanations of human behavior, particularly from a conservative evangelical orientation, begin with a different set of assumptions than do naturalistic, positivistic scientists. Theologians seek to understand humans in reference to their Maker. Bible-centered theologians do not deny the valid role of science, empirical thinking, and research. In fact, theologians would suggest that science, even the social science disciplines of psychology, sociology, and anthropology, have a rightful function in the study of human beings as a part of God's natural revelation. But they would not limit reality to the natural realm. Instead, theologians assume the existence of a supernatural reality along with a natural one.

Theologians hold that God established the natural order, including the principles and laws that govern nature, to function in a systematic and continuous manner. His orderly character is the basis for those laws, and His clever design and sustaining will is the reason they exist at all. But those laws and the boundaries of the physical universe do not limit God. He is able, when it fits His good and perfect will, to suspend His own laws and do miraculous things. As the Creator of human beings, God is able to work His plans through whatever means He might choose, although never in violation of His own divine attributes. He is able to enter into human affairs to relate to and communicate with His creation. He has done so in a diversity of ways, but most significantly in the person of Jesus Christ and in the pages of the Bible.

Understanding people demands, therefore, that we gain knowledge of the natural laws that govern space and time as well as knowledge of the principles and teachings of the Scriptures. In fact, it is Scripture that must have the preferred place of authority in our thinking, as we discussed in the first chapter. In the pages of Scripture we discover truth about people that we could know through no other means. We could not reason our way to it; we could not empirically discover it. God had to make it known through the special revelation of His Word.

Theological explanations of issues such as Karen's behavior, struggle, and death go beyond scientific explanations about eating disorders to include biblical understanding of human beings and human suffering. Science is of invaluable help in understanding many of the biological, sociological, and psychological factors that were at work in Karen's life, but it is the organizing truth of the Bible that helps to give clear understanding to the causes of Karen's deeper sufferings. Let us consider a theological understanding of human suffering and problems as we discover the perspective of the Bible.

A THEOLOGICAL UNDERSTANDING OF HUMAN STRUGGLES AND SUFFERING

In the previous chapter we looked at some of the biblical dimensions of human personality. We sought to understand people as God created them. In this section we will expand that understanding to include the attributes of human personality that contribute to our brokenness, pain, and suffering. We will also explore those physical and spiritual forces outside of human beings that shape us and sometimes hurt us. We might begin this theological study by asking, "Why do people have problems in the first place?" and "What are the reasons we hurt, have inner turmoil, or face personal struggles?"

In a real sense we could point to the fall of Adam as the ultimate reason for human sufferings. It was Adam's sin that brought God's wrath and banished humans from the perfect Garden and the wonderful daily presence of God (Gen. 3). It was Adam's failure that brought judgment and hardship on the human race. The original condition of mankind was altered by that one act of disobedience to God. As a result, human beings face many unfortunate realities that flow either directly or indirectly from that event.

These realities include such facts as broken human relationships, the daily struggle to survive, personal suffering, and even physical death. We know too that Adam's sin affected even the natural; creation fell with Adam and now groans for the time of final redemption (Rom. 8:22).

Had Adam and Eve not each taken that bite from the forbidden fruit, there would be no need for counselors, nor would there be the problems and predicaments faced by human beings. But sin did enter the human race, and things did change. What we must now explore is how those changes explain human struggles. We would suggest three primary sources of human suffering that are linked to the fall of Adam. Theologians have historically categorized these using three biblical terms—the world, the flesh, and the devil.

The *World:* External Forces That Bring Human Suffering

According to the writers of Scripture, we humans suffer because of forces that reside outside of ourselves. The Bible uses the term the *world (cosmos)* to refer to these external, environmental factors. The Greek term *cosmos* can reference the physical Earth, the human race, and collective forces of evil that work through the world social order against the kingdom and people of God. *World* is a broad term that most often applies to any force external to the person that works to mold that individual in some damaging way. The world does this through natural forces, human forces, and societal forces. We will briefly consider each.

Human Struggles Can Be Attributed to Natural Forces

Our world is not always kind to us. The physical world, and the natural forces that are at work within it, bring suffering to people's lives. Earthquakes, volcanoes, tidal waves, and floods all bring suffering to humans who come in contact with their natural fury. Drought or storm, tornado or typhoon, fire or freezing all put human life at risk, sometimes bringing injury and death. Famine, starvation, and disease continually threaten human life somewhere on our globe. In 1976 an earthquake rolled across China, killing some 250,000 people. In 1985 a dormant volcano erupted in Columbia, taking twenty thousand lives. In 1988 in Armenia forty-five thousand died in another massive quake. Again a quake in Iran took twenty-nine thousand lives in 1990. More than six thousand died in the Kobe quake in Japan in 1995. Closer to home, the eruption of Mount Saint Helens, earthquakes in San Francisco and Los Angeles, floods and tornadoes in the Midwest, hurricanes in the Southeast, and winter storms in the Northeast are all reminders of the enormous power at work in nature and the devastation that can come when humans are in the path of a storm. How are we to understand the suffering brought through these natural forces? Is God angry? Is He rendering judgment? Are these just examples of the "wildness" of nature at its worst?

To understand human suffering as the result of natural forces we must understand something of God's work in preserving life on this planet. Numerous passages address the gracious act of God in preserving creation from its own destruction. In Nehemiah 9:6 we learn that God as Creator of the heavens and the earth preserves His creation. Paul also indicated that the continuance of creation depends on the will of God when he wrote, "He is before all things, and in him all things hold together" (Col. 1:17). The author of Hebrews communicates a similar thought saying that the Son "upholds all things by the word of His power" (Heb. 1:3 NASB). The point of these passages is that creation is not self-sustaining. Rather, God is active, willing the continuance of this creation.

The biblical concept of the natural world is this: Apart from divine preservation, due to the destructive and unfaithful nature of fallen creation, the world would be consumed violently were it not for God's mercy. As David C. Toole put it, "God holds back the chaos evoked by human wickedness so that the natural rhythms can proceed" (556). His point is that every natural disaster is a reminder of God's mercy and that God remains involved in His creation, preventing the complete and total destruction of human life. The fact that natural disasters are the exception rather than the rule demonstrates God's long-suffering and mercy. Creation has a propensity for destruction that is restrained by God's will.

With that said, we ought to remind ourselves of God's lovingkindness and provision for His children. Jesus was clear in His teaching regarding God's providential care over His children's lives. In Matthew 6, Jesus reassured His followers that if the Father cares for the birds of the air and the flowers of the field He would surely do the same for them. His point is that we ought to seek His kingdom and righteousness rather than being anxious about food and clothing. Paul likewise indicated that God cares for His children in such a way that we cannot be separated from His love (Rom. 8:35–39). It is reassuring to know that God is actively at work providing, protecting, and delivering His children from evil. This is important to note, for we know that believers are not always spared from danger, trial, persecution, and suffering (Rom. 5:3–5; James 1:2–5; 1 Peter 1:6–7; 4:12–13). These may be a part of our lives. But when trials or suffering come into our lives, not as a result of personal sin, God has a purpose and we can depend on His integrity that He is at work on our behalf. Like Job, we must conclude that God is God and can be trusted regardless of our immediate circumstances (Job 13:15; 42:3–6).

Natural disasters and the resultant suffering occur because of the forces of the created order. But that does not mean that God simply set those forces in motion and is operating the world on autopilot or cruise control as the Deist might suggest. Although natural laws do govern the universe and those forces work on both Christians and non-Christians alike (gravity is gravity, and it applies to the just and the unjust), God uses those forces to achieve His will in ways that differ between Christian and non-Christian. For one, God may be forming character or testing commitment (Job), while at the very same time He may be bringing judgment to another. We cannot easily discern God's ways in these acts, but we do know that even when apparently innocent persons suffer, God's integrity remains. In suffering and in disaster, God is at work both judging and saving. Remember that we worship the God who understands suffering. His Son both judged sin and saved sinners through the suffering on the cross.

Is it possible that Karen suffered due to natural forces with God's permission? Without the discernment of the Spirit of God it would be difficult to see such a connection, but we do know that as God's child, Karen's suffering was with His knowledge. Karen's body functioned as it was designed, and natural processes operating within her body had to affect her condition. Karen literally starved to death—a decision and habit for which she is ultimately responsible. But the process of starvation was the force that finally brought her death.

Anorexia deprives a person's body of the needed nutrients to sustain life. A number of natural physiological results follow. Heart disease is the most common medical cause of death in people suffering with anorexia nervosa. Starvation causes the heart to develop dangerous abnormal pumping rhythms and slow rhythms known as *bradycardia*. This reduces blood flow and blood pressure. The heart muscles starve, losing size while cholesterol levels rise. Minerals such as potassium, calcium, magnesium, and phosphate are normally dissolved in the body's fluid. Calcium and potassium are essential in maintaining the electric currents that make the heart beat regularly. Dehydration and starvation from anorexia reduces fluid levels and mineral content, a condition known as electrolyte imbalance. This eventually brings death because the electrical messages from the brain that keep the heart beating cannot be transmitted. Before the point of heart failure, people with severe anorexia may suffer nerve damage, experience seizures, and develop disordered thinking. Brain scans indicate that parts of the brain undergo structural changes and abnormally high or low activity during anorexic states.

And so it is correct to say that natural forces brought about Karen's death. These natural processes were the result of Karen's will and God's permission. Christians can take hope in the knowledge that even in the death of this child of God, God was at work to achieve His purposes through Karen's life and death.

Human Struggles Can Be Attributed to Human Forces

Sometimes people struggle with problems due not to their own sin, but the sin of another. It might be a parent, a spouse, an employer, or an employee. It could be a teacher, a pastor, a politician, or a leader. We relate to many different people in the course of our lives who, in one way or another, impact us for good or for ill. When those who influence our lives choose destructive acts of sin, we too can suffer and struggle. Take Andrea's situation for example.

Andrea is now twenty-six years old and married. Andrea grew up in a home that was marked by the damaging behavior of an alcoholic father. Because of the unpredictability of her father's moods and his frequent fits of rage, Andrea lived much of her young childhood in fear and emotional isolation. At times Andrea heard her father come home drunk late at night. Soon an argument ensued between Andrea's mother and father. The yelling would turn to violence, as her father physically abused her mother. Andrea covered her head with a pillow and prayed that God would change her father and protect her mother. It seemed to her that God heard her prayers because the next day her father always apologized and her mother forgave him. He would be better for a few days, but then the pattern began again. The cycle of drinking, abusing, apologizing, and forgiving became a way of life.

In Andrea's family there wasn't much communication. She never really could talk about what was going on in her life. "Dad is tired," her mom would say when she tried to talk with him or show him the work she had done in school. That was code for "Dad is too drunk to listen." When Andrea tried to tell her mother of her feelings toward her father, her mother would say, "You really don't feel that way" or "You really don't think that, do you?" Soon Andrea learned that it was best to say nothing at all.

Andrea rarely invited friends over. Her father's drinking embarrassed her. And besides, she knew that her mother did not want their "family secret" known, so it was best not to let too many people into their home. At one moment her father could be loving and kind, the next angry and nasty. She concluded that his behavior was too erratic to chance having a school friend come by.

College provided an escape for Andrea. She selected a school as far from home as possible with the hopes that she could start fresh and put her father's alcoholic binges and her parents' marital conflict behind her. It was at college that Andrea met Tom. His smile won her heart. He was a pre-med student and a solid believer. She always wanted to meet a Christian man who was considerate, kind, and attentive. Tom fit the bill exactly. In the summer between her junior and senior years they were wed, but very quickly their marriage faced problems.

Don't talk—don't trust—don't feel. Those were the lessons of her childhood. Now they were the obstacles to her marriage. Because she learned growing up that talking about problems only brought on more problems, she rarely spoke directly when various issues and problems came up in the relationship. She kept her thoughts and feelings to herself. She was sure that to talk openly would make matters worse. Over time the relationship suffered. She became distant and depressed. She was emotionally numb and simply went through the motions of married life. Eventually her goal became just making it through the day. Despondent and feeling very alone, Andrea finally turned to a counselor for help. Slowly she discovered how the patterns she learned as a child were affecting her life and marriage as an adult. With the help of a caring counselor using principles rooted in the Bible, Andrea was able to make changes and regain her ability to feel a wide range of emotions. She is still growing and her marriage is getting stronger. Daily she learns to experience the renewing work of Christ in her life.

Sometimes the actions and the sins of others are the human forces that bring personal struggles to our lives. Sometimes others victimize us, and we must wrestle with the results of that victimization. Andrea was a victim of her father's sin. As a result, she had carried damaging patterns of thinking, feeling, and behaving into her new role as a wife. As the adult child of an alcoholic, Andrea suffered lingering emotional strife.

Scripture is filled with examples of the actions of one person damaging the life of another. Take, for example, young Joseph sold into slavery by his brothers. Their sin robbed Joseph of his relationship with his father, forced him into service to the Egyptians, and eventually landed him in prison. It is interesting that although his brothers quite intentionally meant to do evil toward Joseph and he suffered for a period because of their misdeed, Joseph recognized the hand of God even in this wrongful event. "As for you, you meant evil against me, but God meant it for good in order to bring about this present result, to preserve many people alive" (Gen. 50:20 NASB). It is important for the counselor to remember that suffering in human lives can come as the result of the sinful actions of others, but even in such situations, God works providentially to achieve His will.

Human suffering can be attributed to human forces in our world. This may occur in overt sins like those of Andrea's father or less obvious and unintentional actions of those who love us. Let us again consider Karen, the young girl we introduced at the beginning of this chapter. Research indicates that one reason anorexics initially go undetected as having a serious mental disorder is that the early symptoms of the disorder are similar to their parents' values. If parents place excessive value upon physical appearance, shape, weight, and achievement, girls who manifest these signs are simply seen as living up to parental expectations and their "good girl" image. Such children are more likely to develop anorexia (Romeo 71–76). If Karen lived in a highly "enmeshed" family structure where parents were controlling, freedom to make independent choices were minimal, and expectations to achieve were high, it is possible that her anorexic disorder was a resultant outcome. Counselors working with an anorexic person like Karen must come to understand the family dynamics involved in the person's life. Although it is altogether possible that a normal, stable, and even model home life is involved, those who seek to help the anorexic must come to understand whether family values and parental expectations are playing a role in the problem.

Human Struggles Can Be Attributed to Societal Forces

It is true that we were finite even before the Fall. Humans have always been less than God and limited by that fact, but since the Fall, human finiteness has radically affected human experience. Before the Fall, Adam and Eve experienced a warm and intimate fellowship with God. As a result, His personal care for them minimized their limitations. He provided the food they needed. He created a rich environment. So long as He was their God, their needs would be met. But after the Fall that intimate relationship that offered so much security was shattered. Driven from the Garden, Adam and Eve no longer had the security of divine protection. They lived in a hostile world and sometimes lacked the needed wisdom to overcome their inherent limits. Banished from the secure environment of the Garden, something new entered human experience, something our modern world would call *stress*.

Apart from direct acts of sin, some of the problems faced by human beings are rooted in pressures of life outside the Garden. We have too many things to do and too little time to get them done. We struggle with knowing how best to rear children, we deal with our own experience of aging, and we wrestle to find the best means of caring for our aging parents. We strive to maintain a home, hold down a job, make ends meet, and fulfill the demands of running a business. Deals to close, production schedules to keep, things to fix, and a myriad of other human concerns fill our lives—all of which lead to the buildup of stress. Just the thought of it all is stressful. Stress is a reality, and it is a contributing factor in human struggles. We ought to take care, therefore, in our counsel, not to automatically equate stress with personal sin. Such human tensions are actually quite predictable and the result of circumstances. Our approach should be one of helping those we counsel to deal with stress effectively.

Could stress have been a factor in Karen's condition? Could demands and schedules have contributed to her eating disorder? It is likely that the pressures of college life exacerbated her problems. Papers due, late nights, missed meals, and distance from those who cared most about her could well have been components in her dilemma. This is not to say that stress caused her disorder or that she would have survived her battle with anorexia had she remained at home. But for those who counsel, such stresses must be considered and weighed. Our understanding of human beings and their problems must recognize that this experience is common to us all. It is interesting that when stress befell Moses because of the great demands of his work, God's answer came through the counsel of Moses' father-in-law, Jethro (Ex. 18:13–24). Jethro advised Moses to divide the load. It seems that even those in touch with God can face the demands brought on because of life outside the Garden. Stress weakened Moses and made him less effective as a leader. Jethro understood that excessive stress, left unchecked, eventually leads to greater human suffering.

Societal forces can include more than the stresses of life in this world. They can involve cultural values and social institutions that corrupt, compromise, or condemn us. We live in a fallen world, and that world system is set against human beings in many ways. Jesus and Paul witnessed to the hostility and opposition of the world toward Christ, the believer, and the church. Jesus said that "the world hates" Him along with any who are His disciples (John 7:7; 15:18–19). According to Paul, the world's way of thinking is distorted and stands in opposition to the mindset that Christians should have through the ministry of the Spirit of God (1 Cor. 1:18–25). We know, too, that the world is an organized force, a power or order that fights against the kingdom of God. Paul made it plain in Ephesians 2 that the course of this world system leads to death (vv. 2–3). James warned believers to remain unstained by the world (James 1:27) and not to become friends with the world or risk becoming an enemy of God (4:4). John commanded his readers not to love the world or the things in the world (1 John 2:15–17). Truly, the message of the New Testament is that the world we live in is an enemy seeking to bring failure and suffering to the lives of those who would adopt its distorted outlook.

The world we live in seeks to undermine the Christian at every turn and does indeed bring suffering to our lives. The messages of the media, pop culture, special interest groups, scientists, politicians, and mental health professionals often run counter to the message of Scripture. These messages seek to take believers captive. Because of this oppositional relationship, the believer must be cautious of accepting the contemporary teachings and ideas of our culture in a wholesale manner. But we must also reject an avoidance approach to the world. We need not approach our world with a defeatist mind-set. Instead, we should shine as lights in this dark world (Phil. 2:15) and allow our good deeds to expose the evil deeds of the world (John 3:19–21). We are to be salt and light in this world.

The biblical judgment of our world is clear. It is doomed. The world will face judgment even though now it hates and judges God's people. Believers need not be overcome by the world but can instead be overcomers (1 John 5:4–5). The use of the word overcome in this passage indicates that the life in this world is not an easy one. Jesus warned, in fact, "In this world you will have trouble. But take heart! I have overcome the world" (John 16:33). The believer need not continue under the power of the world. Its power is broken in the work of Christ. When we do suffer because of this world, we must recognize that such suffering is part of life in this fallen environment and that God, through Christ, can equip us to be victorious in the worst-case situations.

The world system, with its values, institutions, perspectives, and corporate sin, works to bring suffering to human beings. Racism, misguided nationalism, ethnic conflict, immoral government systems, injustice, and oppressive laws all can contribute to evil and suffering. Often the world works as an immoral force and a negative environmental variable in human experience. It is important that we link such factors to the Fall. The toil of work, the thorns and thistles that infest the ground, and the pains of childbirth are all clearly mentioned as results of the Fall. But the corruption of the world due to Adam's rebellion is not limited to the curses mentioned in Genesis 3. The sad fact is that because of the collective sin of the human race, we see lives broken, twisted, and distorted from what God originally intended.

The *Flesh:* Internal Attributes That Bring Human Suffering

The term *flesh* is used in many ways in the Bible. It can refer to our physical body, and it can describe our fallen nature. In some contexts the term is placed in opposition to the Spirit of God within us. We use it now in its broadest sense to describe sin-damaged human attributes. We will consider the attributes of our flesh that include our frail bodies, our flawed judgments, and our fallen condition.

Human Struggles Can Be Attributed to Our Frail Bodies

My back is killing me! Well, actually it is my leg. As the result of digging out after one of Chicago's largest snowstorms on record,

I (Gary) strained my back and was flat on the floor in howling pain. Two bottles of muscle relaxant and painkiller later I was up and around again. But ever since that last shovelful of snow, my leg has been bothering me. Even as I sit and write these words I have to frequently get up and walk around or the pain gets to be unbearable. It's a pinched nerve I'm told, and in time it may require surgery. But it is also a reminder. It is a reminder that these physical bodies of ours have been damaged as a result of Adam's sin. We live in frail bodies, bodies that are subject to genetic abnormalities, physical deformity, injury, and organ failure. We must contend with life-threatening illnesses and unexpected physical conditions. Ultimately, we will face the inevitable process of dying and death itself. These frail frames of ours are often the source of human struggles.

Jill has Alzheimer's disease. She is seventy-three years old and in every other way is the picture of health. She is in great physical condition, walks every day, and swims twice each week. But she is facing a progressive, degenerative disease that alters the brain, causing impaired memory, thinking, and behavior. Jill's experience with Alzheimer's disease has progressed over a span of three years since the onset of her first symptoms. Its effect is gradual. Her symptoms now include cognitive difficulties (memory loss) and the decline of intellectual abilities severe enough to interfere with the activities of daily living. The causes of Alzheimer's disease are under research, and no definitive answers exist yet. But researchers have found that a genetic predisposition and abnormal protein deposits in the brain play a role in the development of the disease.

It is getting difficult for Jill to function, and it is sad to see the toll that the disease is having on her. Her once outgoing and people-centered personality has been altered to a more reclusive and introverted one. She avoids old friends for fear she will not recall their names. Jill's family members and caregivers are starting to experience increased burdens and overall distress as the disease progresses. They know that the disease will eventually leave Jill completely dependent upon others and that caring for Jill as an Alzheimer's patient will demand a high emotional, social, and financial cost. But Jill is not alone. Approximately ten million people worldwide are affected by Alzheimer's disease. It is a leading cause of death for the elderly, behind cardiovascular disease and cancer. Nearly 10 percent of people sixty-five years of age and older are personally affected by Alzheimer's disease. There is no known cure for the disease, but Jill's family has hope that newly available therapies might slow down her symptomatic decline and enhance her cognition, activities of daily living, and basic functioning.

Jill's condition is not the result of personal sin. The stress that Jill's husband and children feel in caring for her is not sin either. In our view, the universal principle of Adam's sin is ultimately to blame for the decay of our mortal bodies, but it is the frail, mortal human body that is immediately the culprit. As we care for others in a counseling capacity, we must always be aware of the fact that some of life's struggles and human personality disorders are directly related to our physical bodies and our dying condition. Physical death is linked to the Fall (Gen. 3:19). As a result of Adam's disobedience, sin entered the entire world and with it death (Rom. 5:12). Although it can be debated whether Paul was speaking of physical death or spiritual death, it seems plain in Paul's first letter to the Corinthians that physical death is defeated through Christ's resurrection (1 Cor. 15). Although it is conceivable that Adam could have died while still in the Garden, outside of the Garden it was a foregone conclusion that he would die. No longer did God protect him from disease and the host of other forces that would bring about physical death and suffering.

We take heart to know that Paul tells us that someday all of creation will be liberated from the impact of the Fall. "The creation itself will be liberated from its bondage to decay" (Rom. 8:21). In the meantime we live in these mortal bodies, and we face the inevitable frailties of our mortal physical existence. Whether it be disease, injury, brain dysfunction, genetic abnormalities, or the normal process of aging, the human body plays a significant part in our emotional, social, and even spiritual health.

Kerry Wood was the 1998 Major League Baseball rookie of the year. He deserved the honor. At only twenty years of age, Wood started the season in the minor leagues but was eventually called up to play for the Chicago Cubs. In just his fifth major-league start, Wood pitched what one commentator called "arguably the best pitched baseball game in history." Wood struck out twenty batters in just nine innings, more than two strikeouts per inning, a National League record. This is a remarkable achievement when one considers that there are only twenty-seven outs per side in a baseball game. The only hit against him was a ball that never left the infield. It bounced off the third baseman's glove. For reasons best known only to himself, the official scorekeeper marked it as a hit. Given this momentous start it was a great disappointment to Wood when he injured his pitching arm and had to sit out the play-offs.

In his first 1999 spring training start, Wood again injured his pitching arm, tearing a ligament from the elbow. It was announced that he would be out for the season. It was moving to see this very young man in tears on the evening news as he struggled with the fact of his injury, his impending surgery, and the potential of a promising career in doubt. Wood openly described his depression and disappointment. Was Kerry Wood's problem a spiritual one? Was it an emotional one? Was it a physical one? In reality it was all of these. Kerry Wood is a total being. He is more than a well-conditioned athlete with a ninety-eight-mile-per-hour fastball. He is a human being—physically, socially, intellectually, and spiritually. If Kerry Wood is to deal with this event and return to the mound successfully, those involved with him must treat more than his arm. Surgery can well mend his damaged body, but there is more to this young man that needs care. Kerry's confidence and spirit must also be rebuilt. Surely his physical state affects his entire state of mind and outlook on life. We are all made that way.

Could physical factors have also played a role in Karen's battle with anorexia? In all likelihood physical issues were at work. Although emotional factors may have led to her self-imposed starvation, the process of starvation itself had to impact her judgments—a fact that the counselor must bear in mind. Anorexia nervosa is like a whirlpool. Once ensnared, it tends to suck a person under. Because of the effect of starvation on the brain, the capacity to make sound judgments is hindered. Not only is the person caught mentally and emotionally in destructive patterns, he or she simply does not think in logical ways that might enable him or her to overcome the disorder. Often this means that decisions must be made for the person being treated.

Recent research indicates that some children with anorexia have abnormal blood flow to parts of their brain. The idea that a physical defect, rather than cultural or genetic factors, can predispose people to eating disorders is controversial to be sure. Most specialists admit that the basic causes of anorexia are unknown, but this possible linkage has raised significant issues as to the role of brain chemistry as a cause of this disorder.

A second study found a surprising connection between autism and anorexia nervosa. Autism and anorexia are radically different disorders, but a trail of research evidence has led scientists to a common physical connection at least in some persons: a case of strep throat. The infection itself isn't to blame. Antibodies produced by the body to fight strep, in some people, mistakenly attack the basal ganglia, an area in the brain that is involved in the control of movement and emotion. It is believed that this damage leads to obsessive or compulsive behaviors. In the autistic individual it shows itself in a tendency for constant repetition, and in the anorexic person it is seen in the need to exactly and compulsively regulate calorie intake (Talan 20).

Physical issues affect human struggles, problems, and predicaments. Those who seek to offer counsel must recognize that human personality is directly linked to physiology. Although we may not be able to become medical doctors, we must be aware that factors related to the human body are significant in shaping our personality traits. Human struggles are attributable to several sources, but undeniably our frail bodies are a key point of origin for problems in our lives.

Human Struggles Can Be Attributed to Our Flawed Judgments

"I thought I could make it across the tracks before the train," were the words of a stunned truck driver after the crash of an Amtrak passenger train carrying more than two hundred people on March 15, 1999. The train dubbed "The City of New Orleans" crashed into a truck loaded with steel bars, killing eleven persons at the scene as people in a sleeper car were engulfed in flames. More than one hundred others were injured, some critically. The flawed judgment of one truck driver was the catalyst for enormous suffering for individuals on the train and the many families they represented. It was a poor judgment call. Not intentional, not an act of a sinful person trying to damage the lives of others, but a faulty decision. Many human struggles grow out of miscalculations and flawed judgments. As the saying goes, "To err is human." Often we wish we could have the opportunity to reverse those mistaken choices, but, bound in time, we cannot.

Sometimes flawed human judgments forever affect our personalities. Lisa Merit will never be the same since her auto accident. The young mother was busy Christmas shopping when she misjudged the distance and speed of an oncoming car while making a left turn into a mall parking lot. In that awful moment she became a different individual. Comatose for several weeks and suffering from significant brain trauma, Lisa lost many of her memories of her past, several of her characteristic skills, and even some of her fundamental personality traits.

It has taken time, but Lisa, her husband, and their children have coped with the accident's results. She has relearned how to cook, clean house, do the laundry, and manage a household. In what has been a difficult experience, she and her husband, Pete, have had to forge a new marriage relationship. She has had to become newly acquainted with her own children. Slowly memories return and skills reappear, but in this cognitive ordeal, Lisa has developed a very different personality. Lisa and Pete have struggled not because of the direct result of personal sin but because of flawed judgments like those all of us make. Sometimes we suffer and those we love suffer with us in significant ways because of those momentary lapses of judgment. It is part of our human condition. We make mistakes. But we can take encouragement even in this kind of suffering and difficulty that God is still governing our lives. Even in the accidental actions of persons or the misjudgments of finite people, God still works to achieve His purposes in the lives of His children.

In Scripture we see that human errors can bring suffering. Consider for example the biblical concept of the city of refuge. In Exodus 21 and in Numbers 35 God established cities where those who accidentally took the life of another could flee. There the person was safe from revenge. Why create such cities? Because God recognized that accidents do occur. Such accidents can bring enormous suffering, but they are in themselves understandable human experiences.

In Karen's case were faulty judgments at work? It is always difficult to look back and act as "Monday morning quarterbacks" on other people's decisions. We might ask, Was Karen wise going to college with her condition still plaguing her? Should she have been in a treatment program instead? Should the school have required her to enter a program and then return to college when her disorder had been treated? Looking back, it is likely that flawed judgments did contribute to Karen's succumbing to anorexia's final battle. Some of those judgments were Karen's own decisions, and others were the decisions of parents or school officials. Flawed humans make flawed decisions. It is just that way. We ought not to be surprised to discover that such errors of judgment marked Karen's case as well.

Human Struggles Can Be Attributed to Our Fallen Condition

A third attribute of the flesh that brings pain, sorrow, and suffering to people's lives is the indisputable fact of our sinful condition. Through Adam sin entered the human race and has been passed along as a fundamental condition of human nature ever since (Rom. 5:12). Our sin nature gives us a propensity toward sin. We sin because we are born with a sin nature. The hard truth is that these personal acts of sin consistently destroy lives.

Sin has been defined in several ways. Millard Erickson defined sin as "any lack of conformity, active or passive, to the moral law of God" (578). He went on to state that "Sin is failure to live up to what God expects of us in act, thought or being." Sin can take three different forms. First, it can take the form of immorality. That is to say that sin can be an act that violates the character or will of God. Second, sin can take the form of selfishness. Selfishness is, according to Strong, "the choice of self as the supreme end which constitutes the antithesis of supreme love to God" (Strong 567). A third form of sin is idolatry. Idolatry involves the displacement of God and unbelief. We are idolatrous when we choose to make something, someone, some cause, or some concept the god of our lives and then live to serve that god. We are idol worshipers when we fail to acknowledge God as God and substitute some other god before Him (Ex. 20:3).

Sin in any form damages people and ultimately brings trials. It is true that for a period sinners can get away with their sin and even appear to prosper, but more often than not sinful acts come quickly back against us to weaken and finally defeat us. Even those sinners who prosper will eventually pay the price for their rebellious hearts. In the end, the Scripture is correct when it says that "each one is tempted when, by his own evil desire, he is dragged away and enticed. Then, after desire has conceived, it gives birth to sin; and sin, when it is full-grown, gives birth to death" (James 1:14–15).

For many this is the path to their own life turmoil and problems. One need not look any further than the morning newspaper or the evening news to see how the destructive power of sin is at work in human lives. Stories of domestic violence, abused children, gang killings, alcohol- and drug-related traffic fatalities, prominent leaders' credibility and reputations destroyed by extramarital affairs, theft, racial violence, child pornography, and terrorist bombs all fill the news on a weekly, if not nightly, basis. Dr. Laura Schlessinger is a radio talk show host who invites callers to tell their personal moral dilemmas each day on her syndicated radio program. Person after person tells of moral choices that have brought chaos to their lives. Sometimes the real stories of human failings are more tragic than a movie script. Over and over the words of James's epistle ring true. Our desires once conceived give birth to sin, and sin does bring death.

Nicholas began his marriage and his career with every hope of success. He and Kate were high school sweethearts. It was a natural progression of events that led to their marriage and eventual family. Nick worked for a major auto parts producer and traveled to larger auto parts stores around the South as a salesman. And a great salesman he was. In just four years Nick became the company's regional sales leader. He and Kate enjoyed the benefits of Nick's skills. They purchased a large home in a prestigious suburb of Nashville where they settled in to raise their two young children. A member of an evangelical church and a teacher in the adult Sunday school, Nick was a solid believer who openly discussed his faith with others.

Traveling meant a great deal of time away from home for Nick. For the first three years in Nick's sales position he found it was hard to be away so much, but he and Kate seemed to make it work. It was in the fourth year of travel that Nick's life took a turn. It began with an in-room movie. Nick was enticed by the preview channel to watch a pornographic video. It only seemed at the time like a minor failing. He had not sinned against his wife by straying sexually, he thought. He had only watched a movie. But then his interest grew. He began to develop an appetite for more and more hard-core pornographic material. In time Nick found himself in the grip of this binding sin. Eventually his addiction grew to the point that he would stop his travels early in the day just so he could fulfill his lust for more sensual content. He missed appointments and he lost sales. In just a few months, Nick went from a sales leader to a failure. His sales dropped so severely that his boss asked him if he was having any personal problems. Of course, he said no and promised a better second half of the year.

The second half of the year was as bad as the first. By this time Nick was ordering videos, buying books, and using the Internet to feed his addiction. His relationship with Kate was also paying the price. Kate could sense that something was wrong, but the problem became painfully clear to her when she opened an unmarked package that arrived at their home. It was filled with materials that literally made her sick. That evening, Kate mustered the courage to confront Nick about the package. At first he pretended not to know where the package came from or why it was sent to him. But then the weight of his sin became crushing. He confessed his sin to his wife and together they went for counseling to help Nick deal with his addiction. Nick understood that his desires had given birth to sin and this sin would ultimately lead to death—the death of his marriage, his career, and his ministry. Through professional Christian counseling Nick gained the help he needed. Today he is victorious over this besetting sin, but he remains cautious of situations that might draw him back to this destructive lifestyle.

Our sins are not always as blatant as Nick's, but they can be equally destructive. It might be the sin of gossip or pride. It could be an arrogant spirit or a hateful heart. Whatever the sin, the end is the same. Sin brings struggle, sorrow, and suffering to people's lives. Paul spoke of the acts of our sin nature as "sexual immorality, impurity and debauchery; idolatry and witchcraft; hatred, discord, jealousy, fits of rage, selfish ambition, dissensions, factions and envy; drunkenness, orgies, and the like. I warn you, as I did before, that those who live like this will not inherit the kingdom of God" (Gal. 5:19–21).

What about Karen? Was her anorexic battle the result of personal sin? To some measure that may be the case. Although it is presumptuous to think that we could or should point to a particular sin that factored into Karen's situation, it is likely that sin played some role. Was she taken in by the distorted values of our culture, which attribute worth to women based on their bodies rather than the inner beauty of a life dedicated to Christ? That is possible. Could her sin have involved a form of perfectionism or excessively high standards of performance often found in anorexia patients? We don't know, but perhaps. What we do know is, like all human beings, Karen was a sinner and sin marked her life as surely as it does each of our lives. Could destructive sinful habits or tendencies have been at work in her life? It is altogether reasonable to assume so.

The *Devil:* The Enemy Who Brings Human Suffering

Since the temptation in the Garden of Eden, Satan and his fallen angels have worked to oppose and damage human beings. The Hebrew word for the devil, satan, is derived from a verb that means adversary. The Greek term is a transliteration of the Hebrew word. The Greek term means devil, adversary, and accuser. Other terms used of the devil include tempter, enemy, Evil One, deceiver, father of lies, and murderer. Each of these names for Satan points to his character and activity against God and humans. Satan is the chief of the demons who seek to disguise themselves as angels of light (2 Cor. 11:14–15). His goal is to blind the minds of unbelievers (2 Cor. 4:4), hinder Christians in their service (1 Thess. 2:18), and bring physical, mental, and emotional ailments to people in order to destroy people's lives (2 Cor. 12:7).

The devil and his subjects bring suffering to human beings in a number of ways. They tempt and deceive, leading humans into destructive choices (Luke 22:3). They inflict disease and disabilities such as deafness and muteness (Mark 9:25), blindness (Matt. 12:22), paralysis and lameness (Acts 8:7), and convulsions (Mark 1:26; 9:20; Luke 8:29). Demonic activity is linked to disturbed human behavior as well. Bizarre behavior including public nakedness (Luke 8:27) and self-destructive actions can be results of demonic control (Matt. 17:15; Mark 5:5).

It is important to note that the Bible does not attribute all illness to demon possession. For example, Luke told his readers that Jesus distinguished between two different types of healing—one involving the casting out of demons, the other simply bringing a cure (Mark 1:34; 6:13; Luke 13:32). Although seizures are sometimes linked to demonic activity, epilepsy is a physical condition (Matt. 4:24). In a number of cases Jesus healed persons who were ill or deformed without reference to demonic spirits.

What about today? Do demons still bring suffering to human lives in modern times? For those of us who accept the Bible as inspired and authoritative, there is no reason to believe that demon possessions are restricted to the times of the biblical text. There are cases even today that can only be explained by the ongoing work of Satan and his demons. When we read of unspeakable crimes committed by persons such as Richard Speck, John Wayne Gacy, Jeffrey Dahmer, or Charles Manson, we have little difficulty recognizing demonic forces at work within these individuals. When we study human history and recall the horrific acts performed in Hitler's concentration camps or the genocide in Cambodia, we can readily agree that demons are still active in our world today. But we must, at the same time, be careful that we do not equate all aberrant physical conditions or psychological disorders with demon possession.

How about in Karen's case—did Satan or demonic forces influence her battle with anorexia? Without a doubt Satan would have desired to work his woe in her life and would have so afflicted her if God would permit it. But we know that as a child of God, Karen was protected from the direct attack of the Evil One unless he had God's permission (Job 1:10; 1 John 4:4). While Satan could not directly possess Karen, he could oppress her and work to tempt her to take actions that were self-destructive. Was Satan working through her human flaws and failings? That is a reasonable position. What we do know is that God can even take the contrary acts of Satan and turn them for His glory should Satan have been a factor in Karen's struggles. Karen could have been the victim of spiritual warfare, but she was not, in the final analysis, the loser as a committed believer in Christ.

Yet Another Reason for Human Suffering

We come now to the conclusion of our rather brief study of the factors that are at work bringing suffering to people's lives. We have observed that *the world* brings suffering because of natural forces, human forces, and societal forces. We also noted that *the flesh* is a contributing factor in human suffering through our frail bodies, our flawed judgments, and our fallen condition. Finally, we recalled that *the devil* "seeks to work us woe" as Luther wrote in his famous hymn "A Mighty Fortress Is Our God." We noted that Satan works against humans directly and through his demonic servants to bring suffering, temptation, and failure. These three—the world, the flesh, and the devil—are the sources of most human suffering and are the points on which we must focus our ministry as we seek to bring spiritual direction to people's lives.

We would be remiss if we did not point out another potential source of suffering. That source is God Himself. Suffering that finds its source in God can come to us in four ways. First, suffering and trials can be a means by which God cultivates character in our lives. Sometimes our trials are the "learning vehicle" that God employs in order to produce maturity in our lives (James 1:2–4). Trials can often produce godly character in the suffering Christian (Rom. 5:3–5). Second, suffering can be a means by which we share in the redemptive work of Christ (Rom. 8:17). Third, suffering can be the result of divine discipline. Suffering brought because of God's chastisement of the believer is not an arbitrary exercise of power. It is a form of parental punishment (Hos. 11:1–9), and its purpose is disciplinary and corrective. "Know then in your heart that as a man disciplines his son, so the Lord your God disciplines you" (Deut. 8:5). This precept is picked up in the New Testament and reaffirmed (Heb. 12:5–6). Always, despite the pain of the moment, the purpose of the divine discipline is a restoration to spiritual health and personal wholeness. Finally, suffering can be due to divine judgment. God is sovereign and that sovereignty is expressed in God's role as judge *(shofet)*. God's judgment is both forensic, occurring after the fact of sin, and active in nature as He exercises His sovereignty in the very actions of leaders, nations, and natural disasters (Ps. 98:9; Isa. 33:22). God judges human actions, not just at some future time, but even in our present world and personal lives. He is at work through many different means overthrowing oppressing powers, establishing justice, bringing peace, and punishing sin.

Many times God uses one or more of the previously discussed factors—the world, the flesh, and even the devil—to work His purposes through human struggles. We must at times take refuge in the knowledge that God is a God of integrity who does that which is both just and merciful. Not one or the other, not justice or mercy, but always both and always together in every life event. The sufferings of the present age cannot be accounted for adequately, only on the basis of God's punishment for human sin. Any pastor who has ever done regular hospital visits knows that to be true. People suffer for many reasons, some of which defy human understanding. In the Old Testament, the book of Job stands as witness to the inadequacy of simplistic explanations of human suffering.

— *The End of the Matter* —

The conclusion is clear: Human suffering is as complex as human nature. Just as we are multifaceted beings, suffering is a multifaceted occurrence in our lives. Simplistic answers to human struggles are usually faulty because suffering is most often the result of a composite of multiple-layered and intertwined issues. As those who counsel and seek to bring spiritual counsel to people who face various life struggles, we should take note that solutions are rarely the result of a single action or a simple answer. Often godly counsel will require that we deal with several aspects of a problem, layer by layer or strand by strand. Personality develops over time, and changes in personality generally occur as a process as well. To be sure, we can be confident that our all-sufficient Lord and Savior, Jesus Christ, can address the web of factors at work in human struggles when we give counsel under the authority of Scripture. The process of change may at times occur miraculously as an instantaneous act of God, or it may, like many physical afflictions, involve a step-by-step, day-by-day process of gradual healing.

However God elects to work in human lives, one thing is certain. Jesus Christ is the Messiah—we are not! We must recognize our own inability to heal anyone. That is Christ's role. Our function is to serve Him as He works through us to care for others and to offer spiritual counsel to suffering people.

NOTES

Erickson, Millard J. *Christian Theology.* Grand Rapids: Baker, 1990.

Romeo, Felicia F. *Understanding Anorexia Nervosa.* Springfield, Ill: C.C. Thomas, 1986.

Strong, Augustus H. *Systematic Theology.* Westwood, N.J.: Revell, 1907.

Talan, Jamie. "Antibiotics for Anorexia?" *Psychology Today* (May–June 1998): 200.

Toole, David C. "Divine Ecology and the Apocalypse: A Theological Description of Natural Disasters and the Environmental Crisis." *Theology Today* 55.4 (Jan. 1999): 547–61.

SOCIAL SCIENCE FOUNDATIONS OF HUMAN PERSONALITY

— Chapter 4 —

WINDOWS FOR SEEING:
The Value and Evaluation of
Psychological Theories

We work together in the heart of Chicago. Harry Shields and I (Gary Bredfeldt) serve together as professors at the Moody Bible Institute. Located just north of Chicago's Loop, Moody is situated on a twenty-six-acre campus. Like most colleges, it has academic buildings, dorms, a library, administrative buildings, an athletic center, and a student commons. What is unique about Moody's location is its view.

Moody stands between two cities really, one of wealth, the other of poverty. If you look from windows on the east side of the campus your view will include skyscrapers, high-rise condominiums, and upscale neighborhoods. Chicago's Gold Coast borders the north side of the campus with its "magnificent mile," rehabbed greystone houses, and affluent shops. To the south are the Merchandise Mart, the LaSalle Street financial district, and the heart of Chicago's corporate business presence. Wealth north, wealth east, wealth south—that is one Chicago. But look now up the side streets to the west and you will see another Chicago. It is the Chicago of poverty, crime, and the Cabrini Green high-rise public-housing project. Drugs, gangs, shootings, and fear are the words most readily associated with life there. And so it is—two different views, two different cities.

Like windows in a building, theories offer us multiple views of the world. Just as the different windows on the Moody Bible Institute campus provide diverse perspectives on the city of Chicago, contrasting personality theories give us alternate understandings of human nature and human need. In the chapters that follow, we will introduce you to several theories of personality development. Each one provides its own picture of human nature and behavior. Each one describes a slice of the vastly complex world of mind and emotion that comprise God's unique creation, human personality.

At points we will discover that personality theories disagree. Some "biblical counselors" would contend that such disagreement renders theories of human personality unreliable and thus unprofitable for the Christian caregiver's study and application. We take another approach. Rather than bemoan the fact that the social sciences, including psychology, are comprised of diverse and sometimes even conflicting theories with opposing inferences and conclusions, we prefer to recognize the limitations and assumptions that govern each theory. In this way, we can judge the validity and the contributions of the theory in question. We believe that common grace and general revelation enable nonbelievers to make meaningful discoveries about creation, including human beings. In fact, we would not expect social scientists to agree with each other. People are far too complex to be so easily understood. It is exactly because people are complex that no single theory could ever completely encompass the vast array of characteristics, qualities, struggles, and strengths that are part of human personality. Just as windows on all sides of a building offer a more complete view of the world surrounding that structure, so too do multiple theories of human behavior give us a more complete view of people.

THE VALUE OF THEORIES:
WHY STUDY THEORIES OF HUMAN PERSONALITY AND DEVELOPMENT?

Charles S. Pierce, a pragmatic philosopher, once said, "There is nothing more practical than a good theory." What did he mean by that rather strange quip? His point is that theories are useful in explaining the causes of events and development of people. Likewise, theories give us a basis for the development of a logical response to those events and people. Although facts are essential, facts in themselves do not explain events or behaviors. For that, we need a plausible theory.

For example, consider the efforts of the investigators in discovering the cause of a jet crash. They can know the facts surrounding the crash of an airliner, yet not have an explanation as to why it crashed. That explanation must come in the form of a theory. Details can be gained from the analysis of a flight data recorder or cockpit voice recorder and the scene of the wreckage. Eyewitnesses can give their account. Survivors, if there are any, can tell of what they experienced. All of this constitutes the collection of facts. Although each of these facts may be accurate, they still must be forged into a coherent theory that best organizes and explains the facts.

It is important to remember that it is possible for more than one theory to be developed from the same set of facts. Maybe it was a bomb, maybe a mechanical malfunction occurred, or maybe it was the result of pilot error or of sabotage. Each answer represents a theory, a way of viewing the facts. The task of investigators is to evaluate each theory to see which is most plausible and consistent. We call that *theoretical validity* in social science research. Researchers can gather facts and agree on those facts, but they may propose diverse theories about the meaning of those facts. In that case, our task becomes one of judging the theoretical validity of each theory.

But one might be tempted to ask, "Why bother with formulating a theory at all? Why not just collect the facts and leave it at that?" We formulate theories, as in the case of the airline crash, because theories enable us to explain the past and to better predict and, possibly, even alter the future. It is hoped that, through the development of a plausible theory as to why the jet crashed, questions of cause can be answered and a repeated tragedy averted. In this way, theories are practical. Theories give us answers, direction, options, and solutions to life's issues and events. So too, theories in the social sciences are practical. They can offer answers, direction, options, and solutions for those who seek to understand and care for people.

In much the same way as an investigator seeks to understand why a plane falls from the sky, personality theorists hope to discover why some personalities soar while others crash and burn. Why do we suggest that you spend your energies in the study of personality theory? Because such a study will broaden your own understanding of people and give you a further underpinning for your caregiving response to people in need. Specifically, we would suggest five motivations for your study of personality theory.

Theories Organize Facts and Make Them Useful

Facts are like a pile of bricks. Although bricks have the potential to become a building, without organization it is still just a pile of bricks. But when a plan is applied, when design is involved, when the bricks are carefully organized and combined with other necessary materials, that pile of bricks becomes a structure. Similarly, design and order give meaning to a collection of facts. Social scientists can collect data about people, but they cannot draw conclusions from that data until they attempt to place their information in a reasoned framework called a *theory*. In this way theories benefit those who minister to others. They bring facts together in such a way that they can be discussed, analyzed, and understood. From this process of logical ordering of facts into theory, counselors are given frameworks to think about human problems and predicaments.

For example, we might know factually that children learn to speak near the end of the first year of life and that they gain a basic understanding of grammar during the second through fourth year of life. Knowing these facts is interesting, but that knowledge does not explain how children acquire language. Some theorists contend that language is innately part of human beings and that it develops as the product of inborn maturational processes. Others argue that language is entirely learned by observation and conditioning. There is no dispute over the facts, just over the meaning of the facts. This is where theory comes into play. Theories organize those facts and offer an explanation of the cause of those facts. The role of a theory is organization and interpretation of facts. Knowledge of the various theories of language development can help a parent or a childcare worker assist children struggling with language acquisition. Parents and professionals will encounter diversity of language theory. But in that diversity comes greater understanding. Each theory can aid those who work with children to assess the progress of children in their care.

The world is filled with facts about human behavior and the struggles faced by those whom we seek to counsel. By studying the variety of theories that exist about human development and personality, people helpers can think about those facts in an orderly way. We need not agree with a theory in totality to benefit from it. The real benefit of theoretical study comes in the opportunity to think logically about facts and possible interpretations of those facts. Facts do not organize themselves for our review. Facts do not automatically stamp their meaning into our minds. Facts simply pile up. Order comes from the development of a theory about those facts. From that order then come ideas for treatment and response.

Consider Angela for a moment. Angela is collecting data relating to teenage suicide. She has studied numerous cases of student suicide attempts. Her data include the details of the events leading up to each attempt, the methods each young person employed in attempting to take his or her own life, and information about the outcome of each attempt. What must Angela do with her information if she is to use it to explain teenage suicide and prevent future suicide attempts? She must organize her data, seek to discover patterns within the data, and draw tentative conclusions about what might be driving students to suicide. From her tentative hypotheses she must establish a research approach that will either confirm or deny her speculations. Eventually, she must put forward a theory about the causes of teen suicide attempts and potential preventative actions. She must do all of this because her facts cannot organize themselves and cannot automatically produce conclusions. Her theory need not be fully supported at every point to be of value. No theory will be entirely correct. But if she develops a good theory, her work can make a contribution to our understanding of teens and the cause of their self-destructive behavior. Out of that theory can then come potential help to teens who may be moving toward such acts.

Theories Make Private Knowledge Public

Let us assume for a moment that you have discovered a counseling technique that helps couples in damaged marriages resolve their conflicts and establish growing and successful marriages. You are finding that your technique is working with nearly every couple you serve. One couple at a time, your approach to marriage counseling is having an enormous impact.

As good as your approach to marriage counseling might be, until you make it public, it cannot affect the direction of marriage counseling in the future or affect many people for the long term. So how will you make it public? Well, you could have every person that you have worked with go out and tell others. This evangelistic-type approach will spread information about your counseling technique by word of mouth and might succeed in communicating the technique to a wider audience. You could go on a speaking tour or go on the radio. But for your technique to truly affect others, you will probably have to formulate it into a written marriage counseling theory. It can then be published and evaluated by those who read it and try to implement it. By doing so, you will have taken your private knowledge of marriage counseling and made it public knowledge. That is what happens when we move from private experience to public theory.

Consider even the message of the gospel. It is interesting that despite the essential role of personal evangelism and the one-to-one way that the gospel is spread, God still put the message in writing. The Bible is, in a sense, the publicizing of the private knowledge of the apostles and prophets. By putting the facts about Jesus in writing, the authors of the Scriptures enable readers to understand and interpret the significance of those facts. Expressing the message of salvation in written form allows it to be considered, contemplated, understood, and, preferably, accepted.

Jean Copply is a reading specialist who works with children who are having trouble mastering basic reading skills. In her work, she must diagnosis students' reading struggles and decide how best to help them. Although it might be informative for Jean to speculate as to why Johnny doesn't know how to read, it is far less productive than to study a carefully developed and scrutinized theory that seeks to explain how children in general learn to read and why they fail. She could conjure up an explanation for Johnny's reading problem based on his poor home environment and uninvolved parents, but this private information will not serve her as well in helping Johnny as will the public information found in the form of theories about reading. It is better for her to take knowledge gained from studying hundreds of Johnnys and Jennys than to simply speculate with regards to her one pupil. From learning theories that specifically focus on reading, she can begin to understand how to diagnose Johnny's deficiencies and determine a means by which they can be corrected.

Theories Challenge the Bias in Private Knowledge

Private knowledge is found in personal experience. Public knowledge comes to us through lectures, libraries, education, books, journals, magazines, and the Internet. Public knowledge is available to everyone and is readily transferred from person to person and situation to situation. Private knowledge is untested and often biased toward a particular perspective, anecdotal event, or stereotypical understanding. Public knowledge can be openly discussed, debated, researched, and scrutinized. Private knowledge is typically assumed to be factual by the individual who possesses it and is often held without criticism. When we explain other people's behaviors and experiences based on our personal views it is often self-satisfying but may be self-deceptive as well. Because private knowledge is limited to one's personal point of view and experiences, it is a less reliable source of knowledge than is a carefully researched question.

All of us have personal opinions about the causes of human behavior or the nature of human events that, most often, are based upon our own personal experiences. For example, Andrew is a fifth-grade teacher in a Christian elementary school. Recently, the school decided to experiment with an inclusive education program wherein handicapped children were integrated into regular elementary classrooms. Not long after the program began, Andrew received complaints from parents about classroom disruptions. Parents told him that they were concerned that the handicapped children would disrupt the learning for "normal" children. After hearing the concerns several times, Andrew decided to keep a log of all daily disruptions, including the name of who was involved in the disruption and the nature of the disruptive behavior. His discoveries were interesting. He found that nearly all disruptions were from the so-called normal children. Handicapped children were less likely to be disruptive than were the other children. After further research, Andrew found that his data coincided with data from classrooms around the country. It seems that there is a difference between common personal opinion (private knowledge) and behavioral research findings and what we might call *public knowledge*.

Sometimes personal bias distorts our understandings of what is really happening, and research can correct those distortions. By developing theories of behavior, we can test our personal knowledge against the larger collection of public knowledge represented by the theory.

Let's take another example. Cathy and Mitch O'Connor adopted two children. Both boys have grown up to be well-rounded individuals, and both are now grown and raising their own families. But there was a time when Brent, the younger of the two boys, gave his mom and dad some major moments of parenting frustration. Often during Brent's high school years he was in trouble. On more than one occasion his father and mother had to deal with Brent's problem behaviors. Once he was arrested because he was in a fight with another student. Another time they found beer cans under the seat of his car. For Cathy and Mitch, it seemed it was one act of rebellion after another. Raising Brent was no easy task.

On occasion Cathy and Mitch tried to discuss the struggle they were having with Brent with others who attended their small group Bible study from the church, but they were hesitant to do so. It wasn't that they were alone in their concerns about raising adolescent children. Others in the group had their stories of adolescent parenting woes as well. But on more than one occasion people had referred to the fact that Brent was adopted. Once, in fact, one of their group members asked, "Do you think Brent's problems stem from his being adopted? I've heard that a lot of adopted children have problems, you know."

Cathy was tired of hearing comments that connected her son's problems to his adoption, so she began to research the matter for herself. She discovered that no statistically significant differences exist in the mental health or social behavior of adopted children as compared with nonadopted children. In fact, some research pointed to just the opposite conclusion. Often adopted children have a more clearly defined sense of identity and fewer problems related to matters of self-esteem. This may be due to the fact that adoptive parents so strongly desire children and are quite ready to welcome an adoptive child into their home. In this case, private knowledge of adoptive children and their problems is based on faulty information. A cause-and-effect relationship is assumed between adoption and personal problems that cannot be supported from the public knowledge gained from careful research of adopted children.

Here then is one of the clear advantages of the study and development of theory: Theories subject personal claims of knowledge and truth to more rigorous scrutiny. The result is that our narrow personal perspectives of the causes of human behavior are challenged and sometimes changed.

Theories Are Less Complex Than People

Why does my child struggle to make friends? Why is my wife so outgoing? Why is my husband so reluctant to take a risk? Why are my parents so restrictive and controlling? Why do children join gangs? What causes people to become depressed and suicidal? What is the cause of learning disabilities? Why are some people leaders and others followers? How do we explain people who molest or abuse children? Why are our children shooting each other in their schools? The list of questions about people and why they do what they do is endless. People are highly complex beings, and simple answers are rarely adequate or complete. It is difficult to explain an individual's actions or characteristics. Theories help us sort through the complexities that are so characteristic of people.

Theories help us to simplify, analyze, predict, and even solve problems. Through these windows on people, theories allow us to more accurately discuss, compare, contrast, and draw conclusions about human behavior. Here is a concept that is hard to grasp, but true. The mind cannot produce ideas that are more complex than itself. Therefore, theories are less complex than the mind they seek to understand.

The human mind is not capable of perfect self-reflection. In other words, it cannot perfectly know itself and its own properties. That means two things must be true. Human beings cannot fully know their own true nature, and the theories that human beings develop are less complex than actual humans. It is also true that a system can only be understood fully by a higher system. This is a strong indicator that only God can fully understand us. We are dependent on His revelation of that which we cannot know on our own. And so, theories are less complex than people and are never fully adequate explanations of people. They are simpler than the totality of human nature and behavior. A theory can provide us some insight into people, which simplifies the task of knowing ourselves, though it is always limited.

Sometimes we think of theories as difficult to understand. Although they may stretch us and we may have to work hard to consider all of the various aspects of a theory, no theory of human personality is as complex as the real thing. Consider the development of the mind of the child. Although researchers like Jean Piaget may be able to give us insights into the cognitive development of a child, Piaget could never fully conceive of the developing mind of any one child, let alone children in general. This fact

supported by research, it is wise for us to consider its merits. We should not avoid such scientific findings even if they are difficult for us to comprehend, synthesize, or apply. When a theory moves closer to a true understanding of human beings and it is shown to be consistently supported by research study after research study, the Christian caregiver would do well to consider the implications of such a theory on ministry.

In the course of considering theories, we must ask questions regarding the way the research was conducted and the accuracy of the conclusions in light of the quality of research. We must be sure that scientific theories are based on good scientific methodology.

Testability

Because theories are less complex than people, they can be tested and critiqued. At least in principle, theories can be tested but private opinions cannot be. Each theory we present in the chapters that follow offers claims and principles about human nature. By putting a theory into writing, theorists open their views up to evaluation. This many times comes in the form of testing. Private knowledge does not have this self-correcting benefit. This book is a good example. Later in this book we will be presenting a model or theory of counseling. It is designed to aid laypersons and pastoral leaders who seek to minister to hurting persons. We believe that the theory we propose is sound. It is well tested in our own counseling experience and in the counseling ministry of those we have trained. But you can't just take our word for it. You will have to judge the theory we present in this book for yourself. The very fact that it appears in print gives you that opportunity. The same is true of the various personality theories presented in the next segment of this book.

Testability is one of the most important factors in evaluating the scientific worthiness of a theory. In order for a theory to be testable, the concepts it presents must be clear and subject to objective verification. It is interesting to note that a theory that is testable yet proven wrong may have greater scientific value than one that can never be tested at all. If a theory is not testable, there is no way of finding out whether it is right or wrong. A theory that is not testable could be entirely correct or incorrect, but no one would ever know for sure.

To be testable a theory must have measurable claims and predictable outcomes. Even psychological theories must stand up to standards of testing and predictability. Measurement and predictability are not absolute, however. They are a matter of degree. Those theories that achieve a higher degree of predictable results when applied are more worthy than those that have inconsistent results. That is the scientific criteria for worthiness. Science demands careful measurement and replicable results. If a theory lacks these, it does not prove the theory wrong. It simply means that it does not have the same degree of scientific worthiness as another theory. Take for example the work of Piaget as compared with the work of Freud. Freud speculated about the subconscious mind as a major aspect of human personality. But based on its very nature and definition, the subconscious cannot be measured. Piaget focused his research on cognitive development stages. He used experiments to demonstrate the development of thinking at various stages. Almost anyone can replicate his work and achieve the same results. One can measure the results of his experiments and draw some consistent conclusions. On a testability scale, therefore, Piaget's theory is more scientifically worthy than is Freud's.

External Validity

By external validity we mean that the theory corresponds with the real world as an accurate and plausible explanation of real events. Let's think about Newton's explanation of falling objects as an example. Newton explained falling objects as a function of three variables: mass, distance, and force. His theory is scientifically worthy because it consistently fits reality. If one increases the mass of an object, the distance it falls, or the force with which it is propelled, one can consistently produce and predict the same results or reality. So Newton's theory is sound. But Einstein also described the same problem of falling objects. He used the variables of space, time, and energy. Again, his theory has scientific worthiness in terms of external validity, despite the fact that both theories are radically different in their frame of reference. Here we have an example of the same phenomena being understood through the lens of different theoretical models. Both are judged to be accurate descriptions of reality. Both, therefore, can be said to have external validity even though they view the same facts in divergent ways.

Consider now the theory of Erikson with regards to psychosocial development. He describes eight stages of development that involve crucial social or psychological achievements if one is to grow up healthy and move progressively from stage to stage. Research seems to show that Erikson's theory has strong external validity. Erikson seems to consistently describe human developmental experience. This would mean that on this point at least, Erikson has scientific worthiness.

Predictive Validity

Similar to external validity is the criteria of predictive validity. Predictive validity describes the ability of a theory to accurately predict future events. For example, Newton's theory of gravity has high predictive validity, so much so that it can even be considered a scientific law. Each time one drops an object, it is possible to predict exactly when the object will hit the ground and at what rate of speed. Such a theory has extremely high predictive validity.

Skinner's behavioral theory is an example of a theoretical approach with moderately high predictive validity. Behavior modification techniques can produce behavioral change and have predicable outcome results in most cases.

Internal Consistency

If a theory is scientifically worthy it must be noncontradictory. If a theory contradicts itself or its parts are not rationally interconnected, it is not considered a scientifically worthy theory. Three factors determine internal consistency: (1) the number of exceptions that are acknowledged, (2) the relative simplicity of the theory (the more complex the theory, the more likely it is to have internal inconsistencies), and (3) the prominence and consistency of a central theme. Internal consistency is like the rules of a game. If the rules are constantly changing, the quality of the game is suspect. Likewise, if a theory is constantly undergoing modification, it is probably due more to internal inconsistencies than new discoveries.

Theoretical Economy

Was O. J. Simpson guilty or not? Would he be found guilty, or would he go free? Those questions divided our nation throughout most of 1994. Two theories were proposed. One was rather simple. Nicole Brown Simpson's blood was at the scene of the crime and on Mr. Simpson's vehicle. It was also present at his home. Various items of circumstantial evidence pointed to Simpson as the killer. It seemed like an open and shut case. Yet a jury found him "not guilty." They chose to believe that a conspiracy against Mr. Simpson had been at work. It was a conspiracy that required the involvement of the Los Angeles police, the coroner, and the crime lab that processed the blood samples. Which theory was more scientifically probable or worthy? Was it a conspiracy, or was Mr. Simpson involved in a homicide?

The principle of theoretical economy would point to guilt rather than the conspiracy theory. The principle of theoretical economy says: If two explanations of an event or phenomena fit all the facts equally well, then the simpler explanation is the more likely one. Based on this principle, conspiracy theories are considered to be doubtful explanations of most events. So whether we are considering a criminal verdict, the cause of a jet crash, or the scientific worthiness of a personality theory, simple is better than complex when the simpler theory adequately explains the phenomena being studied.

Of course, theoretical economy is a principle, not a law. Some phenomena are complex and require complex explanations. Sometimes simple explanations are too simplistic and cannot adequately account for the many variables shaping an event or behavior. As we examine the social science theories of human personality we should keep in mind that we are looking at highly complex aspects of human beings and, therefore, complex theories may have greater merit.

Fruitfulness

We need to recognize one more factor that makes a theory a good theory. It is known as fruitfulness. A theory is fruitful when it generates more research and leads to new discoveries. Fruitfulness is not a measure of a theory's accuracy but of its worthiness. It is important to note that a theory that contributes to human understanding, even if errant, can be scientifically worthy. Freud's theory might well be considered a fruitful theory of scientific study. It has made a contribution in that it has generated and continues to generate research and factual understanding of people. It is on Freud's shoulders that a researcher like Erikson has stood. And so we study such theories and value their contributions, even though we may not agree with them in their entirety.

Evaluating Theological Compatibility

Christians have a second issue that they must consider when examining theories of personality. It is the matter of theological compatibility. Personality theories should be reviewed in light of the explicit teachings of the Bible and historical tenets of Christian theology. Three specific points of review are essential if we are to think Christianly about social science research.

Foundational Assumptions

It is important to carefully consider the foundational assumptions any theorist brings to the study of people. All theorists have views about human nature, the origin and destiny of human beings, the possibility and process of change in people, the responsibility and freedom of people to make that change, and the ultimate purpose of people in the world. These assumptions, along with assumptions about the existence of God, the nature of truth, and the means of knowing truth, shape the conclusions the theorist draws from his data. These assumptions are not proven facts. They are unproven beliefs. As such, they represent a worldview and are inherently theological in nature.

It is important that we understand the assumptions that lie behind a theory. For example, it is important to know that Skinner denied human freedom, worth, and dignity. He had no problem equating a person with a pigeon or a mouse with a man. In his theory, humans are merely more complex organisms governed by the same behavioral principles. As Christians, we must recognize the faultiness of his assumptions theologically. It is essential that we compare Skinner to the teachings of the Bible and point out where his research is biased by his theology of man and of God. This is not to reject all aspects of his theory, but to be wise and discerning in understanding and applying his theory.

Core Concepts

Each theory of personality development has, embedded within it, certain theoretical components that comprise its theoretical architecture. For example, Erikson has the concept of conflict or crisis built into his theory. He holds that all stages of human development place the person in a tension between a healthy and an unhealthy response to a pressing life issue. Failure to successfully negotiate each of these life issues creates a tendency to fail in negotiating the next life issue. Erikson believed that there is a need for people in counseling to return to earlier points of failure in order to resolve the issues of a previous stage in a healthy way. In this way a person can be freed to move on in healthy personality development. Is this biblical? Must a person return to past failures in order to have future success? These are the kinds of questions we must raise as we consider the theories presented in this text.

Research Conclusions and Applications

Research assumptions drive research conclusions. We must be discerning when we read of conclusions and research discoveries. Many of these conclusions are not driven by data, but by worldview bias. Researchers filter information through their own grid and tend to produce conclusions that are consistent with their original assumptions. Before we jump on a theoretical bandwagon, we must be sure that conclusions are indeed derived from the data and not simply an application of the unproven assumption of the theorist supported by his research data.

Consider Skinner's behavioral applications as an example. Before we simply embrace his conclusions, we ought to know how they were derived and how well they stack up against the teachings of the Bible about human beings. We cannot simply implement his findings through the use of behavior modification techniques without careful consideration of the theology behind his methods. Does the use of conditioning techniques dehumanize people? Are Skinner's programmed instruction approaches appropriate in light of a biblical view of people? Should societies be engineered so that all behaviors are predictable and trained? These are important questions that are only answered theologically. Because scientists cannot tell us what is moral, because science can only deal with what is, not what ought to be, Christians must be careful to evaluate all conclusions and applications from a theory against a biblical theology. This is not to say that Skinner is devoid of truth or has no contribution to make to the Christian counselor, parent, or teacher. It is not even to say his methods do not work. What it means is that we cannot take Skinner without careful scrutiny and biblical discernment.

Social science theories of human personality cannot provide us with the ultimate truth about human nature. The best they can do is to provide a systematic means to approach it. Theories have inherent limitations both scientifically and theologically. Understanding these limits can help us make effective use of theory in the counseling care of others. (For a more detailed treatment of the value and evaluation of psychological theory, see Michael Green, *Theories of Human Development*.)

— Five Theoretical Paradigms —

In the next four chapters we will review five theoretical paradigms that help in understanding people. In chapter 5 we will consider the biological and behavioral paradigms. We will study these together because they are linked by a common set of assumptions about human nature. In chapter 6 we will consider the psychoanalytic paradigm. The psychoanalytic paradigm explores the conscious and unconscious thoughts that motivate human behavior. The phenomeno- logical or humanistic paradigm that recognizes human value and dignity and seeks to understand how people reach their greatest potential is studied in chapter 7. The cognitive paradigm, which investigates the thought processes that precede and direct human behavior, is the subject of chapter 8. Let us consider the contribution of each paradigm as we widen our understanding of human personality.

Chapters 5 through 8 include several theories of personality development. Some of these theories we significantly disagree with, whereas others we find more convincing. In all cases, what each theorist proposes is an alternative view of the facts surrounding human personality development. We offer a study of these theories as a means of furthering your understanding of human beings and their behaviors. It is entirely likely you will find that some theories are theologically faulty and that most have flaws. But this should not keep you from understanding these proposed views of human personality.

Because we believe that both Christians and non-Christians can discover truth and that the social sciences are a legitimate field for human inquiry, we encourage you to reflect on the work of a number of theorists. We believe that each theory under review will likely expand your understanding of people in some way. Each makes a contribution, but each has weaknesses and limits. We will explore several theories in this book, but we do not expect that you will fully embrace any of them. We hope you will approach this section seeking truth and discerning error. In the end, we believe you will become a better people-helper because you made the effort.

— Chapter 5 —

PERSONALITY PARADIGMS I:
Biological and Behavioral Approaches

Jennifer Cain is a volunteer in the two-year-old room in her church Sunday morning preschool program. She has found it interesting to note the wide range of characteristics present in the different children in the group. One little girl, Korrine, has a hard time when she is dropped off each Sunday morning at the door to her room. She will not let go of her mother's leg, and when she is finally separated from her mom, she is very slow to warm up to the children's workers. Matthew is Korrine's opposite. He is friendly, outgoing, talkative, and playful. He has no difficulty at all with the transition when he arrives at the door. He moves quickly into the room to play with the toys after giving his father a hug and kiss good-bye.

Korrine and Matthew both elicit responses from the children's workers. Korrine is welcomed lovingly by the workers, but the workers respond to Matthew more easily because of his easygoing disposition. Korrine is given wonderful care and loving attention, but she is thought of as a difficult child. Many times she spends the entire hour on someone's lap so that she will stop crying. Although the workers look forward to Matthew's arrival, they are not nearly as receptive to Korrine. In fact, most workers would admit a measure of relief the Sundays that she is absent.

As Jennifer observes the children and the response that adults have to each of them, she wonders how these traits will play themselves out in the developing personalities of each little one. She wonders what shape their personalities will take and how she might minister to each child as they grow into the distinctive individuals God is making them to be.

Personality is a term used by researchers in human development to describe the constellation of characteristics that define an individual. Personality involves the sum total of physical, cognitive, psychosocial, and spiritual qualities. It is the product of our physical strengths and limitations, our innate temperament, our upbringing, our personal choices, our life experiences, and the larger cultural and historical context in which we live. Personality is the complete individual, the whole person—material and immaterial. Scientifically speaking, we are a personality; we do not possess a personality.

Personality is a term psychologists use to describe the enduring individual differences in people. Over the years, researchers have debated how to study personality, how best to understand personality, how personality develops, and how personalities can change. As a result of this ongoing disputation, five families or paradigms have emerged in the field of human psychology (table 5-1). Each of these paradigms has a measure of support and a degree of truth that commends it to our study. Each contributes to our understanding of human beings. But each must be considered against the theological grid we have established in chapters 2 and 3. Where appropriate, those concepts that are compatible with a biblical view of people can be integrated into our knowledge of human development and into our ministry of counseling. In this chapter we will examine two of these basic paradigms. We group these because of their common materialistic and monistic understanding of human nature.

TABLE 5-1
Understanding Human Personality: Five Theoretical Paradigms

1. The Biological Paradigm
   - Influential Period: 1950s–present
   - Principal Contributors: Allport, Murray, Cattell, Eysenck
   - Subject Matter: Physiological bases of behavior in humans.
   - Basic Premise: Personality can be explained in terms of the brain structures, biochemical processes, and genetic tendencies that underlie behavior.

2. The Behavioral Paradigm
   - Influential Period: 1913–present
   - Principal Contributors: Watson, Pavlov, Skinner, Bandura
   - Subject Matter: Effects of environment on behavior and personality.
   - Basic Premise: Only observable stimulus-response relations can be studied scientifically. Stimuli can be both overt (direct) and covert (modeled). These observations can explain all human behavior.

3. The Psychoanalytic Paradigm
   - Influential Period: 1900–present
   - Principal Contributors: Freud, Jung, Erikson
   - Subject Matter: Unconscious factors that determine behavior.
   - Basic Premise: Unconscious motives and experiences in early childhood govern personality and mental disorders.

4. The Phenomenological Paradigm (Humanism)
   - Influential Period: 1950s–present
   - Principal Contributors: Maslow, Rogers, Frankl, May
   - Subject Matter: Unique aspects of human experience that distinguish them from animals. Normal development as opposed to personality abnormalities.
   - Basic Premise: Humans are free, rational beings with the potential for personal growth and positive achievement. Humans are fundamentally different from animals and are capable of moral and creative actions.

5. The Cognitive Paradigm
   - Influential Period: 1950s–present
   - Principal Contributors: Piaget, Chomsky, Simon, Adler
   - Subject Matter: Mental processes and their impact on human behavior.
   - Basic Premise: Human beings construct a cognitive view of their world which becomes the primary basis for explaining their behavior.

THE BIOLOGICAL PARADIGM OF HUMAN PERSONALITY

The biological approach to understanding human personality development places genetics, hormonal activity, and neurological function as the foundational basis of personality. From this vantage point, personality, in all of its facets, is the production of one's biology and is best explained through the study of neuropsychology and physiology. This paradigm has expressed itself in two ways. First, it is reflected in a variety of theories of human personality called *dispositional theories*. The dispositional approach is the oldest and the most persistent means of viewing human personality. Dispositional theorists describe personalities as having certain characteristics or traits that identify both similarities and dissimilarities between people. For example, some persons may be referred to as extroverted, whereas others are introverted. Some may be identified as highly analytical, while others deemed to be more intuitive in nature. Because such traits are considered to be inherent in the person's biology, these traits are believed to have a pervasive influence over a person's life and choices.

The second way in which the biological paradigm has been understood has been through the lens of neurology and brain research. This variation of the biological paradigm reduces people to physical beings who can be fully understood by their chemistry and neurological functioning. The popularity of the biological paradigm has grown in recent years with the development of the neurosciences. Brain research findings have brought dramatic advances in understanding human personality. Such technological wonders as magnetic resonance imaging (MRI) have enabled scientists to observe brain activity and have opened new vistas for the study of personality. At the same time, rapid advancements made in drug development, primarily for the treatment of personality disorders, have occurred. These new drugs, and their positive effects, have brought increased support for the biological paradigm. Writing in the *British Medical Journal*, A. M. Daniels has this to say about psychopharmacological advances.

Gordon Allport

Maybe you have heard someone make a statement like this one: "Jan is very conscientious in her work." Or, you have yourself said something like "Dr. Smith is very outgoing. That's why I like him as a teacher." Whenever we assign descriptors to people's personality characteristics we are referring to what Gordon Allport would term a *personality trait*. Allport was among the first to systematically explore the concept of personality traits. Born in 1897 in Indiana, Allport grew up in Cleveland, Ohio. Allport described his home life as the son of a country doctor as one characterized by "plain Protestant piety and hard work." Allport attended Harvard where he concentrated his studies on both psychology and social ethics. In his spare time he ran a boys' club in Boston's West End and served as a volunteer probation officer. Upon graduation, Allport left for Istanbul, Turkey, where he taught English through a program that was a forerunner of the Peace Corps. In 1922 he returned to Harvard, where he received his Ph.D. His dissertation, "An Experimental Study of Traits of Personality," was the first American study of personality traits.

Allport identified 17,953 words in the English language descriptive of personality traits. He narrowed this list to some fifty personality definitions. Recognizing that such a complex understanding of personality would have little ultimate value, Allport brought order to the chaos of characteristics by identifying three levels of traits.

A *cardinal trait* he identified as a dominant trait that characterizes a person's behavior. For example, consider Jeff for a moment. Jeff is a die-hard Cubs fan. He is a true believer. Despite the Cubs' long-standing history of disappointing seasons, Jeff is always sure this will be their season to win it all. But those of us who have grown up in Chicago know that the Northside Cubbies have an uncanny way of snatching defeat out of the jaws of victory. We still love our Cubs, but winning is not something we have come to expect. Once when Jeff was visiting his brother Mark, they attended a Cubs game together. The boys in blue pinstripes were getting roundly beaten by a score of nine to two. When the eighth inning rolled around and things looked bleak, Mark suggested that the two leave early to get a jump on the crowds and the traffic. Jeff would hear nothing of it. The eternal optimist, Jeff asked, "What, leave now and miss their rally?" How do you explain Jeff's optimism? According to Allport, it is a *cardinal trait* of his personality. To Jeff, seven runs represent a minor obstacle. Anything is possible. That is the nature of his temperament.

Allport's second level of personality traits is what he terms *central traits.* These are prominent traits and general dispositions but are not as powerful in ruling behavior as cardinal traits. A tendency to be a sensitive and caring individual or the tendency toward independence or irresponsibility would be examples of Allport's central traits.

Allport's third level of characteristic traits of personality he termed *secondary dispositions.* These are situational responses in our lives. For example, a man may be domineering at home but submissive when faced with a police officer who is writing out a ticket. One's personality traits affect the way one responds in a given and specific situation.

Henry Murray

Born in New York on May 13, 1893, Murray was a contemporary of Gordon Allport. Murray grew up in a privileged home, spending his winters in the city and his summers on Long Island. Unlike Allport, Murray was not formally trained in psychology. Murray was trained in medicine at the Columbia University School of Medicine where he graduated top in his class. Later he received a Ph.D. in biology from Cambridge University. As a biologist and medical doctor, Murray was convinced that personality was not a real entity separate from the physical body, but instead, he believed personality to be dependent on brain processes. We could call Murray a neuropsychologist because of his belief that neurophysiological processes are the source of human behavior.

Murray extensively researched human needs as a force shaping human personality. Murray defined a *need* as a construct representing a force in the brain that organizes our perception, understanding, and behavior in such a way as to change an unsatisfying situation and increase our satisfaction. From his study, Murray constructed a list of twenty basic human needs (table 5-2). According to Murray, some needs, such as hunger or thirst, are more powerful in shaping human behavior if unsatisfied. Murray also recognized that forces within the environment help and hinder persons in meeting their needs. He terms these environmental forces an *environmental press*. An example of an environmental press might be poverty or religious training. In both cases, these environmental factors influence how a person goes about meeting a fundamental need. Later, humanistic psychologist Abraham Maslow picked up on Murray's research. Maslow categorized needs based on the order in which people seek to meet them. He published his needs theory in his now famous hierarchy of needs.

Raymond Cattell

A third researcher who is associated with the biological paradigm of human personality is Raymond Cattell. Born in Stafford-

TABLE 5–2
Murray's List of Needs

Dominance	To control one's human environment
Deference	To admire and support a superior other
Autonomy	To resist influence or coercion
Aggression	To overcome opposition forcefully
Abasement	To submit passively to external force
Achievement	To accomplish something difficult
Sex	To form and further an erotic relationship
Sentience	To seek and enjoy sensuous impressions
Exhibition	To make an impression
Play	To relax, amuse oneself, seek diversion and entertainment
Affiliation	To form friendships and associations
Rejection	To snub, ignore, or exclude another
Succorance	To seek aid, protection, or sympathy
Nurturance	To nourish, aid, or protect a helpless one
Infavoidance	To avoid humiliation
Defendance	To defend the self against assault, criticism, and blame
Counteraction	To master or make up for a failure by restriving
Harmavoidance	To avoid pain, physical injury, illness, and death
Order	To put things in order
Understand	To give meaning by asking and answering general questions

shire, England, in 1905, Cattell enjoyed a very happy early childhood. Cattell received his undergraduate training at the University of London in chemistry and physics. His graduate work was also undertaken at the University of London where he earned a Ph.D. in psychology.

Cattell was interested in the physical and neurological components that influence behavior and personality. He distinguished between *surface traits*, which he held were clusters of overt behavior responses that tend to appear together such as honesty, integrity, and self-discipline. *Source traits* are the underlying traits that seem to determine surface trait expressions—such as "ego-strength" in the case of the traits listed above. Using a sophisticated statistical technique called *factor analysis*, Cattell reduced Allport's massive list of more than fifty traits to just sixteen variables (table 5-3). He then devised equations that he believed would predict how a person would respond to a given stimulus based on the person's constellation of traits. Cattell believed that, in time, by applying appropriate rules of research, psychologists would eventually be able to predict human behavior in various situations as accurately as astronomers predict the stars and the planets.

Based on Cattell's work, current research has further reduced Cattell's source traits to what have become known as the "Big Five." Researchers McCrae and Costa have delineated *openness, consciousness, extroversion, agreeableness,* and *neuroticism* as the five primary factors that form the basic structure of human personality (Weiten 473). These five basic traits can be remembered with the little mnemonic device "OCEAN." The Big Five have become widely accepted as the dominant conception of trait theory of personality in contemporary psychology.

Hans Eysenck

Hans Eysenck was born in Berlin, Germany, in 1916, of parents who were renowned stage actors. When his parents divorced when he was only two, Eysenck was given to his grandmother to rear. Raised a Lutheran, Eysenck was often taunted by his classmates as a "white Jew" because he sympathized with the plight of Jews in Germany. He left Germany when he was eighteen years old

TABLE 5–3
Cattell's Sixteen Basic Source Traits

Outgoing	Reserved
More intelligent	Less intelligent
High ego strength	Low ego strength
Assertive	Humble
Happy-go-lucky	Sober
Strong conscience	Lack of internal standards
Adventuresome	Shy
Tough-minded	Tender-minded
Trusting	Suspicious
Imaginative	Practical
Shrewd	Forthright
Apprehensive	Self-assured
Experimental	Conservative
Group-dependent	Self-sufficient
Casual	Controlled
Relaxed	Tense

when the Nazis came to power because, as an active Jewish sympathizer, his life was in danger. Eysenck settled in England where he attended the University of London and received his Ph.D. in psychology in 1940. During World War II, he served as a psychologist at an emergency hospital, where he did independent research on the reliability of psychiatric treatment and diagnosis. The results led him to a lifelong antagonism toward mainstream clinical psychology, particularly Freudian psychotherapy. Eysenck wrote seventy-five books and some seven hundred articles, making him one of the most prolific writers in psychology.

Eysenck's theory is based primarily on physiology, neuroscience, and genetics. Although he was a behaviorist, he considered personality differences to be the result of genetic inheritance, not reinforcements. He was most interested in understanding the nature of various human temperament types. Eysenck's original research found two main dimensions of temperament that he termed *neuroticism* and *extroversion*.

Neuroticism describes a person's emotional stability, ranging from calm and collected at one end of a continuum to nervous and easily distraught at the other. He found that highly nervous and easily flustered people tended to suffer more frequently from "nervous disorders" called *neuroses*. Eysenck described a neurotic individual as a person who has little emotional control and is excessively anxious, unpredictable, and emotionally unstable. He was not saying that people who score high on the neuroticism scale are all neurotics, however. He just believed that because they have neurotic tendencies they are far more susceptible to neurotic problems.

Eysenck was convinced that the emotional or neurotic dimension of personality is genetically based and physiologically supported. Because of this viewpoint, he turned to physiological research to find possible explanations. He felt that the most logical place to find the cause of this personality tendency was the *sympathetic nervous system*. The sympathetic nervous system is a part of the autonomic nervous system and functions separately from the central nervous system. It controls much of our emotional responsiveness to emergency situations. The sympathetic nervous system is the part of our nervous system that prepares us for "fight or flight" situations. When you walk down a dark alley at night and your heart races, your pupils open wide, and you feel a surge of adrenaline coursing through your blood to your muscles, you are experiencing the effects of the sympathetic nervous system. Eysenck hypothesized that some people have a more responsive sympathetic nervous system than do others. Some remain calm during emergencies, while others feel considerable fear or tension. In the extreme, Eysenck believed those who have panic attacks or neurotic disorders have hyperactive sympathetic nervous systems.

His second dimension was *extroversion*. The extroversion versus introversion dimension reflects the degree to which a person is outgoing or shy. This dimension he also believed had physiological explanation. Eysenck hypothesized that extroversion-introversion is a matter of the balance of "inhibition" and "excitation" in the brain. *Excitation* is the brain waking itself up, getting into an alert, learning state. *Inhibition* is the brain calming itself down, either in the usual sense of relaxing and going to sleep or in the sense of protecting itself in the case of overwhelming stimulation.

Extroverts, he hypothesized, have strong inhibition capability. When confronted by traumatic stimulation the extrovert's brain inhibits itself, becomes "numb" to the situation or the trauma. Often the extrovert will forget the details of a trauma quickly. Introverts, on the other hand, have weak inhibition capability, so when a traumatic situation occurs their brains are slow in bringing a self-protective response. Instead, they are highly alert and able to learn and remember everything that happens. When in a car crash, for example, introverts will report that the crash seemed to happen "in slow motion." Eysenck found that introverts were more easily traumatized by something like a car crash, may be slow to drive after such an incident, and may even avoid driving altogether.

Eysenck identified four temperament types that he felt coincided with the four dispositions identified by Greek physician Hippocrates. Using Hippocrates's terms, *choleric, sanguine, phlegmatic,* and *melancholic,* Eysenck created a model for understanding personality temperament types. Taking the two major personality trait dimensions already discussed—neuroticism verses emotional stability and extroversion versus introversion—Eysenck placed these dimensions on intersecting axes (figure 5-1).

Additionally, Eysenck recognized the ingredient of psychoticism in human personality. A psychotic person is unable to distinguish between reality and fantasy. A psychotic person may have disturbances in thought, emotion, or behavior, as well as hallucinations or delusions. He believed that all persons exhibit some psychotic behavior and that people range from low to high on the psychoticism scale.

Evidence Supporting the Biological Paradigm

What evidence supports the biological paradigm for understanding human personality? Researchers point to three lines of proof that biology is at the root of our personality qualities.

First of these includes the clear connections between the physiology of the brain and personality traits.

For one hundred and fifty years, researchers have been discovering causal links between the brain and personality. This quest

FIGURE 5–1
Eysenck's Intercorrelation of Traits

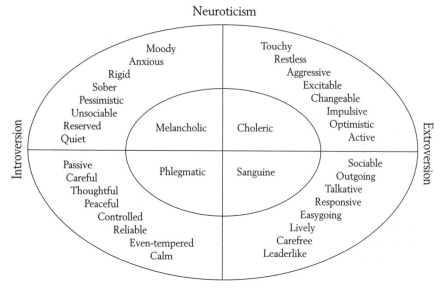

Neuroticism

Introversion — Extroversion

Moody
Anxious
Rigid
Sober
Pessimistic
Unsociable
Reserved
Quiet

Touchy
Restless
Aggressive
Excitable
Changeable
Impulsive
Optimistic
Active

Melancholic   Choleric

Passive
Careful
Thoughtful
Peaceful
Controlled
Reliable
Even-tempered
Calm

Phlegmatic   Sanguine

Sociable
Outgoing
Talkative
Responsive
Easygoing
Lively
Carefree
Leaderlike

Emotional Stability

to understand the nature of the brain can be traced to a rather remarkable incident that occurred in September 1848, in Cavendish, Vermont. Phineas P. Gage, a twenty-five-year-old railroad foreman, was using explosives to clear the way for new track. In preparation for blasting he was packing an explosive charge into a drill hole with a thirteen-pound, three-and-a-half-foot-long tamping rod. An accidental spark ignited the charge prematurely, sending the rod through his left cheek and out the vault of his skull. It landed more than thirty yards away. Gage survived the experience but faced several weeks of infection, fever, and semiconsciousness. His condition became so poor that a coffin was prepared for him. But in the fifth week his condition improved. Gage regained consciousness but was blind in the left eye. What made this case noteworthy was not Gage's survival, however; it was the change in Gage's behavior due to the brain damage that occurred.

Before the incident, Gage was well liked by friends and was considered to be honest, trustworthy, hardworking, and dependable. When that tamping rod plowed through Gage's skull, it took a part of his brain tissue with it and, in the process, something of Gage's former self. After the accident Gage's doctor described him as "fitful, irreverent, indulging at times in the grossest profanity (which was not previously his custom), manifesting but little deference for his fellows, impatient. . . . A child in his intellectual capacity and manifestations. . . . His mind was radically changed, so decidedly that his friends and acquaintances said he was 'no longer Gage'" (Harlow 327–47).

From that point until today, brain researchers have sought to understand how the brain affects personality. In 1861, French surgeon Pierre-Paul Broca discovered a region in the left hemisphere of the brain that, if damaged, causes various speech disorders. That part of the brain became known as Broca's area. Thirteen years later a neurologist named Carl Wernicke discovered a second area of the brain that affected language, involving the continued ability to speak but the loss of understanding of language. These early brain studies, along with more recent studies of brain hemispheric functioning, have generated an ever growing knowledge of the relationship between brain and personality.

Brain damage changes people by changing their abilities and their personalities. There is an intimate connection between the health of our brains and the health of our personalities. We often take it for granted that personality is indelible and unchanging, but this is incorrect. Although personality is stable, it is affected by the state and health of those two handfuls of grayish matter called the brain. Neurochemical transmitters, synapse connections, dendrites, and axons are all terms that now are used to describe the growing understanding of the brain-mind-personality relationship. Diseases such as Alzheimer's and Parkinson's, split-brain patients and pharma-psychological treatments, all underscore the undeniable role of the brain in human behavior and personality.

A second line of evidence for the biological paradigm is the inheritance of temperament traits.

There is clear and strong evidence that temperament traits are transmitted genetically. Studies of the personality traits of adults and their children and studies of identical and fraternal twins raised together and raised apart consistently point to the significant role of biology, especially genetics, in forming our personality characteristics. Take, for example, the recent study of leadership traits in identical twins. Researchers at the University of Western Ontario made the discovery that leadership has a genetic linkage. After comparing the results of personality tests of identical twins (having the same genetic blueprint) with fraternal twins (who share the same environment but have different genetics), they found that identical twins achieve similar scores for leadership traits such as charisma and the ability to inspire others. They found that this was not true in the case of fraternal twins (Matthews).

In studies in Sweden and the United States, researchers have found that identical twins raised apart have more similar personality types than fraternal twins raised together. Even preference in clothing style, personal interests, body posture, body language, speed and tempo of talking, sense of humor, and recreational habits were discovered to be more common among the identical twins studied. Such research lends a support to the biological paradigm of human personality (Bee 251).

The third line of evidence for the biological paradigm is the consistency of temperament over time.

Some have linked temperament to genetics and then defined personality as temperament plus environment. Generally speaking, when we go to bed at night we do not expect to wake up the next day with a radically changed personality. Biological psychologists would explain this as the result of unchanging genetics and consistent neurochemistry. Although abrupt changes do occur, these are often due to trauma of some sort, either physical or emotional, which changes brain physiology in the case of an accident or brain chemistry in the case of a traumatizing event. More often, humans experience a stable, consistent personality, which is predictable from day to day. Biological psychologists believe that this is because of the stable nature of our brain hardware. Clearly, it seems that there is no refuting the fact that inborn genetic and physiological patterns underlie human personality.

Problems with the Biological Paradigm

The biological model has some significant shortcomings that make it inappropriate as the sole paradigm for understanding human personality for those who would counsel under the authority of Scripture.

The first problem is found in its materialistic, monistic assumptions.

You will remember that materialism is a belief that the only true reality is the material world and that monism is the belief that humans are comprised of one element. Biological psychologists tend to take a materialistic, monistic position when it comes to the constitutional nature of human beings. They do so because of the belief that all human behavior can be understood when all of the workings of the brain are understood. As monists, they contend that human personality and self-awareness are simply the result of brain functioning, whether chemical or structural. Although certainly there is a causal relationship between brain, behavior, and personality, it is important to note that philosophical materialism, not just brain research, lies behind the biological paradigm. This brand of modern science chooses to dispense with immaterial souls and spirits altogether, making the brain the only explanation for the mind and the spirit.

The biblical teaching regarding human nature includes both physical and spiritual dimensions. The Bible teaches that humans are a unified whole consisting of both material and immaterial attributes united together to become a "living soul." The separation of body and spirit is unnatural and is the essence of death. Understanding human physiology and brain functioning is essential if one is to have a growing awareness of the nature of human personality, but to deny the spiritual aspect of human nature is to leave out one of the foundational moorings of a biblical anthropology.

It is interesting to note that even neuroscientists do not universally agree with a monistic biological view of personality. Restak presents an engaging account of several prominent neuroscientists who have concluded that the mind cannot be explained only in terms of the physical brain. He cites persons such as Wilder Penfield, Sir John Eccles, and Karl Pribram as prime examples of formerly materialistic monists who have adopted a dualistic position late in their careers (348-49). Why the change? Each of these researchers has come to reject the reductionistic views of the biological paradigm. They have concluded that biology alone is an insufficient means of explaining the uniqueness of human beings' thought and behavior.

Some Christians who study and work in the field of neurology and neuropsychology have embraced the biological paradigm despite its monistic and materialistic problems. Arguing from a *perspectivist* viewpoint, they conclude that the descriptions of human nature in the Bible and the descriptions in science cannot be related to each other in any direct sense. Perspectivists argue that these descriptions represent radically different understandings even if, at times, they employ the same or similar terms (e.g., mind, body, heart, etc.). Their point is that the biblical description of humans is much like the Bible's description of the movement of the sun across the sky (phenomena). Biblical writers simply described the world and people as they appeared to them. Scientists, on the other hand, speak of the earth's movement around the sun and neurochemical activity of the brain (empirical facts). They contend that the difference is one of purpose, suggesting that the Bible's purpose is theological and, thus, one cannot use the Bible to understand humans in a scientific way. Neuroscience is given final authority, and biblical descriptions are reinterpreted to accommodate those findings.

In the process of accommodating neuroscience, perspectivists find themselves having to attribute the biblical account of an immortal soul to the influence of Greek thought in the New Testament. In the end, such an accommodation requires them to depart from historic Christian views of an immaterial spirit, the intermediate state, and the eternal punishment of hell. (See chapter 2 for a more detailed discussion of this position.)

A second problem with the biological paradigm is ethical in nature.

Although brain diseases, such as Parkinson's disease, may be treatable, treatments sometimes involve ethically unacceptable actions. In the case of Parkinson's, this includes the use of fetal tissue. Research evidence shows that fetal tissue transplanted into the brains of Parkinson's patients can relieve some symptoms. This is because the fetal cells establish new neuro-networks and produce a missing chemical, dopamine. But the treatment is at the cost of the life of an unborn child. For the materialist, such a cost is simply a trade-off, but for the Christian who recognizes the presence of an immaterial soul in the unborn child, such treatments are barbaric. No matter how beneficial the result, sucking brain tissue from an unborn child in order to treat a Parkinson's patient is a murderous act. Similar ethical issues arise regarding genetic engineering, cloning, some methods of infertility treatment, and the use of psycho-pharmaceuticals for personality alteration.

If people can be reduced to bodies only and there is no spiritual dimension to their nature, then how would one logically argue for the existence of a sin nature, the worth and dignity of the individual, and the sanctity of life? If, as the semimaterialist holds, the immaterial aspects of people are simply derived from the brain and brain states, how can one argue for the full humanness of the unborn or mentally disabled? Whether for materialistic monism or semimaterialistic monism, the monistic explanation of human nature creates far more problems than it solves.

Contributions of the Biological Paradigm

Because of its monistic, materialistic perspective, one may wonder how a biological approach to human personality could contribute to counseling ministry. In reality, there are four significant contributions of the biological paradigm. The first of these is *valuable empirical research*. There is an abundance of beneficial research into brain function and the correction of damaged or diseased brains. This benefit holds out a promising hope to patients suffering from brain-related problems or neurochemical imbalances and to their families who must care for and relate to them. Additionally, research into the genetic links to various human conditions and behaviors may open heretofore untapped avenues of treatment. Second, the biological paradigm contributes a *balancing to spiritual reductionists* that would, like Job's counselors, make every human problem an issue of personal sin. Third, the biological paradigm *puts into perspective the nature of human success and suffering.* If the differences between people are more than their will, and include their biology, then we can be less critical and more understanding of those who may not act as we may desire or learn as we learn. Although tolerance has been far overstressed in our culture today because of philosophical pluralism, it is not a quality that is without merit. Understanding a biological paradigm can generate appropriate tolerance for human differences that would serve us well.

The fourth contribution of the biological paradigm is probably the one that has been most readily accepted by Christians. It involves *personality type testing.* Such tests as the MMPI (Minnesota Multiphasic Personality Inventory), the 16PF (based on the sixteen personality dimensions identified by Cattell), the NEO-PI (Costa and McCrae's Big Five personality inventory), and the MBTI (Myers and Briggs Type Indicator) have been widely used in Christian premarital and marital counseling. Likewise, pastors, Christian counselors, and Christian educators have used these tests in a number of other counseling situations. Based on the concept of personality types, numerous inventories and personality profiling instruments have been created over the years to aid individuals in understanding themselves and others. Some have taken the concept of personality types and have expanded it to develop parenting style, leadership style, learning style, and even spiritual gift inventories.

We need not dismiss out of hand all of the findings of those who embrace the biological paradigm. To hold that persons are born with certain personality traits is in keeping with a biblical view of human beings. Clearly, the benefits of the biological paradigm are many. What those who would counsel under the authority of Scripture must do is reject the assumptions of the biological paradigm that are contrary to the teachings of the Bible. At the same time, those discoveries and treatments that can enhance ministry should be understood and further explored.

THE BEHAVIORAL PARADIGM OF HUMAN PERSONALITY

The printed advertisement in the weekend paper was tough to ignore. "Computerized collar created world's first radio-controlled dog." The one-page ad, written to look like a newspaper article, told of the effectiveness of what it called "Instant Fence." The system consists of a radio transmitter that sends out an adjustable circular signal, a radio receiver collar, training flags, and instructional videotape. The wireless system transmits a signal that the collar detects. When the dog moves close to the end of the signal area, the collar beeps. A few more feet and it gives the dog a momentary static shock similar to one a person would receive when touching something metal after walking across carpeting. Using flags as a temporary visual cue, the dog is trained over several days to know where the safe area is and where a shock will occur. The final result is a dog that will remain in a fenceless yard. Like most animal-training techniques, the system is built on behavioral conditioning.

The behavioral paradigm of human personality understands the development of personality qualities in humans as taking place in very much the same manner as our furry friend learns his backyard boundaries. The behavioral paradigm sees people as behaving organisms, as animals who are simply more complex in nature and more advanced in mental capacity. The correction and reinforcements do not come from electronic collars but from everyday experiences and forces in the environment, which serve to shape our thinking, attitudes, behavior, and personality.

Most of us are behaviorists to some degree. When we heard of or saw the live television coverage of the student shootings at Columbine High School in the Denver suburb of Littleton, Colorado, in April of 1999, we asked one another, "What would cause a child to become so violent?" Behind our question was a behaviorist assumption. The assumption was that something in the environment "caused" the boys' deviant behavior. Was it the video games they played? Maybe it was the music they listened to. Could it have been their involvement in an antisocial group, the "Trench Coat Mafia"? Was it the Gothic subculture, a fringe countercultural youth movement? Was it the movies they watched over and over that depicted similar behaviors? Maybe it was the treatment they received from other young people at school. Or was it their parents who seemed to have little understanding of their children's actions? The speculations went on and on. All of these "causes" had one thing in common—a belief that environment causes or even determines behavior. Such assumptions are at the heart of the behavioral paradigm. Let us examine the major propositions that define this paradigm.

Basic Propositions of the Behavioral Paradigm

Like the biological theorists discussed earlier in this chapter, those who hold to the behavioral paradigm are typically materialistic and monistic in their understanding of the nature of human beings. The significant difference between biological and behavioral psychologists arises, however, in their understandings of the causes of human behavior. Biological psychologists see behavior as a result of brain functioning and innate personality traits. Behaviorists believe that personality traits are determined by causal factors within the experience of the person rather than in his biology. *Behaviorism* is a theoretical orientation based on the premise that scientific psychology should study only observable behavior. Behaviorism holds that all behaviors are caused and that by studying behavior one can come to systematically understand how behaviors are learned and changed. Four proposition statements will help us understand this highly influential perspective regarding the nature of human personality.

Proposition 1: Experience and learning are the primary forces that shape human behavior and personality.

Also known as learning theory, the behavioral paradigm emphasizes that the dominant factors in the development of human personality are the environment and learning experiences. Behaviorists do not reject biology, but they believe that human development is primarily exogenous in nature, meaning that changing occurs from forces outside the person rather than forces within. Humans are pliable, and nurture is the means by which people are shaped.

Julia is three. Like most three-year-olds, Julia has a way of needing attention at the most challenging times. She seeks attention while her mother is fixing dinner. Constantly she tugs at her mother saying, "Mommy, I'm hungry." Her mother offers her something healthy so as not to ruin her dinner. But Julia wants a cookie, not a carrot. Finally, in desperation, Julia's mother relents and provides the cookie. What has Julia learned? What has her mother reinforced? What kind of personality might Julia develop if this interaction is typical of other encounters between mom and child?

Behaviorists would suggest that learning is occurring in this social dance. Julia is learning how to get what she wants and is being reinforced by her mother's actions. But Julia is not the only one who has learned through reinforcement. Julia's mother has also discovered through the daily social exchange that when she gives in to Julia, Julia will stop whining. Because giving in is negatively reinforced for Julia's mom by Julia's more pleasant behavior, it is likely that her mom will give in next time as well. Imagine this exchange repeating itself night after night. It is easy to see how this mutually reinforcing behavior can shape both mother and child for the long haul. Mother becomes less authoritative while her child is shaped into a demanding and noncompliant child who rules the roost.

Behaviorists hold that in such experiences of daily life, personality qualities are formed and habits learned. Whether it is the tendency toward aggression or shyness, whether it be socially desirable or undesirable behavior, the behaviorist would point to experience and to conditioned and observational learning as the reasons for these personality markers.

Proposition 2: Humans are born with a "blank slate" mind that immediately begins to form associations from worldly sensations.

John B. Watson, behaviorism's founding father, once offered a tongue-in-cheek challenge that he could take any child and turn him or her into anything from a doctor to a beggar.

Give me a dozen healthy infants, well-formed, and my own special world to bring them up in and I'll guarantee to take any one at random and train him to become any type of specialist I might select—doctor, lawyer, artist, merchant-chief, and yes, even beggarman and thief, regardless of his talents, penchants, tendencies, abilities, vocations and race of his ancestors. (82)

Watson's statement is extreme, but the sentiment of his words is characteristic of the behaviorist perspective. For Watson and other behaviorists, the exercise of a free human will is not a factor, nor is conscious decision making. Instead, each child is seen as a tabula rasa (blank slate) subject to the conditioning forces in the environment. Through experiences beginning at the moment of birth, children are believed to establish associations within the mind between behaviors and various rewards. These associations become the basis on which personality is built.

Proposition 3: Human behavior and personality are the cumulative result of learned associations and reinforcements.

Over time and repeated reinforcement, ideas and behaviors are connected in ways that become inseparably bonded. For example, in a word-association game the word *bread* will more often elicit the response "butter" than it will the responses "milk" or "wheat." Why is that? It is because the association between bread and butter has been consistently experienced and eventually learned. In the same way, associations between various behaviors and their reinforcements are learned and become part of one's personality.

Sixteen-year-old Stacy is a prime example. She is known for her bubbly nature and wonderful sense of humor. Behaviorists would suggest that these qualities are present because of the favorable attention she gains from them. Since her laughter generates positive responses in others, a kind of reward, she continues the behavior until it becomes so much a part of her as to be a habit. These reinforced associations shape personality until the individual is conditioned to respond in a consistent way. Experience by experience, reinforcement by reinforcement, children learn to behave as they do and form the personalities we come to know. Behaviorists would suggest that through understanding these kinds of associations, all behaviors can be understood and, in fact, reshaped as desired.

Proposition 4: Children learn new behaviors and personality patterns through the modeling behavior of others.

Many years ago a commercial for the American Cancer Society was aired for the purpose of convincing parents that their smoking habits increased the likelihood that their children would smoke as well. Throughout the commercial the words "like father, like son" were repeated. A young father is seen washing his new car. As he takes the sponge and washes a wheel, his little boy, maybe three or four years of age, follows his example and does the same. "Like father, like son" proclaims the voice-over. The dad then washes a headlight while his ever-watching little one mimics his actions on the other headlamp. "Like father, like son" we hear again. Then they pick up the hose to rinse the car and again the familiar phrase is heard, "like father, like son." Finally, both, tired and hot, sit down under a nearby shade tree. The father sighs. The son sighs. Then the father pulls out a package of cigarettes. He lights the cigarette and places the pack between him and his son against the base of the tree. The boy looks at his dad and then at the pack. As the boy reaches out to take the pack, the announcer again states, "Like father, like son." It is a powerful commercial about parental role modeling and the learning of behavior through observation.

Behavioral researchers have extended behaviorism beyond simply stimulus-response and reinforcement understandings of learning. Many behaviorists would argue that a full range of social behavior is learned by watching others, not just by direct reinforcement. For example, a child who watches her mother as the mother prepares a casserole for a new widow learns generosity and Christlike service. Similarly, a child who observes parents belittling others or using violent means to solve problems will likely learn the same solutions. Parents are not the only role models. Television, teachers, siblings, peers, sports, and music personalities all provide examples from whom behavior can be learned.

Jefferson is a nine-year-old boy living in a Near Westside Chicago neighborhood. His world is one of street gangs, shoplifting, drugs, and nightly shootings. His older brother steals hubcaps from cars and carries a handgun for protection. Jefferson's continuous exposure to crime and antisocial behavioral models makes it much more likely that Jefferson will pursue a similar life path. Why? Because the power of observational learning is indisputable.

Whether in real life or vicariously through the media, role models have a powerful influence on human learning and behavior. Despite the arguments from the producers of America's media violence that their products do not cause deviant behavior, the overwhelming weight of evidence is that such depictions of violence do affect the choices that children make. One estimate of the relationship between violent television viewing and behavior is that it is about the same as the relationship between smoking cigarettes and lung cancer. Certainly there is not a one-to-one correspondence, but the association is so strong as to be a predictive variable in understanding human behavior. It is important to note that children learn not only overt behavior, but also ideas, expectations, internal standards, and self-concepts from reinforcement and modeling.

Proponents of the Behavioral Paradigm

The leading and most influential proponents of the behavioral paradigm have been B. F. Skinner and Alfred Bandura. We will briefly summarize each of their theories.

B. F. Skinner

In a town of just two thousand persons it is a rare occasion when an event occurs of worldwide significance. Situated at a bend in the river just a few miles south of the New York and Pennsylvania state line, Susquehanna, Pennsylvania, can claim just a distinction. Born March 20, 1904, to Grace and William Skinner, Burrhus Frederic Skinner received a liberal theological upbringing and eventually became a self-avowed atheist during his college years at Hamilton College in Clinton, New York.

A 1931 Harvard University Ph.D. graduate, Skinner first came to the public's attention in 1938 with the publication of his book *Behavior of Organisms*. Later, after World War II, Skinner published a novel entitled *Walden Two*, a story of a behaviorally controlled utopian community. In it he presented his philosophical views regarding the application of behavioral psychology to social institutions. Also noteworthy are his works *Beyond Freedom and Dignity* (1971) and *About Behaviorism* (1971) in which Skinner challenged concepts of an inner person, free will, and human dignity. In response to these writings, *Time* magazine described Skinner as "the most influential of living American psychologists, and most controversial contemporary figure in the science of human behavior, adored as a messiah and abhorred as a menace."

Skinner's concept of human learning and personality can be historically traced from Pavlov's *classical conditioning* through Thorndike's *instrumental conditioning* to Watson's *environmentalism*. Pavlov (1849–1936), a Russian psychologist, researched the relationship between stimulus and response. In his famous classical conditioning experiments, Pavlov trained dogs to salivate at the ring of a bell by associating the sound of the bell with the presentation of food, demonstrating that behavior can be conditioned through the process of association.

Thorndike (1874–1949) took Pavlov's concepts further. He postulated three laws of behavioral learning: the law of effect, the law of readiness, and the law of exercise. The most significant of these is the *law of effect*, which simply states that behavior is strengthened when followed by pleasure and weakened by displeasure. John B. Watson (1878–1958) drew on the work of Pavlov and Thorndike, proposing that environmental controls could determine a child's development, personality traits, beliefs, behavior, and even career choice. Taking an extreme position on the matter, in Watson's view all human behavior is determined by environment.

Based on the work of these predecessors, Skinner also concluded that environmental circumstances, not heredity, temperament, or even personal choice determine human behavior. Skinner believed that all human personality traits and habits are the result, not of inner processes, but of external forces that shape, reward, and reinforce behavior. In Skinner's theory of human personality, "brain" substitutes for "mind," and "behavior" for "conscious thought." People are simply organisms like any other organism, only more advanced. The fundamental assumption behind Skinner's theory is deceptively simple: People tend to repeat responses that lead to positive outcomes, and they tend not to repeat responses that lead to neutral or negative outcomes. Working with laboratory animals and with his own daughter, Skinner showed that, by using reinforcements, he could control behavior.

Reinforcement is the key concept in Skinner's theory. A *reinforcement* is anything that strengthens a desired response. It could be something as simple as verbal praise, a grade on an assignment, or even the feeling of accomplishment or satisfaction in a completed task. Not all reinforcements are positive in nature. Skinner also described negative reinforcements. A *negative reinforcement* is any stimulus that results in the increased frequency of a response because of the desire to have the stimulus withdrawn. For example, when a child cleans his room because he can no longer tolerate his mother's nagging he has been negatively reinforced.

One of the distinctive aspects of Skinner's theory is that it attempts to provide behavioral explanations for a broad range of cognitive phenomena. For example, Skinner explained motivation in terms of deprivation and reinforcement. Skinner, likewise, tried to account for language within the operant conditioning paradigm by pointing out that parents reinforce their children's efforts to speak.

Skinner's students eventually applied his behavioral principles discovered primarily in animal research to complex human behaviors. Over time, the principles of behaviorism became widely used in business, schools, prisons, mental health treatment programs, and counseling.

Alfred Bandura

Canadian by birth, Alfred Bandura was born in 1925 in northern Alberta. He studied psychology at the University of British Columbia and did his graduate study at the University of Iowa. In 1952 he moved to Stanford to become a psychology professor. Bandura's interest was directed toward an understanding of how social situations and the observation of others affect the formation of behaviors in children. His theory is known as social-cognitive learning theory.

> Learning would be exceedingly laborious, not to mention hazardous, if people had to rely solely on the effects of their own actions to inform them what to do. Fortunately, most human behavior is learned observationally through modeling: from observing others one forms an idea of how new behaviors are performed, and on later occasions this coded information serves as a guide for action. Because people can learn from example what to do, at least in approximate form, before performing any behavior, they are spared needless errors. (Bandura 22)

Bandura's theory focuses on observational learning (modeling) rather than a pure stimulus-response-reinforcement approach that is characteristic of Skinner's theory. According to Bandura, humans differ from animals in that they have the ability to remember, understand, and interpret symbols and experiences, thus setting them apart from the stimulus-response limitations of the animal world. Because of this ability, people are able to learn by observing others. This is called *modeling*, which he believes could have as much of an impact on an individual as direct experience.

Have you ever been to an elaborate formal dinner where several eating utensils are provided? Different forks, knives, and spoons are arranged around the plate, each with a different purpose. Now, what would you do if you were not quite sure which piece of silver was appropriate for which food item? If you are typical, you would probably look for someone around you, maybe the hostess or a more cultured friend, to model the correct selections. You do not have to learn by doing; you can learn by observing. Maybe you have read of a child acting out a violent scene in a movie or a child abuser who turns out to have been abused himself in childhood. In countless situations from the classroom to the boardroom, human behaviors are modeled in a way that changes the behaviors of those doing the observing.

Although Bandura agreed with most of Skinner's conclusions, he believed that an individual's cognitive processes are active in shaping behavior and personality. The fact that many of our most persistent habits and attitudes result from simply watching and thinking about the action of others convinced Bandura that learning is more complex than simply the reinforcement of behaviors. Because of the inclusion in his theory of active mental processes and the ability of persons to observe and evaluate the experiences of others, Bandura was much less deterministic in his outlook than was Skinner.

Bandura continued to hold that reinforcements are the major motivating force in human behavior. He recognized three types of reinforcements. The first he termed *direct reinforcement*. Direct reinforcement occurs when an individual is reinforced as a direct result of following a model. This is similar to Skinner's concept of reinforcement. Let's say you are coaching a Little League baseball team. You show the players how to make a force-out at second base when fielding a grounder. Then they follow your example and try it themselves. When they make the play correctly you praise them by saying "great play." Each child is being directly reinforced by your comment.

The second type of reinforcement is *vicarious reinforcement*. Vicarious reinforcement is when a person observes how another person is reinforced for certain behaviors and then adjusts his or her own performance accordingly. Let's say Tommy hears you say "great play" to Johnny. As a result, Tommy tries harder in order to perform as well as Johnny. In this case, Tommy was vicariously reinforced. Your comment to Johnny actually motivated Tommy's behavior.

The third type of reinforcement that Bandura observed he termed *self-reinforcement*. Self-reinforcement occurs when a person sets personal standards for his own behavior and then controls his own reinforcers. Some children are highly dedicated ballplayers. They set personal standards of performance and then work over and over on their skills until they reach their desired level. Their own sense of accomplishment is their reinforcement when they meet their own standard. When Tommy spends hours throwing the ball against a wall, counting the number of catches he has made, and feels good about his improvement, he is reinforcing his own behavior by choice. This is self-reinforcement.

Evidence Supporting the Behavioral Paradigm

In this section we have examined the behavioral paradigm for understanding human personality. We must now turn our attention to the question of the validity of the behavioral perspective. Is there evidence that supports the behavioral paradigm? Two significant lines of evidence should be noted.

The Effects of Reinforcements

Probably the single greatest support for the behaviorist paradigm is the abundance of research data indicating that human behavior and personality are shaped by reinforcements. Recognition, attention, praise, hugs, smiles, raises, grades, awards, prizes, and applause are all examples of behavioral reinforcements. Research shows that human beings are motivated by and respond to positive reinforcements and that positively reinforced behavior is more likely to be repeated than behavior that is not reinforced. These are facts that most teachers, parents, and counselors have come to understand and use. Because of the power of reinforcements, numerous behavioral approaches to therapy, education, coaching, teaching, and even church ministry have been developed.

Patricia is a new teacher in an inner-city school in New York. Struggling in her first year on the job, she asked for assistance from a seasoned teacher, Sue, with regards to classroom management techniques. Sue's advice to this new teacher was further evidence that reinforcements are powerful tools in shaping and controlling behavior.

Dear Patricia:
The easiest system that I've found is use a chart and fill in a smile face each time that you "catch" the child acting appropriately. With 4-year-olds I would start with checking every 15 minutes or so. If that doesn't work try 10 minutes. Set it up with the whole class so one child is not singled out. Once you start drawing in the smile faces the kids catch on quickly and they shape up. The charts are available commercially or just draw one up yourself. The ones I use are 5x5. When a child earns 5 faces I give them a reward. It can be something like a sticker, first choice at a game, first in line, sit by me—most any thing. When you

first start this you should plan on completing a row in one day. After a few days you can slow down and just use it a couple of times each day. Good Luck. Sue

Reinforcement-based behavior modification programs have been used to assist people with stuttering problems, depression, hyperactive behavior, aggressive behavior, procrastination, academic difficulties, eating disorders, phobias, and various anxiety disorders. Parenting programs have taught mothers and fathers the value of natural and logical consequences in disciplining their children. In each of these examples and countless more, the evidence is massive that people respond when reinforced.

While never truly behavioristic, even in Scripture we see the use of cues and reinforcements to encourage and discourage behavior. We see the use of cues or reminders to establish a mental link between an object and an event or concept. For example, the Passover celebration was filled with reminders of God's faithful and good work to protect and preserve His people. Such remembrances are learning devices for the nation of Israel that they might continue to walk faithfully with the one true God (Ex. 12:25–28). Likewise, the Israelites were reminded of their special relationship with God and of their dependence upon Him through the practice of building altars. This act and resulting object served as a cue that God had done something for His people and was worthy of worship (Deut. 27:1–7; Josh. 8:30–31). We might consider the Lord's Supper as another example of a behavioral "cue." Jesus instituted the ordinance as a memorial of His redemptive work and as motivation that believers would continue in right relationship with Him until His promised coming (Matt. 26:29).

In Scripture we also discover the use of consequences for behavior. Such consequences serve to reinforce some behaviors and discourage others. Paul's use of encouragement is a form of reinforcement for godly behavior (1 Thess. 1:2–10). Similarly, his admonishments and corrections serve as negative reinforcements to undesirable behavior that veers away from God's principles (1 Thess. 5:14). Although we want to be careful not to suggest that behaviorism is supported by these passages, we can see that it is true that reinforcements have a powerful affect on human behavior and that the Scriptures recognize this fact.

The Effects of Modeling

By watching others we can learn much and form many of our personality qualities. Research supports the fact that modeling is among the most potent means by which human beings learn and develop. For example, we do not have to find out for ourselves that an iron is hot by suffering a burn. We can see that a hot iron should be avoided by simply observing how others react when they receive a burn. Through the use of correlation studies, researchers have been able to demonstrate the relationship between watching a model behave and the behavior of research subjects. In his famous study of nursery school children, Alfred Bandura demonstrated that children follow adult demonstrations of behavior. Children were shown a film in which adults punched, kicked, called names, and threw objects at a "Bobo" doll (Bandura, "Influence"). After watching the film, children imitated the behaviors they observed in the film. Another group of children was shown a similar film, but this time positive behaviors were modeled. Children responded by imitating the positive behaviors as well. This experiment and numerous studies like it indicate that observation of others shapes behavior. Research on the effects of television violence on children's behaviors indicates a relationship between viewing violent acts and an increase in aggressive behavior (Reiss and Roth 371). It seems clear that, for good or for ill, role models do indeed influence how followers behave, leading to the shaping of human personality traits.

Many passages in Scripture point to the importance of observational learning. In Luke 6:40, Jesus stated that "a student . . . who is fully trained will be like his teacher." John cautions us to be careful who we emulate (3 John 11). In His daily relationship with His disciples, Jesus modeled servanthood as He healed the sick and cared for the lowly. His most powerful lesson in this regard came not in the preaching of a message, but in the demonstration of servanthood when He washed His disciples' feet (John 13). Understanding the power of role modeling, Peter told pastors that they should not be authoritarian rulers, but should be examples worthy of imitation by those under their authority (1 Peter 5:3). These and other passages exhort us not just to profess faith, but to live it and demonstrate Christ's power at work within us (James 2:14–26). Why? Because modeling is a valid and effective means of affecting the lives of others.

Problems with the Behavioral Paradigm

Materialistic, Monistic Assumptions

In this chapter we have covered both biological and behavioral paradigms of human personality. We have included them together for a reason, that being their materialistic and monistic assumptions. Like the biological model we examined earlier, behaviorism cannot serve as the working model for one who would seek to counsel under the authority of Scripture. This is because it reduces humans simply to the status of behaving organisms. In doing so, behaviorism denies the existence of the immaterial nature of human beings, a concept fundamental to a biblical understanding of persons. This monistic weakness was addressed extensively in our previous evaluation of the biological paradigm, so we will not repeat ourselves here. We should point out, however, that such a view of people is far too low and limiting to correlate adequately with the scriptural description of human beings.

Denial of Human Freedom, Dignity, and Worth

One of the impressive things about Jesus is the dignity, freedom, and value He gives to people. He did not force or cajole His disciples to follow Him. He did not manipulate them with rewards and reinforcement. He was not focused on modifying their behavior. He gave people the freedom to make their own decisions and afforded them the dignity of personal choice. On occasion He gave people the freedom to walk away from Him in unbelief. He wasn't interested in commitments that came only when the water was being turned to wine or the miracles were numerous. No, He sought disciples who would sacrificially follow even to death with no immediate reinforcement in sight. Jesus knew that changing behavior was insufficient. He focused on the inner person, on motives and on character. He sought to change the total person, not just behavior. Jesus' view of people was a far cry from the view embraced by Skinner and the radical behaviorists.

One of the foremost problems of behaviorism is its denial of human freedom and dignity. Skinner's operant conditioning theory reduces complex behaviors and higher order thinking processes to simple and discrete behaviors that can be studied, manipulated, and controlled. If the environment is seen to control human behavior as Skinner suggests, then freedom is an illusion and all human behavior is environmentally determined. His view results in the elimination of the biblical concept of autonomous persons who act and are responsible for their actions. Because humans are not free, their actions can hardly be considered moral or immoral. No spiritual dimension in the human being remains. Dignity is also a concept that is lost in the behaviorist paradigm. If people are shaped by reinforcements and models, without choice or responsibility, then from where is human dignity to arise? None is nobler than another is. People simply respond to the environment as it affects their lives. Such a view of people does not fit the perspective of Scripture, which gives to people a distinct status in the created order—created in the image of God.

Reductionistic Treatment of People

Wittingly or unwittingly, Evangelicals have adopted many behaviorist concepts. Beyond its philosophical problems, the behavioral paradigm can treat people in ways that dehumanize them. Here, caution is essential. It is tempting to seek to change a person's behavior and think we have changed the person. In fact, we may have only achieved a temporary compliance or a surface level behavioral conformity. A classic example of this is the use of behavioral models in theological education. When Bible colleges and seminaries employ behaviorist models of curriculum development in an effort to produce a consistent "product," they run the risk of treating their students like raw material in a factory or like Skinner's rats in a box.

At a recent meeting of a college academic planning committee, the discussion turned to the question of the school's mission. As the conversation continued, one participant stated that "we need to clearly define our product and then build our curriculum in a way that will consistently mold students toward that end." Another committee member used the term "raw material" to describe the incoming student. Although such terms are appropriate in describing the production of steel, the molding of plastic, or the assembly of digital cameras, they are out of place when discussing human beings. Behaviorist concepts are easily embraced in Christian ministry because they promise systematic change in people. The problem is, at what cost! As counselors, we must remain cautious of behaviorist therapies even if they pragmatically work. We may be guilty of creating persons who are changed on the outside but whose hearts rebel. We must not treat people as organisms to be conditioned rather than as people to be nurtured, cared for, and challenged.

A small boy was standing on the chair at the kitchen table one night when his family joined together for dinner. His father instructed him, "Calvin, sit down in your chair!" The boy folded his arms defiantly and did not budge. His father remarked a second time, "Calvin, if you do not sit down now you are not going outside after dinner to play." Not wanting to lose his play privileges on a such a warm summer evening, Calvin complied. He then commented, "I am sitting on the outside, Daddy, but I am standing on the inside." Calvin was making an interesting point. His father could condition his behavior with reinforcements and bring about compliance, but he could not enter the boy's heart and change his attitude. And so it is with behaviorism. By ignoring the inner person, behaviorism simply changes one's actions, often a short-lived result.

Contributions of the Behavioral Paradigm

Can one accept the findings of the behaviorists without accepting their worldview? Are there legitimate research discoveries within this paradigm that can lead to more effective counseling ministry? Can one employ the techniques of behavioral counseling approaches without devaluing people? The answer to all of these questions is a qualified "yes." We would suggest that, as is the case with all of the theoretical paradigms we will study, Christians must take care to maintain a clearly biblical view of people and must use behaviorism, especially Skinnerian approaches, with caution.

Behavioral principles are easy to grasp and to master. Add to this the fact that they are effective in many situations, and you have a very inviting paradigm. Yet there is more to human beings than the behavioral paradigm would claim. Although Skinner may not hesitate about using behavioral programming methods, as believers we cannot reduce people to raw material or organisms to be conditioned. Jesus would never treat people in such low, "ratomorphic" ways, and neither should we. So what then are the genuine contributions that behaviorists have brought to people-helping circumstances? We would suggest two major contributions of behaviorist research.

Preventative Applications

Behaviorist principles can help prevent human problems and struggles. Let us take parenting as an example. A wise parent can learn that through the careful use of appropriate reinforcements, positive habits can be encouraged. Likewise, teachers can use behavioral principles to create positive environments to encourage appropriate classroom behavior and to motivate learning and task completion. Take for example the simple "Book It" program offered by schools across the country in cooperation with a major pizza chain. Students earn coupons for free pizzas by reading a specified number of books per month. By reinforcing reading with a personal pan pizza, teachers can motivate a student to read who may not otherwise be willing. Counselors can offer encouragement and praise to a counselee who is making progress and can set up self-reinforcement plans with clients to encourage continuance of a desired behavior.

The applications of positive role modeling are even more exciting. Big brother and big sister programs, mentoring programs, and even programs like the Boy Scouts or Girl Scouts can have a wonderful preventative place in working with children. In church ministry, premarital and marriage counselors can use mentoring couples to assist other couples who may be struggling. In countless ways behavioral principles can be employed in positive, preventative situations.

Corrective Applications

At times there is a need to change behavior. Rooted in behavioral theory but not identical with radical behaviorism is *behavioral therapy*. Behavioral therapy does not refer to a specific theory or method but to an approach that seeks to apply the findings of behaviorist research to the modification of abnormal or undesirable behaviors. For the behavioral therapist, the goal in counseling is the reduction and reconditioning of maladaptive behaviors. In this regard, behaviorism does offer some helpful techniques. Behavioral therapy can help a person facing a reoccurring behavioral struggle. For example, a man who fears air travel but must travel for his job can gain needed help in modifying his behavior and desensitizing his fears. Using behavior modification approaches, counselors and teachers can help children learn to control inappropriate behaviors and learn greater social skill.

Behavioral concepts have been applied to education, business, counseling, and parenting. Educational applications include curricular development models, educational objectives, classroom management, programmed learning, and outcomes assessment. Business applications include productivity enhancement, incentive programs, training programs, and strategic planning. In counseling we have already mentioned behavior modification, behavior therapy, and reality therapy as examples of the influence of behaviorism. Parenting programs such as Parent Effectiveness Training (P.E.T.) and Systematic Training Effective Parenting (S.T.E.P.) are two examples of behaviorism influence. Given its wide-ranging usage, it can be seen that behaviorism has played a significant preventative role in working with people.

— *A Final Thought* —

*B*rain or behavior, biology or environment—all of the paradigms discussed in this chapter share common assumptions about human nature. These include a materialist, monistic, and a deterministic outlook on human personality. Such foundational notions make the wholesale adoption of either of these paradigms an unwise position for the counselor who places God's Word as the ultimate authority in ministry practice. And yet, we have seen that each offers a measure of truth. Each grants the counselor insight into human personality development. And each provides tools that can be of benefit to the Christian who seeks to help others face life's problems and predicaments.

NOTES

Bandura, A. *Social Learning Theory.* Englewood Cliffs, N.J.: Prentice-Hall, 1977.

———. "Influence of Model's Reinforcement Contingencies on the Acquisition of Imitative Responses." *Journal of Personality and Social Psychology,* 1, 589-95, 1965.

Bee, Helen. *The Developing Child.* 8th ed. New York: Longman-Addison Wesley Longman, 1997.

Daniels, A. M. "The Promise of the Neurosciences." *British Medical Journal* 317.7174 (19 Dec.–26 Dec. 1998): 18.

Harlow, J. M. "Recovery from the Passage of an Iron Bar Through the Head." *Journal of the Massachusetts Medical Society* 2 (1868): 327–47.

Hinrichs, Bruce. "Brain Research and Folk Psychology." *The Humanist* 57.2 (Mar.–Apr. 1997): 26–31.

Kagan, J. *Galen's Prophecy.* New York: Basic, 1994.

Matthews, Robert. *Our Leaders Have It in Their Genes, It Seems.* 1999. 20 Apr. 1999 <http://www.smh.com.au/cgi-bin/archive.cgi>.

Reiss, A. J. and Roth, J. A. (Eds.) *Understanding and Preventing Violence.* Washington, D.C.: National Academy Press, 1993.

Restak, Richard M. *The Brain*. New York: Bantam, 1984.

Watson, John B. *Behaviorism*. New York: Norton, 1930.

Weiten, Wayne. *Psychology: Themes and Variations*. 3rd ed. Pacific Grove, Calif.: Brooks/Cole, 1995.

— Chapter 6 —

PERSONALITY PARADIGMS II:
The Psychoanalytic Approach

*H*is childhood should have been idyllic. Born an especially beautiful baby to strong, intelligent, handsome, and wealthy parents, little "Teedie," as he became known, was a healthy child at the outset with a life of great promise before him. But as time progressed he became ill. Severe asthma, constant colds, coughs, and fevers began to take their toll. Forced by his asthma to sleep sitting up, he sometimes came dangerously close to death because of a lack of oxygen. In addition to his asthma, Teedie had very bad eyesight and, from early childhood, was forced to wear thick wire-rimmed glasses. Weak, sickly, and nearsighted, he was easy prey for boys looking to harass someone.

One day two boys, both Teedie's age, stopped him as he walked down a country road. They picked on him verbally, threatened him, and eventually beat him. Nowhere near their match, Teedie could not defend himself. Despite the beating, that incident became the turning point in Teedie's life. Never again would someone overpower him! No, from now on he would do all he could to become stronger. He began to lift weights, eat more carefully, exercise, and take boxing lessons. Teedie planned to change, and he did. Slowly he became healthier, stronger, and more fit. By the time Teedie went off to college at Harvard, few people would recognize him as that once weak and frail boy.

At college he won several athletic contests. After his college years he lived briefly as a North Dakota cowboy. He loved the great outdoors and enjoyed both hikes and horseback rides in the Black Hills of South Dakota. After his Harvard days, he practiced law, became a successful New York assemblyman, served as the commissioner of the New York police, was appointed the assistant secretary of the navy, and had an illustrious military career as a lieutenant colonel commanding a famous fighting unit. After his military service, he became the governor of New York and published a best-selling book. What is most remarkable is that weak and frail little Teedie did all of this before the age of forty. Later, he was nominated as William McKinley's vice presidential running mate. In 1901, after McKinley was assassinated in Buffalo, New York, at the Pan American Exposition, Theodore Roosevelt was sworn into office and "Teedie" became the twenty-sixth and youngest president of the United States. As commentator Paul Harvey would say, "And now you know the rest of the story" (retold from Boeree, *Adler*).

How is it that someone so sickly and frail could become so healthy, vigorous, and successful? How did Teedie's past influence his future? How much did his past affect his personality development? These are the kinds of questions that fascinate those who embrace the psychoanalytic paradigm. Looking for the connections between past, present, and future is at the core of this theoretical model. Psychoanalytic theorists believe that human personality expressed in the present is the composite result of past life events. Let's take a closer look at this personality paradigm.

The terms associated with psychoanalytic theory are so much a part of American culture we use them without even being aware of their origin. Maybe you have heard some the following statements or have even said them yourself:

- "I think *unconsciously* he wanted that to happen."

- "She is using a *defense mechanism* so she won't be hurt by the truth."
- "Through counseling, he has discovered a number of *repressed memories.*"
- "The accident was so traumatic, he's still in *denial.*"
- "She is *projecting* her anger on others around her."
- "He is trying to *rationalize* his behavior."
- "She is doing that to *compensate* for the loss of her father."
- "I think he is going through an adolescent *identity crisis.*"
- "Sorry, that was a *Freudian slip.*"
- "Let's do a little *free association* here, shall we."
- "Boy, does he have an *anal retentive* personality."

Seeking to understand human personality by probing the reaches of human consciousness is the heart of the psychoanalytic paradigm. Comparing human personality to an iceberg whose tip is visible but whose bulk is hidden underwater, Freud and other psychoanalytic theorists focused their study on the hidden aspects of human motivation and behavior. Believing that "there is more to a human being than what meets the eye," psychoanalytic theorists point to these hidden factors as the most critical in determining one's personality type and functioning. The psychoanalytic paradigm emphasizes the role of unconscious forces, instinctual drives, and internal conflicts in understanding the nature of human personality development. In order to better understand and evaluate the psychoanalytic perspective, let us consider the four basic propositions that define this paradigm. As we do, we will discover a description of human personality that is a curious blend of truth and error.

BASIC PROPOSITIONS OF THE PSYCHOANALYTIC PARADIGM

Proposition 1: Unconscious, as well as conscious, motives and experiences in childhood govern personality development and mental disorders.

Psychoanalytic theory suggests that one's basic personality structure is determined through the early years of life as a dynamic process and that much of that process is hidden from the conscious understanding of the individual. As a result of this assumption, researchers in the psychoanalytic camp seek to understand the nature of the underlying structures and processes of human personality development. They would hold that some of these unconscious personality structures and processes exist at the time of birth, while others develop in a stagelike way throughout childhood. We will examine two of the leading psychoanalytic proponents later in this chapter, but clearly the most renowned of the psychoanalytic theorists is Sigmund Freud. Freud proposed that an unconscious, instinctual sexual drive that he called the *libido* is the energy behind virtually all human behavior and personality traits. Others, such as Erik Erikson, rejected Freud's concept of *libido* in favor of unconscious and conscious social and cognitive factors that shape human choices.

Anna was a highly intelligent twenty-one-year-old woman. Over a two-year period, Anna had developed a number of physical and mental disturbances that baffled her doctors. Her symptoms included paralysis of the right arm and leg, distorted vision, an inability to hold down liquids, and a more than occasional inability to speak or to comprehend speech. She would have periods of amnesia and occasional changes in her personality so radical that she was labeled a "hysteric."

Using what was known as "the talking cure," Anna's doctor helped Anna to explore her past in order to discover what might have brought about this change in her otherwise normal life. Anna began to tell her doctor recollections of her childhood years. She told him about her father who experienced a lengthy illness and eventual death. She told him too of her childhood efforts to care for her ailing father. In the course of their conversations she revealed a long forgotten memory of an event that occurred while she was caring for her father. As she recounted the event, she told of a poisonous snake common in her part of the country that had made its way into her father's room. She recalled trying to drive the snake away from her helpless father but finding herself paralyzed with fear, unable to take action. It was as if she could not move her arm. She tried to call for help, but nothing came out. In this moment of fear, she failed to protect her father. He was bitten and eventually died. In her guilt, she was stricken with her array of symptoms. Finally, after being able to tell of her repressed experience, she was completely and dramatically cured. (It's worth noting that our culture has taken the idea of repressed memories far beyond original theories of the concept and that in recent years psychology has challenged and balanced those extremes.)

Underlying the psychoanalytic approach is the concept that events and happenings in our lives evoke strong feelings. Because these events are painful or guilt-ridden, we resist their recollection to the point that they are buried deep in the recesses of our minds. Because these events and their associated feelings are so powerful, one cannot avoid the lasting impact they have on personality development even though the memory is no longer conscious or vivid.

Proposition 2: Personality structure develops over time as a result of interactions between the individual's inborn drives/needs and the responses of the key people in that person's world.

Freud postulated that children's inborn instincts, drives, and desires motivate human behavior. He also proposed, however, that children are restrained from achieving instant gratification of their various drives by key persons in their life. As a result children are forced to develop new skills—planning, talking, delaying, and reasoning—in order to allow gratification in more indirect ways. In this way, various qualities and traits become part of the child's personality mix. This process of desire/restraint/development becomes the means by which individual personality is formed or distorted. A child naturally desires something, is restrained by significant adults, and, in turn, develops socially acceptable means to achieve satisfaction of his desire. Over time, the child incorporates adult standards into his thinking processes and learns to restrain himself as a part of his own personality.

Proposition 3: Development of personality is fundamentally stage-like with each stage centered on a particular task or basic need.

One of the distinct characteristics of psychoanalytic theory of human development is the concept of stages of human development. Generally these stages are centered on a particular developmental tension or task. By tension, we mean a crisis to resolve or a struggle to overcome. By task, we mean a social skill or an achievement to learn or master. For example, Erikson described the adolescent period as a time of *identity formation*—the task of developing a unique sense of self is achieved through a crisis of self-discovery and definition. He believed that a period of testing and trial is necessary in the adolescent's life. It allows the individual an opportunity to become a person distinct from his or her parents with a personal set of values and goals. Through this testing process, the child who is successful in establishing a personal value system moves on to become an independent functioning adult.

By studying the various issues and tasks of development, researchers can identify various stages of human development. Freud thought that these stages were influenced primarily by physical maturation and human sexuality. Erikson disagreed. He proposed that various social-cultural forces place demands on children at various ages and, as a result, influence the child's development in a stagelike way. Each child moves through a fixed sequence of tasks or dilemmas that propel him from stage to stage. In both Freud's theory and Erikson's, the critical point is the success or failure experienced by the child in negotiating each of the various stages. Both believe that either success or failure has a lasting impact on later developmental outcomes. Thus, they conclude that present personality concerns are rooted in previous life experiences.

Proposition 4: The specific personality qualities that a person develops depend on the degree of success the individual experiences in traversing the various stages.

During each stage of development, the child must negotiate a particular crisis or task. The environment created by caregivers can encourage success in resolving the stage-specific dilemma facing the child, or it can be lacking and nonsupportive, causing failure and personality disorders. Each stage is important, but early childhood is considered most critical because of the essential relationship that must develop between the child and the caregiving adult. How the child negotiates these early stages places him on a developmental pathway through the remaining stages.

Mike was born into what would be considered a "Christian home." He had two loving parents, both of whom were active in his life from the beginning. They were supportive in all aspects, attending school functions and hardly ever missing one of Mike's sporting events. As Mike grew up, he excelled both academically and athletically. This pattern continued until around his seventh-grade year when his mother, who had worked outside the home for most of his life, had to increase her workload due to financial difficulties. This led to more time away from home for his mother and to a feeling of isolation and loneliness on Mike's part. In an unconscious effort to gain his mother's attention, Mike's grades began to drop and his behavior became a problem. During that year, Mike was taken out of that school, so he finished junior high at another school. His parents made this move believing a change in atmosphere would be beneficial, but Mike's problems did not cease. Mike chose friends often considered to be "troublemakers." His attitudes toward his parents and others continued on a downward slope. He went on into high school where he dropped out in the middle of his junior year.

Mike's friends became the driving force in his decisions, so much so that he would, at times, sacrifice his own happiness to cover for his friends' wrong deeds. It seemed to those who cared about Mike that little could be done to control or regulate his actions. Mike began to smoke heavily, and drinking became a way of life. He would often be late to work or absent altogether because he had overslept after coming home at around three or four o'clock in the morning in a drunken stupor. By this time, Mike's life had no direction. He had no goals or dreams. He just worked (when awake), hung out with his friends, and slept.

Through the concern of a friend who exercised tough love, Mike began to see the error of his adolescent choices. Encouraged by his Christian friend to get his life back together, Mike took some actions to establish a new sense of identity and purpose. Mike began his way back by obtaining his GED and, eventually, by attending a community college. He found a steady job, became in-

191

volved in sports, and, most significantly, returned to his Christian roots.

This case study reveals the developmental pattern observed by psychoanalytic researchers. Mike successfully negotiated the stages of development that marked his early years, but when faced with the crucial adolescent task of establishing a sense of personal identity, Mike failed. This failure set a pathway that led to adult failures and life problems. When Mike's friend helped him return to the matter of establishing his identity in a healthy way, Mike was freed to pursue the next stage of development in a healthier and more successful manner. We can see from Mike's case that our choices and our past do indeed play a role in our present and our future and that by discerning where those choices have gone awry, one can move ahead with greater fulfillment.

PROPONENTS OF THE PSYCHOANALYTIC PARADIGM

We have already mentioned two of the most prominent psychoanalytic theorists. We will now expand our treatment of each of these persons, their personality theories, and their impact on the fields of counseling and developmental psychology.

Sigmund Freud

Sigmund Freud, the oldest of eight children, was born in 1856 in Moravia, the central part of what is now the Czech Republic. When he was four years old his family moved to Vienna, where Freud worked until the last year of his life. Although Freud had very wide-ranging interests and professional training, he always considered himself to be, first and foremost, a scientist. At the age of seventeen, in the year 1873, Freud entered medical school at the University of Vienna. There he studied physiology for six years under the famous German scientist Ernst Brücke, director of the university's physiology laboratory. His medical training stressed *biological determinism*—a view that attributes all human thought, personality, and activity to biological/neurological causes. This training inspired him to conduct research on the brain's neurology. Freud completed his medical-degree training in 1881. In 1883 he became engaged and, in order to meet the financial needs of his family, reluctantly turned from research to private practice and service as a doctor at Vienna General Hospital.

While at Vienna General and in private practice, Freud began to experiment in the treatment of mental disorders. In 1885–86 Freud spent part of a year in Paris, where he became aware of the work of the French neurologist Jean Charcot. Charcot was, at that time, using hypnotism to treat hysteria and other abnormal mental conditions. When Freud returned to Vienna, he experimented with hypnosis, but did not find it to have long-term benefits for his patients. Instead, he adopted a method suggested by the work of a colleague and friend, Josef Breuer. Breuer had discovered what he called "the talking cure."

Breuer found that by allowing patients to talk about their problems and past struggles, he could cure their mental disorders. In collaboration with Breuer, Freud formulated the idea that many neuroses (phobias, hysterical paralyses and pains, some forms of paranoia, etc.) had their origins in past traumatic experiences. Freud theorized that these experiences, although forgotten and hidden from consciousness by the individual, were the root cause of mental disorders. He proposed a treatment that enabled the patient to recall the experience to consciousness, confront the experience, and eventually to discharge it from its control over the person's life. His theory launched a radically new conceptual and therapeutic framework for the understanding of human psychological development and the treatment of abnormal mental conditions called *psychoanalysis.*

Eventually, Breuer found that he could not agree with Freud because of what he regarded as the excessive emphasis that Freud placed upon sexual origins of neuroses. The two friends parted company, but Freud continued to work alone to develop and refine the theory and practice of psychoanalysis. In 1900, after a period of personal self-analysis, he published *The Interpretation of Dreams,* which is generally regarded as his greatest work. But his work was not immediately recognized for its importance.

Quietly suffering under the anti-Semitic persecution of turn-of-the-century Austria and his deliberate exclusion from learned societies throughout Europe, Freud remained relatively obscure in the early years of the twentieth century. But his professional standing was to change dramatically when in 1909 he visited America and delivered a series of lectures at Clark University. His presentation propelled him to international fame and prompted the University of Vienna to appoint him to a full professorship. For three decades, Freud was able to develop his theory in relative peace, but then in 1939 the Nazis invaded Austria. At first Freud refused to flee but, when both the American and German ambassadors encouraged him, he left for London. He died there of cancer in 1939, unaware that his sisters had been murdered in Hitler's concentration camps.

Sigmund Freud was a physiologist, medical doctor, psychologist, and the father of psychoanalysis. He is generally recognized as one of the most influential thinkers of the twentieth century. To understand Freud's theory of personality we must understand some of the influences that shaped Freud's worldview. Freud's theory of personality developed as a process influenced by a variety of factors. Two of these formative factors have already been discussed—his research into neurological brain structure and his interest in the psychic curing techniques of Charcot and Breuer. But other less obvious forces helped to shape Freud's thinking as well. We will consider these briefly.

Freud lived and worked in a world of change—change from a religious and philosophical world to a scientific one. When Freud was four years old, Charles Darwin published his world-shattering work, *Origin of Species*. This book made Darwin the most towering and controversial scientific figure of the nineteenth century. Darwin's evolutionary doctrine radically challenged and eventually changed the prevailing conception of man. Before Darwin, man had been seen as distinct from the animal kingdom by virtue of his possession of an immortal soul. But that changed with Darwin's theory. Humans were seen as part of the natural order, different from nonhuman animals only in degree of developmental complexity. This worldview shift made it both possible and plausible to treat human beings as objects of scientific investigation rather than creations of God. Additionally, evolutionary theory made it possible to understand human behavior in terms of natural causes and scientifically logical motivations. Because of Freud's enormous esteem for science and his antireligious orientation, he accepted this worldview implicitly. Thus, Freud moved away from a biblical worldview toward a scientific one.

An even more important contemporary influence on Freud came from the field of physics. Physics as a science underwent monumental advancement in the second fifty years of the nineteenth century, largely initiated by the formulation of the principle of the conservation of energy. According to this principle of physics, the total amount of energy in any given physical system is always constant. The energy within that system can change forms but not be annihilated, and consequently, when energy is used in one part of the system it must reappear in another part. Energy then is not lost or expended—although it may become unusable; it is moved within the system. The application of this principle of physics led to new and significant discoveries in other fields of study such as thermodynamics, electromagnetism, nuclear physics, and their associated technologies. Freud applied this principle of conservation of energy to the human mind.

Now at this point in our discussion of Freud you may recall the name Ernst Brücke. He was the scientist Freud worked under at the University of Vienna. In 1874, Brücke published a book that proposed the view that all living organisms, including human beings, are essentially energy systems and that, like inanimate objects, the principle of the conservation of energy applies. Freud adopted this new "dynamic physiology" concept of Brücke's with great enthusiasm. Freud took Brücke's concept still further. He theorized that there is such a thing as "psychic energy" and that the human personality is an energy system. He also theorized that it is the function of science, through the field of psychology, to investigate the modifications, transmissions, and conversions of "psychic energy" within the personality. By doing so, Freud held that one could work with each individual's psychic energy system to change and develop human personality. In fact, this concept became the foundation of Freud's psychoanalytic theory.

Freud's theory is comprised of three foundational systems that work together to form an individual's personality. The first of these is the *dynamic system*. The dynamic system involves instincts and drives that motivate behavior. This is the psychic energy system that drives human beings as surely as organic energy keeps the human heart beating. Freud believed that sources of psychic energy included the need for food, water, comfort, sleep, pleasure, and sex. Freud theorized that these basic instincts are the ultimate source of nearly all behaviors. When unfulfilled, a tension arises within the individual, creating psychological discomfort. The effort to satisfy these longings motivates the individual to take action. Freud believed that most of these motivations are unconscious and unknown to the individual, but very real. According to Freud, these instincts, especially the libido or sexual instinct, motivate a wide variety of phenomena—from war and individual acts of aggression to benevolence and self-sacrifice.

The second psychological system underlying the development of human personality is the *structural system*. The structural system balances the dynamic system. Beyond the idea that human beings are driven by powerful instinctual drives or forces, Freud also believed that mental structures help to control and channel those forces for the person's benefit. The architectural structure of the mind, according to Freud, includes *id, ego,* and *superego*.

Id is his term for the basic, innate drives mentioned above. The *id* is raw psychic energy, driven toward self-satisfaction and need achievement. The *id*, Freud held, is primitive, uncivilized, and irrational. The *id* has but one goal, pleasure. Its desires are powerful, but unharnessed. To Freud, this is the nature of the child at birth.

Ego is the reasoned, conscious, and sane dimension of the personality structure. The *ego* develops after the child is born. As a result of the constraints of society and parents in particular, the child begins to understand how to appropriately meet personal needs. The *ego* logically informs and controls the *id* so that needs are met in acceptable ways. Freud called this the *reality principle*, which serves to balance the *pleasure principle* of the *id*. Like the rider of a wild horse, the *ego* brings the *id* under control and channels its energy into constructive pursuits. The *ego* develops as a by-product of social order and controls and is an essential humanizing factor, according to Freud, keeping people from pure animal aggression.

The *superego* is the greater side of people, the moral, ethical, value-driven side. As the *ego* arises out of the *id*, so too does the *superego* arise out of the *ego*. Whereas the *ego* controls the *id* in the "here and now," the *superego* is more long-term. This dimension of human personality structure adapts to the social conventions and moral values of a culture. *Superego* is the human conscience, providing prohibitions, values, and higher ideals.

The third system at work forming the personality of the individual is what can be termed the *sequential system*. Freud contended that all of this development occurs in five sequenced stages. Each stage, he felt, is a critical period of development that sets the climate for the next stage. Therefore, failure to negotiate a stage successfully will diminish the level of success at all subsequent stages. Freud believed that sexuality plays the primary role in motivating behavior and thus, his stages reflect that belief.

Freud's first stage is the *oral stage*, which begins at birth and continues until one year of age. During this stage the lips, mouth, and tongue provide sexual pleasure to the infant. Freud contended that if this stage isn't completed successfully, then some libidinal energy will remain unexpressed at the oral stage. This he called *fixation*. Fixation is possible at any stage of development.

The next stage is the *anal stage*, where the child's sexual energy focuses on the anal region. The anal stage occurs between one year and three years of life. According to Freud, sexual pleasure is associated with elimination of body wastes. Freud argued that tension arises for the child when toilet training is instigated, because the child must choose between the pleasure of immediate elimination and the pleasure of parental approval.

The third stage is the *phallic stage*. Occurring between ages three and five, the genitals become the focus of the child's sexual interest and energy. Freud believed that this was the critical period for the development of socially sanctioned sexual roles. Freud held that a pivotal event, the Oedipus complex, occurs at this stage. The Oedipus complex occurs when the child feels a sexual attachment to the parent of the opposite sex and views the same-sex parent as a rival. These feelings are unconscious and eventually the child responds to them by a process that Freud called "identification." This involves the child's incorporating aspects of the behavior of the same-sex parent into his or her own personality structure through the process of imitation.

When the *phallic stage* is complete, there is a resting period of sexual energy known as the *latency stage*. This stage occurs between five and twelve years of age, during which children identify with the same-sex parent and the same-sex peer group. Freud identified this stage but gave minimal attention to it. Ironically Freud, it seems, underestimated the importance of sexuality during this stage. Post-Freudian researchers have shown that children in this stage are intensely interested in sexual matters, but may not have the social comfort to address their interests directly or openly.

When children reach puberty, their sexual energy again becomes focused in the genital region, where it remains through adulthood. Sexual energy is now directed toward obtaining sexual pleasure with another person. Freud believed that heterosexual relationships are normal results of development, and he considered homosexuality to be a dysfunctional result of failure to negotiate each stage successfully. Freud believed that romantic love and attractiveness to a particular person resulted from an unconscious desire to seek a mate who possesses some of the key qualities of our opposite-sex parent.

Human personality is the result of the interaction of these three systems—the dynamic, the structural, and the sequential. Different types of personalities are, according to Freud, determined by how individuals work through each stage. Treatment of personality disorders involves systematically exploring the past to discern the point at which dysfunctionality began. Then, by making the unconscious conscious, the counselee is guided in the process of restructuring his or her personality (Green 33–65).

Erik Erikson

A second figure who has helped to shape the modern psychoanalytic paradigm of human personality was Erik Homburger Erikson. Born in the city of Frankfurt, Germany, in June 1902, Erikson was reared by his mother and stepfather. Erikson's biological father abandoned him and his mother, Karla, before his birth. In Erik's early childhood years, Karla married Dr. Theodore Homburger, the physician who had delivered Erik just a few years earlier. But it was not until Erik's adolescent years that he was told that the man he had known as his father was not his biological father. This revelation brought a period of significant personal identity crisis to young Erik's life, so much so that he adopted his biological father's name and became Erik Erikson. His uncertain sense of identity, coupled with persecution he experienced among his peers in an anti-Semitic Germany as the child of a Danish Lutheran mother and a German Jewish stepfather, led Erik to set out to answer his fundamental life question, "Who am I?"

His quest led him to travel Europe as an adolescent, seeking his initial goal to be an accomplished artist. His paintings revealed an obvious talent, and he soon found himself gaining a reputation as an exceptional painter of children's portraits. It was, in fact, due to his renown as a children's artist that he was asked to paint a portrait of the child of a well-known Austrian doctor named Sigmund Freud. This assignment was the turning point in Erikson's life. Although he felt shy and stumbling in Freud's presence, he found himself involved in lengthy, informational discussions with Dr. Freud while he painted. As a result of their conversations, Freud asked Erikson to join the Psychoanalytic Institute of Vienna. Eventually, he found himself under the training of Freud's daughter Anna who accepted him because she had approvingly witnessed Erikson's work with children in a small private school, both as a private tutor and a teacher.

Freud's influence helped shape Erikson's understandings of human personality, but the two theorists differed on some important points. Freud believed that cognitive skills were products of need gratification, whereas Erikson believed that cognitive development was independent of gratification needs. He placed emphasis on the process of creating a personal sense of identity. Freud emphasized physical maturation in his psychosexual theory, whereas Erikson focused on changes in the social environment in his psychosocial theory. Thus, for Freud, sexual drive is the prime determiner of personality development. Erikson disagreed. He did not hold that personality was based solely on sexuality. A significant difference in Erikson's theory is that his stages were based upon a series of social, rather than sexual, conflicts that all individuals must successfully master. This means, from Erikson's perspective, that we are products of our society and must, therefore, understand the realities of the social world to understand normal patterns of personality growth.

Erikson's theory consists of eight stages that drive and define human development. A conflict or "crisis" that must be resolved by the individual characterizes each stage. These crises arise when the environment makes new demands on people. When a person is faced with a choice between two ways of coping, one adaptive and one maladaptive, the outcome of that choice brings a change in the personality, for better or for worse. If a person can successfully negotiate the challenge of the stage he is presently traversing, he will move with confidence into the next stage of development. But if a person is unable to resolve a conflict at a particular stage, he will confront and struggle with that problem or issue later in life until he successfully resolves the matter.

Each life conflict must be properly dealt with in order for the person to be prepared for the next life conflict. The person who does not deal with a life conflict properly may encounter problems in the future. Erikson also believed that these crises are cumulative and build upon one another. Given this emphasis on the past and its effect on the present and future, Erikson's theories have been identified within the psychoanalytic paradigm. According to Erikson, children's experiences in early relationships establish their basis for social or personality development.

Stage 1: Trust Versus Mistrust (Birth–1.5 Years)

Each baby comes into the world helpless and with biological needs and drives. But this helpless appearance and his ability to cry inspire others to care for him, bond to him, and develop a relationship with him. These first caregiving relationships, according to Erikson, have a profound influence on the development of the child's personality by determining how well he will trust others in the future.

The important event in this stage is feeding. According to Erikson, the infant will develop a sense of trust only if the parent or caregiver is responsive and consistent in meeting basic needs. The need for care and food must be met with comforting regularity. If the infant's needs are being met on a regular basis, then the infant will develop a sense of trust of the parents, thus promoting a general sense of trust toward people. If, on the other hand, the infant's needs are not met, a sense of mistrust will be promoted, leading to a general sense of mistrust toward people. If the degree to which a child mistrusts is great, then the child could have a tendency to be timid, withdraw, and have little faith in his own abilities.

Stage 2: Autonomy Versus Shame and Doubt (1.5–3 Years)

According to Erikson, self-control and self-confidence begin to develop at this stage as young children learn to do more on their own. Toilet training is the most important event at this stage, but children also learn to feed and dress themselves and to do some basic life tasks. In this way, toddlers begin their quest for autonomy or independence. Erikson would suggest that it is essential for parents not to be overprotective at this stage. He believed that a parent's level of protectiveness influences the child's ability to achieve autonomy. At the same time, if a parent does not reinforce the child's successes or magnifies the child's failures, the child will feel shame and will learn to doubt his or her abilities. Erikson believed that children who experience too much doubt at this stage will lack confidence in their powers later in life.

Stage 3: Initiative Versus Guilt (4–5 Years)

The preschool and kindergarten years are the approximate time frame for this third phase of life. The most important achievement of this stage is a growing sense of independence. The child continues to be assertive and to take the initiative. Playing and hero-worshiping are forms such initiative efforts can take. Most children in this stage are eager for responsibility, have new abilities to achieve, and can build on past achievements. They can now run and take actions that demand more coordinated control over the body. Children of this stage can also speak more clearly and with more skill and thus are typically less frustrated and frustrating than in the twos and threes. These newfound abilities give children much pleasure and confidence, but also allow the possibility of failure and guilt.

According to Erikson, it is essential for adults to confirm that the child's initiative is accepted no matter how small it may be. If the child is not given a chance to be responsible and do things on his own, a sense of guilt may develop. The child will come to believe that what he wants to do is always wrong. When the child has completed this stage, he seems ready to enter into life of the world outside of home.

Stage 4: Industry Versus Inferiority (6–11 Years)

During the fourth crisis stage, the developing child moves from the world of home to the educational setting. In addition to parents and families, primary social agents now include the child's teachers and peers. In this stage the child is struggling between feelings of industry (success) and feelings of inferiority (failure) based upon a comparison of his own achievements with those of others. It is typical for children to measure themselves by their young peers' achievements and to decide for themselves how well they compare. Although these comparisons may lead to discouragement, they may also lead to a sense of accomplishment.

Children can learn the satisfaction of a task completed successfully. As students, children have a need to be productive and do work on their own, and they are both physically and mentally ready for it. The child for the first time has a wide variety of events to deal with, including academics, group activities, and friends. Difficulty with any of these often leads to a sense of inferiority if the child fails to achieve competency. These feelings can often linger throughout life or until this stage is successfully completed. This stage will often affect the behavior of the child, setting up a pattern for how the child will act and react to those around him in the future. Failure is very real, and the desire to avoid it is strong.

Stage 5: Identity Versus Role Confusion (Adolescence)

From Erikson's perspective, this is perhaps the most difficult stage of development. Failure to successfully negotiate this stage can create identity and role confusion throughout one's entire life. This stage is a kind of crossroads where childhood and adulthood intersect. Confusion often characterizes this stage in that the child is in a desperate search for his new identity. This identity is the person's true sense of self. Am I the person others have told me I am? Who am I really? What are my values? What do I really believe? What is the purpose and direction of my life? These are the critical questions that are addressed in this stage of development.

There is an uncertainty about occupational, social, sexual, religious, and political roles, and this stage is the point at which those issues are sorted through. As a result of this stage, the adolescent will develop a personal sense of identity that will lead him or her into adult life. According to Erikson, healthy resolution of earlier conflicts can now serve as a foundation for this search for identity. The level of trust one has developed, the degree of self-doubt or personal confidence one possesses, the willingness one has for taking initiative and risk, the sense of industry one has achieved, and the degree of inferiority one feels all factor into the sense of identity the person will develop. It should be clear how important the adolescent years are in formation of adult personality. During these years, the patterns that are formed come to characterize the way life is conducted from this point forward.

Stage 6: Intimacy Versus Isolation (Young Adulthood)

In this stage, the most important issue of life is the establishment of meaningful and intimate relationships. The young adult must come to understand the nature of true intimacy in which one gains the ability to relate to another human being on a deep, personal level. An individual who has not developed a sense of identity usually will fear a committed relationship and may retreat into isolation. It is important to mention that Erikson did not equate intimacy in a relationship with sexual intimacy. Erikson recognized that people can be sexually intimate without being committed and open with another and thus not experience true intimacy. Erikson believed that this more profound intimacy of relationship requires personal commitment. Erikson found that human beings who make such commitments to another are free to seek a deep, meaningful relationship and, as a result, find greater mutual satisfaction from the increased closeness.

Also characteristic of these years (ages 20–40) is a focus on settling down, starting one's own family, and launching a career path. If this stage is successfully completed, the person is able to become stable and relational. The individual who doesn't successfully complete this stage will struggle with feelings of loneliness, isolation, insecurity, and an unsettledness. With success or with failure, the young adult becomes a full member in society.

Stage 7: Generativity Versus Stagnation (Middle Adulthood)

Erikson's seventh stage includes the ages of approximately 40 through 65. In this stage, generativity refers to the adult's ability to care for another person. This most often is learned in the experience of parenting in which the adult gives more than he or she personally receives back from the parenting task. Often, middle adults find themselves caring for aging parents as well as their children and, as a result, must sacrifice their personal desires for the benefit of others. This transition from self-interest to sacrificial caregiving is essential to healthy personality development. The "crisis" in this stage then is one of learning to sacrificially serve or to become self-absorbed and self-serving. Each adult must have some way to satisfy and support both the next generation and their parents' generation.

Through this period, life either takes on greater meaning or leads one to stagnate in a self-centered world of personal goals, desires, wants, and indulgences. Generativity gives purpose to one's work, parenting efforts, and marital relationship. Stagnation brings sorrow, discontent, self-indulgence, and disappointment. Erikson observed that often people pursue material things and personal pleasures in this era of life only to discover that these offer a shallow sense of fulfillment. He held that there is an intrinsic need for each generation to care for the next and for each person to make a contribution to that task. Success in that endeavor sets up the person for a positive resolution to the final stage of life, whereas failure sets one up to end life in a despairing way.

Stage 8: Ego Identity Versus Despair (Senior Adulthood)

This final stage of maturity occurs between 65 years and death. Senior adults are forced by their own mortality to look back at life and evaluate whether life has been meaningful, productive, and happy or a disappointment, unfulfilling, and replete with unrealized goals. The success or failure of one's life experiences and relationships will determine the outcome of this final life crisis. The most important issue at this stage is coming to terms with one's whole life and reflecting on that life in a positive manner. According to Erikson, achieving a sense of integrity means fully accepting oneself and one's impending death. This requires that the individual accept responsibility for his life, recognize that he cannot undo the past, and achieve a significant degree of satisfaction with the self he has become. The inability to do this results in a feeling of despair.

This stage is most effectively negotiated when a person believes he has taken care of successfully raising the next generation and can look with pride on what has been done in this life. Despair occurs when one frets about how little time is left, how much was left undone, and how damaged life's relationships have become. Erikson suggests that the end of life is similar to the beginning of life in the eventual need to again trust in others. Those who have developed significant generativity in the prior stage seem better equipped to traverse this final stage with a sense of personal dignity (Green 66–89).

It is clear from this brief review of Erikson's work that he offers the counselor or people-helper a basic framework to think about healthy personality development. Knowledge of each of these stages can provide a foundation for effective ministry emphasis in both preventative care and redemptive treatment of persons who struggle to negotiate various life crises. Erikson's contribution is one of identifying the process of personality growth that is typical of most individuals and gives us hints as to where that process might have gone off course. Erikson shows us how each step of life is a basis for the next step and how our past affects our present and our future.

PROBLEMS WITH THE PSYCHOANALYTIC PARADIGM

The value and validity of the psychoanalytic approach to understanding human personality has been questioned since its inception in the early 1900s. Critics dispute many aspects of the psychoanalytic paradigm, including its scientific worthiness, its approach to data collection, and its effectiveness as an approach to treating mental disorders. It is important in critiquing the psychoanalytic approach to recognize that, as a paradigm for understanding people, it has changed over the course of the last century. We will focus our critique on Freud's work since it is foundational to the paradigm, but we should underscore the fact that neo-Freudians have brought important correctives to Freud's original theoretical efforts.

Problems with Scientific Worthiness

Scientific criticism of Freud's theory can be grouped into three categories: criticisms of Freud's evidence, criticisms of Freud's methods, and criticisms of Freud's theoretical validity. Freud's evidence is limited to very few case studies primarily used as illustrations of his theory, rather than carefully presented scientific observations. Freud's sample was demographically restricted and faulty in its design. Lack of a control group and lack of precision in recording observations hindered Freud's research. Evidentially speaking, Freud's evidence is suspect and his data polluted.

The second concern over the scientific worthiness of Freud's theory is related to the way he collected his data. Using "free association" in which the patient speaks about any subject matter that comes to mind and the analyst interprets the patient's statements results in anything but objective data. The goal of "free association" is to access the patient's repressed memories. The problem is that it is difficult to distinguish between actual memories and those that are constructed due to the influence of the analyst's leading questions. The result is contamination of the data due to the method of collecting the data.

The third scientific criticism that has been leveled against Freud's research is its lack of testability. You will recall from chapter 4 that the degree to which a theory can be tested is a measure of the scientific worthiness of that theory. How does one measure "psychic energy"? How can one test for aspects of the "unconscious mind"? How can one determine if a "repressed memory" is genuine? Clearly, the problems of testing the most central concepts of Freud's psychoanalytic theory are obvious, pervasive, and unsolvable.

Although substantially more support exists for the work of Erikson and other modern psychoanalytic theorists, even these modern approaches are subject to similar criticisms. It seems that scientifically speaking, the psychoanalytic paradigm is highly questionable even if it does offer a number of interesting ideas and constructs.

Problems of Theological Compatibility

You will recall that, in chapter 2, we identified four boundaries essential to a Christian worldview—humans are created beings, humans are divine image-bearers, humans are multifaceted beings, and humans are broken and hurting beings due to the impact of sin. Given these boundaries, it should be clear to the reader that the psychoanalytic paradigm falls short as the answer to the nature of human personality and the treatment of mental disorders. This is not to say that research and conclusions from a psychoanalytic perspective are devoid of truth. It is wise, however, for believers to exercise caution as they discern truth and implement treatment approaches based on the psychoanalytic model. What are some of the theological cautions appropriate in our evaluation of the psychoanalytic paradigm?

First, the psychoanalytic approach is *naturalistic* in its approach. Freud believed that supernatural beliefs in God are the result of early childhood fantasies. Maturity, for Freud, meant growing beyond the childhood need for a fatherly caregiver and "letting go" of our religious mythology. Most Freudians reject the supernatural, including God, and accept a naturalistic explanation of religiosity. Religious experience is believed to be based on an unmet need or repressed desire within human beings. The reality is that letting go of God is not a step to maturity. As Paul Vitz has said, "It is this rejection of God that is really adolescent. All modernism can be seen as a giant adolescent rebellion, with a focus on sex and aggression. As we mature and come out of it, we recover the wisdom of childhood" (Cromartie 6).

The second theological problem with the psychoanalytical paradigm is the tendency to overemphasize the past, producing a *deterministic* outlook on life. Because early childhood influences are excessively emphasized, psychoanalytic counselors tend to make their counselees slaves to their past. The past is important; it is, of course, the stuff that present personality qualities are built upon. But the past does not determine our future. "It's my parents' fault or the fault of a traumatic childhood experience." Such conclusions can turn human beings into permanent victims unable to move beyond their present situation. One of the things that the psychoanalytic approach has done has been to make people believe that they are not responsible for their personal behavior. Scripture presents human beings as free moral agents, responsible for their behavior and, therefore, destined for judgment (2 Peter 2:4–10). It presents believers as those liberated from bondage to the past (2 Cor. 5:17).

A third theological problem with the psychoanalytic paradigm, Freud's in particular, is the reduction of human nature to *animalistic* drives, especially the sex drive. Denying both the image of God in humans and our sin nature, Freudians reduce human motivation to raw animal instinct. By diminishing human nature to that of a sexually driven animal, Freud has emphasized sexuality far beyond its biblical importance. According to Freud, sexuality is repressed in humans and must be brought into the open. Many human psychological disorders are a result of those repressed urges. This emphasis has brought about the modern sexual revolution and widespread acceptance that humans are fundamentally and primarily sexual beings.

As we discussed earlier, Scripture teaches that we are made by God to honor God. We do that in many ways, including through the sexual aspects of our being. But we are more than sexual beings. We are divine image-bearers. We are more than people driven by animal urges. We are influenced by the very moral characteristics of God Himself. We are multifaceted beings. Biblical Christianity elevates the worth and dignity of people even though it understands that we are fallen image-bearers with the tendency toward self-interest and sin. Rather than understanding people as multifaceted beings, the psychoanalytic approach minimizes human personality, defining it down to an *animalistic* level.

We can see then that because of the naturalistic, deterministic, and animalistic emphases of the psychoanalytic approach, it is outside of the boundaries of a biblical view of human personality. This being the case, does it have any redeeming contributions or ideas that are worthy of the attention of one who seeks to counsel under the authority of Scripture? We believe there are some worth noting.

CONTRIBUTIONS OF THE PSYCHOANALYTIC PARADIGM

Although there are a number of problems with the psychoanalytic paradigm from both a scientific and a biblical perspective, the psychoanalytic approach has brought significant contributions to our understanding of human personality. To be accurate in our review of the psychoanalytic paradigm we must distinguish between a Freudian approach and the post-Freudian approach of Erikson and others. Post-Freudians are those psychoanalytic theorists who build their theories on Freud's basic tenets but reject his more extreme views. Erikson is a post-Freudian researcher, as are persons like Carl Jung, Erich Fromm, and Alfred Adler who also draw from Freud's foundational concepts. The first four contributions identified below come to us directly from Freud. The remaining items are contributions derived from post-Freudian psychoanalytic researchers.

Level of Consciousness

Is it possible to take action based not only on our conscious choices and thoughts but also upon our unconscious and preconscious ones as well? Freud argued that unconscious drives, impulses, and fears motivate conscious thoughts and behaviors. In other words, Freud reasoned, we sometimes behave not fully knowing the motives that push our behavior. Some have called these "blind spots" referring to our tendency to be oblivious to our own deeper layers of drive and motive. Freud believed that "slips of the tongue" could reveal our true feelings and that dreams often express our hidden desires. Feelings and conflicts often influence us, Freud held, without our being aware of their presence and power. He held that our conscious thoughts about life and our interactions with others are incomplete and even unreliable.

Freud identified three levels of consciousness: conscious thoughts, preconscious thoughts, and unconscious thoughts. Conscious thoughts consist of whatever one is aware of at any given moment. Preconscious thoughts contain mental material just below the surface of awareness that can be easily retrieved. Unconscious thoughts contain memories, experiences, desires, and motives that we are not aware of but that are nonetheless exerting influence on our behavior. For example, I am conscious of my thoughts about Freud as I write this chapter. Someplace in my preconscious mind are thoughts about the wonderful autumn day outside my window and the many things I need to do to get my home ready for another Chicago winter. It is not difficult to bring these to the conscious level. Unconscious thoughts might include my motives for writing this rather than going for a walk or raking the leaves. I may not be fully aware of the deeper motives that encourage my efforts. According to Freud, all of these levels of consciousness affect me at any given moment.

Many have found this construct helpful in explaining human behaviors. It certainly is the most enduring of Freud's theoretical ideas. In fact, despite its original frosty reception by scientists at the time Freud proposed it, his concept of levels of consciousness has gained widespread acceptance today.

Defense Mechanisms

Defense mechanisms, according to Freud, are largely unconscious responses that protect a person from unpleasant emotions.

They are a kind of mental maneuvering or self-deception that allow us to rationalize negative experiences or personal behaviors. In essence, a defense mechanism is a shield that protects the individual from emotional discomfort. By distorting reality in some way, people are able to deceive themselves so that reality does not seem quite so threatening.

Freud's defense mechanisms are considered by many to be a landmark discovery about human nature. We have even come to use some of his terms in everyday speech: repression, denial, projection, identification, and rationalization. We speak of a person repressing a bad memory or in denial about a loved one's impending death. We talk about a person being able to identify with another or projecting his feelings on another. Each of these common expressions is rooted in Freud's theory of personality.

Take Kendra's response to her grades as an example of a defense mechanism at work. Kendra is a student at Moody where we teach. She is not doing very well in her freshman courses and is in danger of flunking out of school. Initially, according to her own later description, she denied her situation, blocking out the possibility of flunking. In this way she could fend off the anxiety of her situation for a period of time. As a way of coping, she would daydream about getting spectacular scores on her final exams. By living in her daydream world, she could avoid dealing with the real truth that she is desperately behind in getting her work done and that she has an almost insurmountable way to go to get her grades to a passing level. Rather than deal with the situation, she denied it and enjoys life as if all will be well in the end. What Kendra's mind has done is bend reality so that she need not deal with it. Freud called this "denial."

Denial and other defense mechanisms are normal. Everyone uses them, and on a fairly regular basis. Those who work with people facing life struggles and difficulties can readily attest to the common use of these coping strategies. Most often, they provide temporary relief from some difficult and stressful problem. But defense mechanisms are avoidance approaches, and avoidance rarely produces a genuine solution to troubles. Counselors know that defense mechanisms must be addressed or greater problems can result—problems like poor health and even death. Socially, defense mechanisms can bring about an inability to form a deep, human bond. Sometimes defense mechanisms can produce wishful thinking, excessive compensation behavior such as overworking or overeating, and fantasy approaches to life.

Freud's discovery and description of defense mechanisms is one of his enduring contributions to people-helping. Those who work with persons facing difficult life struggles should be aware of Freud's work in this area and the many studies that have been done to confirm this theoretical concept.

Stage Theory

It is difficult to imagine that at the turn of the twentieth century there was little interest in studying human development and the stages associated with social and emotional changes in people. Infants and children were regarded as simply miniature adults or as organisms driven by primitive instincts. Freud changed all of that by introducing the revolutionary idea of developmental stages. Although we would certainly challenge the details of his stage theory, we cannot fault his insight into the development process. His theory generated a widespread interest in understanding how infants develop their unique personality and how childhood experiences contribute to adult behaviors. Although we think of developmental stage theories as common sense today and think of infancy, childhood, adolescence, and adulthood as eras in human development different from one another, before Freud such concepts were anything but common. Today's commonsense understandings of developmental stages were, at the time of Freud, new and unheard-of ideas.

Psychotherapy

The search for scientific cures to mental illnesses comes as a result of Freud's efforts. Psychotherapy is a therapeutic technique that served as a forerunner of modern psychiatry. Although we may well dispute the effectiveness, appropriateness, and biblical correctness of psychotherapy, we cannot deny its impact. Freud's treatment approach has served as the basis for many later variations of psychological treatment. It can even be claimed that Freud's approach to treatment of abnormal behaviors spawned the field of psychopathological treatment. We might conclude that the therapeutic has come to replace the life-changing role of the Word of God in many people's lives, but we should at least acknowledge its enormous place in our modern world.

Healthy Personality Development

Building on the work of Freud, but looking not at abnormal development but at healthy personality, was Erik Erikson. Erikson has contributed one of the most researched and attested-to theories of human development, his so-called "eight stages of man." His view was that human beings are basically emotionally healthy and that they are not doomed to anxiety and conflict-ridden lives. He held that people could live happy and satisfying lives provided they resolve eight psychosocial "crises" or choices, one in each stage of development. Each choice leads the person in either a negative direction, which is *inward, backward, or downward,* or positive direction, which is *outward, forward, or upward.*

Identity Crisis

Without a doubt, Erikson's most significant contribution is his concept of the adolescent identity crisis. Surely this must be the most researched aspect of the psychoanalytic approach. Today, most literature on adolescence acknowledges the reality of the quest for a sense of personal identity. Most counselors, whether Christian or non-Christian in their theology, recognize the vital place of identity formation in the adolescent's developmental process. Researchers such as James Marcia have taken Erikson's theory further to study the elements that make for a healthy sense of personal identity and the results of a failure to establish that sense of personhood. Studies have revealed that a failure to establish a personal set of values and a sense of life purpose has a profound effect on later adult life functioning.

Here again is an example of a "commonsense" understanding of teens that was not so common just a few years ago. The research and theorizing done by Erikson and Marcia has served to shape much of our thinking about the period that we call adolescence. As a result, this conception of adolescence as a quest for personal identity has shaped how many people work with teens. Youth pastors, social workers, teachers, and parents have all developed a greater tolerance for the struggles sometimes experienced by young people. We seek to understand clothing fads, music choices, adolescent egocentrism, and even doubting of parental beliefs as part of a process leading to the establishment of an individual adult with a sense of identity. We know now that most teens experience these moments of testing, and that, with guidance, the vast majority will negotiate the adolescent years with success.

Individual History

Chief among the contributions and evidences of the psychoanalytical model is the concept that every individual has a personal history that helps to explain that person's present. I am a teacher. Often I have to remind myself that my students did not come into existence the moment they entered my classroom. Each comes with a history all his or her own. For some it is a history that includes a wonderful Christian home, supportive parents, a solid school experience (possibly even Christian school), healthy friendships, and a strong church. For others, their personal history is the polar opposite: broken homes, abusive parents, poor schools, negative relationships, and failing churches. We all have a history that, added together, brings us to our present. We cannot ignore the power of that history, nor can we easily shake it if it was negative.

The wise people-helper understands that human beings live in the present moment of an ongoing process. Life is the process of living. We grow one step at a time, inch by inch, moment by moment. As we work with people, we must seek to understand from whence they have come so that we can guide them toward their future. Life is much like rowing a boat across a lake. We must look back and keep a clear focus on where we have come from so that we can move forward to where we are heading. We need reference points from the past to guide our future. We need markers to help keep us on course. Many Christians would seek to deny the past, ignore it, and move ahead. The thought is that our past is overcome by the work of Christ and is no longer relevant. Citing passages like Philippians 3:13 where Paul says, "Forgetting what is behind and straining toward what is ahead," some have argued that the past is not important to the Christian and that we are not bound by it. Yet such approaches to biblical exegesis neglect the wide array of passages that call us to remember the past and to learn from it.

— *A Final Thought* —

The psychoanalytic paradigm has been a lightning rod for criticism and attack. From Christians who challenge the psychoanalytic worldview to scientists who question the scientific worthiness of the model, psychoanalytic perspectives are under fire. But, despite its critics, the psychoanalytic paradigm has had a profound influence on American culture. Recognizing the influence of Freud and those who followed, the Library of Congress planned an exhibit that was scheduled to open in 1996. The exhibit was titled "Sigmund Freud: Conflict and Culture." But the exhibit was temporarily postponed due to a petition signed by a number of scholars who called for the exhibit to reflect the wide-ranging disagreement with regards to Freud's contributions and scientific worthiness. Eventually the exhibit opened in October 1998. The New York Times editorialized, "Never-ending backlash against Freud confirms the potency of his theories." They have a point. Freud and the psychoanalytic theorists have had an enormous impact. As Christians seeking to counsel under the authority of Scripture, we should understand that impact, for good or for ill.

NOTES

Boeree, C. George. *Alfred Adler.* 1997. 1 Oct. 1999 <http://www.ship.edu/~cgboeree/adler.html>.

Cromartie, Michael. *Freud Analyzed: A Conversation with Paul Vitz.* 1999. 23 Dec. 1999 <http://www.eppc.org/library/articles/cromartie/mcvitz.html>.

Green, Michael. *Theories of Human Development: A Comparative Approach.* Englewood Cliffs, N.J.: Prentice-Hall, 1989.

— Chapter 7 —

PERSONALITY PARADIGMS III:
The Phenomenological Approach

The view was breathtaking. Hiking for the first time in the Colorado mountains was a wonderful experience for the Monroe family who live in the flatlands of Joliet, Illinois. They were impressed with the grandeur of the towering 13,000-foot peaks that surrounded them. They were awed by the emerald beauty of the cold mountain lake in which they dangled their feet. Massive boulders made up the shoreline of the remote glacial pond. No one complained of being too tired to go on, despite the two-mile walk to the lake. On this sunny day in early June, even the children were up for more hiking.

Helen Monroe called the children. "Mark, Andrew, Amanda—time to move on!" Mark and Andrew responded immediately. They were just a few feet away skipping stones on the calm lake's surface. But little Amanda was nowhere to be found. Just moments earlier, six-year-old Amanda had been in plain sight playing happily. "Where is Amanda? She was with you two just a minute ago!" Helen asked, starting to become concerned.

Helen and her husband, Steve, searched the nearby trails, but there was no sign of Amanda. They called her name, but heard no response. Steve decided to go for help before darkness fell. Helen and the boys stayed back in case Amanda found her way again to where the family had rested. They decided they would meet in two hours at the intersection of two trails. Two hours later, Steve returned with a ranger. Helen was frantic. The mountains that Helen had found awe inspiring only hours before now had become her enemy. Why? Because her little girl was missing and because her child was far more valuable than even the most scenic natural wonder.

We understand that, don't we? We understand that both children and adults have value, worth, and dignity. We know inherently that each person, wonderfully made by God, is more than simply a behaving organism. Each human being is made in the image of God and is the pinnacle of divine creation. And so it is right to value life—to count each life as sacred. It makes sense, perfect sense, that the Colorado government would invest numerous man-hours and a great deal of money to search for Amanda in that very dangerous environment. We know intuitively that there is more to a person than simply a functioning physical body that responds to environmental stimuli and reinforcements. There is an immaterial aspect to each person that distinguishes people from animals and bestows enormous value on human life.

For nearly thirty-six hours, including one long night, Amanda was on her own, lost in the rugged mountain terrain. Fortunately, the story ended well. This little child, the object of intense search, was found, cold and frightened but safe. Wisely, she had taken shelter in a small hollowed-out rock area. She knew that when it turned dark the temperature would drop, so she found a place away from the mountain winds. Conscious of the fact that people would be looking for her, Amanda stayed in one place as her parents had instructed her to do in such a situation. In time, she was found.

We tell this story to introduce a chapter focused on the phenomenological paradigm of human personality. Combining humanistic and existentialistic approaches to understanding human personality, the phenomenological paradigm focuses on the role of personal experience in shaping personality. It is interesting to note that the humanist and the existentialist and the Christian would all agree that Amanda is a person of intrinsic worth and enormous value. Each would agree that an extended search for this little one was appropriate, and each would surely participate in that search, driven by a worldview that elevates people beyond the level of mere organism. Each would see something more in Amanda.

On this point, Christian and humanist and existentialist should agree: People have worth, dignity, and potential. But although they may agree with the conclusion, they would disagree as to the source or basis of that celebrated view of persons. In this chapter we will review the phenomenological personality paradigm. We will discover a very high view of people and their potential. Although this view neglects the balancing truth of human depravity, it does offer us a very different understanding of personality from those paradigms already presented.

The phenomenological paradigm, with its roots in humanistic and existentialist thinking, emerged in the 1950s and 1960s. It was a corrective to the dark, pessimistic, and essentially negative view of people proposed by the psychoanalytic paradigm of the Freudians and the mechanistic, robotic, and dehumanizing views of Skinnerian behaviorists. Freud had studied persons with severe emotional illnesses and devised his theory of personality from these unhealthy personalities. Skinner studied rats, pigeons, and Pavlov's dogs. His emphasis was on the study of lower life-forms in an effort to understand people. The result of both theories was a faulty and limited understanding of personality. The study of emotionally crippled people (Freud) led to a crippled psychology of people. The study of lower life-forms (Skinner) yielded a materialistic and animalistic view of people, devoid of consciousness and free will. Both produced a view of people that diminished the uniqueness of the human being.

Humanist and existentialist psychologists proposed what has been called the "third force" in psychology. It has been seen as an alternative to the behavioral and psychoanalytic approaches. Under this heading fall the need-centered concepts of Maslow and the person-centered therapy of Rogers. We include also the work of Viktor Frankl and Rollo May, both existentialists, because their philosophical underpinnings are very similar to those of the humanists. The common thread between the humanistic and existentialistic approaches is a belief that the perceptions of a person about himself and his situation are as important to the mental health of an individual as the reality of the situation itself. Likewise, both views seek to empower people to "rediscover a sense of self" and take personal responsibility. Both approaches have a common respect for people and their ability to make constructive, conscious choices. Both approaches have a common vocabulary with words like freedom, choice, values, personal responsibility, autonomy, purpose, and meaning frequently cited.

Those who hold this view have been termed "phenomenologicalists." Their focus is on studying the phenomena of conscious human experience, as people perceive it. Phenomenologicalists hold that a person's perception of his experience in the world defines the nature of his personality. For the phenomenologicalist, perceptions are as real as reality itself.

Humanism is a worldview that sees human beings in a positive and optimistic way. Humanistic psychology, therefore, is a value orientation that holds a hopeful view of people and of their self-determining capacity. Foundational to humanistic psychology is the conviction that ethical values are strong psychological forces and basic determinants of human behavior. Because of this belief, humanistic psychologists emphasize choice, creativity, responsibility, and the inherent trustworthiness of human beings.

Existentialism is also a worldview that believes that man is nothing more than what he makes of himself. Freedom of choice is the focus. This openness to choice means, for the existentialist, that people can make lives for themselves that are either pleasurable or painful. Although existentialists still hold hope for people and their capacity for positive action, they are more pessimistic than the humanists. Humanists expect people to make positive choices given the right environment. Existentialists emphasize personal experience and its role in shaping the individual's view of self. To the existentialist, each person carves out his own destiny and is responsible for his own actions. Feelings of powerlessness paralyze individuals. The solution is to rediscover a sense of "selfhood."

We will further examine these viewpoints later in this chapter when we look at the proponents of this paradigm and their theories. First, we shall examine the basic propositions that undergird the paradigm.

BASIC PROPOSITIONS OF THE PHENOMENOLOGICAL PARADIGM

Termed the phenomenological paradigm because of its emphasis on human experience and the person's subjective understanding of that experience, this paradigm focused on four foundational premises or propositions.

Proposition 1: Human beings are fundamentally different from animals and are driven by generally positive dispositional tendencies.

The phenomenological paradigm is built on a belief that people are fundamentally resourceful, self-directed, trustworthy, and productive. It holds that people differ from animals in their conscious awareness of their own existence and in their ability to enhance life through positive decisions and choices. People are not determined, but are able to determine their own future. Typically, human choices are positive and constructive. Those who hold this view believe that most psychological study has wrongly focused on unhealthy persons who are in the minority and has ignored the overwhelming examples of happy and healthy human beings. The misguided attention of psychological research to maladjustment problems, aggression, neuroses, and disturbed behavior has led to a skewed understanding of people. The result, according to the proponents of this paradigm, is a sick and crippled view of human nature. By basing psychological theory on a sick population, a faulty sense of the disposition of the human personality has been conceived.

Alternatively, this paradigm suggests that human personality should be viewed with a far more positive outlook. People are capable of tolerance, compassion, autonomous behavior, humor, inner-directedness, intense interpersonal relationships, and generally positive actions.

Proposition 2: Humans are free, rational beings with enormous potential for personal growth and achievement.

Whether it is determinism of genetics as proposed by the biological paradigm, determinism of environment as predicted by the behavioral paradigm, or determinism of fundamental nature as the psychoanalytic paradigm would suggest, all of the previously examined views see people as entrapped and incapable of self-improvement. But the phenomenological paradigm would disagree. People are free. They decide their own future. Through their own creative abilities, positive emotions, acts of care and compassion, and peak personal efforts, people can bring about enormous positive results. Highly optimistic, this paradigm holds that change is in the hands of the individual. By even small course corrections, major life changes are possible. People can make rational decisions to better their situation and the lives of others.

Imagine an aircraft flying from California to Hawaii. It is just the matter of a few degrees on the compass between a plane's landing at its destination in a sunny, lush tropical paradise and ditching out of gas in the ocean. In the same way, a minor life change can bring enormous change over the long haul. And so too is the hopeful perspective of the humanistic and existentialistic psychologists when it comes to human problems. Growth and change can occur as people learn to make needed adjustments in their outlook and view of their own potential.

Proposition 3: Human beings are active, creative, and resilient creatures who respond to current perceptions, relationships, and encounters in predictable ways.

Imagine a plant growing from a rock outcropping at the mouth of a rugged ocean cove. Wave after wave breaks over the rocks with a merciless violence and spray. With each wave the plant is bent over, its leaves drawn straight by the rushing waters. Then, as the waves recede, the plant again returns to its upright stance, tough and resilient in its ability to cope with the crushing world around it. Incredibly, hour after hour, day after day, the beating continues. Yet the plant remains. But more than that, the plant grows and reproduces; it extends its domain and enhances its place on the rock.

This is the view of human life and personality held by the phenomenological paradigm proponents. It is a view of human beings that sees hope in the midst of constant environmental challenges. It is a view that sees life as a thrusting forward against incredibly hostile circumstances. It is an adaptive, developmental, and buoyant view of human personality. This is the essence of the humanistic and existential outlooks on human beings. People are capable of great things and great acts even in the midst of an incredibly pounding environment that would seem to break them. It is this tenacity of life that they embrace.

Such a view of the human spirit can be seen in the film *Life Is Beautiful*. It is the story of Guido, an Italian Jew, and his family, who are taken to a Nazi concentration camp during World War II. Guido shields his son from the horrors of the camp setting by turning the whole situation into a game. He tells his son, Joshua, that when one person collects one thousand points the winner will receive a tank. He concocts the story to protect his son, who in the end survives the experience. The Germans kill the father in the final moments of the film while Joshua is hiding out of harm's way. Alone in the camp, Joshua emerges from hiding and greets the liberating Allied troops. He is reunited with his mother when he spots her while riding in the arms of an American tank driver who gives the boy a ride out of the concentration camp on board his tank. Joshua's final line is spoken as a reminiscent adult. He says, "This is the gift my father gave me." The film is a touching story of human sacrifice and the spirit of resilience within people. Like the plant on the rock, Guido, his wife, and their son grow despite the horrible setting where they find themselves.

Rather than focusing their interest on the evils that drove the Germans, the humanistic and existentialist psychologists prefer to look at the active, creative, and resilient qualities within those persons who survived the Nazi atrocities. They would seek to minimize evil action in favor of an emphasis on the potential within people. The humanist especially holds out the hope that people are moving toward a brighter future. As one humanist put it, "The missing link between the ape and civilized man has been discovered. It is us."

Proposition 4: Human personality is the result of one's self-concept, level of self-esteem, and environmental factors that either encourage or retard development toward self-actualization.

We will never go beyond the limits we place on ourselves.

Megan is a teenage girl living in the Blue Ridge Mountains of West Virginia. Her community is a depressed coal town with no real industry or employment opportunities. Her county has one of the highest unemployment rates in the country and the lowest per capita income level in her state. It is interesting to note that it also has one of the highest teenage pregnancy rates in the entire country. With opportunity minimal, income scarce, and the potential for self-improvement difficult to imagine, there is little for a young woman to lose by getting pregnant as a teen. It has been said, "The most effective birth control is hope." If a young person has plans, goals to reach, and a serious sense that those goals can be reached, he or she is far less likely to risk them with behaviors that would hinder those ends. Hope is a powerful preventative. It keeps children from actions that are self-damaging. But a lack of hope, a sense of personal incompetence, and a lack of personal life potential can all contribute to a sense of resignation. Megan's self-image and sense of personal potential can shape her future. Is self-esteem a cure-all? Not at all! But it is a factor in establishing a range of options that define a person's future choices.

According to the phenomenological paradigm, both self-concept and environment can promote or discourage healthy personality development. Neither is deterministic, but both can create strong tendencies toward certain life options, behaviors, and outlooks. Helping people see their potential, including their ability to change their situation, is at the core of the phenomenological paradigm. It is held that instilling a strong self-concept, high self-esteem, and a sense of personal potential, while providing an environment where the positive is promoted, will lead to a self-actualized life. Negative thoughts and a negative environment, it is contended, will retard that end.

224

HUMANISTIC PROPONENTS OF THE PHENOMENOLOGICAL PARADIGM

Abraham Maslow

Although humanistic psychology has no single founder, Abraham Maslow has been described as its father and single greatest proponent. Maslow described humanistic psychology as the "third force" in American psychology. He criticized both the radical behaviorism of Skinner and the pessimism of Freud. He proposed an emphasis on the positive in human beings and their potential, rather than immaturity, unhealthy behaviors, and mental illnesses.

Abraham Maslow was born in 1908, the first child of seven born to his Russian immigrant parents. Initially, Maslow's family moved into the slum neighborhoods of Brooklyn, New York, but as his father's business prospered, his family moved to a lower-middle-class neighborhood. Like many other Jewish psychologists, Maslow found himself the target of anti-Semitic taunts as a young boy. Unpopular, friendless, isolated, and lonely, Maslow found the library a safe place. The books on the shelves became his companions, and his time was spent discovering the wealth of knowledge they contained.

Maslow lived in a dysfunctional home. He respected his father, but feared him. His mother was mentally ill, easily provoked, and abusive. She would punish him severely and verbally berate him. Once, when Abraham brought home two stray cats, she killed them by smashing their heads against a wall. Maslow hated his mother. They were never reconciled and, in fact, he did not even attend her funeral. Fortunately for Maslow, he did have a compassionate and devoted uncle who cared greatly for young Abraham. He was the lifeline that kept Abraham sane during his rather difficult childhood years.

Maslow's life took a positive turn when he married and began his studies at the University of Wisconsin. It was there that he was trained in laboratory research and did his doctoral dissertation on the dominance characteristics of monkeys. After receiving his doctorate, he left Wisconsin in 1934 for New York, where he served on the faculty of Brooklyn College.

He arrived in New York during changing times. Many European psychologists and psychiatrists had come to America, specifically New York, to escape Hitler and the Nazi regime. This brought an interesting climate to the intellectual world. In the natural and the social science departments of New York's colleges and universities, an eclectic mix of ideas percolated.

The Second World War propelled Maslow's interest in psychology. He wondered about the causes for the war and its resulting horrors within the human heart. At the same time he contemplated the reasons for the flashes of heroism he read about. As a result of his mental wrestlings, he decided to research the nature of human personality more fully, with the goal of ultimately improving on it. He hoped that his studies might show that human beings are capable of something better than war, prejudice, and hate.

Maslow is probably best known for his hierarchical theory of human needs that was published just prior to his death. Maslow believed that human beings are fundamentally good and that evil acts are actually predictable and radical responses to frustrated attempts to meet genuine human needs. Maslow theorized that human beings are driven by fundamental needs. Once a need is met, a new need moves in to take its place. Immediately, we again seek satisfaction of that new need as well. Need after need, desire after desire, each one gains our attention until it is satisfied. This constant process creates a push toward growth, happiness, and satisfaction that he called *the drive to self-actualize.* This principle is at the core of Maslow's human motivation theory. Man is a "wanting animal" as Maslow phrased it.

Maslow proposed a hierarchy of needs based on the principle that the most pressing and essential of our needs will be pursued before lesser demanding concerns. In order of their strength, Maslow identified five basic needs in human beings (figure 7-1).

Briefly presented, the first level of human need Maslow terms *physiological needs.* Physiological needs are the strongest. This level pertains to basic survival. The need for food, water, sleep, oxygen, shelter, and sex are fundamental needs that Maslow suggests. Maslow held that if these needs are threatened, most of our en-

FIGURE 7–1
Maslow's Hierarchy of Needs

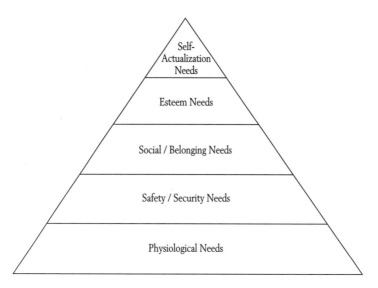

ergy will be focused on meeting them or defending against those who would threaten us. Take, for example, the experience of the three astronauts aboard Apollo 13 in April 1970. When an explosion caused the loss of power and threatened the lives of those on board, the attention of the astronauts was focused on mere survival. Their mental, emotional, and physical energies were directed toward that goal. The quantity of oxygen remaining, the amount of power in the batteries, and the temperature of the capsule were their primary concerns. Without attention to these needs, the matter of life purpose and goals for the future held little significance. All that mattered was meeting the basic needs of life. First things first. In a similar way, James implied that an unmet physical need hinders people's responsiveness to higher needs. "Suppose a brother or sister is without clothes and daily food. If one of you says to him, 'Go, I wish you well; keep warm and well fed,' but does nothing about his physical needs, what good is it?" (James 2:15–16).

The next level of human need that Maslow identified was the level of *safety needs.* Safety needs involve those aspects of life essential to an orderly, secure, and stable environment. Maslow observed that human beings need a measure of order in their world. This includes routines and structure, but also a sense of protection and a secure environment. If that sense of safety is threatened, anxiety results. Time is invested in regaining a sense of security.

We can see this in the national response to the Y2K bug. It is estimated that the United States collectively spent 100 billion dollars preparing for the potential of a national computer shutdown. Fears of the loss of basic needs and a secure environment drove many to stock up on supplies and even to purchase weapons and generators. Our sense of security and safety was in jeopardy. As it turned out, the single worst event associated with Y2K was a very poor made-for-TV movie that people watched a few weeks before the New Year arrived.

Maslow's third level of need he termed *belonging and love needs*. Once physical and safety needs are addressed, people are free to consider the matter of love and belonging. According to Maslow, the individual seeks acceptance and affection. Deeper still is the need to be a part of a group and the need for intimate interaction with others. According to Maslow, it is this need that motivates adolescents to join gangs and adults to build family units. Of course, sex could more appropriately be categorized here, as one way an adult shows love to a spouse, rather than in level one as a purely physiological need.

The fourth level of Maslow's hierarchy of need involves *esteem needs*. This level can be subdivided into two kinds of esteem needs, the need for the respect of others and the need for self-respect. Maslow believed that self-respect grows out of the development of competencies, confidence, success, achievements, recognition, advancement, independence, and freely made choices. Respect from others comes from recognition, status, appreciation, and personal achievements. According to Maslow, when this need area is not satisfied, a person feels a sense of inferiority and discouragement. Maslow postulated that the need for recognition from others decreases as we age and as recognition is achieved. At the same time, the need for self-respect becomes more important with age. A lack of adequate self-esteem will hinder a person from reaching a sense of fulfillment in life and can lead to self-depreciation and further failure.

The fifth level of need Maslow termed *self-actualization needs.* Once the human needs are met at the lower levels in the pyramid, a need to fulfill one's highest potential emerges. Self-actualization is a personal thing because individual giftedness and values define it. Self-actualized persons are emotionally healthy individuals who enjoy a sense of fulfillment and a deep sense of purposefulness. Maslow identified a number of factors that describe self-actualized persons, and he grouped them into four basic categories: awareness, honesty, freedom, and trust. Maslow believed that the number of people who experience true self-actualization is relatively small.

Although we certainly would reject many of the premises upon which Maslow's humanistic views are built, we would agree that human needs motivate actions. We agree, as well, that when those needs are unmet, people will sometimes be moved to meet them in inappropriate and sinful ways. We cannot agree, however, that human needs are so compelling as to control human behavior or dictate human life satisfaction. We would suggest that it is quite possible, for example, that a person who has unmet physical and safety needs can yet enjoy a fulfilled life. Scripture is clear that the fulfillment is found in doing the will of God and in pleasing Him. This could lead us to very unsafe situations that include times of suffering and deprivation.

Like Paul, we believe that a truly "self-actualized person" is one who has learned contentment and is no longer the "wanting animal" that Maslow described. "I have learned to be content whatever the circumstances. I know what it is to be in need, and I know what it is to have plenty. I have learned the secret of being content in any and every situation, whether well fed or hungry, whether living in plenty or in want. I can do everything through him who gives me strength" (Phil. 4:11–13).

Carl Rogers

Born in 1902, the fourth child in a family of six, Carl Rogers grew up in the Chicago suburb of Oak Park, Illinois. He grew up in a family where a fundamentalist, Protestant faith dictated an environment in which emotional and private thoughts were unexpressed. Rogers's family was loving, but legalistic and controlling. Oak Park is, and was at the time, a city of broad viewpoints and liberal thinking. That put Carl's family at odds with the prevailing moral tone of the community. His mother would quote Scripture to Carl and his siblings with the hope that it would keep them from the dangers of the world around them. "Come out from them and be ye separate," she would say (2 Cor. 6:17). She would quote as well from Isaiah 64:6, "All of our righteousness is as filthy rags in thy sight, O Lord." Interestingly, Carl Rogers's views are polar opposites of those his mother tried to instill. He taught that persons should openly express thoughts and feelings and that people are fundamentally good, not sinful.

When he was twelve, Rogers's family moved to the country to a farm thirty miles west of the city. The move to the country created a new interest for Carl. He gained a love for the natural world and a scientific interest in agriculture. In 1919, Rogers left home to go to school at the University of Wisconsin at Madison, another institution noted for its liberal orientation. There he began his studies in the field of agriculture. In Madison he stayed in a youth hostel operated by the YMCA. In the 1800s the YMCA (Young Men's Christian Association) was an evangelical organization with the mission of evangelism through social service. But by the turn of the century, the YMCA had become a social agency supported by liberal mainline denominations. It too became an influence in Rogers's life away from the conservative theology of his parents.

Rogers was compassionate and desired to serve others. He worked for a boys' club and eventually became a student delegate representing the United States at a conference of the World Student Christian Federation in Peking, China. He lived six months in China, during which time he forged greater independence from his parents and their fundamentalist views. Sadly, by this time in his development, he had come to conclude that "Jesus was a man like other men—not divine!" After expressing his views to his parents, he announced his plans to go to New York to attend seminary. His father offered to pay his way through Princeton Seminary, the center of Protestant conservatism at that time. Instead, he chose Union Theological Seminary, the most liberal in the country in that era.

Rogers valued his seminary training, but he felt it was a decision based upon an emotional response to appeals at student conferences. He saw his training as a widening and deepening of his personal understanding of life. But he did not go into the ministry. Across the street from the seminary was Columbia University's Teacher's College. He decided to take some courses there. At Teacher's College he studied the psychology of Freud and the work of the behaviorists. He saw two radically different worldviews, neither of which, he believed, was appropriate for understanding and counseling people. He felt that people were more than animals, driven by instinct. He held that people could be viewed more optimistically, with personal potential for change and success.

After his studies at Columbia, Rogers began twelve years of service in Rochester, New York, at the Society for the Prevention of Cruelty to Children. There he occupied the role of child psychologist in the child study department of the agency. During this time he developed an approach to counseling that allowed the client to set the direction in the counseling setting. He came to believe that open expression of feelings along with a belief in the potential in people to grow and change was the most effective approach in helping people with psychological problems.

The next step in Carl Rogers's life journey took him to Ohio State University, where he became a professor in 1940. There he formalized his approach to helping hurting people and eventually offered his alternative approach to the behavioral and psychoanalytic paradigms of human personality development. It is easy to see why the work of Rogers is so vehemently rejected by the nouthetic or biblical counseling proponents. How could one who denied Christ, denied the sin nature in man, and so clearly rejected conservative Christianity have a contribution to make to those in counseling ministry?

Like Freud, Rogers's theory is a clinical one in that it is drawn from his experience with clients. But distinct from Freud, Rogers considered people to be naturally good and mentally healthy. He believed that mental health is the normal progression of life and mental illness, hurtful and evil deeds, and criminality are distortions of that natural tendency.

Rogers held that people possess what he termed the *actualizing tendency*. This he believed was the fundamental force of life. He defined it as an innate tendency in every life form, humans included, to develop to its fullest possible potential. For Rogers, this is the reason that people seek medical cures for illnesses or develop new technologies to enhance life. Like a weed growing through the cracks of a sidewalk, life seeks to extend itself and improve its position. This *actualizing tendency* is what leads most people to generally healthy and growing lives.

Rogers contended that people create society and culture in an effort to work together in pursuing actualization. We are social creatures, and it is our nature to relate to one another, he suggested. But once created, culture and society take on their own life. Culture can become a force that shapes people and, at times, can interfere with individual actualization. Culture and society are not inherently evil. The problem is that they can become so complex that they lose their very purpose and benefit to the individuals within them.

As an evolutionist, Rogers believed that adaptation was the force behind social and cultural advancement. But even good adaptations can be taken to extremes and become negative for the individual, Rogers held. It is something like a bird found in the jungles of Papua New Guinea. The colorful plumage of the male birds is designed to distract potential predators from the female birds and their young. But the feathers are so elaborate that the male bird cannot get off the ground to fly! The result is that the male becomes the target of predators. Rogers believed that in a similar way, our complex and technological cultures intended to help us can themselves become our own undoing, possibly even destroy us in the end.

Rogers held that organisms generally know what is good and do that which is in their own natural best interest. He gives the example of our sense of taste to illustrate his point. We can trust our tastes to determine what is good and bad for us in most situations. When hungry, we seek not just any food, but food that tastes good. We reject foods that taste bad. Why? Because it is more likely that such foods are spoiled, rotten, or unhealthy. This natural ability to discern good and bad Rogers called *organismic valuing*. This organismic valuing applies to other matters beyond food. We instinctively value the love, affection, attention, and nurturing of others. This need for and honoring of love and attention is part of our lives from birth. Rogers termed this the *value of positive regard*. Likewise, we value feelings of self-worth, achievement, and personal accomplishment. This value he termed *positive self-regard*. Without such self-regard, people experience feelings of helplessness and incompetence.

According to Rogers, human personality problems and disorders result from faulty environments. For Rogers, our home environment may lead us astray by putting conditions of worth upon us. As we grow up, our parents may give us what we need only when we show we are "worthy." Such conditions distort our development. For example, we may get love and affection if we "behave." Love may be withdrawn if we don't. Because of our need for the positive regard of others, our positive self-regard becomes conditioned as well. We like ourselves only if we meet the standards others have applied to us. We give up true actualization in exchange for the feelings of acceptance.

Rogers believed that human beings have two conflicting views of themselves, one he called the *real self* and the other he termed the *ideal self*. The *real self* is the one that follows genuine actualizing tendencies. It is the self that has the potential of becoming great and reaching its full potential. It is the self that is undistorted by environment, culture, and society. The *ideal self* is the one that is distorted by conditional positive regard and conditional self-regard. It is the self that seeks to live up to the standards of others or of our own making that can never be met. Rogers believed there is a gap between the *real self* and the *ideal self*, which he termed *incongruity*. The greater this gap, the more incongruity we feel. This incongruity is what Rogers means by *neurosis*. It is a sense of being out of sync with one's own self that brings one to say, "I really don't know who I am anymore." It is a sense of lostness and aloneness in a vast sea of people.

Rogers suggested, like Freud, that in an effort to cope with incongruity within ourselves, we establish personal defenses. These are devices that we use to keep us from situations that threaten our sense of self. When we face a potentially threatening situation we feel anxiety. When we feel anxiety we tend to find ways to run from it psychologically. We tend to use one of two defenses in our psychological flight: denial and perceptual distortion. Denial is blocking out the threatening situation altogether and pretending it did not occur or is not occurring. Perceptual distortion is a matter of reinterpreting the situation in a way that makes us feel more comfortable. Unfortunately, if we persist in denial or perceptual distortion we are unable to deal with reality and, in fact, may move into a world all our own.

But Rogers held that most people do not become so distorted. Instead they tend to live happy and fulfilling lives. He calls this a *fully functioning person*. Fully functioning persons, according to Rogers, are marked by (1) openness rather than a defensive attitude, (2) living in the here and now, that is, in the real world, whether good or bad, rather than in a world of self-creation, (3) trusting in one's own instincts, (4) a realistic sense of freedom and personal responsibility, and (5) creativity.

Carl Rogers is best known for his approach to therapy. His approach has had three different names over the years, but its essential core has not changed. Originally, Rogers termed his approach *nondirective therapy*. He used this term because he believed that counselors should not lead, but rather be there to monitor progress. He believed that people have the capability of discovering their own solutions to problems, but they need someone to listen and to whom they should be accountable. Later, he changed the name of his approach to *client-centered therapy*. He meant by this that counselors should take their cues from their clients, allowing the clients to take responsibility for their problems and their solutions. Today, most people simply call this approach *Rogerian therapy*. The goal of the counselor is to be a support and not try to reconstruct the person's life for him. The counselor functions something like a parent holding the seat of a child's bicycle as the child learns to ride. The goal is to let go as soon as possible so the child rides for himself, but a wise parent will not let go until the child is ready. The parent running behind the bike provides support and a sense of security until the child can take off on his own.

One of the common techniques used by Rogerian counselors has been called *reflective listening.* Reflective listening involves hearing the person's concern and then restating it back to the person without further comment. For example, if your child were to say to you, "I hate school," you might respond by saying, "It sounds like you are not happy at school these days." This communicates that you are listening and allows the person to respond with further feelings or information. The goal is to aid the person in thinking through his own solution to the problem. To respond by saying, "Oh, you really don't hate school, you just had a bad day" short-circuits the process and ends a free expression of feelings and thoughts.

To Rogers, therapy or people-helping is first and foremost listening. People have within themselves the capability to solve their problems. He believed that people are not generally looking for or in need of advice; they are looking for support. Often Rogers is correct in his observation. Listening is a gift we can give others in need. We do not believe that it is a sufficient approach to counseling, but we do believe that reflective listening can be a technique used by Christians who seek to help others. (Some of the information about Carl Rogers was taken from Boeree, *Rogers.*)

EXISTENTIALIST PROPONENTS OF THE PHENOMENOLOGICAL PARADIGM

Maslow and Rogers represent humanistic psychology. Viktor Frankl and Rollo May are examples of the existentialist branch of the phenomenological paradigm. We turn our attention now from the humanists to the existentialists.

Viktor Frankl

Frankl, like many of his colleagues in the field of psychology, faced persecution from the Nazis because of his Jewish ancestry. But rather than letting the experience break him and turn him bitterly against people, Frankl used the experience of life in a concentration camp as a laboratory to study the inner person.

Viktor Emil Frankl was born March 26, 1905, in Vienna. Until 1942, his father served as the director of the Austrian Social Affairs Ministry, a position he obtained by working his way up from a stenographer position. In high school Viktor's interests were in politics, philosophy, and psychology. Frankl earned a doctorate in medicine in 1930 and was placed in charge of a ward in a treatment facility for female suicidal patients. When the Nazis came to power in 1938, Frankl was reassigned to the only Jewish hospital in Vienna, Rothchild Hospital. There he directed the neurological department.

In 1942, the Germans deported Frankl, his pregnant wife, Tilly, his parents, and his brother to a concentration camp near Prague. Eventually, they were moved to Dachau and on to Auschwitz. Frankl was interned at Auschwitz until the end of the war. When liberated in 1945, he learned that he was the lone survivor within his family. His parents, brother, and wife had all died at Auschwitz sometime in 1943.

Frankl had survived three years of starvation, disease, and fear, but he was not defeated. He had learned that the human spirit can defy even the worst of circumstances. He once said, "It does not matter what we expect of life, but rather what life expects of us." He had discovered that those who lost hope became apathetic and fell into a kind of depressive paralysis. He found that once people were in a state of "giving up," their end was near. Those who survived (assuming they had the opportunity) were the ones who held on to a purpose for life and who chose to remember those people and goals that were once the focus of life. He urged his fellow prisoners to replay memories of their pasts, of a morning sunrise, a youthful first love, or the thought of a little child at play. In these experiences of life were found the hope needed in order to keep on living.

Frankl recorded his experience in his best-selling book *Man's Search for Meaning*, which sold more than 10 million copies and was printed in twenty-six different languages. In it, he wrote a poignant account of the nightmare-like experience he endured in the camps where people were treated like animals. He related the difficulties of daily life and the twists of fate that kept him from the gas chambers and the crematoria. He wrote of the spirit within prisoners that, despite the personal risk of beating and even death, smuggled food to those who were in even worse condition. In the worst of situations, Frankl saw both the most evil and the best in people. It is from these observations that his theory developed.

Following the war, Frankl returned to Vienna, remarried, and had a daughter. There he became the head physician over the neurology department at the Vienna Polyclinic Hospital. He remained at the hospital for twenty-five years as both a practicing physician and a professor of neurology and psychology. Frankl became the author of thirty-two books and was a faculty member at five universities in the United States including Harvard and Stanford. He taught with vigor at the Vienna University until he was eighty-five. A mountain climber and private pilot, Frankl was active until his death on September 2, 1997, at the age of ninety-two.

From his years at Auschwitz and Dachau, Frankl concluded that people are in search for meaning in life. Those who find meaning survive as healthy persons in even the worst of times. Those who do not find meaning fail to thrive even in the best of times. Without that sense of meaning, people cannot weather the inevitable storms of life without despair. But on the contrary, Frankl observed that those people who have a reason for living are able to withstand nearly any living situation. Frankl understood that the most important question in life is not *how* we live, but *why* we live.

Frankl disagreed with Freud, who taught that human beings are driven by *a will to pleasure*. He disagreed with Adler, who felt people were driven by *a will to power*. In Frankl's view, human personality is marked by *a will to meaning*. Rather than seeking to reduce stress and tension within people as Freud would suggest, Frankl believed that inner stress and tension are necessary for mental health. Tension moves us toward meaningful existence, Frankl contended, by forcing us to evaluate our life purpose. Stress can move us toward revised activities and eventually toward positive ends by pushing us to evaluate daily pursuits. Counselors, therefore, should not try to solve people's problems by focused advice or simplistic solutions.

Rather, Frankl believed, the role of the counselor is to help people grow through problems. Counselors are not to be "shrinks," as they are commonly called. They are to stretch people. The counselor should seek to move clients to face their problems directly and help clients see their struggles as a catalyst for change. For Frankl, life struggles are the material out of which character is fashioned.

Frankl believed that at the core of human nature is an *existential vacuum* that human beings seek to fill. Meaning is what all people desire most out of life, even if they are not fully aware of their search. Frankl believed that people today are experiencing empty, meaningless, and purposeless lives because of the modern quest for material things. He believed that most people are striving for something, often anything, to fill this hole and emptiness within. Because of this vacuum of meaning, people are on a quest to fill their empty spirits. We use sound, entertainment, houses, cars, technology, and even other people to try to fill the vacuum within us. We try to fill our need for meaning with pleasure, food, alcohol, drugs, promiscuous sex, power, and money. We become busy, conform to the world around us, live for the moment, and avoid stopping for any length of time to contemplate, for fear that we will discover how meaningless our attempts at self-satisfaction actually have become.

Frankl believed that the surest sign of the existential vacuum is *boredom*. We become like the child who received everything he wanted for Christmas but two days later complains of being bored. He points out that once people have the things they long for, those things lose their motivational power. Momentarily we are satisfied, but not ultimately and restfully satisfied.

So how do we find meaning? By developing a sense of values. Frankl discussed three legitimate value categories wherein he observed that people found meaning in their lives. The first is through *experiential values*. Experiential values involve the recognition of beauty, worth, dignity, character, or magnificence in something or someone. This can include such experiences as viewing great art, listening to a masterpiece of music, or being awed by a natural wonder. Most important, it involves experiencing the value of another person. When we see people in a loving, generous, and compassionate way, Frankl believes that we discover something of the meaning of life.

The second avenue of discovering meaning is through *creative values*. Creative values are found in "doing a deed," as he puts it. Meaning can be found in the life efforts to which we give ourselves. Meaningful pursuits add meaning to life. But this can be a two-edged sword. If meaning is found in our doing, then we must continually be producing something to retain a sense of meaning. The problem arises when we lose our ability to achieve or produce. Aging, an accident, or another unpredictable life occurrence can prevent us from doing what we find most rewarding. In this case, creative valuing becomes a weak foundation on which to build our sense of life purpose.

The third way of finding meaning is in our *attitudinal values*. Frankl believed that meaning can be achieved in suffering through how we handle the experience. When a loved one dies, we experience pain. By suffering that pain with dignity and by developing character through the experience, Frankl believes that we give purpose to suffering. Frankl gives an example of this concept. A friend whose wife had died was in a deep sense of despair. Frankl asked him, "What if you had died first; what would it have been like for her?" His friend replied that it would have been very hard on her. Frankl pointed out that by her dying first, she was spared additional suffering in dealing with his death. As an act of love, he can now mourn her passing. Grief is the price paid for love and is the price his friend would have to pay to allow his wife to avoid suffering. This thought gave his friend a sense of purpose in his own grief and in his wife's passing ahead of him. Frankl believed that by suffering bravely, we give suffering purpose.

According to Frankl these levels of meaning are not the answer to the ultimate meaning of life. Experiential, creative, and attitudinal values are surface-level manifestations of that ultimate meaning that he termed *supra-meaning*. These surface-level experiences of life meaning can fulfill for a period, but not for the long haul. We need something deeper. It cannot come from within, either. It must be independent of our lives so that it can continue to provide meaning regardless of what life brings. *Supra-meaning* is not individually created; it must be universal. There is but one ultimate meaning to life for all persons, and it cannot be found within the individual or differ from person to person. It is external. We cannot create it; we can only detect it. It is not dependent on others, life projects, or dignity in suffering. Frankl held that ultimate meaning is found in God and is spiritual in character. In this way, Frankl's existentialism is far different from that of the atheistic existentialists who suggest that life is ultimately meaningless. Frankl believed that the answer is not found in a resignation of the spirit to a sense of *meaninglessness* of life. The answer is found in learning to endure our inability to fully comprehend ultimate meaningfulness of life. In faith, we must accept that there is an ultimate meaning to all of life that we may not fully comprehend.

Frankl's approach to counseling is interesting. He believed that many of our problems grow out of our efforts to fill the *existential vacuum*. We become anxious about something and create a self-destructive cycle that keeps us from obtaining a satisfying sense of purpose. He concluded that three major causes were at work bringing about psychological disorders in people. The first he termed *anticipatory anxiety*. This is a fear of an experience that leads to failure at the experience. Take test anxiety as an example. We have students who are so afraid of tests because they have done poorly in the past that they inevitably do poorly on tests because of the mental paralysis caused by their fears. So each poor test result reinforces the fears, and a cycle of failure is developed.

The second cause of emotional disorder he calls *hyper-intention*. Simply put, hyper-intention is trying too hard. Let's take writing this chapter as an example. The harder one tries to overcome writer's block, the more difficult writing actually becomes. It is like the problem of insomnia. If you can't sleep, trying to fall asleep simply won't help. It is counterproductive. Generally, it is when we stop trying so hard that we are actually freed to do that which we are trying to do.

The third cause of psychological disorders, according to Frankl, is *hyper-reflection*. Hyper-reflection is "thinking too hard." If we give too much thought to something it can begin to control us or can become a self-fulfilling prophecy. For example, if a person thinks he is going to fail at a task, he actually increases the likelihood of failure. Our daughter is an ice-skater. For a skater, confidence is key. A fall can hinder that confidence. Once, when competing with a precision skating team, she took a fall. As a focused and accomplished skater, this was unusual for her. She knew the program well and had skated it countless times in practice. The problem was not a skating problem, but a problem of confidence. By excessively focusing on just one small aspect of a larger program, she had magnified that moment in her thinking. The more she thought about falling, the more likely she was to fall. The answer was found in refocusing her thoughts away from her fall to the larger program and its overall success. By regaining confidence in her skating ability, she was able to skate through the incident and succeed.

Treatment, Frankl suggested, involves helping a person to take the emphasis off of self, learning to laugh at some of the difficulties in life, and then finding rest in the belief that there is an ultimate meaning or purpose to life. Frankl believed that cycles of failure, despair, and doubt must be broken. Actions need to be taken that reflect a sense of confidence and meaning in life's situations. People must take responsibility for life by making changes in attitudes and actions that lead to their goals and life purpose. It is through a shift in personal values that life issues are addressed, and it is through ultimate meaning that life struggles take on purpose. For Frankl, counseling isn't eliminating problems from people's lives, but helping them to grow through those problems.

Frankl termed his approach to treatment *logotherapy*. The Greek word *logos* means "word, principle, study, or meaning." Frankl held that, through the development of a sense of meaning and in the application of truth principles to life, healthy psychological development can occur. (Some of the information about Viktor Frankl was taken from Boeree, *Frankl*.)

Rollo May

Born at nearly the same time but in a very different world than Frankl, Rollo May grew up with his five brothers and his sister in Marine City, Michigan. Born April 21, 1909, in Ada, Ohio, Rollo lived in a middle-class American context of the industrial Midwest.

It was a region and a time of anti-intellectualism. His childhood was an unhappy one; his parents fought often and eventually divorced. During his childhood, his sister had a psychotic breakdown that his father attributed to "too much education."

During his youth, May was interested in ancient Greek civilization, an interest that he believed helped to shape his view of human nature. After a brief enrollment at Michigan State University, where he was asked to leave because of his involvement in a radical student magazine, May transferred to Oberlin College in Ohio. There he received a bachelor's degree. Following graduation he went to Greece, where he lived for three years and taught English at Anatolia College. During the summers he traveled with a group of modern artists, painting and studying European peasant art. Briefly, he went to Vienna and studied under Alfred Adler.

He returned to the United States and entered Union Theological Seminary, where he was highly influenced by his friend and teacher Paul Tillich, an existentialist theologian. He did not go to seminary with the intent of becoming a preacher. His purpose was to ask questions, questions that had filled his mind during his times in Europe. He felt that by asking questions about despair, suicide, anxiety, and misery he might come to understand the nature of joy, courage, hope, and peace. He believed that seminary would be the place to discover answers.

May left Union Theological Seminary briefly when his parents divorced. He returned to East Lansing, Michigan, to care for his mother, his sister, and a brother. During that time, he served at Michigan State as a student adviser. Finally, he was able to return to Union to finish his studies. It was there during his senior year that he wrote his first book, *The Art of Counseling*. He graduated from seminary in 1938 and briefly became a pastor in Montclair, New Jersey.

In 1949, Rollo May received a Ph.D. in clinical psychology from Columbia University. During his work on his doctorate May contracted tuberculosis. Since there was no reliable treatment at that time for TB, May was forced to stay in a sanatorium in upstate New York for two years. It was a difficult time emotionally since he did not know whether he would live or die. While there, he read several books. Two books in particular influenced his thinking. The first was *The Problem of Anxiety* by Freud. The second was *The Concept of Dread* by Kierkegaard, a theistic existentialist philosopher. He felt that Kierkegaard's book captured the common human experience of life crisis, which he could readily relate to, being in the midst of his own physical struggle. During this time, he wrote his own book *The Meaning of Anxiety*. He went on to write twelve more books presenting his existential approach to therapy.

Over the next several years May went on to teach at City College of New York, New York University, Harvard, Yale, and Princeton. After a career as counselor, writer, and teacher, May retired to Tiburon, California, where he died in October 1994.

The personality theory of Rollo May reflects an interesting merger of psychology and philosophy. He is not scientific, and his work lacks scientific rigor. We include May because of his impact in the counseling field and to complete our picture of the primary influences on modern approaches to therapy.

May believed that most human personality problems result from feelings of "powerlessness" and a sense that the individual can do little to affect the course of culture and economics. He also held that anxiety and the loss of traditional values compound these feelings of powerlessness. May observed that many of his patients suffered from a sense of emptiness and fear. They felt that change was impossible because they lacked the power to make change in either the world or their own lives. He reasoned that a sense of powerlessness leads to apathy and that apathy leads to isolation.

Of major concern to May was the loss of traditional values in American society. He did not argue that traditional values should be reinstated, but that the loss robs people of emotional and psychological moorings. He argued that because traditional values are no longer present, society faces a problem—the need to affirm a new set of values upon which individuals can build their daily lives. This is where his existential views come into play. Because he believed that we have no ultimate "essence, " there are no absolute, pre-established values to be learned. For May, values are determined in the course of our existence and historical situation. Ethics are entirely situational. Since values are devised, we are responsible for them. We should not withdraw in anxiety, fretting about the loss of traditional values, May would contend. We should take action by developing a new society with new values.

May's answer to individual value dilemmas and our sense of powerlessness was a rediscovery of "self." He believed that this rediscovery occurs through conscious choices and commitments. Rediscovering self requires that we get in touch with our feelings and desires. According to May, self-understanding makes emotional health possible. For May, this understanding of self means that we must face what he called our *daimons*. A *daimon* is anything in our life that has the power to control us. The term is, of course, a depersonalizing of the concept of demons. He used the term to speak of negative, controlling factors in people's lives. For example, sex, anger, the craving for wealth, and the lust for power can all take us captive, making us pawns to our own destructive tendencies.

May's theory postulates that certain things are needed in order to establish a sense of self. The first is *freedom*. Freedom is the awareness that we are not determined, but are able to choose our own personality. The second quality needed is a sense of *destiny*. May believed that people are responsible for their own destiny. People with a sense of destiny acknowledge the need to make choices with regard to their future life course. They make choices rather than live as if circumstances or the will of others controls them. Third, May argued that people need *courage*. He believed that courage is not a virtue, but a foundational capacity to move ahead in spite of despair. Fourth, people must exercise *creativity*. The world, for May, is always in a state of being created, including our personal lives. We must fight the belief that acting creatively will bring failure or the wrath of others if we venture into new frontiers. Fifth, May believed we need a *life narrative*. A life narrative is a story that we use to make sense out of life. He termed this our life "myth." For example, those people who packed their wagons and moved to the frontiers of the Old West did so because of a mental image of a new life: a life of opportunity, vast spaces, and new beginnings. Those mental pictures and stories of the frontier motivated action and gave a sense of purpose to the lives of those early settlers. Like those pioneers of old, we too need a life myth to motivate us.

Psychological treatment then, from May's perspective, involves helping people pursue these five basic goals. The quest, in the big picture, is one of being human and becoming self-aware. May believed that when people recognize their potential and commit their will to achieve that potential, personality growth will occur. At the same time, people must face the *daimons* that hinder their success and health.

Although May's idea may have a number of interesting thoughts, conjectures, and observations, it is not a scientific theory. It does not present hypotheses to be tested or an empirical procedure to be followed. It does not offer data to be analyzed or conclusions to be evaluated. It is, in fact, a philosophical presentation of human nature. (Some of the information about Rollo May was taken from Boeree, *May.*)

EVIDENCE SUPPORTING THE PHENOMENOLOGICAL PARADIGM

If you are like many Christians, when you read the word "humanist" in this chapter, you may be tempted to conclude that every idea presented is counter to the teachings of the Bible. That is because the term *humanist* has been so misapplied in Christian writing and preaching. It has come to be used of virtually any concept that Christians find disagreeable. We speak of humanistic education and humanistic scientists. We hear of humanistic politicians or the humanistic media. In most cases, the term is used pejoratively and without definition. Although creators of "The Humanist Manifesto" and some other humanistic individuals have been strongly antireligious, humanism is usually known more by its positive thinking about people than for whether or what it believes about God.

Humanistic thinking and existential thinking have threads of truth that should be recognized. For example, the notions that people have dignity, worth, and value; that people need to take personal responsibility for their actions; that people have potential; that people make choices that affect their lives; that people are not trapped in determinism; and that people seek meaning in life are all concepts that are consistent with the teaching of the Bible. Although we cannot accept the premises of the phenomenological paradigm, we should consider its evidence, problems, and contributions. Evidence for the paradigm can be summarized in five general categories.

First, the phenomenological paradigm is supported by the fact that *human beings are capable of positive actions*. Although these acts have no meritorious place in terms of gaining God's favor or our salvation, they are amazing and laudable. Selfless acts of courage and valor, works of compassion and care, and gifts of mercy and love are found mingled with the hideous acts of the sinful heart. As Jesus said, "If you, then, though you are evil, know how to give good gifts to your children, how much more will your Father in heaven give good gifts to those who ask him!" (Matt. 7:11).

As Christians we believe that those flashes of goodness are a result of the image of God that remains within us, even though that image is marred by sin (see chapter 2). Out of the divine image come positive and beneficial qualities. We can join with the humanist to celebrate a measure of optimism about people. It is certainly tempered with the reality of sin and the ultimate end of unbelieving man, but we can agree that people have a side to them that produces positive actions.

Second, the phenomenological paradigm is supported by the fact that *human beings have an innate longing for purpose and meaning*. People everywhere long for a reason for their existence. This longing comes home most pressingly when death, disaster, or suffering strikes. It can be seen in the innate quest for religious experience, philosophical understanding, or even scientific exploration. The *why* question plagues people. And so, at this point we would agree. Meaning is essential to mental and spiritual well-being. The so-called God-shaped vacuum in all of us is evidenced in the scientific observations of persons like Frankl and others.

Third, the phenomenological paradigm is supported by the fact that *human beings are free, rational beings with enormous potential*.

We make choices, and those choices affect our lives. Because of that, we are responsible. In fact, the very word *responsible* literally means "response able." If we are to hold people responsible for their behavior, then they must have had the ability to respond or choose in the first place.

When humanists and existentialists emphasize freedom and responsibility, we must concur. The overwhelming evidence of daily life supports their assertions. Determined? No! Influenced? Certainly. But in the final analysis, it is our choices that define the people we become.

Fourth, the phenomenological paradigm is supported by the fact that *human beings are active, creative, and resilient creatures.* It is amazing how creative people can be. When I look at the power of my laptop computer and consider the human genius that went into its design, I am astounded. To look at a sculpture, see a painting, hear a piece of music, listen to a poem, or observe a 747 streak across the sky is to marvel. People are capable of unbelievable creativity—something our animal friends cannot experience. As Christians, we know that all of these talents are gifts from the Father of lights who by His common grace made them available to all people, Christian and non-Christian alike (James 1:17).

We believe that the humanists are correct when they suggest that human potential and creativity should be celebrated. We celebrate with them. We too are amazed at the resilient qualities that God has built into people so that they can withstand poverty, criminal threat, natural disaster, hunger, and abuse and still become capable, contributing individuals. We are stunned by stories of survival in the Nazi concentration camps and recognize something in people that kept them functioning despite horrifying treatment. People are indeed uniquely capable creatures of God.

Fifth, the phenomenological paradigm is supported by the fact that *human beings are influenced by their perceptions of their situation and themselves.* Evidence supports the notion of the phenomenological paradigm that perceptions count. If a teacher perceives a child as a "behavior problem," it is likely that she will interpret even innocent childlike errors as acts of intentional misbehavior. Similarly, if we see ourselves as incompetent or potential failures in some regard, it is probable that our own attitude will sabotage us through self-doubt.

PROBLEMS WITH THE PHENOMENOLOGICAL PARADIGM

What are the weaknesses with the phenomenological paradigm? Beyond the naturalistic worldview held by Maslow, Rogers, and May, which make this paradigm unacceptable for Christians, are four significant additional points of criticism. First among these is the matter of *scientific worthiness*. With the exception of Maslow's hierarchy of needs, it is important to note that little true scientific inquiry lies behind the phenomenological paradigm, at least not in the sense of verification studies. Because these theories are not presented in a way that allows them to be submitted to empirical testing, it is difficult to falsify any of the theories in this chapter. If a theory cannot be falsified, it cannot, by definition, be considered a scientific theory. Rather, these theories are best understood as philosophical in nature. This is the point made by Paul Vitz when he described many psychological theories as "applied philosophy of life" (*Psychology*). This is not to say that this paradigm offers no valuable insights or totally lacks scientific support, but we do not place the theories within this paradigm in the category of true scientific study.

A second problem with the phenomenological paradigm is its *theology of human nature*. Those who embrace this paradigm have a far too lofty view of human beings. This optimism does not match the clear teachings of the Bible regarding our fallen nature. Although humans have the potential for good acts resulting from the enduring image of God within, Scripture teaches that the natural inclination of the human heart leans predominantly toward sin (Rom. 7:12–20). Idealistic optimism about people was certainly not the view of Jesus, who saw human nature through the lens of reality. After many responded to His ministry, we read an interesting statement made about Jesus by John. "But Jesus would not entrust himself to them, for he knew all men. He did not need man's testimony about man, for he knew what was in a man" (John

2:24–25). As Christians counseling under the authority of Scripture, we too must realistically include the biblical view of fallen man in any ministry endeavor.

A third problem with the phenomenological paradigm is its *emphasis on the "self" and personal autonomy.* Biblically speaking, self-absorption is the crux of many human problems. An unbridled self-interest leads to narcissism where "self" becomes the all-consuming focus of life. True freedom is the result of dying to self and submitting our will to the will of God (Rom. 6:6; Eph. 4:22–24; Col. 3:9–10). The problem with this paradigm then is an overemphasis on self, self-esteem, personal needs, and self-actualization. The goals of complete personal autonomy and self-rule are not compatible with the believer's goal of a life fully devoted to Christ. We recognize that even Jesus denied His own interests in favor of God's plan when He said, "I tell you the truth, the Son can do nothing by himself; he can do only what he sees his Father doing, because whatever the Father does the Son also does" (John 5:19).

The fourth problem with the phenomenological paradigm is its *emphasis on finding oneself by "getting in touch with one's emotions."* This concept is found primarily in the theory of Rollo May. Although the open expression of our emotions has an important place under the correct circumstances, Christians believe that emotions cannot be the controlling-center of our lives. If we study the Gospels examining the emotions of Jesus, we will discover His expression of anger, sorrow, compassion, grief, disappointment, and loneliness. But all of His emotions were expressed in their proper place. It is also important to recognize that we are to submit our emotions to the lordship of Christ. We are to be Christlike in how we express our emotions. We cannot release emotions as they arise. Sometimes we must rein in our anger, our jealousy, and our resentment as an act of self-denial as Christ works in us (James 1:19–21).

CONTRIBUTIONS OF THE PHENOMENOLOGICAL PARADIGM

Of the theorists presented in this chapter, it seems clear that Christians can most easily accept Frankl's work. Through his research, Frankl points us to a psychology of meaning rather than a psychology of healing. His emphasis on meaning is biblical. When reading his observational research conclusions, we are reminded of similar conclusions expressed by Solomon in the Old Testament book of Ecclesiastes. In it, Solomon tells of his pursuit of meaning. He had sought meaning in wealth, things, a sensual lifestyle, his work, and human relationships. He concludes that none of these have meaning. "Meaningless! Meaningless!" is his cry to God. It is only in God that a true sense of life purpose can be found. Additionally, Frankl contributes by recognizing the value that is present even in suffering. His approach brings balance, and his life brings credibility to his views.

Beyond Frankl's contribution to understanding human nature, other contributions are apparent as well. We have already pointed out the value of Maslow's hierarchy of needs for those in ministry. He underscored the fact that people are complex and that they have a complex range of needs that motivate their actions. He emphasized the importance of addressing basic needs as a means to meeting the more advanced and essential needs. His emphasis on the meeting of the needs of the whole person is compatible with a biblical perspective as well. Finally, his concept of growth is worthy of our study. He believed that to grow, people had to make choices, choices for which they must take responsibility. This is certainly in keeping with a biblical view of human development.

Another contribution of the phenomenological model is found in its emphasis on personal responsibility. There is no victimhood in this model. People are to make responsible choices and then take responsibility for the results of those choices. Recognizing that we are not determined by our circumstances, our genetics, or our parentage is an important point consistent with God's Word. Like Joshua we too must "choose this day whom you will serve" (see

Josh. 24:15). That is a genuine choice. Life is filled with important and pivotal choices that demand careful consideration, decisiveness, and a willingness to accept the consequences for those choices. This is the emphasis of the phenomenological paradigm and of the Word of God.

Finally, the emphasis within this paradigm on human potential is one of its enduring contributions. By looking at what healthy people can achieve rather than only at problems of unhealthy individuals, this paradigm brings an important perspective to our understanding of human personality research. As believers, we know that lives fully devoted to Christ have potential beyond that which we can achieve in our flesh. People are enormously capable and gifted. It is encouraging to consider the potential in the life of those we seek to counsel. We can, at times, get so focused on the negative baggage in people's lives that we fail to see what they can become. It is important to recognize the sin nature in people and its ability to pull people down, but it is equally important to remember the potential in the people we serve.

TIME FOR SOME SELF-ASSESSMENT

Consider the following statements. Which do you agree with?

1. People are capable of highly creative acts. Agree or Disagree?
2. People should take responsibility for their behavior. Agree or Disagree?
3. People are capable of making meaningful change. Agree or Disagree?
4. People have dignity and worth. Agree or Disagree?
5. People can do both good and evil. Agree or Disagree?
6. People long for purpose and meaning in life. Agree or Disagree?
7. People are gifted with talents and abilities. Agree or Disagree?

If you agreed with any or all of the preceeding statements, you have something in common with the humanistic and existentialistic orientation of the phenomenological paradigm of personality.

NOTES

Boeree, C. George. *Carl Rogers*. 1998. 6 Jan. 2000 <http://www.ship.edu/~cgboeree/rogers.html>.

———. *Rollo May*. 1998. 5 Jan. 2000 <http://www.ship.edu/~cgboeree/may.html>.

———. *Viktor Frankl*. 1998. 5 Jan. 2000 <http://www.ship.edu/~cgboeree/frankl.html>.

Vitz, P. C. *Psychology as Religion: The Cult of Self-Worship*. 2d ed. Grand Rapids: Eerdmans, 1994.

— *Chapter 8* —

PERSONALITY PARADIGMS IV:
The Cognitive Approach

*E*ach one of us tends to interpret life and all of its experiences through a filter of his or her own creation. Like the filter on the lens of an expensive camera, our cognitive filters allow certain images to pass through and others to be filtered out. Over time, our filters have been constructed out of our personal daily experience and learning. These filters define for us the meaning of events in our lives, the actions of others, and even our own sense of self. They color our opinions and establish what others see as our personality. At least, this is the view of the *cognitive paradigm* of human personality, also known as the *constructivist* view.

There is something satisfying about a really good cup of coffee. Because of this, gourmet coffee shops have sprouted up from Seattle to Miami offering the simple luxury of a fine cup of coffee at somewhat inflated prices. What determines the quality of a cup of coffee? Generally speaking, it is the quality of the grounds through which the water has been dripped. Water is poured through coffee grounds that rest in a filtering element. As the water passes through the filter it picks up the taste of the coffee and, as a result, we get that aromatic and flavorful product that we so enjoy. But fill that element with poor quality coffee and you will get a poor quality product.

In much the same manner, cognitive theorists suggest that our minds are the primary source of our personalities. Personality is the product of our thoughts. The thoughts that saturate our minds become like the coffee grounds through which life is filtered. Therefore, if we desire to change our personality (the product), we must change our thoughts (the filter). But changing our mental filtering system is not such an easy task. It has been "constructed" over a lifetime. We have come to think in certain ways. We use familiar categories and constructs to interpret life and are not quick to give up these comfortable patterns even when they fail to produce the best results.

John Dewey wisely said, "One of the easiest things we can do is think. One of the most difficult things we can do is think well." Up to this point, we have looked at four paradigms that have been used by researchers to explain human personality development. One obvious weakness in each of these four paradigms has been a lack of attention to the role that the human mind plays as a factor in personality development.

The *biological paradigm* told us we are only brain, not mind. Our brain chemistry and neurological activity explain us. We only appear to have a mind. Similarly, the *behavioral paradigm* claimed that we are simply behaving organisms, responding in predictable and mechanical ways to stimuli in our environment. Again no mind is present, only brain tissue. The *psychoanalytic paradigm* asserted that personality is derived primarily from our response to innate urges and need-seeking responses. The mind, it is contended, is something created from a conflict between our desires and the limitations of family, culture, and society. The mind is "product," not creative force. The *phenomenological paradigm* proponents pointed us away from the mechanistic view of the behaviorists and from the instinctual drives suggested by the psychoanalytic camp. They suggested that we are people of emotion and that we are motivated by a deep need to achieve. For the phenomenologist, emotions, not mind, shape our personality.

What is missing in each of these approaches to understanding people is the recognition of the role that intellectual processes and rational thinking play in shaping human personality. The cognitive paradigm takes a different angle on human personality. According to cognitive theorists, our mind with its thinking processes is the most significant factor in determining our personality development.

Let's summarize the cognitive paradigm with four foundational propositions.

BASIC PROPOSITIONS OF THE COGNITIVE PARADIGM

Proposition 1: People are primarily active, rational beings who develop their potential through rational thinking and, therefore, can intentionally shape their own environment.

Cognitive theorists believe that people are, by nature, curious and inquisitive creatures. We are not fundamentally good, as the humanist would contend, but we do have an innate desire to learn and make sense out of our world. To the proponent of the cognitive paradigm, children are active rather than passive participants in their own development. They are not merely recipients of environmental stimulation. Instead, children actively seek some forms of stimulation and avoid others in an effort to organize their own world and to make sense out of their life experience. Human beings are adaptive by nature and make rational decisions about their situation. It is not the environment that has the primary role in shaping personality; it is the individual's mental state and understanding of the events occurring in his environment.

Amy is five years old. She has three siblings, all older. Amy has learned how to get her parents' and siblings' attention. She knows that if she talks sweetly in her little five-year-old voice, she can get her older siblings and her parents to respond to her will. As an active participant in shaping her own world, she can get others to do things for her—tie her shoes, get her a glass of water, read her a story, play a game, or let her have the last cookie. She has figured out that she can shape her world almost as effectively as her world can shape her. She is an active participant in family life. She is not simply a creature responding to reflex actions or instinctive drives. She is a vigorous force in her own world. This includes learning. Amy can choose whether and what she wants to learn and can use her curiosity to explore avenues of learning of her own making. She can make decisions as to whether she will play a learning program on the family computer or look at her favorite picture book. She can decide if she will explore the wonders of her backyard or the beauty of a newly opened box of crayons. All of these choices and actions are rooted in her cognitive capacity. Amy is a rational creature, and it is that rational ability that makes her the most potent factor in her own personality development.

Proposition 2: Human beings develop a set of personal mental constructs, which in turn become the basis of their belief system used to order and understand the world.

Constructivists believe that each person builds a mental grid through which life is processed. Those mental constructs are called *schemata* (singular, *schema*). Our conceptualization of the world is developed over time as we seek to understand the nature of events, actions, and experiences. We build our mental understandings like stair steps, one upon another, and use prior understandings to help explain new situations. As children, our schemata are limited, less complex, and formed through trial and error experimentation. Once we gain the ability to use language, schemata can be formed both experimentally and intellectually as we consider the ideas of others. They expand as we age and gain knowledge and experience. Those that worked in childhood eventually become inadequate as we mature. New schemata replace old as we gain deductive and systematic reasoning skills.

Despite the fact that maturation brings improved understanding, each of us comes to accept some constructs that may be incorrect. For example, Christina has come to think of herself as "stupid" because she struggles in school. The fact is, Christina has enormous ability with people, possessing a different kind of intelligence than the academic variety. But her mental construct regarding her ability limits her from seeing her potential and her unique people skills. She needs a different way of thinking about herself. She needs to sift data about her successes and failures through a new mental filter. By creating new mental constructs about herself, Christina can open new avenues in her life and new dimensions to her personality.

Some mental constructs serve as the core of our value system. Those constructs become the basis of a personal worldview and serve as the filter through which we make decisions regarding personal behavior, moral issues, and even life direction. For example, if I come to accept the construct "All human beings are made in the image of God and are divine image-bearers," then I must gear my approach to counseling accordingly. I must treat a person I counsel with the dignity and worth of one who possesses the very image of God. My thinking about people serves as a filter in selecting appropriate counseling techniques and in rejecting others. Using this construct, I can order my thinking about counseling.

Proposition 3: Dysfunctional behavior and personality weaknesses are the result of irrational thinking, incomplete knowledge, patterns of ineffective thought, and a faulty belief system.

According to this paradigm, people have problems because they do not think correctly, do not know enough, have fallen into thinking patterns that are unproductive, or have a basic belief system that is inadequate to deal with the real world.

Consider Joanne for a moment. Joanne is a thirty-two-year-old mother of three. She married when her husband was in seminary and worked to support him while he completed his studies. Now she is a pastor's wife. Once an outgoing and well-liked person, Joanne has become despondent, a loner, and very quiet. She was very active in the previous church and loved to teach a women's Bible study group each week. She was an extrovert, joyful and poised. Joanne is a gifted person but is now struggling with an enormous sense of self-doubt. She feels inadequate in her role and does not seem to be comfortable in the church her husband leads. Joanne is becoming more and more distant from people. She has pulled back from her involvement in the church. She avoids contact with people throughout the week and can hardly wait until the morning services are over so she can return to the safe environment of her home. What has changed? Why is Joanne no longer functioning as she did at her previous church, effectively teaching and ministering to others?

Through the insightful counsel of a Christian psychologist in the community, Joanne discovered the basis of her dysfunctional behaviors. She came to understand that her move from their former church in rural West Virginia to her present church in suburban Philadelphia was a factor in her problem. Her previous church was in a poor community. Educational opportunity was limited, and life was hard for most people. Her new church is in a wealthy suburb. Most families have two incomes. In many cases, both husband and wife hold professional positions. The new church pays her husband nearly twice his previous salary. When the opportunity came up, she thought the move would be an easy one because their income level would rise and the new community offered so many benefits. But her experience has been just the opposite of what she had predicted. She found that she was among a handful of women in the church who stayed at home with their children. She discovered, as well, that she was one of very few women who had not completed college, and she was the only woman in the church without professional training of some sort.

Through the help of her counselor, she began to see how her view of herself had changed because of the comparative standard she had adopted. She no longer saw herself as a woman with multiple gifts and abilities, but as a person less competent than those she came to serve. Her problem, the counselor said, was her mental perspective.

Joanne's capabilities had not changed, but her thinking about herself certainly had. In time, her faulty thoughts about her own abilities and limitations worked their way into her behavior. No longer seeing herself as the gifted person that God had made her to be, Joanne accepted a new and damaged understanding of herself, an understanding that diminished her standing and status as a human being to the point that it handicapped her personality. She had come to accept a life script that was written in the ink of wrong thinking.

Proposition 4: Personality change results from a change of attitudes, values, beliefs, and thought patterns.

Cognitive theorists reason that if thinking can be changed, lives can be changed. Again, consider Joanne's case. With the counselor's assistance, Joanne explored the Scriptures, seeking new insights into God's craftsmanship in her life. Once she regained a biblical understanding of her worth, dignity, status, and giftedness, she was able to again allow her people-centered personality to manifest itself. Over time, with the help of her husband and a small group of fellow Christians, Joanne began to see her perspectives change. By recasting her self-thoughts, she was able to recapture her strengths. For Joanne, right thinking gradually produced emotional freedom.

Treatment, then, involves recasting and rescripting one's thought life. If one is immersed in destructive or inaccurate thinking, behavior must become skewed over time since our behavior is preceded by our thoughts. If parents, counselors, pastors, and teachers can help people to think in new, more productive ways, personality change can occur. But just telling someone to think differently does not work. As we will see in this chapter, cognitive growth and development is a process. New thought structures must be built one step at a time.

PROPONENTS OF THE COGNITIVE PARADIGM

We could cite numerous proponents of the cognitive approach, but in this chapter we will focus on two key people—Jean Piaget and Alfred Adler. These men stand out as having had the greatest impact on the field of human personality theory from the cognitive perspective. We begin with an individual who is arguably the world's most influential cognitive psychologist of all time, Jean Piaget.

Jean Piaget

Born August 9, 1896, in the mountains of Neuchâtel, Switzerland, Jean Piaget was just a child when he first began his journey into scientific research. At the young age of eleven he wrote and published his first work growing out of his early interest in biology, a paper about an albino sparrow. Eventually, his elementary scientific interests graduated into a renowned theory of the cognitive development of human beings.

Jean Piaget was the son of Arthur Piaget, a professor of medieval literature at the University of Neuchâtel. His mother, Rebecca, was described as quiet, intelligent, devoutly religious, and a strict Calvinist. His mother took him to church, which he attended reluctantly. His experience in church brought him to the conclusion that religious arguments are childish, close-minded, and anti-intellectual. Rejecting religious and theological thought, he turned to the study of philosophy and logic. But he concluded that this too failed as a reliable source of truth since one could reason to any number of philosophical conclusions. He decided that science offered the surest understanding of the real world, and so it was science he pursued until his death in 1980.

In Europe, Piaget was well known even from his days as a student at the University of Neuchâtel, where he obtained his Ph.D. in Natural Science in 1918. After completing his Ph.D. work, Piaget attended a semester at the University of Zurich. There he developed an intense interest in psychoanalysis. He then traveled to Paris, France, to further his inquiry into the study of human psychology, especially the study of intelligence. He worked for two years at Ecole de la rue de la Grange-aux-Belles, a boys' institution created by Alfred Binet. At this elementary school he was able to study, apply, and develop Binet's intelligence testing theories.

For Piaget, the fascinating aspect of his research was not found in observing students' correct answers, but in their incorrect responses. He found that children consistently answered questions wrong but, strangely, in the same manner. He discovered that children universally made the same errors of logic using similar reasoning approaches. His conclusion from this observation was that children process their answers to problems in predictable ways and that their responses showed a progression of logic moving, step-by-step, toward adult reasoning. He came to believe that children's logic and modes of thinking are entirely different from those of adults. Piaget published his first article on the psychology of the intelligence of children in *Journal de Psychologie* in 1921. Later, he published five books based on these early observations. Piaget had a remarkable career, spanning sixty-five years. The author of sixty books and more than one hundred articles, Piaget was a prolific writer. But it was not until his works were translated into English in the 1950s that he was discovered in North America. (Some of the information about Jean Piaget was taken from Boeree, *Piaget*.)

Figure 8-1 helps us understand Piaget's theory of personality development. Piaget held that children are not empty vessels to be filled with knowledge, but are instead explorers or scientists actively building their own knowledge and interpretations of the world. To do this each child builds a schema. But schemata are not simply unchanging, stagnant boxes. In a certain sense, they are best understood to be thought categories open to constant review and updating.

FIGURE 8–1
Piaget's Theory of Personality Development

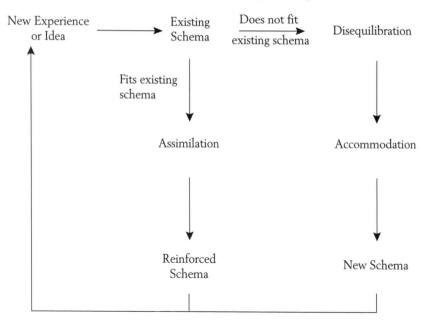

When Keith was eighteen months old, his parents took him on a trip through Wisconsin to his grandparents' home in Minnesota. For Keith, the trip was an adventure. As he peered out the window of the car, he spotted several cows in a nearby pasture. He yelled with excitement, "Doggies!" His parents patiently corrected him. "No, Keith, those are cows." Again, with just as much excitement, Keith cried out, "Cows!" What had just happened was a revision in Keith's mental schema. Keith had only one category for four-legged animals—the doggy category. By creating a new category, Keith expanded and ordered his knowledge and further developed his cognitive schemata.

Piaget held that schemata change as the child grows. These changes occur in three basic ways: assimilation, accommodation, and equilibration. *Assimilation* is the process of *taking in* new experiences to an already existing schema. For instance, when Keith sees a bird and labels it as a bird, he is assimilating his observation into the already existing "bird" category. The result is that Keith's schema is reinforced, making it more reliable for future observations. Assimilation then is best understood as the mental action of placing an event or experience into an already-existing schema. Consequently, this involves grouping new ideas with similar ideas that are already present.

Accommodation is the second means by which children order information and seek to make sense out of their world. Accommodation occurs when an existing schema is changed or reorganized as the result of new information or experiences—resulting in heightened understanding and skill. When Keith called out "doggies" and his parents corrected him, Keith developed a new category of thought. He accommodated the new information and changed his thinking structures.

Accommodation is often far more difficult than is assimilation. When we accommodate new information or events, we must change in some way. Consider, for example, the story of Paul. Paul was a student at Moody Bible Institute several years ago. Paul was a relatively new believer when he came to Moody and was a bit lost when it came to the theological vocabulary being used in his classes. Nancy, a fellow student, noticed that Paul was struggling in class, so she helped him by explaining terms that were unfamiliar to him. Little by little, Paul was able to create mental categories for the information he received in class. Paul's expanding understanding of theology came from his willingness to accommodate his thinking to the new material. Over time, Paul was able not only to understand the concepts taught in the course, but also to interact with others about controversial matters using the new mental categories he had created.

The third means of cognitive development, according to Piaget, is the quest for *equilibration*—that is, "balance." Piaget observed that human beings seek coherence in life and strive for a kind of balance between questions and answers. Equilibration involves the person's striking a balance between his current schema and his experience of life. When an idea or event enters our lives that cannot be easily assimilated or accommodated, it brings a sense of disequilibrium. Out of this disequilibrium comes the motivation to search for answers.

Disequilibrium is hard, and it is not a desirable experience, but it is the catalyst for personality growth and maturation. Our student friend from Moody, Paul, experienced disequilibrium firsthand. Paul and Nancy grew interested in each other and began to date. By the end of the fall term they had become very close and even began talking about the eventual possibility of marriage.

Nancy and Paul each went home for the Christmas break, but only Paul returned for the spring term. He learned when he arrived on campus that Nancy had been killed in a car crash just a day before school was to resume. Paul was emotionally trampled. He had never experienced death up close. His faith was shaken. Why would God allow such a thing to happen to Nancy? Why would God allow this to happen to him as well? The event of Nancy's death pushed Paul's theology of God's grace, mercy, and providential care to a different level. He now had to seek answers that balanced his difficult questions and, in so doing, make his beliefs personal. His schema was tested. To right the balance, Paul was driven to new levels of learning and growth. As a person, Paul will forever be different. Disequilibrating experienc
do that.

At the beginning of his book *The Child and Reality*, Piaget posed the question: What is the role of the life cycle in the development of a child's understanding of his world? Piaget concluded that many characteristics in human beings require time to develop and thus are influenced directly by the child's rate of development. He reasoned that much of our understanding of the world comes to us in a step-by-step, building block process. For example, children do not immediately understand that objects continue to exist independent of their perception of the objects. One can hide an object from a young infant's view and the object will cease to exist in the mind of the child. But with time, children become aware that objects have a quality of permanence about them. This means that objects hidden from view can be searched for and recovered.

Piaget called this quality *object permanence*. The significance of this, and the many other cognitive observations made by Piaget, is that it demonstrates that cognitive development proceeds in predictable ways. As a result of his observations, Piaget came to understand cognitive development in children as stagelike in nature. This means children develop in sequential, invariant steps that can be observed, understood, and encouraged. Piaget identified four stages of cognitive development.

Sensorimotor Development (Birth–2 Years)

Piaget termed his first stage of cognitive development the *sensorimotor stage*. This stage occurs between birth and approximately two years of age. During this period, children do not have language; therefore, learning is primarily sensory in nature rather than reasoned. It is also during this period that language is learned. Once language ability is gained, new horizons of learning are opened to the child.

Using their growing motor skills, infants actively engage their environment through the use of the five senses. In this stage, babies kick, pull, suck, shake, and push as a means of gaining a simple understanding of cause and effect relationships. For example, Tiffany is eleven months old. Her mother set a toy near her on her blanket. Using the blanket, Tiffany pulled the toy to her and then shook it to see what sound it would make. Using her skills of movement and her ability to hold and shake an object, Tiffany was able to discover something about the nature of her world. For sensorimotor children, learning is primarily experiential. The use of language and logic is yet to be developed.

Preoperational Thinking (2–7 Years)

The second stage in Piaget's theory of cognition is termed *preoperational thinking.* In Piaget's theory, the word *operation* refers to logical processes or sequences of thought. From ages two through seven, children are prelogical in their thinking. They do not think in ways that are consistent with adult logical processes, but, instead, children think in a manner that is termed *transductive* reasoning. Adults typically use either inductive reasoning, that is thinking from details to a general principle, or deductive thinking, that is reasoning from a principle to various potential applications. Children in this age group tend to reason from detail to detail. The result is a childlike logic that is quite unlike adult thinking and sometimes a bit humorous.

When Amanda was four, her mother had to travel to Chicago to care for Amanda's grandmother, who had suffered a heart attack. Standing at the terminal building in Toronto, Amanda's father and Amanda stood side-by-side watching as the plane taxied out to the runway and took off. They watched as the plane began to disappear into the distant sky. As the plane grew increasingly distant, Amanda began to cry. Amanda's father offered encouragement. "It's OK. Mommy will be back soon."

Amanda responded, "But Mommy is getting so small!" Amanda had focused on the ever decreasing size of the plane as it appeared to her and concluded that her mother must be shrinking. Amanda was using transductive logic. Her thinking was based on appearances rather than on logical inference.

Preschoolers are easily confused by changes in appearance. For example, if Elise's mother pours juice from a wide glass to a tall, narrow glass, Elise will think that more juice is present in the tall glass because it appears to have more in it. By the time she reaches age seven, she will have grasped a cognitive principle that prevents her from making this error of logic. This new intellectual ability is known as the principle of conservation. At six or seven years of age she will understand that the amount of juice stays constant when poured into a different sized glass or that the amount of Play-Doh remains the same even if reshaped. As basic as this principle may seem to adults, it is fundamental to logical thinking and develops over time in children.

The apostle Paul spoke of this shift from one schema or paradigm to another in his first epistle to the Corinthian church. He wrote, "When I was a child, I talked like a child, I thought like a child, I reasoned like a child. When I became a man, I put childish ways behind me" (1 Cor. 13:11). Paul recognized that the thinking process of a child differs from that of an adult. Old, childlike ways of thinking will not work in adulthood. In time, childlike reasoning gives way to adult logic, and we are not so easily fooled by appearances. Instead, as adults, we consider prior knowledge about the attributes of the object and conclude that the object retains those attributes despite our perception to the contrary.

Concrete Operational Learning (7–11 Years)

Children ages seven to eleven are in the stage of cognitive development that Piaget entitled *concrete operations*. Concrete operational children can think logically and sequentially, but they require "concrete" hooks or helps to aid their thinking. They are beginning to classify and categorize things. They can also arrange items in sequence and are beginning to reverse processes. They can begin to theorize about the world. They are able to think about potential results of actions and can anticipate what will happen, make guesses or estimates, and then experiment to test the outcomes.

At the younger end of this age range, children begin to more effectively explore their physical environment, ask questions and find the answers, and, in time, acquire more complex, sophisticated forms of thinking. But for six- to eight-year-olds, understanding of symbolism and abstractions is still limited unless these concepts are related to physical objects or events.

Nine- to eleven-year-olds can observe more accurately than younger children and reason more logically. They are more self-reliant and have become inquisitive explorers. They enjoy discovering answers to their many questions and are alert and eager to learn anything new. According to Piaget's theory, these children have advanced in their reasoning capacities and are capable of doing more in-depth thinking than younger children do. They classify, categorize, and manipulate mental data with more ease and greater skill. They can estimate, theorize, and master logical operations, but they think concretely and literally. Symbols and abstractions can be taught with familiar examples, concrete props, and visual aids. Those ministering to this age level must not assume children understand these concepts without explanation. Skillful questioning, careful listening, and paying close attention to the ways these children try to solve problems will teach us a great deal about how they think and learn.

Mrs. Martinez is a third-grade teacher who understands how concrete operational children learn best—through hands-on, concrete links to abstract or complicated ideas. Take, for example, the time she taught a science unit on the solar system. Using diagrams, the NASA Internet Website, her textbook, and a desktop-sized model, she carefully explained to her class how each planet revolved around the sun. Wanting the children to fully grasp the relationship of the planets to one another, she came up with a creative idea for learning. She decided to make a gymnasium-sized model of the solar system where the children could actually become the planets in motion. For several days the class fashioned each of the planets and the sun out of papier-mâché. They painted each planet to match pictures they had downloaded from NASA and then took them into the gymnasium. Half of the class watched from the bleachers. Ten children took their places on the gym floor. Each walked at a different rate around the sun in the center. The child holding Mercury walked quickly, but Jupiter walked slowly. From the stands, the children could see firsthand how the planets revolved around the sun, each at its own rate. By providing a concrete model, Mrs. Martinez helped her children understand this difficult and somewhat abstract concept, one that her concrete thinking children could not otherwise grasp.

Formal Operational Thinking (Adolescence)

The fourth stage of cognitive development makes its appearance in the adolescent years. Piaget used the words *formal operational thought* to describe this level of understanding. The formal operational stage begins somewhere around age twelve for most children and continues to develop throughout adulthood.

According to Piaget, early adolescents are at the developmental stage where they are increasingly more capable of serious, logical, and sequential thinking. They are developing their ability to grasp relationships and solve more complex problems. But although they grow significantly in practical wisdom, in judgment, and in common sense, often their ability to reason outstrips their experience, resulting in unwise choices.

Formal operational thinking is qualitatively different from the thinking of childhood. Formal operational thinkers use new problem-solving skills, consider abstract ideas, and engage in reflective thought. When Julius was seven, his mother read him the book *The Lion, the Witch and the Wardrobe* by C. S. Lewis. To a young boy it was the story of a group of children on a fantasy adventure. He saw no deeper meaning. But at age fifteen, Julius picked up the book again and reread it. This time he read at a different cognitive level. The lion he recognized to represent Christ and the witch, Satan. He was discovering the story behind the story. He had ventured into abstract thought.

Rachel has undergone a shift from thinking only about the actual and concrete world to thinking about the possible, potential world. Instead of thinking only about things that she has experienced, she begins to think about things that she could experience. She imagines herself going to college, taking a job at a law firm, and maybe getting married. A few minutes later, she envisions herself as a teacher, leading an elementary classroom filled with second graders, traveling during the summers, and maybe staying single. No longer are her dreams just a childlike wish. Now she can begin to conceive a way to get from where she is to where she wants to be. She begins to imagine the consequences in the future for the actions that she takes now. She is now capable of seeing the possibilities that are before her and the potential outcomes of her decisions.

Rachel can also think in terms of "if-then" relationships. She can reason that *if* she becomes sexually active, *then* she could get pregnant or that *if* she acts selfishly, *then* she will have fewer friends. Using this form of thinking, she is gaining the ability to do systematic problem solving and can reasonably evaluate various options before taking action. Instead of the typical trial and error approach of childhood, she makes a mental hypothesis about each option before her and selects a course of action based on that potentiality. Unfortunately, she does not have enough experience or wisdom to make the best choices at each opportunity, but she now has the capacity for hypothetical reasoning.

As an adolescent, Rachel has a growing ability to deal with the abstract. She can handle more symbolic ideas along with the concrete. She is able to consider much more challenging concepts and is forming opinions of her own. Rachel now finds that discussions in Sunday school designed to seek out her opinion are far more interesting than sessions where the teacher tells her what to think. All of these intellectual skills are the result of formal operational thinking, according to Piaget. Rachel can now effectively shape her future by making logical, adultlike decisions.

Piaget's theory is a *constructivist* theory. He believes that children gradually develop their own mental framework or schema through which they view and process life. As we have discovered, Piaget believed that cognitive development parallels physical development and follows a predictable path through sequential stages. People who work with children, youth, and adults in teaching or counseling roles therefore must match their efforts with the natural developmental processes of the individual. Because thinking drives behavior, we must understand and work with people at their various levels of cognitive development.

Alfred Adler

Alfred Adler was a middle child, a fact important to understanding Adler and his theory. Born in Vienna on February 7, 1870, Adler was the third child in a family of six. This middle-child status meant that Alfred lived in his older brother's shadow. Add to this a series of childhood illnesses and two life-threatening accidents, and you have the story of a child who considered himself to be inferior to his brother and playmates. From his experience as the "hidden child" came Adler's concept called *the inferiority complex*, for which he is best known.

Beyond his physical limitations, Adler also experienced feelings of inferiority in the classroom. An average to below average student in most subjects, he achieved only mediocre grades and did so poorly in mathematics that he had to repeat the course one year. Not believing him to be smart enough to make it in the academic world, Adler's teacher advised his father to take him out of school and find him an apprenticeship as a shoemaker. As sometimes is the case, this experience motivated Adler. Rather than have his teacher be proven correct, he compensated for his earlier failures by studying zealously. Before long, he became the best mathematics student in the class.

Having overcome his feelings of self-doubt, he eventually went on to a much more stunning academic career. Adler studied medicine at the University of Vienna, where he graduated in 1895 near the top of his class. The academic environment provided an opportunity to explore political ideologies. Adler was interested in socialism and joined the campus socialists club. In the club, Adler met Raissa Timofeyewna Epstein. Alfred and Raissa married in 1897 and had four children, two of whom became psychiatrists.

Shortly after graduation, Adler established his practice in a lower-class neighborhood of Vienna. Seeking to make his socialistic idealism a reality, Adler offered low-cost medical care to people of the community, many of whom had never seen a doctor before. Because his office was across from a combination amusement park and circus, most of his clients were circus people. The unusual characteristics of this group of people gave Adler a fascination with human nature. In time, this interest led him to the field of psychiatry.

In 1902 Adler wrote an article in a local newspaper defending the views of Freud. As a result, Freud invited Adler to join the Viennese Analytic Society. Freud eventually named Adler the first president of the group and editor of the group's newsletter. Then he wrote a number of articles concerning aggression instinct and feelings of inferiority in children. Because these papers questioned Freud's notion that human personality is the result of sexual drives, Freud became incensed. A debate between Adler and Freud was arranged by the society. Although no winner was determined, a falling out occurred between Adler and Freud. In 1911, Adler resigned from the society to form the Society for Free Psychoanalytic Research, a name that was a direct reference to Freud's demand for strict adherence to his theory. Later that year the organization was renamed the Society for Individual Psychology.

World War I had an enormous impact on Adler. As a physician in the Austrian army assigned to the Russian front, Adler saw the carnage of war firsthand. Later, when reassigned to a children's hospital, he cared for children who were victims of the war. Through these experiences, Adler came to believe that human beings were capable of both evil and self-sacrificing heroism. This observed tension increased his interest in understanding personality.

After the war, Adler worked in school counseling clinics and was involved in teacher training. In 1926, he came to the United States to teach medicine at Long Island College of Medicine and at Aberdeen University. It was during a break period in one of his lectures that Adler suffered a heart attack and died on May 28, 1937. (Some of the information about Alfred Adler was taken from Boeree, *Adler.*)

Superiority and Inferiority

Adler believed that the primary motivation in life is to gain a better way of life. Rather than seeing personality battling id, ego, and superego as Freud did, Adler held that both the conscious and the unconscious mind work in union toward meeting this most basic goal of life. He held that a single "drive" or motivating force was behind all human behavior and experience. Initially he termed this drive "aggression drive." Later he used the term "striving for superiority." Finally, he settled on the phrase "striving for perfection." By this he was referring to the desire within human beings to achieve, be self-assertive, and gain recognition.

According to Adler, feelings of inferiority cause people to fall short of their potential. These inferiority feelings come to us from several sources. One source he calls *organ inferiority*. Adler believed that each person possesses both weak and strong aspects to his or her anatomy, physiology, and intellect. For example, if a child is born with a physical disability, is very tall or very short, or lacks cognitive capacity, such physical qualities can hinder that child in reaching his or her desired goals. In response, Adler contended, people tend toward one of two reactions. First, individuals can *compensate* and seek to make up for deficiencies by developing alternative skills or functional personality styles. Second, failing to overcome limits or problems, people can become despairing and in time develop what Adler called *psychological inferiority*.

According to Adler, *psychological inferiority* arises out of others' comments and out of life experiences. Take, for example, Krista. She has struggled in math at school. Once a teacher told her she "just doesn't have a head for math." She now has come to believe that she cannot learn math, so she does not even try. She is not cognitively disabled, but she feels she is "dumb." This feeling is a form of psychological inferiority that hinders her from achieving success in the area of math. Krista's thoughts about her inability in math become a self-fulfilling prophecy. Adler suggests that if someone hears something demeaning long enough, over time the person will come to believe those evaluations and live them out.

Adler recognized a third form of inferiority that he called *natural inferiority*. He believed that all children have some feelings of inferiority simply because they are children. Children are by nature smaller, weaker, and less socially and intellectually competent than adults. Adler believed that because of this, they long to be like adults and they feel themselves inferior to adults. He pointed out that children's toys, games, and fantasies reflect a desire to be an adult (or did in his day). These, he believed, are indicators of the natural inferiority felt by children simply because they are children. But Adler also believed that a few people never move beyond those feelings of childish incompetence. The result is that they remain dependent on others. As an example, he pointed to those who spend their entire lives on social assistance programs.

Always dependent, the child looks to the parent for income, food, housing, clothing, health care, entertainment, and all of the other aspects of life. The result is a person forever deemed inferior by both himself and society.

Adler believed that people who are overwhelmed by feelings of inferiority could develop an *inferiority complex*. As a result, they are less able to succeed and perform at their best. They tend to consider others to be more capable and themselves to be worthless, without talent, and the victims of more competent people around them.

Alternatively, Adler also held that feelings of inferiority could be a wellspring of creativity and potential in people. Adler believed that *what* we were born with is not really the issue. It is more important *what we do with* the potential that we were born with. Adler's perspective is grounded in a growth model of human personality, that people grow to become someone different over time. By recasting perspectives and perceptions of oneself, one's situation in life, and one's attitudes, individuals can change to become more competent and achieve greater mastery of life's challenges. Adler believed that weaknesses could be turned to strengths as people learn to compensate in a strong personality area for a shortcoming in another area.

Adler claimed that each person has a unique *lifestyle*. Lifestyle is the term that Adler used to identify each individual's personality or orientation to life. People's lifestyles are a kind of road map for life or plan of life that they follow. Lifestyles are comprised of our goals, strategies for living, and the themes around which we build our existence. Our lifestyles also include our views about ourselves, our behaviors and habits, and the unique events that shape our thinking. No two people develop the same lifestyle because each person is an active creator and responder to life's situations.

Personality Types

Adler embraced the concept of individual uniqueness but, for the purpose of discussion, identified four lifestyle categories. Each category is a personality type that represents a rough estimate of the similarities between people. Three of the lifestyle types are negative in nature; one is positive or healthy.

The first negative lifestyle is that of the *ruling type*. Ruling types are dominators by nature. As the title suggests, they seek to rule over and control others. This is accomplished by diminishing the dignity of others, by aggressive and competitive behaviors, and by pushing for their way. Often ruling types are high achievers and are driven to accomplish goals. But achievement can have its price. Rulers can be seen as hurtful bullies who care little about the people. Some ruling types turn their controlling and abusive behavior inward, resulting in addictions and suicidal tendencies.

Adler's second type is the *getting type*. Getting types are takers rather than givers. These people adopt a passive attitude toward life, are dependent on others, and exhibit low energy levels. Adler believed that pampering of children by parents encourages this lifestyle. Pampering, he believed, creates children who are unable to carry life's difficulties and who depend excessively on others.

The third mistaken lifestyle is the *avoiding type*. Avoiding types assume that by avoiding life's problems, they can avoid potential failure or defeat. Avoiding types are perceived by others as distant, cold, disconnected, and loners. Avoiding types sometimes retreat entirely into their own worlds, becoming psychotic in their behavior.

The fourth lifestyle type is the *healthy type*. Contrary to Freud's tendency to see mental health as the exception rather than the rule, Adler believed that healthy types include the majority of people. Healthy types are socially useful, emotionally balanced, and willing to accommodate others. Healthy types contribute to society by giving of themselves. Healthy types believe that they are basically in control over their lives and choices and thus do not feel their lives are externally determined. They see life as containing good and bad, positives and negatives, advantages and disadvantages. They recognize that both kinds of experiences are simply a part of life and they accept that reality.

Parenting Styles

Adler recognized two significant outside shaping influences on children—parental style and birth order. While Adler believed that each individual has a free will, he contended that it was parents who play the most significant role in shaping their children. Positive parenting styles can encourage the development of a healthy lifestyle, whereas negative parental behaviors can encourage unhealthy lifestyles. Negative parenting approaches tend toward one of two extremes: pampering and neglecting. Pampered children become spoiled children. Neglected children become self-doubters unable to complete tasks. In both cases the result is adults who seek indulgence and further pampering.

Birth Order

In addition to parenting style, Adler believed that birth order influences the development of certain personality characteristics. Although many researchers beside Adler have pointed to parents as a significant variable in child development, it was Adler who extended the study of family influence to sibling interactions.

Adler considered four possible birth order positions. These included *the only child, the first child, the middle child,* and *the youngest child.* Adler observed that the *only child* is a pampered child receiving full attention of his or her parents. Although the only child is often indulged, he is also highly encouraged. Only children have great self-confidence and receive the resources needed to achieve their goals since there are no other children who must share those resources. Since only children do not have to share, they often fail to learn relational skills. As a result, only children tend to be less capable of bending for others, are more self-absorbed, and do not function well in give-and-take situations.

The first child is the "pacesetter" for all children in the family. First children are first to walk, to talk, to ride a bike, or to enter school. They live a life of firsts. The first child is the parenting guinea pig. Adler believed that parents learn to parent by trial and error. It is the first child who is the subject of early parenting successes and failures.

The *first child* begins life as an only child. Once, as the only child, he enjoyed the full attention of parents. Then, a new baby comes along. That's when the first child is bumped from his only child status. Some children will fight fruitlessly to regain their lost position. In that effort, they may replay old baby-like behaviors with the assumption that, like the new baby, they will again gain Mommy and Daddy's undivided attention. But their once cute baby behaviors are not so endearing now that they are toddlers. The behavior is rejected by parents as they are told to "grow up."

The *middle child* is the invisible child. He or she must compete with the "pacesetter" first child. Unlike the first child, the middle child is compared to the standards and achievements set by an earlier child. Middle children can be lost between the "firsts" of the first child and the attention given to the baby of the family. As a result, middle children can feel less significant and less competent than their older or younger siblings as they drift into the hidden middle.

The *youngest child* is typically the most pampered. As little princess or little prince, he or she is the only one who is never dethroned! Youngest children can be significant sources of trial to their parents. Parents may lose energy and become more indulgent. On the other hand, the youngest may also feel inferior to the older siblings. If the older children have excelled, a child may have several "pacesetters" and never be able to keep up.

Adlerian Counseling

So, given these views, how would Adler approach counseling? Adlerian counseling involves exploring with a client mistaken thinking, faulty assumptions, and misdirected goals. It then requires that a reeducation occur wherein the client develops constructive goals and plans for achieving those goals. Adlerian counselors do not view their clients as "sick" and in need of a "cure." Rather, they believe most people can respond well to a process that involves providing information, teaching, guidance, and encouragement. Adlerian counseling seeks to retrain thinking and reshape long-established false beliefs.

Adlerian counseling follows a four-step process to overcome personality faults and life problems. The first step is to *create and maintain a genuine and positive relationship with the client.* Often this is achieved by aiding the client in examining personal assets and strengths rather than dealing directly with personality deficits and liabilities. In the initial phase of counseling, the Adlerian approach suggests that the counselor listen, show interest, and demonstrate respect for the client. Counselors should communicate their belief that the client is capable of change and that the counselor's role will be one of support and encouragement. Asking questions like, "What has brought you to see me?" or "What have you done about your problem until now?" begins to create a relationship with the client. Follow-up questions such as "How would your life be different if you did not have this problem?" and "What are your expectations from our meeting together?" can then take the initial relationship a step further. By attending to and listening to the client, the Adlerian counselor demonstrates a genuine interest in the problem the client is experiencing.

The second step in the process, once a relationship is established, is to *explore the client's life dynamics, including his or her lifestyle and goals.* Using a variety of assessment approaches, the counselor comes to understand how the client is functioning in his or her day-to-day world. Exploration of the client's family situation and relationships, early childhood history, and private interpretations of his or her life situation helps the Adlerian counselor gain insight into the causes and negative thought patterns that may be generating the client's personality struggles.

Adlerian counselors function as psychological explorers who are invited by the client on his or her life journey. They seek to understand the client as a person in light of his total life context. In this way, counselors can be an external reference point to the individual, giving unbiased input to balance the individual's private interpretations. From this exploration and independent point of reference, the client is to gain an awareness of his options for growth and potential paths that lead to greater productivity and a constructive future.

The third step is to *encourage insight and self-understanding.* Adlerian counselors are both supportive and confrontational. Together with the client, they seek to aid the client in discovery of self-defeating behaviors, mistaken life goals, and faulty thought processes. They help the client interpret situations by stating their views as hypotheses that the client can consider. The goal is to bring the client to personal insights upon which behavior changes can be initiated. After a client talks about a problem and gives his insights into his own situation, an Adlerian counselor might make the comment, "I have a hunch I'd like to share with you" or "Could it be that . . . ?" and then wait for a response from the counselee. If the person invites further comment, the counselor will give more observations or explanations. Humbly, the counselor allows the client to decide if the insight is correct or inaccurate. Counselors do not avoid truth telling; they just will not allow counselees to bait them into taking control of the counselee's problem. The goal in this step is get the client to recognize his role and responsibility in identifying and solving his own problem.

The fourth step in the Adlerian counseling approach involves *helping with restoration*. This is an action-oriented stage in which reeducation occurs and action plans are developed. Clients make decisions with regards to how they will address their problem and establish the means by which old patterns of ineffectiveness are to be broken. In this counseling phase, concrete action is the focus. Insights must be translated into new goals and specific courses of action. A variety of techniques is used to aid clients in this step, all of which are pointed at restoring the person to a more functional and effective life.

Alder advised that therapists never allow the patient to force them into the role of an authoritarian figure. If this happens the patient will begin to look to the therapist as a "savior" rather than as a supportive helper. He believed that therapists must avoid taking a "savior role" so that the counselee does not become dependent on the counselor. If a relationship of dependence is established, Adler believed, patients are then justified in blaming the counselor for their continued problems and personal failures.

Adler recognized that some counselees would be resistant to counseling even though they had come for counsel. This resistance is seen in forgotten appointments, late arrivals, demands for special favors, or stubborn and uncooperative interactions. Adler believed that a patient must come to understand the nature of his or her lifestyle and its roots in self-centered fictions. This understanding, he believed, could not be forced, but should come with guidance and responsiveness from the counselee. A counselor should communicate a desire to listen and understand, but not communicate the power to control or resolve the patient's problem. The counselor is to bring the patient to the point of willingly taking responsibility for his or her own choices.

EVIDENCE SUPPORTING THE COGNITIVE PARADIGM

After considering two of the leading proponents of the cognitive paradigm, we now come to the matter of supporting evidence. What evidence supports the theories of Piaget, Adler, and others who see cognition as the most significant component in the development of human personality? Two lines of evidence are most convincing.

Scientific Worthiness

Remember that scientific worthiness is determined by examining five matters: a theory's testability, external validity, predictive validity, internal consistency, and theoretical economy. On all counts, the cognitive paradigm, particularly the work of Jean Piaget, stands up to these tests of scientific worthiness.

On the question of testability, cognitive theories are among the most tested and verified of personality theories considered in this book. After the introduction of Piaget's theory in the United States in the 1950s and 1960s, a flurry of Piagetian replication studies were launched. Interestingly, between 1969 and 1972, more than 20 percent of the articles in the journal *Developmental Psychology* cited books written by or about Piaget. Add to this the less formal but still impressive fact that nearly every first-year college student of developmental psychology has replicated Piaget's research. This is because of the reliability and predictability of the results that are obtained when doing Piaget's experiments. Such predictability enables college professors to use these experiments to help students understand the nature of cognitive development firsthand. On balance, cognitive theories are far more testable than are the theories of Freud or Erickson, though less testable than, say, Skinner or Bandura.

Piaget's theory of cognition has a high degree of external validity, meaning that it accurately and consistently explains human phenomena. Many of Piaget's concepts have become accepted facts. Object permanence, cognitive egocentrism, conservation, number concept, and hypothetical reasoning are all examples of Piagetian concepts that are readily accepted as valid by the vast majority of researchers and theorists.

In addition to high testability and high external validity, Piaget's research has high predictive validity, meaning that Piaget's theory can be used to predict human behavior. What will a child most likely do when his toy is hidden from view? Piaget's theory tells us. How will a six-year-old mentally process the death of a grandparent? Again, Piaget's theory can give us a likely prediction. From the classroom to the counselor's office, Piaget's theory has aided professionals in understanding and predicting human thinking and subsequent behavior. Cognitive theories offer us great insight into human beings because they so readily predict how people will process ideas, think about experiences, or behave in given situations.

Cognitive theories are internally consistent. This means that they are not self-contradictory. Cognitive theories hold together logically and retain a consistent application of fundamental assumptions.

Finally, cognitive theories rank high for theoretical economy. This is because they make only a few assumptions about people, seek to introduce a limited number of concepts and terms, and focus only on the role of cognition in personality development rather than try to explain all aspects of human beings. In other words, cognitive theories are among the simplest and most easily understood of the personality theories examined in this text. Albert Einstein once said of Piaget and his theory, "It's so simple that only a genius could have thought of it" (Papert 11).

Theological Compatibility

From a theological perspective, the cognitive paradigm is most easily harmonized with biblical teachings on human nature. Solomon wrote, "As he thinketh in his heart, so is he" (Prov. 23:7 KJV). Scripture teaches that our minds are the key linkage to our behavior. Wrong thinking can produce destructive actions. Speaking of the depravity of the human mind and its ability to impact behavior, Paul wrote of the linkage between thought and action. He indicates that a debased mind will produce debased behavior.

> Furthermore, since they did not think it worthwhile to retain the knowledge of God, he gave them over to a depraved mind, to do what ought not to be done. They have become filled with every kind of wickedness, evil, greed and depravity. They are full of envy, murder, strife, deceit and malice. They are gossips, slanderers, God-haters, insolent, arrogant and boastful; they invent ways of doing evil; they disobey their parents; they are senseless, faithless, heartless, ruthless. (Rom. 1:28–31)

Conversely, Paul says that a mind set on the things of God will free us to do the will of God. In Romans 8:5 he wrote, "Those who live according to the sinful nature have their minds set on what that nature desires; but those who live in accordance with the Spirit have their minds set on what the Spirit desires." Later in Romans, Paul wrote, "Do not conform any longer to the pattern of this world, but be transformed by the renewing of your mind. Then you will be able to test and approve what God's will is—his good, pleasing and perfect will" (Rom. 12:2). Clearly, Paul links mind and actions in each of these verses from his epistle to the Roman believers.

Again Paul indicated a belief that one's thoughts affect one's behavior. In his letter to the church at Philippi he wrote, "Finally, brothers, whatever is true, whatever is noble, whatever is right, whatever is pure, whatever is lovely, whatever is admirable—if anything is excellent or praiseworthy—think about such things" (Phil. 4:8).

PROBLEMS WITH THE COGNITIVE PARADIGM

It Has Received Some Scientific Criticisms

The work of Piaget and other cognitive theorists has been criticized through the years. Piaget's theory is criticized for underestimating the cognitive ability of young children, for describing the lower stages of cognitive thinking in terms of what children cannot do rather than what they can do, for overestimating the thinking capabilities of adolescents, for being culturally biased, and for the inaccuracy of his stages. Others have criticized the cognitive approach for being too simplistic and excessively focused on the role of the mind in human personality. Some would suggest that cognitive theories neglect the subjective aspects of human emotion, innate drives, and environmental influences. They would contend that simply telling people that a reconstruction of their thinking will resolve their problems ignores realities outside of the person's thought world. Such advice fails to help people understand that actions are based on factors other than our immediately retrievable thoughts.

Truth Can Become Personal, Rather Than Absolute

From a Christian perspective this is an important criticism of the cognitive paradigm. Cognitive theories rest on a constructivist view of the mind; thus, knowledge is understood to be an invention of the mind. In the cognitive-constructivist model, knowledge is seen as relativistic since knowledge is a constructed entity. Each person constructs his own understanding of the world that works and makes sense to him. Perception and organization of information within the individual is based on each person's own unique worldview. Knowledge differs with time, space, and circumstance and, therefore, cannot be held to be absolute for all time, all people, and all places. This goes against the Christian contention that truth exists apart from the perceiver of truth. Christians would insist that God is the Author of truth and truth is external to the individual. People discover truth; they do not create it. Although our perceptions of the truth may be limited and fallible, truth itself does exist distinct from those doing the perceiving. Although our construction of truth may indeed be personal and inaccurate at points, Christians would say that absolute truth exists despite our inability to apprehend it absolutely.

Morality Can Become Individual, Rather Than Universal

Because cognitive theorists see truth as relativistic, so too must they see morality as relativistic. They would contend that moral codes are created by human beings as an outgrowth of their construction of the truth. My personal moral code reflects my understanding of reality. Because each person has a differing construction of knowledge, each person has a different moral code or basis for moral choices. Morality is seen as a mental construct and not as something independent of the individual. We can pass along moral thoughts as we do any other thought, but cognitivists would contend that each individual must establish his own code based upon the way in which he constructs his understanding of the world. Christians believe that morality is not rooted in our mental constructs, but in the character of an unchanging God. Morality is an extension of God's nature. Although application of that moral code requires discernment and careful, logical thought, there is a morally correct answer to every situation, and that is the action that is consistent with the character and will of God. Our problem is one of discernment, not one of moral relativism.

CONTRIBUTIONS OF THE COGNITIVE PARADIGM

The contributions of the cognitive paradigm are many. We will focus on three major contributions in this segment of the text.

Recognition of the Role of Cognition

Although it is true that other theories have recognized the importance of cognition in the formation of human personality, they have not made it the central focal point. This emphasis on the role of cognition is certainly one of the contributions of the cognitive view. The cognitive paradigm has a number of properties that distinguish it from the other paradigms examined in the previous chapters of this book. First, it is a constructivist model of human personality. As such, it views individuals as actively involved in organizing and structuring their own personality as they create their personal understanding of the world. Second, it is developmental in nature. This approach sees human beings as progressing from less adaptive to more adaptive stages of development. People develop dysfunctional personality characteristics as a process and, likewise, resolve problems as a process. And third, this approach sees faulty choices as the primary backdrop or cause of personality problems. Since knowledge is constructed by the individual and is adapted to individual experience, the individual invents his or her own understanding of the world. Because this is the case, the individual's perspective can become colored or skewed by misunderstandings. Therefore, counseling assists persons in rethinking their worldview. By bringing thoughts more in line with reality, people can reorder life by thinking in more accurate and effective ways.

Cognitive-paradigm-oriented counselors tend to reject the behavioral treatments that simply reduce therapy to the extinction of undesired behaviors and the acquisition of alternative, more desirable behaviors. Likewise, they reject the notion that counseling is simply a quest toward self-knowledge and personal satisfaction. Cognitive paradigm proponents are committed to the concept of transformation of the individual over time, as a gradual process, by restructuring one's thoughts and worldview. In this manner, it is contended, real change occurs. This kind of change matches reality and permeates the entire personality of the individual. The key is a transformed mind. Cognitive theorists believe that transformation of the mind will lead to transformation of experience.

Counseling Theory and Techniques

One of the major contributions of the cognitive paradigm is found in the counseling theories and techniques it has spawned. We have already mentioned Adler's four-step approach. Others have suggested therapies based on the cognitive paradigm. George Kelly (*Personal Constructs*) proposed a method of treatment that involves a "reconstruction" of people's mental templates through which they organize and act upon life experiences. This process involves aiding people in reinterpretations of their world and personal life events.

Albert Ellis ("Personality") proposed a counseling approach called *REBT* (rational emotive behavior therapy). REBT involves aiding a person in considering perceptions, feelings, thoughts, and behaviors toward a given problem and then recasting these in light of the individual's value system.

Aaron Beck (*Cognitive Therapy*) devised a therapy approach he calls *cognitive therapy*. Beck's premise is simple. He believes that how one thinks largely determines how one feels and behaves. Beck believes that an individual's personality is the result of the person's cognitive organization and structure, which is the result of both biological and social influences. Beck recognizes the role of biochemical and neurological factors in shaping human beings as well. He sees these as constraints to personality development and sometimes the basis for a predisposition to certain psychological problems, but he also sees one's chosen cognitive perspectives as equally, if not predominantly, involved in forming personality. His approach involves helping people see that errors of logic make people victims of cognitive distortions.

Robert Kegan (*Evolving Self*) proposed what he calls *natural therapy*. Natural therapy is an approach to counseling that is rooted in the work of Piaget. Kegan introduced a five-stage process of counseling that seeks to restructure people's thinking about their problems. Kegan attempts to aid clients in seeing their problems as opportunities for growth disguised as problems. By helping the client see the problem as a means to growth, the counselor enables the client to move through the difficulty rather than simply try to solve or remove it. Kegan sees problems as inevitable in life and, therefore, as the very stuff out of which character is developed. By giving support and perspective to clients going through disequilibrating situations, counselors enable individuals to see purpose, and even personal gain, in the difficulty. Problems are a natural process that actually produce a more mature and competent person.

Application to Education

The contributions of the cognitive paradigm have extended beyond the realm of counseling. Piaget and the constructivist ideology have had an unparalleled impact on education. In education this paradigm is termed *progressive education*. The progressive educator views the child as a scientist-philosopher who seeks to make sense out of the world and his experiences. Progressives maintain that logical reasoning and problem-solving abilities develop as a result of cognitive struggles within the student. By wrestling with cognitive problems, students gain cognitive skills. Progressives seek to train students how to think, not just tell them what to think. In so doing, they believe they can promote cognitive growth and development. With this growth comes the capability of improved logic and more value-driven moral judgments. When viewed from a Christian perspective, critical thinking is an important skill, but not at the expense of truth. It is dangerous if students are allowed to create their own values without a basis in true issues of right and wrong.

Educators who attempt to apply the cognitive paradigm, especially the work of Piaget, to the classroom typically include methods that promote student involvement, discussion, research, and experience rather than just didactic instruction. Students are encouraged to become inquirers, questioners, and investigators of truth, rather than simply receptacles of facts. Instructional content is not avoided in teaching, but is matched to the student's maturation level. Learning is as concrete as possible for children, moving toward greater abstraction in teaching youth and adults. Teachers help students construct knowledge by giving feedback and by creating learning problems that students must consider and solve.

Of course there is a risk in a wholesale application of Piaget's student-centered approach. The risk is one of minimizing both the teaching of truth and the authority of the teacher. Piaget is correct that critical thinking is important to learning and that children, adolescents, and adults are not merely data-storage devices. The mind is to be active in learning, but we must also remember that truth is not created by the individual; it is discovered. Truth exists separate from people, and facts do matter. Ultimately, the aim of education is the application of truth to life in a way that transforms both the student and society.

Where Do We Go From Here

We come now to a pivotal point in our text. In chapters 1 through 3, we identified a biblical and theological perspective on human personality. In chapters 4 through 8, we have considered scientific theories and research into human personality. At this juncture we turn to more practical matters. We seek now to present an approach to counseling that we believe is informed by both science and theology. It is an approach that seeks to place Scripture squarely at the core of counseling ministry. But in reality, we would prefer to coin a new term for this approach, one that recognizes the authority of the Scriptures in counseling and the spiritual nature of human beings.

In the chapters that follow, we will introduce you to an approach to people care that we will usually call spiritual counsel. By this we do not mean to compartmentalize people into only the spiritual domain. Instead, we are referring to a total-person approach to people-helping ministry that recognizes the fact that human beings are indeed spiritual beings, not just material. In selecting this terminology we hope to move away from "biblical counseling versus Christian counseling" word wars. Frankly, we are convinced that a Christian worldview offers a unique dynamic to those who seek to help others who are dealing with an array of human problems and challenges. By embracing the Bible as authority, we do not fear psychological research, but neither do we believe it has the ultimate answers to human needs. We believe that the practice of providing spiritual counsel is an appropriate ministry with a rich heritage. It speaks of ministering the grace of God to people in the midst of life struggles.

We are targeting persons who may not themselves be professional counselors, psychologists, or psychiatrists. We believe there is a valuable place for these professionals and are definitely not on a campaign to attack or demonize any who help people using the techniques of modern social science. In fact, we are grateful for their good efforts to serve persons in need. It is true that we may not always agree with their approaches, but we want to debate those matters with charity as we recognize our common people-helping goals. Both of us have been pastors, and we know from experience the benefits that modern social science research can bring to the lives of people God has called us to serve. So then, our focus is on pastors, Christian laypersons, teachers, those involved in discipleship ministry, and those who simply want to help a friend.

We propose, in the coming section of this book, a simple approach that we believe will help many people. As you read on in this book, you will see that this approach is heavily influenced by the cognitive paradigm that we presented in this chapter. In fact, the people-helping steps we present come very close to the four-step process proposed by Alfred Adler (table 8-1). We do not claim that our approach is derived from Scripture, but we do believe that it is consistent with the principles of Scripture. We invite you now to consider "The Practice of Spiritual Counsel."

TABLE 8–1

A Comparison of Adler's Approach to Counseling and the Spiritual Counsel Model

Adler's Approach to Counseling	Spiritual Counsel Model
Relate (Build a caring relationship with the client.)	*Involvement* (Build a caring relationship with the person you are mentoring.)
Explore (Collect background information on the client in order to aid in discovering the nature of the problem.)	*Investigation* (Collect background information on the person you are offering counsel in order to aid in discovering the nature of the problem.)
Insight (Support the client in discovering the real nature of the problem.)	*Identification* (Support the person you are counseling by helping him or her identify the real nature of the problem.)
Restore (Assist the client in developing realistic action plans that will begin and lead to a restoration of mental health.)	*Initiation* (Assist the person you are giving counsel by developing realistic action plans that will begin and lead to spiritual health.)

NOTES

Ansbacher, H. L., and R. R. Ansbacher. *The Individual Psychology of Alfred Adler.* New York: Basic, 1956.

Beck, A. T., and G. Emory. *Cognitive Therapy of Anxiety and Phobic Disorders.* Philadelphia: Center for Cognitive Therapy, 1979.

Boeree, C. George. *Alfred Adler.* 1997. 1 Oct. 1999 <http://www.ship.edu/~cgboeree/adler.html>.

———. *Jean Piaget* 1999. 14 Jan. 2000 <http://www.ship.edu/~cgboeree/piaget.html>.

Cloninger, Susan C. *Personality: Description, Dynamics Development.* New York: W.H. Freeman and Company, 1996.

Ellis, Albert. "Toward a Theory of Personality." *Readings in Current Personality Theories.* Ed. R. J. Corsini. Itasca, Ill..: Reacock, 1978.

Kegan, R. *The Evolving Self.* Cambridge, Ma.: Harvard Univ., 1982.

Kelly, G. A. *The Psychology of Personal Constructs.* 2 vols. New York: Norton, 1955.

Papert, Seymour. "Time 100: Child Psychology" *Time Inc.* 3 March 1999.

— *Part Two* —

THE PRACTICE
OF SPIRITUAL
COUNSEL

— Chapter 9 —

SPIRITUAL COUNSEL:
The Care and Cure of Souls

Pastor Jim Starr was moving into the second year of his ministry at Faith Community Church. The congregation he inherited was small in comparison to many other churches in his area, but Jim's faithfulness to biblical preaching and the hard work of his one hundred members caused the church to grow faster than he had ever dreamed during that first year. Increasingly Faith Church's facility was being overtaxed. It was one of those problems that the young minister didn't mind having.

What did bother Pastor Jim more than anything else was the fact that more and more people were contacting him about personal problems they were facing as individuals and families. Even one of his deacons, Tom Green, came with his wife to ask for help to deal with conflicts they were having in their marriage. Then there were people like the Joneses, a two-income family that was just making enough money to get by. Their son seemed to be continually having academic and behavioral problems in school. Mary Jones reported that she was often depressed and didn't want to go to work on most days. Her husband, Ralph, was getting more and more frustrated with all that his wife and son were experiencing. Pastor Starr thought about referring them to a nearby Christian counseling center, but he was almost positive that they would not be able to pay the fees for what seemed to him to be a need for long-term counseling.

Pastor Jim had been a diligent student of theology during his Bible college and seminary days. He was also a good preacher. His classmates and college professors had voted him the best preacher in his graduating class. Oh yes, he had taken the basic classes in pastoral theology and counseling, but he never planned to do much counseling once he got into the actual work of ministry. Yet here he was at Faith Church and the problems of people paraded in and out of his office almost every day. He complained to his wife about what was going on, but Jim could never bring himself to tell people to go elsewhere for help. He believed that in many of the counseling situations he faced, people were dealing primarily with matters of knowing and obeying what God's Word taught. He wondered why people didn't simply go out and live what God said in His Word, especially when he tried to make his preaching so applicable to life.

One day after counseling a young man who came to his office, Jim was evaluating what was happening in his ministry. He was convinced that God wanted him to preach and teach the Scriptures. After all, 2 Timothy 4:1–2 was clear that pastors should preach the Word. Other passages of Scripture that he reviewed seemed to confirm this same conclusion. And yet his preaching alone did not seem to alleviate the problems that people wrestled with day in and day out. And if counseling was financially prohibitive to some people in his congregation, who would be available to help these parishioners to grow in Christian maturity?

Pastor Jim Starr decided to talk with his elders at the June board meeting. He informed Ed Smith, the elder board chairman, not to put too many things on the monthly agenda. He wanted the elders to prayerfully consider all that their growing church was facing with respect to this issue of pastoral care. When Ed deferred to Jim, the young pastor started by admitting that he didn't have immediate answers for what he was about to introduce to his fellow elders. But he was convinced that God had something in store for them with respect to the way they were going to do ministry in the future.

Jim explained how his counseling ministry was growing even as the size of the congregation grew. He admitted that he didn't want to turn people away, and yet he wasn't sure how to care for all of the needs of the congregation. He then reminded the elders of some things that they had all affirmed when Jim Starr first came to Faith Church. They had all agreed that the ministry belonged to every believer in the church, not just to the pastor. He also noted that their mission statement and their doctrinal commitments affirmed that life at Faith Church was to be lived out under the authority of God's Word. Jim went on to note that he was impressed with what he had been reading in the Scriptures recently. He reminded them that many of the New Testament letters were written against a background of personal and corporate challenges. Jim assured the elders that he was committed to preaching and teaching the Word of God, but he was even more convinced that people experienced change and spiritual growth through the everyday challenges of life.

It was at that point that Jim Starr took a deep breath. Slowly looking at those men he had grown to love, he spoke very deliberately. "Men, we need to work together on this issue of caring for the flock. I simply cannot do it alone any longer. I am growing tired and even becoming weary with the work of ministry. I don't think that God is pleased with my situation. In fact, I have learned some things from reading the words of Jethro to Moses in Exodus 18. We all know we all have responsibility in caring for the needs of our people, according to 1 Peter 5. So I have decided that I need to devote myself to equipping our elder board, as well as some key people in our congregation, to help me in this task of pastoral care."

Ed Smith held up his hand to gently interrupt what his pastor was saying. "Jim, I agree with what you just communicated. In fact, some of us around this table have been talking about how overworked you seem to be recently. We have talked among ourselves about hiring another staff member. Have you considered this option?"

Pastor Jim nodded that he had. He quickly returned to expressing what was at the forefront of his thinking. "Yes, Ed, I think another staff member could help us. But we need to think about what that person would do. We have needs with the youth, and you and I discussed several months ago the possibility of hiring someone to serve as a worship leader. Whatever we do with staff should not deter us from thinking about involving the elders and other key church leaders in doing pastoral care." Jim went on to cite key texts from Acts 20, 1 Timothy 5, and Titus 1 to substantiate what he had been saying to the elders. All of his elders sat in rapt attention.

Once again Pastor Jim was interrupted with a raised hand at the other end of the table. It was Elliot Bergman, the senior elder within the church leadership team. "Pastor Jim, I don't disagree with where I think you are headed. Maybe you are going to answer this question, but I have a concern about how we are supposed to do pastoral care. You mention all of the people who need counseling in our congregation. Are you suggesting that the elders should become counselors?" Three of the other elders nodded their heads in agreement with Elliot's question.

Jim Starr paused momentarily, then he continued. "Elliot, you raise a good question. My study in God's Word and the reading I have done in the last couple of weeks lead me to answer with a resounding yes. But I think we become apprehensive when we use a term like *counseling*. Let me suggest another expression. It seems to me . . ." Jim paused and spoke more deliberately at this point. "It seems to me that we need to function as elders who carry out the work of providing spiritual counsel. Down through the history of the church you will find individuals who were singled out to provide spiritual wisdom, men and women who came alongside other people in their times of discouragement, confusion, and doubt to help them find God's will for their lives. Some churches are beginning to refer to them as 'spiritual directors' to avoid the confusion of calling them 'counselors.' I am not suggesting that there isn't a place for trained counselors, but quite frankly some of our people can't afford counseling. And many of the problems our people are facing are issues that relate to wrong choices or wrong attitudes about life. What these people need are individuals who will come alongside them and minister to them out of their personal maturity and understanding of the Word of God. I propose that we as elders think seriously about being such people."

There was silence for several seconds. Finally Elliot Bergman spoke once again. "Pastor, I am intrigued about what you are saying about spiritual counsel. Yes, the word *counseling* does scare me just a little bit. But I would still like to have some more information and certainly some training before I tried to minister to people with problems. Can you tell us more?"

Jim thought to himself, *These guys are more receptive than I thought they would be.* He shifted in his chair and drew another deep breath. "Elliot, I'm glad you asked. I wish I could be more specific. But when I started to put some things together for tonight's meeting I had to put them aside so that I could meet with people from the burgeoning counseling load I told you about. If you give me some time between now and our next elders' meeting, I will have some things ready that should answer your questions and concerns." The elders once more nodded in agreement. Jim sensed that they were headed in the right direction. And for a change he felt that perhaps there was a glimmer of hope in dealing with the issue of pastoral care in his church. He quickly reminded himself that he wanted to use the phrase "pastoral care" less often and the phrase "spiritual counsel" more and more, so that he wouldn't intimidate his leaders into thinking they had to be professional therapists or ordained pastors.

A BRIEF HISTORY OF PASTORAL CARE

Is Pastor Jim Starr naive? Should he ever really plan to get other people involved in caring for the needs of people? Why is it that the church and its leaders are resigned to delegating problems to people outside of the local church and its redemptive community?

Pastors raise these issues all of the time. In fact, we have been motivated to write this book because of two practical concerns. First, we realize that many pastors are in the situation portrayed in the ministry of Pastor Jim Starr. They are overwhelmed by ministry needs and don't know what to do. They are not necessarily "anticounseling," but they realize there are barriers to getting so-called professional help for many of their parishioners. They are also motivated in getting all the saints involved in doing works of service (Eph. 4:11–16). We affirm this important biblical goal.

Second, we are motivated by a desire to give basic training in helping Christians, especially pastors and church leaders, care for other Christians facing spiritual and emotional problems in their lives. However, we are also aware of the fact that many of our training institutions do not prepare pastors for the everyday work of caring for people in need. Training in "counseling" is often reserved for those who enroll in specialized degree programs. These students generally plan to enter private practice in marriage and family therapy or some phase of clinical counseling. Instead of becoming staff members in local churches, they join private counseling practices or serve in some sort of community setting. But what about those who become pastors? If their training is primarily in biblical and theological studies, with a few courses thrown in related to preaching and pastoral management, what will they do when people come to them for help? We believe there is a need for training that is concise and effective in meeting the needs of people in our churches.

The reader should not assume that the steps that are outlined in the following chapters will eliminate all human emotional and spiritual problems. There will always be a need for compassionate, well-trained specialists. But church leaders can be more effectively equipped to help people in their time of need. Pastors can also feel more confident about their caregiving skills if they have biblical goals and simple paradigms to follow. We will articulate one paradigm for ministry care in this book, even though we realize it is only one possible approach to helping people.

The return of the ministry to all believers is not a new approach at all. For years leaders in the church renewal movement have been advocating training people to serve Christ and the church. Christian leaders like Gary Collins and Siang-Yang Tan have contributed significantly to the work of training others for this task (Collins

17–28; Tan 82ff.). But the assumption is that caregiving has to focus primarily on psychological issues. This was not always the case when it came to pastoral ministry.

The Bible teaches us that caring for the needs of people is the responsibility of the entire congregation. Paul wrote to the Thessalonians and exhorted them to "warn those who are idle, encourage the timid, help the weak, be patient with everyone" (1 Thess. 5:14). Ministry was not isolated to a handful of theological or psychological experts. Every believer was responsible for ministering to other believers as problems occurred in the community of faith. The text of 1 Thessalonians 5:14 indicates that people were wrestling with laziness, grief, enslavement to besetting sins, and interpersonal conflict (Thomas 289–90). Yet it was the responsibility of the entire body of believers to minister to these personal issues.

The classic text dealing with the ministry of all the saints is found in Ephesians 4:11–12. Speaking of Christ's ascension, the apostle Paul wrote, "And He gave some as apostles, and some as evangelists, and some as pastors and teachers, for the equipping of the saints for the work of service, to the building up of the body of Christ" (NASB). Notice that some were identified with a task that would, in turn, impact others in a positive way. The key word of the text is "equip." We often think of "equipping" as giving people the resources they need to get a specific task done. R. Paul Stevens in his book *Liberating the Laity* helps us to understand the history of this word as it relates to ministry in the local church. Three metaphors related to the term help us to understand what ministry and caring is all about. He wrote:

> Though *katartismos* ("equipping," "preparing") occurs in the New Testament only once (Eph 4:12), the word has an interesting history as a medical term in classical Greek. A Greek doctor would "equip" a body by putting a bone back into its correct relationship with the other members of the body. By reducing a fracture or realigning a dislocated limb, the doctor "equipped" the patient. The task of an equipping minister is to see that members of Christ's body who are in a broken relationship or are wrongfully connected to the body become correctly related. (111)

Again he wrote:

The equipper is also like a fisherman mending his nets in preparation for another night's work. This is the literal use of the verb
katartizō. James and John "were in a boat with their father
Zebedee, preparing [*katartizontas*] their nets" (Mt 4:21). This literal use of the verb *katartizō* has the double meaning of undoing the harm and damage done by previous service and preparing
the nets for further service. (113)

Stevens portrayed a third image related to "equipping" in this way:

Another meaning of *karatizo* is to create or to form. It suggests
the image of a potter fashioning clay. In Romans 9:22, Paul speaks
of objects prepared (*katertismena*) for destruction and compares
these with objects prepared for glory. In the letter to the Hebrews
we read, "A body you prepared [*katertisō*] for me" (Heb 10:5). After believers have experienced some suffering, God "will himself restore you [*katartisei*] and make you strong, firm and
steadfast" (1 Pet 5:10).

Equipping is building into people what they need to function
effectively as servants of God in the church and in the world. This
is God's work in which we have a share. And such molding by
God takes place primarily when people are steeped in the Word
of God "so that the man of God may be thoroughly equipped
for every good work" (2 Tim 3:17). (Stevens, 117)

It is important to see in all of these images that people were
called of God to care for others. Some members of the body of
Christ were to be given to the church to prepare others for ministry. And this ministry took place in the context of everyday challenges. But as people ministered to people, spiritual maturity
occurred. And this ministry was itself a kind of spiritual formation.
People were fashioned to become what God wanted them to be.
Interpersonal conflicts and human heartache were to become the
training labs for people to become more and more like Jesus Christ.
ᶜ ᶜh was the biblical model.

As the church grew and became a major spiritual and social force in history, spiritual formation continued as one of the primary tasks of the church. However, the concept of all believers serving as ministers was relegated to a more professional role for doing pastoral care. Pastors taught the Scriptures and cared for needs as they arose in the congregation. The pastor was viewed as one who was available to give counsel and care for people in times of need. Thomas Oden in his book *Classical Pastoral Care* referred to pastors in the early church as individuals who engaged in what he refers to as "soul care." He likened their work to that of a physician. Oden wrote:

> Soul care is both like and unlike bodily care. The pastoral writers often struggled with analogies between medicine and ministry. They asked how the soul's peculiar diseases were to be diagnosed, how malaises were to be recognized at early stages, how treated without eliciting further complications, and restored to soundness. In all these ways pastoral counsel is similar to medicine, surgery, and physical therapy, even though certain differences are obvious. (52)

Oden complemented the medical metaphor with yet another image of soul care. He wrote:

> The physician metaphor is not complete without the complementary metaphor of guidance. For even one who is well needs a guide through hazardous territory. The soul needs not only a physician for sickness, but a guide through dangerous terrain. In the background of this metaphor is the hazard of the high mountain, the danger of the dark forest, the confusion of the trackless desert, the clamor of the distant city where one does not know the language. To be there without a guide is folly. These are the situations to which the soul's journey is analogous. (58)

He went on to cite such writers as Clement of Alexandria, Augustine, and Origen to substantiate the fact that ministry to people in need was viewed as soul care. And the primary medicine and guidance for weary souls was the Word of God. What is important for the reader to understand is that pastors saw themselves primarily as caretakers of the soul. They provided spiritual formation for people who struggled with life as they encountered it.

Soul care, as we have described it from a New Testament perspective and from the writings of the church fathers, took a dramatic turn by the time the church entered the twentieth century. David Powlison affirmed that the clergy envisioned the cure of souls as the primary means of pastoral care in colonial America. The aim was to overcome sinful temptations and sinful resolves with biblical truth. But the twentieth century seemed to give greater credence to the role of the psychological in religious life. Powlison wrote:

> The "therapeutic" was triumphant. Psychiatry and psychotherapy displaced the cure of souls, reifying the medical metaphor, and so ordaining "secular pastoral workers to take up the task." Emotional and behavioral ills of the soul that once registered dislocations in a moral agent's relationships to God and neighbor were re-envisioned as symptomatic of a patient's mental and emotional illness. Worry, grumbling, unbelief, lovelessness, strife, vicious habit, and deceit came to be seen through different eyes, as neurotic anxiety, depression, inferiority complex, alienation, social maladjustment, addiction, and unconscious ego defense. Hospital, clinic, and office displaced church and community as the locus of cure. (*Competent* 41–42)

As we noted in the first half of this book, knowledge of secular studies is part of the process of learning to subdue the world. But the movement to make soul care a "professional matter" has robbed the church of its important task of equipping the saints to do the work of ministry. Consequently the problems and challenges that people face are referred to sources outside of the church. We would affirm that there is a place for professional counseling. But what about those people whom Pastor Jim Starr meets with all too frequently? And what about those who cannot afford "professional counseling"? We would suggest that there is a need to reaffirm spiritual counsel as a primary task of the church, and a task done both by pastors and laypeople alike.

WHAT IS SPIRITUAL COUNSEL?

If giving spiritual counsel is part of the ministry of congregational care, and if every believer has a responsibility to carry it out in some way, then what is it? How are we to define it?

What will people like Jim Starr be doing when they care for souls through the ministry of spiritual counsel?

Frequently the concept of spiritual formation has been linked with such activities as theological reflection or Christian education, two important tasks indeed. But the New Testament portrays Christians as learning and growing through more informal, spontaneous experiences rather than highly structured programs aimed at spiritual growth. This is not to say that educational and discipleship programs in local churches are unnecessary. They are very important to the growth and maturity of believers. But the New Testament writers addressed people who were struggling with the frequent challenges of life.

The Corinthian church struggled with issues of pride and personality worship (1 Cor. 1:11–17), the revelation of sexual immorality among their membership (1 Cor. 5), and the threat of marital breakup (1 Cor. 7). It is also possible that the Ephesian believers wrestled with their own worth in the program of God (Eph. 2:11–22). The Thessalonian believers grieved over the loss of their loved ones (1 Thess. 4:13–18). And the apostle Peter had to minister spiritual truth in the context of unjust suffering (1 Peter 1:7; 4:12–13). The early church obviously had formal settings in which it interacted over the significance of apostolic revelation. But these first-century Christians learned what it meant to be a Christ-follower in the context of pain, heartache, and disappointment. In these settings spiritual counsel was given. From the New Testament perspective, ministry involved the whole person, not just the soul that needed salvation or the mind that needed educating.

This concept of total person care in the context of everyday experiences can be pictured as a journey of the soul. Frank Stanger, former pastor and educator, described it this way:

> Spiritual formation is a *journey*. It is a dynamic process, always taking place, always progressing toward a desired spiritual objective, always manifesting evidence of personal and relational achievement. The spiritual life is never static; we are alive in Christ. (16)

Stanger's view mirrors what the apostle Paul told the Colossians. He proclaimed Christ in the circumstance of his own suffering. Yet he had a larger goal in mind, the goal of ultimately presenting everyone "perfect in Christ" (Col. 1:28). Paul realized that they were not yet mature, but through ongoing personal encouragement (admonishing) and biblical instruction (teaching) the goal would ultimately be achieved.

Our family (the Shields) has taken a number of cross-country trips over the years. While living in Denver, Colorado, we often drove from our home to visit with family and friends back East. Our children were young at the time, and traveling for hours was not what they viewed as a family vacation. So we made frequent stops along the way. In the process we learned a lot about our own personal shortcomings and irritations as we rode the thousand-plus miles together. Parenting took place in a car, in hotel rooms, and over meals. We visited museums, state capitals, and amusement parks. Fun times were mixed with learning experiences. It was a journey, not a short flight to our destination.

Life is a journey as well, and those who manage the challenges along the way realize that personal growth takes place in both good times and bad times. Everyday situations became classrooms for personal and spiritual growth. And in the journeys of life, people grow best when someone can come alongside to help them understand what is going on around them. Pastors are frequently called upon to join confused and hurting people in life's journey. But other mature believers, whether they are professionally trained or not, can also serve as fellow travelers in the journey toward spiritual maturity.

Consider the following definition of what it means to participate in the ministry of giving spiritual counsel. *Spiritual counsel is that specific ministry of joining people in the various trials of life to help them experience the grace of Christ, which is revealed in the Word of God, administered by the Spirit of God, and communicated through the people of God.*

Several factors must be kept in mind as we understand and implement this definition. First, spiritual counsel is a process. It will encompass all of the years of our earthly existence from the time we come to faith until we enter into the very presence of Christ. Second, it takes place in both formal and informal settings, but for the sake of our study it will focus on maturing through the trials and difficulties that come to every individual (James 1:2). Third, spiritual counsel has as its primary goal becoming more Christlike in thinking and behavior. Those who engage in soul care are not simply concerned with eliminating unpleasant symptoms and circumstances. God wants us to become like Christ (Rom. 8:28–29). Fourth, the ministry of spiritual counsel relies primarily on the resources that God has graciously given to the church. The Word of God will be the primary source for wisdom as to how one can live in a godly and effective manner (Pss. 1:1–3; 119:105). Other information sources might inform the believer about life, but the Scriptures will have the final say in how one should think and act. And in addition, God's Word will be administered to people in need through the Spirit of God (1 Cor. 2:12).

Spiritual growth is not simply a matter of taking in information. The Christian life is an experience of growing in an intimate relationship with the triune God. And it is the Holy Spirit who teaches us the very mind of God (1 Cor. 2) and assures us that we are God's children (Rom. 8:14–16). At the same time, God uses mature people who care deeply about those who struggle with the challenges of life to encourage others to persevere in the will and ways of God (Gal. 6:1–2; James 5:19–20).

WHERE DO WE GO FROM HERE?

It is one thing to have a theory of soul care and spiritual formation, but it is altogether another thing to put it into practice.

If we believe that spiritual counsel is a process of helping people in the context of trials, how will it be done? We are not the first to suggest that the church needs to renew its efforts at raising up many who can participate in the work of pastoral care. David Powlison, a leader in the biblical counseling movement, put it this way:

> "Biblical counselor," however, is not primarily a professional occupation. Pastors and professional biblical counselors, those who have special training experience in applying the Scripture to life, may have been uniquely equipped by God to help with certain problems. However, they are not the ones who will meet the majority of the church's counseling needs. Instead, we call a friend on the phone and ask for prayer, we hear a sermon that changes us, we grow in faith when our small group comes over to help with a house project, we talk to a godly older person about parenting while we have a cup of coffee. ("Biblical Counseling" 4)

Likewise, Larry Crabb has been a strong advocate of returning the ministry of caring to the local church. In a recent interview Dr. Crabb challenged the church with these words:

> There will always be a place for good therapists. But what they are doing is closer to what the Bible calls "shepherding" than what our culture calls "therapy." And that has implications. I envision a community of shepherds and friends with the power to address the underlying issues beneath most of what we call "psychological problems." (38)

Whether one calls it "biblical counseling" or "shepherding," the goal should be the same. Believers are to help other believers in the various circumstances of life to grow in spiritual maturity. As we noted in chapter 2, this is the process of sanctification. It is God's work of changing us. There are a variety of suggestions as to how change will ultimately occur. Some theories advocate an inward investigation of past hurts and relational experiences. Others focus on practicing appropriate behavior and carefully controlled thinking. Common grace, as we noted earlier, has made it possible for people to discover nuggets of truth from a variety of life experiences. However, we are advocating the notion that change will occur as people are led to look at their troubling experiences from the perspective of God's Word. Other disciplines might inform our thinking as to how we can understand people more clearly. But God's revelation will be our primary information source.

WHO WILL LEAD IN GIVING SPIRITUAL COUNSEL?

We are now at a point where we need to ask, "What kind of person will be most effective in helping others in this life journey toward Christlikeness?" Many of us have sought out the counsel of another individual who we thought had wisdom and skill that could help us in those crucial decision-making experiences of life. For instance, a man asks a fellow employee for advice about taking a job transfer. A young mother struggling to keep her toddlers in check seeks insight from a woman who has grown children. A teenager stops by the youth pastor's office to chat about problems he is facing with his parents. All three individuals sought counsel from another individual. But why were these people sought out for wisdom? One might answer that it had to do with their experience, their position, or even their willingness to relate. All such answers are correct.

But if one chooses to be used of God in the process of spiritual counsel, certain qualities are important. Those who serve in local churches as pastors, elders, deacons, and ministry leaders would do well to think about how they can be more effective in their service to Christ and others. It is one thing to talk about improving the way that we do ministry and to focus on techniques of evangelism, discipleship, or pastoral care. But the Bible speaks of the issue of maturity as the primary prerequisite to effective service. Paul told both Timothy and Titus to appoint leaders in the church who demonstrated the development of Christlike character in their lives (1 Tim. 3:1–13; Titus 1:5–9). Spiritual counselors, therefore, need to think about caring for their own souls before they get heavily involved in the lives of others. We will have more to say about this in the epilogue.

There are three basic ingredients, however, that prospective spiritual counselors or spiritual directors will want to pursue if they are going to continually grow in Christlikeness and in the ability to minister to other struggling saints. (Keep in mind that we are assuming that these potential caregivers are born-again Christians.) These three ingredients are faith, hope, and love. You might dismiss this comment and suggest that these are spiritual terms that are impossible to clearly identify in any individual. But we believe that the more we know an individual the better we will be able to discern if such qualities do or do not exist in the person's life. We are *not* suggesting that faith, hope, and love are the only qualities of an effective caregiver, but they should be the primary ones. What is even more important to remember is that these qualities can be developed in the life of a person who takes seriously Christ's call to discipleship.

OK, but what do faith, hope, and love look like? First, *faith* is that quality in a believer's life whereby he or she exhibits increasing trust in God and His promises, no matter what challenges the individual might be facing personally. We see this in people like Abraham, whose growing faith was an example for other believers to emulate (Heb. 11:11–12). Here was a man who was promised an heir even when his wife was beyond childbearing age. Yet he trusted God, even through times of doubt, believing that God was true to His Word. And even after the child was born Abraham was again tested and asked to sacrifice his son on an altar. Apparently the great patriarch had matured in his faith, and he obeyed God—though he stopped short of killing his son when God stopped him—believing that God would do what was best, no matter what circumstances he might have to face.

This same kind of growing faith can be seen in people today as they battle debilitating diseases or unexpected challenges to their well-being. They do not constantly bemoan their fate or complain that God doesn't care about them. They trust in the goodness of God no matter what pain comes their way. I often think of a woman, the mother of five and a former missionary. It was an obvious shock to her when her husband abandoned her, the ministry they had developed together, and his children. The woman returned to one of the churches that had supported her financially over the years of missionary service. For the next several years she reared those children by herself, supported them with multiple jobs, and taught them to follow Christ. Surprisingly, she never spoke ill of her former husband. Most people who know her well view her as a woman of courage, wisdom, and . . . *faith*. Many young mothers called her on the phone or stopped by her office at work to simply chat about life. And what people most respect about her when she gives advice is that she trusts God deeply. In the same way a person who qualifies as a potential caregiver must be a person of faith.

Second, those who will eventually direct others in the ways of God, especially in times of trouble, must be people of *hope* and people who can generate hope. The word is closely associated with faith, but the emphasis is upon the way one views the future. People characterized by hope have a confident expectation about the future, believing that what is up ahead is so good that they are motivated to live Christlike lives in the present. While in prison, the apostle Paul wrote to the Philippian church to encourage them about some of their own unique challenges. Yet he did not live in fear of the circumstances of his imprisonment or possible death. If he died, he would depart and be with Christ. If he lived, he would continue to have fruitful service (Phil. 1:20–26). Paul was a man of *hope.*

In 1991 I (Harry) had the privilege of traveling to Eastern Europe soon after the collapse of the Soviet Union. During that visit I met a number of Christians in Bulgaria who ministered under some of the most difficult circumstances. In one community a young minister and his wife pastored a church of gypsies, people who were ostracized by the society at large. Yet this "outsider" came to minister to those who had been severely marginalized by their society. When asked about his motivations for such service under some very harsh conditions, he would smile and tell us it was Jesus, the One who promised him forgiveness and the hope of eternal life. What was ahead motivated the young pastor for what he did in the present.

I have a friend, Dr. Ken Nichols, who serves as a pastor, an educator, and a counselor. He has a ministry that was established several years ago and is identified by the acronym ALIVE. The letters stand for "Always Living In View of Eternity." When Dr. Nichols counsels with people, he frequently directs them to the believer's relationship with the living God and His promises. "Eternity" plays a crucial role in how he counsels people about their current problems. His is a ministry characterized by hope.

The third quality that characterizes the one who would qualify as a caregiver is the virtue of *love*. This quality is frequently used in the New Testament as the trait that is to distinguish the Christian before a watching world (John 13:34–35). Love might be defined as that action, grounded in the nature of God Himself and demonstrated by the death of Christ on the cross, whereby we seek God's best for another person.

One of the best examples of love as it relates to spiritual formation is portrayed in the ministry of a man by the name of Philemon. We don't know much of his life, other than the fact that he had been the owner of a runaway slave named Onesimus. During his intended escape, Onesimus met up with the apostle Paul and became a Christian. As a result, Paul was sending him back to his former owner and was asking Philemon to no longer receive him as a slave but as a brother in Christ (Philem. 16).

Imagine the struggle that must have gone on in Philemon's mind. Onesimus may have cheated his former master, even robbing him of valuable possessions (v. 18). Yet Paul was asking Philemon to nurture this man in true Christian love. Some church historians believe that nurture did take place and Onesimus became an outstanding leader in the church. If so, it was the result of one man choosing to minister in such a way as to bring about Christlikeness in another person.

People who are characterized by Christian love minister to others not because they feel like it, but because they choose to do so under the lordship of Christ (John 13:34–35). It is what happened in the life of a woman who lost her daughter to a murderous crime spree in Denver. She grieved the loss of her daughter and longed for justice to be done toward the man who ultimately confessed to the crime. Several years after the murder occurred the woman got involved in a project of supplying Bibles to prison inmates. She didn't realize that one of those Bibles was given to the man who had murdered her daughter. He read the Scriptures and became a Christian. It wasn't long until he asked if he could meet with her. After much thought she reluctantly agreed, and a meeting between the two was arranged. What took place defies human logic. The man asked her to forgive him for what he did. And, miracle of miracles, she did! And not only did she forgive him, but she also went on to provide other resource tools for this convict-turned-Christian that enabled him to grow in his life as a believer. Such actions exemplify the maturing quality of love.

It is important to note in describing these three basic qualities that a key part of the defining process has been the use of the word *maturing*. Christians who give spiritual counsel are not perfect, but they are growing—they are in the process of becoming more and more like Christ in the way they react to circumstances around them.

It is also important to notice that faith, hope, and love are basic ingredients to becoming an effective caregiver. They are not the only ingredients. In the chapters that follow we will point out some skills that one will need in order to best give guidance to those who are hurting. We need to know how to listen, how to interpret presenting problems from a biblical perspective, and how to guide people to make godly responses to the challenges they face. It goes without saying that those who help others will want to spend time in regular study of and meditation on the Word of God. They will also spend time in prayer for themselves and those they serve. But as they assist others in making sense out of life, they will be primarily characterized by a faith that demonstrates confidence in God and His Word, a hope that is motivated by eternal things, and a love that responds for the good of others.

— *Things to Ponder* —

Before moving on to the next chapter, reflect on the following questions:

1. After reading this chapter, describe the difference between "spiritual counsel" and what some would refer to as "counseling." Why would these distinctions be important?
2. What are the basic ingredients that characterize a "spiritual counselor" or "spiritual director"? Where do you see these qualities appearing in your own life? Where might they be lacking?
3. Write out a simple strategy describing how you will grow in faith, hope, and love, particularly as it relates to your knowledge of the Word of God.

NOTES

Collins, Gary. *How to Be a People-Helper.* Santa Ana, Calif.: Vision, 1976.

Crabb, Lawrence J., Jr. "Where Healing Begins." *Leadership* 18.2 (Spring 1997): 37–40.

Oden, Thomas C. *Pastoral Counsel.* Grand Rapids: Baker, 1987. Vol. 3 of *Classical Pastoral Care.*

Powlison, David A. "Competent to Counsel? The History of a Conservative Protestant Anti-Psychiatry Movement." Diss. Univ. of Pennsylvania, 1996.

———. "What Is Biblical Counseling, Anyway?" *Journal of Biblical Counseling* 16.1 (Fall 1997): 2–6.

Stanger, Frank Bateman. *Spiritual Formation in the Local Church.* Grand Rapids: Zondervan, 1989.

Stevens, R. Paul. *Liberating the Laity: Equipping All the Saints for Ministry.* Downers Grove, Ill.: InterVarsity, 1985.

Tan, Siang-Yang. *Lay Counseling: Equipping Christians for a Helping Ministry.* Grand Rapids: Zondervan, 1991.

Thomas, Robert L. *I and II Thessalonians.* Grand Rapids: Zondervan, 1978. Vol. 11 of *Expositor's Bible Commentary.* Ed. Frank E. Gaebelein.

— Chapter 10 —

The Process of Spiritual Counsel (Part One)

*J*im Starr was both elated and startled by the reaction of his elder board. He wasn't anticipating such enthusiastic support. He thought that the men who served as his partners in leading Faith Church would be more hesitant to assume pastoral care roles. But strong negative pressure never came. *Hallelujah!* he thought. But almost immediately he was pondering Elliot Bergman's question. How in the world would he teach them how to counsel? Oh yes, he reminded himself that he didn't want to scare his colleagues away by using the term *counseling.* He almost spoke out loud when he said to himself, *How will I teach them to give spiritual counsel?*

Jim looked at the stack of books to the right of his computer. He had already identified some chapters from an old seminary text in pastoral counseling that might be useful. There were three books from the local library that his secretary, Delores Smith, had checked out. Yet Jim didn't want to simply give his elders the labors of someone else's work, as good as it might be. He wanted any training he offered to the elders to be simple and arranged in such a way that these laymen could get a handle on what to do.

But where would he begin? What were his goals? What did he hope would be accomplished in the ministry of providing spiritual counsel?

Jim started to think about what he did when people called and asked for help. His thoughts seemed to freeze in midair. What did he do? And if he did anything valuable, why did it work? While still pondering a training program that he might present to the elders, Jim opened the file drawer behind him. He reached for the folder marked "counseling" and threw it on the desk. He chuckled as he thought about the label. If he was going to be consistent in his terminology, he would have to ask Delores to print another label. Yes, he would ask her to print it in all capitals, SPIRITUAL COUNSEL.

Jim looked through the notes he had collected on the increasing number of people who came for help. He was glad that no one else had access to this folder, especially his old seminary professor who taught the pastoral care courses. His notes seemed to make no sense, other than to remind himself what direction his various sessions had taken. There were notes about a couple who had come to see him on three different occasions. Another page summarized a conversation he had with a single man in the church who struggled with leaving his job at the post office to go back to school. Page after page had information, but Jim Starr couldn't make heads or tails as to the direction of his notes. If he was confused about what he was doing, how in the world could he train his leadership team? Yet the task of caring for this flock of believers was so important that he had to do something. He still had three weeks before the elders would meet again. Perhaps he would attend the conference on pastoral care issues that Tom Parkes, his friend and fellow pastor, had asked him to attend. Yes, that might give him some insight. Time was running out. He knew he had to try to register as soon as possible. He picked up the phone to see if he could still get on the list for the Monday training class.

WHAT'S A SPIRITUAL COUNSELOR TO DO?

As we noted in the last chapter, many pastoral training classes do not provide the hands-on experience that most pastors need to do the work of pastoral care and spiritual counsel. Yet pastors like Jim Starr increasingly find themselves having to deal with people's personal problems, problems common to all of humanity, including Christians. It is one thing to preach and teach the Word of God, but altogether another matter when sitting face-to-face with anxious people, depressed individuals, and people in conflict with members of their own family. In the previous chapter we indicated that spiritual counsel has as its goal moving people toward maturity in Jesus Christ (Col. 1:28–29). But how do we do that? If those who provide spiritual counsel are to go beyond Jim Starr's procedure of taking notes on the events and conversations of any given session, what will that mean?

Starting Point 1: Pastoral Care Issues Are Not All the Same

My (Harry's) son used to enjoy putting puzzles together. From the time he was four until he was about seven he was given a lot of puzzles as gifts. He played with them for several hours almost every day. Sometimes the puzzle pieces were all over his bedroom floor. So when bedtime arrived my wife or I would ask him to pick up the pieces and make his room as neat as possible. As a young child his idea of neatness was not the same as his father's. Nevertheless, he would quickly pick up the puzzles and throw them into a plastic box he kept near his other toys. That meant the pieces from several different puzzles were all mixed together. So if he wanted to play with them the next day he would have to go through the box and sort out each piece according to the puzzle to which it belonged. I used to enjoy watching him arrange all the pieces in specific groups he had formed throughout his bedroom. It took him some time to sort through all of the pieces, but he had learned that if he was to make sense out of all that was in that box, he would have to first gather the pieces according to the puzzles to which they belonged.

Helping people in times of difficulty is a lot like putting several puzzles together simultaneously. As a matter of fact, that is one of the reasons that hurting people come to pastors and other care-givers for help. They have difficulty making sense out of the pain that they are experiencing. The various events of their lives are like scattered pieces of a puzzle. Early on those events do not make sense. And if the caregiver is confused as to where to go next and what to do, then the problem is only intensified. That is why we not only want to talk about various theories of personality devel-opment, but we want to provide a way that spiritual counselors or spiritual directors can think through the process of caring for hurting people. We want to give a picture, so to speak, of how spir-itual counsel might begin and how it might continue toward the goal of helping someone become mature in Jesus Christ. And to get started we need to realize that not all "problem pieces" are part of the same "puzzle."

It is important to keep in mind that problems come to Chris-tians in a variety of different forms. The apostle James wanted to remind his first-century readers that trials would appear in dif-ferent ways, what he referred to as "trials of many kinds" (James 1:2). The principle is still true today. Some people face financial challenges. Others are frequently confronted with fears about their health, their children, or their future. Some face the tragedy of relationships that have been terminated by divorce or death. But no two individuals in a given church face the exact same trials.

To amplify the problem even more, we can categorize the prob-lems that people face by observing that they are either problems that occur as *crisis events* or problems that increase in intensity with the passing of time, what we will refer to as *spiritual/emotional* trials. When we speak of crisis events we are referring to situa-tions that occur suddenly without any warning. They tend to up-set the normal routines of life. And a crisis usually involves some loss, whether the loss is actual or perceived. Lee Ann Hoff de-fines a crisis as follows:

> Crisis refers to an acute emotional upset arising from situation-al, developmental, or social sources and results in a temporary in-ability to cope by means of one's usual problem-solving devices. A crisis does not last long and is self-limiting. (4)

316

Swihart and Richardson define a crisis as

the disequilibrium produced by a perceived threat or adjustment that we find difficult to handle. Here we emphasize "perceived," because if we think a crisis event is going to occur, we have a crisis whether or not the actual crisis event occurs. (16–17)

These two authors go on to concur with Hoff that a crisis ultimately involves a tremendous sense of loss.

Pastors and church leaders are no strangers to crisis events. In fact, they are some of the first ones called when circumstances parishioners face prohibit them from solving the events that come their way. It happens when the pastor receives word that a beloved church member has been killed in a car accident on the way home from work. The parishioner may have been the victim of another individual's carelessness in falling asleep at the wheel. But a grieving family must be comforted. They seem speechless, helpless, and unable to cope. They are obviously in a crisis.

On yet another occasion a pastor receives a call at 10:00 P.M., just about the time he is thinking about going to bed. The phone rings and the message at the other end of the line comes from a familiar voice. The woman informs the pastor that she is at the home of her sister, and she wants to know if he can come as soon as possible. She doesn't say much other than the fact that her sister's husband has just walked out leaving divorce papers on the kitchen table. The pastor agrees to come, but he does not know what he will encounter once on the scene. If he is sure of anything, he knows that a crisis-care situation is just up ahead.

Crises happen to individuals, families, and even organizations. They occur when the sexual misconduct of a husband and father is exposed. They happen in times of death, the discovery of a terminal illness, and the breakup of what appeared to be a stable family. Crises are common to life, and, therefore, they are common to the ministry endeavors of the church. But as Hoff's definition indicates, crises are often short-lived. People regain their ability to cope and move on.

We could spend the remainder of this book talking about crisis care and all of the dynamics associated with the sudden, unexpected traumas of life. But we have elected to talk about the second type of pastoral care issue cited above, the matter of *spiritual/emotional problems.* They are different from crises in that the person facing such problems still has the ability to cope and carry on normal day-to-day activities. However, the problems affect relationships negatively and often may be accompanied by other symptoms such as mild to severe depression, anxiety, and abnormal fear. There may also be physical changes as well—loss of weight, sleeplessness, stomach ulcers, and a host of other features. But two things stand out. The person's spiritual health is usually affected in some way. God seems distant or insignificant from the perspective of people seeking help. What they frequently want from the church is relief, and the sooner the better. And when they talk of their feelings they are anything but positive. Thus we refer to the issues they bring to pastors and lay caregivers as *spiritual/emotional problems.* What these people need is spiritual counsel. And for those who will provide such care, it will be important to determine whether one is dealing with a crisis or a *spiritual/emotional* challenge.

Starting Point 2: Looking Beyond the Problems of Fallenness

Those of us who spend time in God's Word preparing to teach, preach, and evangelize often develop a one-dimensional view of people and problems. We reflect on passages like Romans 3:23 and remind ourselves that "all have sinned and fall short of the glory of God." Pastors like Jim Starr all too frequently encounter people who are discouraged, depressed, and guilt-ridden because of bad decisions that they have made. Christian spouses sometimes cheat on their mates. Believing employees take items from their place of employment. And then they wonder why they are guilt-ridden and unable to sleep. It is possible that medication might increase their ability to sleep and redirect their thought life. But it is safe to say that sin is the chief cause behind the emotional discomfort. But is every symptom of anxiety, depression, fear, or anger a mark of some unconfessed sin?

Christian caregivers must be careful not to quickly diagnose every emotional trauma as "sin." We live in a sinful, fallen world. Everything in the world has been corrupted by sin's impact on the world (Gen. 3:14–19; Rom. 8:19–21). However, that does not mean that every problem is the direct result of some sinful choice that we make as human beings. Some symptoms that we might classify as spiritual or emotional trials can be caused by physical problems that a person is facing. How the person thinks, feels, and behaves results more from a malfunction of physiology than from a problem in the soul. As we pointed out in the first half of the book, it is important to look at human beings from the perspective of unity, rather than trying to make precise distinctions between body, soul, and spirit. When it comes to helping people find spiritual direction, we must be careful to realize that sinful choices are not the only causes behind an individual's emotional pain.

J. Kirk Johnston made a helpful observation about physical problems and their impact upon people's emotional states. He wrote:

> When a person has been receiving counseling or therapy and is not really making progress with his or her problem, the primary issue may not be spiritual or emotional, but physical. Some people go for a complete physical exam before they go to a counselor. Some counselors insist on a physical exam before they will begin counseling anyone. This is not always necessary, but counselors and counselees need to be open to the possibility that in any given situation the root problem could be physical. It is unfortunate that even today there are many Christians and some Christian counselors who refuse to acknowledge this possibility. Some Christian counselors and pastors still believe that all emotional difficulties are a direct result of personal sin. While I admire their willingness to accept sin as a frequent cause of emotional distress, I am concerned that these professionals may unnecessarily increase pain of hurting people instead of helping to relieve it. (18)

Those who write in the area of biblical counseling often use the term *organic* to describe emotional problems that are more

319

physically based than spiritually caused. Later we will discuss procedures that a caregiver can employ when interviewing people about their problems. One of the initial inquiries will be to find out what physical symptoms manifest themselves and how recently the troubled person has had a thorough medical check-up.

But what about the majority of people who enter a pastor's office or sit at the kitchen table of a Christian friend and pour out their problems? To say that sinful choices are the root cause of all such pain can sound simplistic, even though we affirm the severity and all-encompassing power of sin. People are often inclined to blame their parents, their teachers, and even their friends for the problems they experience. We stated earlier that the tragic events of Genesis 3 left all of human history in a spiritual quandary. Sin permeates all of life. However, that does not leave us without responsibility in a fallen world. According to the Genesis record, human beings were created in the image of God. We are vice-regents with God in the world He created and in which He placed us. However, the sinful choice to live independently from God affected all that man was to do, including one's spiritual, emotional, and physical existence (Gen. 3:14–19).

The biblical record consistently portrays God revealing the path to life and blessing. Yet His revelation is followed by the human propensity to live apart from God. Israel was led out of bondage by the mighty hand of God, yet the people chose to complain about their unpleasant circumstances (Ex. 15:22–27). Even in their hardship God revealed to them the way of blessing. It was their choice whether to obey or pursue life on their own. Much of the Old Testament reveals this same pattern of God blessing, then revealing the way of life, followed by Israel's inclination to disobey. Sinful choices were the primary factor in the nation's spiritual and emotional decline. The New Testament reveals a similar pattern. Christ called His disciples to embrace the ways of "kingdom living." At the conclusion of the Sermon on the Mount, Jesus informed His disciples that His way is the way of stability in an unstable world. He makes no promises that life will be problem-free, but He does teach that His words are words of wisdom (Matt. 7:24–27). To obey Him is to find life and then to experience it in all its abundance (John 10:10).

The apostle Paul addressed similar themes when he spoke of living a life in the power of the indwelling Spirit. One can either choose to live independently from God, that is, to live according to one's own view of life, or one can live in the power of the Spirit (Rom. 8:12–17). The Bible gives ample evidence that the quality of our spiritual/emotional existence relates directly to the choices we make. This is not to deny that we are often subject to the choices that others make. An abusive father can bring great pain to his children, and that pain will influence the quality of their lives. People around us can be insensitive, controlling, dishonest, and extremely cruel. However, we also have responsibility for the choices we make that can enhance our spiritual and emotional well-being. Otherwise, why would a loving God call us to Himself and invite His redeemed people to enter into an option of obeying or disobeying His will?

It is important that spiritual counselors keep in mind that problems occur because of crisis circumstances, organic causes, and most often, sinful choices made by the person or someone else. What is interesting with respect to the care and nurturing of people who are in need is that they are not always aware of the sinful choices they are making. That is why simply telling a person that sin is the cause for his emotional discomfort may not be the most effective way of providing spiritual counsel. Very few of us respond to people who accuse us of wrongdoing when we ourselves have perfectly logical explanations for why we do what we do. Even those who have been Christians for a long period of time do not immediately see the sinfulness of their ways. They think that going to church or Sunday school has somehow tamed their sinful tendencies for the rest of the week. So to identify a spiritual/emotional dilemma as having a sin-rooted cause may seem highly offensive, especially to the person seeking help.

Why is this the case? Larry Crabb made the following observation:

> Preachers and counselors can spend their energy exhorting people to change their behavior. But the human will is not a free entity. It is bound to a person's understanding. People will do

321

what they believe. Rather than making a concerted effort to influence choices, preachers first need to be influencing minds. When a person *understands* who Christ is, on what basis he is worthwhile, and what life is all about, he has the formulation necessary for any sustained change in lifestyle. Christians who try to "live right" without correcting a wrong understanding about how to meet personal needs will always labor and struggle with Christianity, grinding out their responsible duty in a joyless, strained fashion. (101)

Does this mean that once we understand biblical truth, change will automatically occur? Obviously not. King David was a man after God's own heart. He surpassed many of his contemporaries when it came to knowing God's revealed will. Psalm 53 reveals a man who was knowledgeable of God's demands for righteous living. Yet his knowledge of the Law did not prevent him from entering into an adulterous encounter with Bathsheba. David pursued a sinful course of behavior, apparently believing that he had a right to certain pleasures because he was Israel's king. After all, he had been in so many battles that he deserved a break from the rigors of warfare (2 Sam. 11:1).

All of David's attempts at covering up his adultery and the murder of Uriah indicate that two belief systems were at work in his thinking. We know from the life of David that he knew the will and ways of God. And at the same time we see David living by another belief system in his encounter with Bathsheba, a belief system that affirmed the right of weary leaders to pursue whatever they want in order to reduce stress or boredom in their lives. We can only speculate about what might have happened if Nathan had met with the king prior to David's sexual rendezvous and accused him of lust. David may have denied any such thinking. Perhaps he would have had the prophet executed for falsely accusing him. What is interesting is that Nathan did confront him in 2 Samuel 12. Yet the confrontation was subtle and progressive. He could have entered the courts of David and said, "You *sinned* when you had an adulterous affair with Bathsheba." But the narrative reveals a more subtle approach. Nathan started with a story. David was drawn in and ultimately condemned himself before Nathan rendered his own verdict.

Someone will respond and point out, "Nathan used confrontation and identified the sin problem." Yes, but it was not immediate. What seems to happen is that Nathan, the prophet and spiritual counselor, confronted David's two-tiered belief system to bring about change. The prophet challenged the king's unrighteous and ineffective way of looking at life. He not only appealed to David's mind but also to his emotions. David had to understand the severity of his wrong behavior before he could begin to act in obedience.

Perhaps other examples will demonstrate a similar pattern of biblical caregiving. Gideon was a fearful man, filled with doubt and reluctant to act on what God wanted him to do. If you were a friend or adviser to Gideon, what would you say to him? Would it be wise to confront him with his sins of doubt and self-centeredness? If you carefully read the account of Gideon's transformation from a man of fear to a man of faith, you will notice that he was never once confronted as being a sinner. Are we saying that he was not? Of course not! What we are saying is that God related to Gideon in such a way that He challenged the reluctant warrior's belief system. He challenged his doubts by getting him to look less and less at Israel's current situation and more and more on what God could do (Judg. 6:36–40; 7:13–15).

We can observe a similar situation in the life of the apostle Peter. John 21 describes one of the post-Resurrection appearances of our Lord before His disciples. John was careful to record in chapter 18 the three times that Peter denied knowing the Lord Jesus. What would your approach be if you were one of the other followers gathered on the shore to eat with the resurrected Savior? We might be inclined to point out how disappointed we were in Peter's actions. "Just look at you, Peter. To think that you have the nerve to join us here in the Master's presence is unconscionable. You'd better confess your wrongdoing as soon as possible." Had Peter sinned? Who would want to deny the charge? But the Lord's approach was not one of confronting him directly with his sin. He didn't even allow Peter to speculate on what the other disciples may or may not be doing. The focus is on the Lord's love for Peter and Peter's love for the Lord as demonstrated in doing what the Savior wanted him to do. Jesus worked to change Peter's perspective, his belief system. That is what Nathan did with David, the Angel of the Lord with Gideon, and Jesus with Peter. We would suggest that wise spiritual directors will do the same with the people to whom they minister.

Dr. Charles Kollar makes an interesting point about the way we approach people in a caregiving setting. He wrote:

> Confrontation, no matter how lovingly offered, is still disturbing. Most people are uncomfortable with it, and to assume that this discomfort is due to sin places the counselee in a double bind. To the counselee the confrontation sounds like this: "I'm the pastor, and I say your problem is a result of sin. I've shown you chapter and verse of the Scripture, so if you don't receive it, or if you're uncomfortable with it, that proves I'm right." Although few pastoral counselors would put it in these words, it comes through loud and clear to the counselee. When ministers and Christian leaders fail to consider their presuppositions, they can find themselves in difficult and often disturbing counseling sessions. (42)

Taking a Deeper Look

It is important that we reiterate our belief that problems occur because we live in a sinful, fallen world. As a result, people face crises and have to cope with events that are beyond their control. Some struggles are organically based, the result of disease and dysfunction that affect the person physically, emotionally, and spiritually. In addition, we believe that people have problems because of the sinful choices that they make (James 1:14–15). But confronting the sin issue or searching for a pattern of sin can be as complicated as trying to discover other causes for a particular problem in a person's life.

People are unique in the way they respond to life's challenges. Spiritual directors must be willing to appreciate the uniqueness with which people approach life rather than focusing on behavior that we are quick to label as sinful. Is it possible that the inspired writers of Scripture saw beyond visible actions to see other factors, faulty core beliefs that might be the primary cause of spiritual/emotional troubles? Consider at least three other factors.

First, some people may be anxious, depressed, or in a constant state of fear because they do not understand the *role of pain* in a Christian's life. No one wants to face pain. In fact, we expend quite a bit of energy trying to avoid it. But God's Word informs us that trials come so that believers might persevere in the faith and mature in their life with Christ. It is interesting that the apostle James did not criticize the early saints for joyless living (James 1:2–4). Instead, he asked them to consider looking at life from another perspective. Notice that he did not tell them that they were sinning. He pointed out that God was using trials for a specific purpose. So what motivated these believers to behave as they did? We might identify their behavior as joyless and ineffective. But it appears that they were motivated by a lack of knowledge about what God was doing in their lives. Something beyond their outward behavior influenced what they did. Spiritual counselors will want to be aware of a believer's lack of knowledge concerning pain and its purposes.

A second motivation that may be behind a person's behavior is the issue of *hidden values.* We identify them as "hidden" because they are not the first things that a person will talk about when discussing the struggles of life. The individual Christian may not even think about these values. Nevertheless, they are powerful forces in empowering people to do what they do. These values have been formulated over a number of years through a variety of experiences such as parental models, educational experiences, and the interpretations a person makes of the major events of life. James addressed these hidden values when he encouraged the first-century believers to look at what was really valuable in life (James 1:9–12). Apparently they were stressed over the fact that others were much better off financially than they were. Why would they draw such a conclusion? They probably had learned that having this world's goods was a positive benefit and something to be pursued. Notice that James never confronted their emotional distress or called it sin. He called them instead to a different belief system, namely by telling them that what they had in their new relationship with Christ was what was really important. Once again, those who give spiritual counsel would do well to look beyond behavior and feelings to see what motivates a person.

One other force that generates behavior is a *lack of faith* to do what is appropriate. This lack of faith can manifest itself in anger toward God or toward other people. Likewise, people who have professed faith in Christ might even withdraw from active participation in the things of God. Kirk Johnston put it this way:

> Many hurting believers say, "I was angry with God, but now I'm just very disappointed with Him." This is where a lot of angry Christians eventually end up. They may start out being angry with God because they conclude that He isn't as loving or as powerful as He should be. But they often move from anger to disappointment. They are deeply hurt that God has failed them, but they realize that one cannot fight with God, so they simply resign themselves to their painful circumstances. This does not improve their lives or their relationship with God. (90)

We would not disagree that sinful actions may be evident in the lives of the kind of people described above. But simply telling people that their actions are sinful will not always resolve the problem. What is first needed is a reexamination of one's beliefs about God's goodness and God's power. Again we turn to the apostle James for insight into the matter of lacking faith. In James 1:13–18 the apostle challenged the mistaken view that God might be the cause behind a believer's being tempted. The context surrounding the text is significant. The writer established the fact that God allows trials to help the believer mature. But in the face of these trials, could it be that the early saints concluded that God wasn't as good as they originally thought? Some might have even started accusing God of leading them into temptation. Their faith in God's goodness and power was diminishing. So what did James do? He refocused their thinking, sinfully distorted as it might have been, on the character and goodness of God. Spiritual counselors will want to do the same thing in dealing with spiritually indifferent believers.

What we are suggesting is that *spiritual counsel requires looking beyond the symptoms* a person brings to any caregiving context.

Consider what happens when a person tries to look only at surface issues in the physical realm. A man awakens one morning and discovers a rash on his chest. He scratches rather vigorously, feeling irritated that his day has to start with such discomfort. He tells himself that a shower will help. But after letting hot water rain over his body for several minutes, he only feels worse. He dries himself off and searches the medicine cabinet for some type of ointment he is sure his wife has stored away. A rather worn tube of white cream informs him that the contents are good for "relieving itching due to infections, hives, and poison ivy." The man rubs it over his chest and hurries to get dressed for a very busy day. But the itching does not go away. Repeating his treatment of showers and applying a special ointment does not provide much relief. After the fourth day, his wife tells him to see their family doctor. When he is ushered into the doctor's office, the physician shows real concern. He asks questions about diet and allergies. Nothing seems out of the ordinary. So the doctor orders tests, a complete blood workup, and a series of X rays. The doctor tells the man that the results of the tests will be back in three days. Our friend thinks very little about what has just occurred, other than to scratch his chest every so often.

And then the test results return. The man is asked to come to the physician's office as soon as possible. Once more he is ushered into the examination room, and the doctor enters just moments later. A brief greeting between doctor and patient are exchanged, and then the news is disclosed. No, it's not an allergy that is irritating the man's chest. Neither is it a bad case of poison ivy. The X ray reveals that a rather large tumor is growing in the man's chest, just in front of the right lung. His body was reacting to the deadly growth with an irritating rash.

Sound foolish? We have a friend who has gone through those exact circumstances. What seemed like a mild irritation to his body had in reality been something much more serious. That is why a hasty diagnosis must be avoided, whether in the physical realm or in the work of spiritual counsel. It is one thing to believe that we live in a sinful world and that people who face spiritual/emotional trouble are sinners. But the essence of a person is more than what he does. Beyond the surface of things, people are motivated by faulty beliefs that must be uncovered and dealt with before the spiritual maturation process can continue.

WHO IS WORTHY FOR SUCH A TASK?

As we noted in the previous chapter when we looked at Pastor Jim Starr's ministry, pastors fear that the average person will be reluctant to engage in the ministry of caring for hurting people, especially people who are depressed, anxious, in conflict with others, or fearful about life circumstances. Perhaps this is so, but we agree with Dr. Larry Crabb and Dr. Dan Allender, who envision a Christian community where every believer functions as an encourager. They wrote:

> Every Christian, regardless of gift or training, is called upon to encourage his brothers and sisters. Whatever the direction in which our particular congregation is moving, church life will include spending time in the presence of other Christians. And when we meet together as God's people, we are to encourage one another, to say and do things that stimulate others to a deeper appreciation of Christ and to stronger commitment to our relationship with Him and with each other. (15)

Crabb's sentiments are what the writer to the Hebrews was saying when he wrote, "Let us not give up meeting together, as some are in the habit of doing, but let us encourage one another—and all the more as you see the Day approaching" (Heb. 10:25). Some would call this lay counseling, and others would identify it as encouragement. We believe that it is part of that long ministry tradition of the church known as spiritual counsel or soul care. And all believers are to participate in this ministry in some way.

But who should be the primary caregivers, especially if there is some organized ministry of soul care? What kind of people should your church be recruiting for ministries of spiritual counsel? Obviously the senior pastor and members of the pastoral staff should be readily available for ministry to hurting people. Likewise, those who serve as elders or deacons (depending on the polity of the local church) would do well to be inclined toward ministries of shepherding. But if a church uses the leaders of the congregation, those individuals should be characterized as people who are effective in guiding people through their pain to greater confidence in the person and power of Christ.

Spiritually Based Characteristics of the Caregiver

Two kinds of qualities should characterize the prospective spiritual counselor, qualities that are spiritually based and those that are skill based. First, the distinguishing mark of any caregiver should be that the individual has that spiritually based quality of having a saving relationship with Jesus Christ. Carol Lesser Baldwin wrote, "The strength of your help is your personal relationship to God. You can pass on only what you have learned yourself" (59).

The dynamic of a life empowered by Christ will draw people to oneself and demonstrate to others what it means to know the Savior intimately. Such a life will be characterized by faith. That is, the person will have moment-by-moment dependence on the finished work of Christ. Paul describes this kind of faith in Romans 8:1–4. The maturing believer no longer puts confidence in a life of works-righteousness but in a new identity with Christ, our righteousness.

This dynamic life will also be characterized by hope. It is a hope that has been forged in the midst of suffering and that realizes that there is something more than what this life has to offer. In Romans 8:18–21 the apostle Paul described a mind-set that sees beyond suffering to God's eternal plans. He was describing the quality of biblical hope that should be evident in everyone who gives spiritual counsel.

Likewise, a potential caregiver will be a person of *love*. He will believe and experience the love of God for him in Christ Jesus (Romans 8:37–39), and then express that love for others in the body of Christ (John 13:35). Faith, hope, and love forged in one's own experience, including trials, will be the primary qualities of an effective spiritual director.

In the same way, the effective spiritual counselor will be one who knows the Scriptures. Paul told young Timothy to present himself as one approved by God, "a workman who does not need to be ashamed and who correctly handles the word of truth" (2 Tim. 2:15). The concept of a "workman" pictures one who labors in a particular craft. In Timothy's case he was to be a diligent student of the Scriptures. And what was true of Timothy should be true of every pastor, every church leader, and yes, every believer in general. If we are to counter the false assumptions and values by which people live, we must know what is absolutely true. The Bible is the only completely reliable source for knowing what is true and what is to be lived out in the everyday challenges of life. The Bible should be studied, not to dispense facts, but so that the Christian can know God better and experience ongoing transformation. For the caregiver, the goal is transformation of the caregiver and those who come in contact with that person's ministry.

Skill-Based Characteristics of the Caregiver

Prospective spiritual counselors should also have some basic skill-based qualities that characterize their lives. Some people may want to serve who do not have the skills to do so. They may even be knowledgeable in expressing theological truth. But at least three other qualities should be present in the work of effective spiritual counsel. For instance, the caregiver should be one who listens well. That means that early on in the process one must not be quick to pass judgment on what a hurting person is saying or doing. There will be time to point out what the Bible says about specific actions and attitudes. But before we can uncover those hidden beliefs we talked about earlier, we need to collect information. That means that careful listening is a must. When implemented with skill, listening not only benefits the caregiver in understanding what is going on in a person's life, but it communicates love to the troubled person as well.

Likewise, an effective spiritual counselor will demonstrate the ability to *communicate truth in love*, yet in a way that guides people to transformation. Regarding truth speaking, Baldwin writes:

Truth speaking has the same two components that are present in biblical love: *comfort* and *confrontation*. Affirmation, support, encouragement, and words of affection all express welcoming comfort to our friends. We must be able to recognize our friends' strengths, to compliment their successes, and to express our care for them. Without the ability to express this type of comfort, we would be like merciless judges, trapping our friends in a prison of condemnation.

Confrontation, the second component of truth speaking, involves giving feedback. We don't ignore our friends' sins, problems, or difficulties. Instead, we help by giving feedback and pointing out these difficulties. (85)

It is not enough to listen to the problems a person might be facing. Those who encourage others according to the principle of Hebrews 10:25 will help them to see that there are more effective and biblical ways of living.

Finally, the effective spiritual director or spiritual counselor will *guide people to appropriate action*. As we stated earlier, we sometimes fixate on a person's behavior. We see it as sin, and most of the time this is correct. But behind every behavior is a way of looking at life, a system of core beliefs that must be changed. When a caregiver helps a hurting person to see those faulty beliefs, action must be taken. As we will see in the next chapter, the action must be appropriate to the new belief that is being explored. This requires creativity on the part of the person providing the soul care.

A person can affirm that something is true and that it may even be needed in that person's life. That doesn't mean that the person will act upon it. For instance, a woman might agree that her fear of being with people is irrational. She can even affirm the right belief that she needs to be with other Christians. But the wise caregiver will not only have her say what is true, but will have her act on the truth. The one who ministers might have her meet with one person to pray, perhaps once a week. The spiritual director might follow this action a week later by having the fearful individual meet with two or three others. Small action steps will complement what one knows to be true. Consequently the one who does the work of soul care will need to have skills that help others to put truth into life.

— *Things to Ponder* —

As you consider your work as a caregiver, you may want to evaluate your own qualities as a potential spiritual counselor. There are a number of formal tests that a church could use, such as the Myers-Briggs Temperament Type Indicator or the MMPI. Siang-Yang Tan identifies a number of testing instruments that organizations could use to assist in identifying specialized ministers for the church (102–6). Many pastors and small churches will not be able to invest time or resources in such instruments. The assessment scale below may be of some help in identifying those who are most qualified to do the work of soul care. The inventory can be used first as a self-test, and then given to one or two other individuals who know the prospective caregiver well. (Permission is granted to photocopy the form for such use.)

A Spiritual Counselor's Personal Inventory

1. *I spend time regularly studying the Word of God.*

   Rarely 1   2   3   4   5   6   7   8   9   10 Frequently

2. *I spend time regularly in prayer, seeking God's will for my life.*

   Rarely 1   2   3   4   5   6   7   8   9   10 Frequently

3. *I have seen God use the trials of my life to transform me into a more mature Christian.*

   Rarely 1   2   3   4   5   6   7   8   9   10 Frequently

4. *I can identify specific Scriptures that affirm God's love for me.*

   Rarely 1   2   3   4   5   6   7   8   9   10 Frequently

   What are those Scriptures?

5. *I have been intentional in showing my love and concern to people both within and outside of my family.*

   Rarely 1 2 3 4 5 6 7 8 9 10 *Frequently*

6. *I am courageous about discussing the gospel with people I know who are not Christians.*

   Rarely 1 2 3 4 5 6 7 8 9 10 *Frequently*

7. *People tell me that I am sensitive and caring.*

   Rarely 1 2 3 4 5 6 7 8 9 10 *Frequently*

8. *People tell me that I have communicated hope to them in their times of need.*

   Rarely 1 2 3 4 5 6 7 8 9 10 *Frequently*

9. *I am comfortable communicating with people who are different from me.*

   Rarely 1 2 3 4 5 6 7 8 9 10 *Frequently*

10. *I can listen to people and the details of their conversations without interrupting them.*

    Rarely 1 2 3 4 5 6 7 8 9 10 *Frequently*

11. *I believe that the Bible has helpful insight for people who are struggling with life challenges.*

    Rarely 1 2 3 4 5 6 7 8 9 10 *Frequently*

12. *It is easy for me to stop what I am doing to listen to people describe their frustrations with life.*

    Rarely 1 2 3 4 5 6 7 8 9 10 *Frequently*

13. *Before telling people to act in a certain way, I try to communicate my concern for the pain they are feeling.*

    Rarely 1 2 3 4 5 6 7 8 9 10 *Frequently*

14. *I am comfortable ministering to others when there are extended times of silence or tearfulness.*

    Rarely 1 2 3 4 5 6 7 8 9 10 *Frequently*

15. *I can listen to people express their anger without becoming angry myself.*

Rarely 1   2   3   4   5   6   7   8   9   10 Frequently

16. *I am comfortable ministering to people who express negative thoughts about themselves.*

Rarely 1   2   3   4   5   6   7   8   9   10 Frequently

17. *People view me as someone who can kindly but firmly direct them to take constructive action.*

Rarely 1   2   3   4   5   6   7   8   9   10 Frequently

18. *I am comfortable listening to people talk about issues of sexuality.*

Rarely 1   2   3   4   5   6   7   8   9   10 Frequently

19. *I can maintain confidences that are shared with me.*

Rarely 1   2   3   4   5   6   7   8   9   10 Frequently

20. *I honestly evaluate my own growth in the Christian life.*

Rarely 1   2   3   4   5   6   7   8   9   10 Frequently

This form is taken from Harry Shields and Gary Bredfeldt, Caring for Souls: Counseling Under the Authority of Scripture *(Chicago: Moody, 2001) and is used by permission.*

Not every Christian will be suited to enter into a ministry of soul care. We strongly recommend that a formal ministry of soul care not become a matter of public announcement or mass recruiting. In many situations, the pastoral staff may want to recruit their own candidates to carry out this very important ministry.

In the next chapter we will look at specific steps that one can take in doing the ministry of spiritual counsel. But before moving on to the specifics of the spiritual counseling process, pastoral leaders and their respective leadership boards (elders, deacons, session leaders, etc.) would do well to heed the instruction of Dr. Siang-Yang Tan. Dr. Tan suggests that those who have caregiving ministries should have three goals for the services provided by the professional and laypeople of the church staff. Those goals are to pursue *competence, confidentiality,* and *choice* (219–21). It is also important that spiritual counselors are growing in Christlikeness. That is, they should be men and women who are committed to the lordship of Christ in every area of their lives. Such individuals will demonstrate a commitment to the authority, inerrancy, and absolute truthfulness of God's Word. Like the Lord Jesus Himself they will have a love for people to see them grow in grace and holiness.

Competence means that pastors who serve as spiritual counselors will seek to get as much training as possible, through both reading and special seminars. At the same time they will carefully select, train, and supervise those who also serve as spiritual counselors.

By *confidentiality* we mean that thoughts, ideas, emotions, and experiences discussed in meeting with a spiritual director will be kept strictly private. One who comes for spiritual guidance and care should be able to sense that what he tells will not be divulged to others, except where information is exchanged in the context of supervision. However, there are limitations to confidentiality. If the person has broken the law, the person who is counseling him is responsible to report that to the proper authorities. Those who counsel with minors are responsible for sharing information with the appropriate individuals. They will want to consult with the senior pastor regarding the appropriate course of action to take. In addition, they will want to inform parents and legal guardians about what has been happening in the child's life. The spiritual counselor will also want to give guidance to these adults as to what would be appropriate action to take.

When it comes to the issue of *choice,* the goal of the spiritual counselor is to develop an atmosphere where those who come for assistance are given adequate information to make their own decisions regarding various circumstances. The aim should not be to put people under compulsion to act a certain way. Rather, people should be guided through various kinds of information to decide for themselves what they will do.

Before entering into any type of caregiver training, check with your church attorney or the insurance company that works with your congregation. Be familiar with the laws of your state and county as it relates to nonprofessional, caregiving services. We would encourage you to avoid using terms like *counseling* and devote your ministry to one of biblically based spiritual counsel. Some states hold churches responsible if they describe their ministry as one of counseling, and some insurance companies discourage the use of the term.

NOTES

Baldwin, Carol Lesser. *Friendship Counseling: Biblical Foundations for Helping Others.* Grand Rapids: Zondervan, 1988.

Crabb, Lawrence J., Jr. *Effective Biblical Counseling: A Model for Helping Caring Christians Become Capable Counselors.* Grand Rapids: Zondervan, 1977.

Crabb, Lawrence J., Jr., and Dan Allender. *Encouragement: The Key to Caring.* Grand Rapids: Zondervan, 1984.

Hoff, Lee Ann. *People in Crisis: Understanding and Helping.* 3d ed. Redwood City, Calif.: Addison-Wesley, 1989.

Johnston, J. Kirk. *When Counseling Is Not Enough: Biblical Answers for Those Who Still Struggle.* Grand Rapids: Discovery House, 1994.

Kollar, Charles Allen. *Solution-Focused Pastoral Counseling: An Effective Short-Term Approach for Getting People Back on Track.* Grand Rapids: Zondervan, 1997.

Swihart, Judson J., and Gerald C. Richardson. *Counseling in Times of Crisis.* Waco, Tex.: Word, 1987. Vol. 7 of *Resources for Christian Counseling.* Ed. Gary R. Collins.

Tan, Siang-Yang. *Lay Counseling: Equipping Christians for a Helping Ministry.* Grand Rapids: Zondervan, 1991.

— Chapter 11 —

The Process of Spiritual Counsel (Part Two)

*J*im Starr and Tom Parkes had a lot in common, but it had been quite some time since they had gotten together. The thirty miles that separated their two churches and the busyness that came with two growing congregations kept the two men in their own respective worlds. But here they were, back together again after almost a year and a half of not communicating until Tom's call last week. The conference they had attended was just what Jim needed, even though he still had a lot of questions. He didn't realize that he had been staring out the car window, almost abandoning his old seminary friend to the task of driving the two of them home.

"Whatcha thinking about, my friend?" Tom asked with a slight grin on his face. "I'll bet you're putting the finishing touches on your sermon for Sunday."

Jim realized rather sheepishly that he hadn't been saying much. "Hey, I'm sorry, Tom. I'm not much of a sidekick, I guess. And no, I'm not working on my sermon. I guess I was reflecting on what Dr. Riley was saying in his talk today. I really want to put some of the principles he presented into practice."

Tom nodded in agreement.

Jim didn't know whether to discuss his thoughts with Tom or not, but he needed to talk with someone. Spiritual counsel and pastoral care were areas he had never intended to pursue as a pastor. And Jim knew that the two of them had disagreed on how ministry should be done when they were taking pastoral ministry classes together at the seminary. Tom was the consummate pastor in Jim's eyes, always taking time to be with people and listening to their troubles. He read a lot of the popular self-help books on counseling. Jim was the Bible student. He had taken every theology class for which he could register. Jim Starr spent his summers reviewing the biblical languages and his theology notes. But now he was realizing that Tom had some insight into how to relate to people that he didn't have.

"You know, Tom, I've been thinking a lot about the conference today and the way the two of us have approached ministry in the past. I have to be honest and say that I wish I were more like you in the way you minister. We have a couple, the Greens, who moved to our community from your church. They sing your praises. Maybe I'm a little jealous, I'll admit it, but they think you're right up there with the apostle Paul. Apparently you helped them in their marriage a while back."

The two men laughed at what the Greens thought of Tom. Then Jim's musings led into a "remember-when" session. Story after story from their seminary escapades broke the monotony of the three-hour ride back home.

As they neared the end of the drive, Jim brought their conversation back to what was originally on his mind. "Tom, I really do wish I had some of your skills. I studied so hard when we were students together. I used to make fun of you when you took so much time to listen and counsel people. I could have learned from you, my friend."

"Hey, the feelings are mutual," Tom said with a very serious tone in his voice. "I don't know how many times I have told my wife that I could have benefited from devoting more time to biblical studies and theology the way you did. It may surprise you, Jim, but I have been trying to read through Calvin's *Institutes* over the last two years. Go ahead. You're going to faint, aren't you?"

"Well, I am a little surprised. What brought this on?"

"Jim, I realized, the more I met with people, that the answers were really issues related to wisdom and the ways of God. I spent a lot of time working on trying to understand human dynamics. I do think I learned some things from all of my reading, but I have come to the conclusion that the Bible gives us the wisdom we need to help people get beyond their problems to serve God. I guess I agree with what Dr. Riley was saying today about the way to be a good caregiver is to be a good theologian. I wouldn't have said that back in seminary, but I sure believe it now. The key is to know how to relate theology to life issues."

Jim's interest was piqued; it was surprising to hear his friend say what he just said. "Yes, I am pleasantly surprised at your apparent change of heart. But I have to admit that I have been wrestling with the issue of relating theology to life in my own ministry. Tom, I thought I would do that almost exclusively through preaching, but boy, have I had an awakening."

"What do you mean?" Tom inquired.

"Well, I discovered that people are really hurting when it comes to their families, their jobs, and life in general. More and more people have been calling, asking me to meet with them. I thought that if I just preached the Word faithfully and people listened, they wouldn't have problems. Boy, was I naive!"

"Hey, don't feel bad, Jim, ol' buddy. I was naive at the other end. I thought that if I had an open-door policy and searched for some hidden secret from people's past that I could expose, they wouldn't have problems for very long. Guess what? People came back, that's for sure, but they didn't seem to improve. Jim, the turnaround in my pastoral care came when I went back to the Scriptures and tried to help people see things from God's perspective. You wonder why the Greens think I'm such a great pastor? If they only knew the truth! In fact, I was so stressed with their slow progress that I actually pulled the Bible out in frustration and told them what they needed to do. Boy, was I shocked when they came back the next week and told me that it really got them to thinking. I don't do that with every parishioner, and I don't think it would work with everyone. But I suspect God was trying to get my attention. That's why I'm reading theology as well as some trusted names in caregiving."

Jim nodded in agreement. Several seconds passed without either pastor saying anything. Then Jim spoke up. "Tom, I still believe in the Word of God to change lives. But I am finding something else out as well. For one thing, people's hearts have to be ready. I came to that after studying Jesus' parable of the sower in Matthew 13. It isn't just getting the Word out. People's hearts have to be prepared. I know that God is the ultimate One to change their hearts, but I am more and more confident that if I meet with people one-on-one, almost as a discipler, not a counselor, I may be used of God to influence change."

Jim paused again, obviously choosing his words carefully. "I have intentionally tried to avoid using the term 'counseling' when I meet with people. I am more comfortable with the term 'spiritual director' or with the idea of a godly person giving 'spiritual counsel.' I know you might think I am 'wrangling over words' as you used to tell me in seminary when we would get into some of our intense debates. I'm even surprised we're still friends." Both men chuckled.

Jim's serious tone returned. "Tom, how do you do pastoral care? I mean, how do you know what to do once you start meeting with people? I believe people are where they are because they make sinful choices. I don't tell them that right away. I also believe that many of the people who come to me are there because of horrible things that have happened to them. But my problem is I don't know what to do from session to session. Any suggestions?"

Tom seemed like he was excited about what his pastoral colleague was telling him. Both men were surprised when they realized they were pulling into the parking lot of Twin Hills Baptist, Tom's pastoral home. "Jim, I think you are on to something with this spiritual counsel thing. You might have your sermon ready for Sunday, but I still have some work to do on mine. Let me loan you a couple of books that might help you to think about process. But my suggestion is that you develop your own approach. You need to own it for yourself instead of duplicating something someone else has done."

Jim looked at his watch and agreed that as stimulating as this conversation was, he too needed to get home. It was already 9:30, and he wanted to get home before midnight. He took up his friend's offer regarding the books then headed to his car. Jim Starr and Tom Parkes promised each other that they would get together again during the next month, especially before the hurriedness of the holiday season captured both of their schedules. Tom especially wanted to find out what his friend was doing for an advent preaching series this year. And Jim wanted to bounce some more of his ideas about spiritual counsel off of his friend. The day's seminar and the interaction in the car had provided the spark that Jim Starr needed to persevere in caring for the people God had placed under his ministry.

THE POWER OF PROCESS

One of the important things about wrestling with ideas, like the kind that our two pastoral friends are facing, is that we eventually have to bring order to the thousands of thoughts that bombard our minds every day. Even when we focus on one task, such as organizing the ideas of a sermon or arranging the parts for a do-it-yourself project, the mind longs for order. The same is true when it comes to caring for people. We can "shoot from the hip," but seldom does a random approach to doing anything pay off in the long run. Spiritual counselors need to focus on a person's feelings, behaviors, and thoughts to discover what is at the heart of any given problem. Many of the books on the subject of caregiving have suggestions for what to do from meeting to meeting. For instance, Everett Worthington suggests a five-step approach. First, the caregiver needs to understand the person. Second, the person needs guidance in rethinking the problem. Third, the person will be guided into making an action plan. Fourth, the person will be supported as he attempts to make changes. And fifth, the caregiver will provide follow-up (57).

Larry Crabb also offers a possible pattern that one can follow. He builds his counseling paradigm on a seven-stage process. In the first stage Crabb suggests that one needs to identify the problem feeling, since most people naturally talk about what they are "feeling" about a given situation. The second stage has to do with identifying problem behavior. Stage three seeks to identify problem thinking. The fourth stage shifts to a more directive process of clarifying biblical thinking. Stage five seeks to draw the person into making a commitment to live biblically. Stage six affirms a plan and process for carrying out biblical behavior. And the final stage helps the person to identify Spirit-controlled feelings (146–60). Crabb's model has a lot to commend it, especially because of its emphasis on thinking and acting in a biblical fashion.

Over the next several pages we are going to look at a suggested model that lends itself to the work of pastoral ministry and lay-pastoral spiritual counsel. It is important to remember that those who do spiritual counsel should not think continually in terms of steps or stages. Such descriptions are helpful in getting a person started in the ministry of helping others. But more important, ministry is a relationship. People do not function like machines, and neither should those who care for them. So keep the following paradigm in front of you only to develop some structure. But the more you employ the format, the more it should become second nature. The process itself should always be dressed in the wardrobe of a loving relationship.

To help you to better understand people and to harness all the confusing thoughts that might come your way, we want to suggest a four-stage process. The four stages can be thought of as four primary questions that the spiritual counselor must ask if adequate ministry is to be provided. It is also important to keep in mind that whatever the pastor does will most likely be short-term. The concept of short-term care means that the pastor or lay spiritual director will attempt to bring biblical solutions to human problems in five to six meetings. In fact, many of those who engage in professional counseling are actually advocating a focus on short-term, solution-focused paradigms (Oliver, Hasz, and Richburg, 11–14).

Pastoral care with respect to spiritual counsel needs to be short-term because of the very nature of pastoral ministry. Most of those who shepherd small churches have multiple roles to fill. They teach two or three times a week, which requires significant por-

tions of time devoted to study. Pastors are called upon to offici-
ate at weddings and funerals and to provide premarital counseling.
And they frequently serve as the chief administrative officer when
it comes to the overall ministry operations of the church. Add
the works of discipleship and pastoral care to a pastor's typical
week, and you discover that long-term involvement in counseling is almost prohibitive. That is why pastors should think less
about doing clinical counseling and do more in the way of providing spiritual counsel. The process of spiritual counsel that unfolds in this chapter lends itself to this focus on short-term care.
Once problems are addressed in any given person's life, the pastor
will want to direct those individuals to ongoing activities of discipleship and nurture that may already exist within the congregation.

Not only are pastors busy, but lay leadership is busy as well.
However, the hectic pace of today's American family does not nul-
lify the Word of God and the need to have every believer involved
in the work of ministry (Eph. 4:11–12). So how can we live and
minister with these two tensions of crowded schedules and the call
of God on our lives? One answer is to keep the training for ministry as simple as possible. Once again, the model for training spiritual counselors developed in this chapter lends itself to short-term
training, as well as short-term care. People will be more inclined
to get involved in ministering to the needs of others if they feel
they have the time to participate in the needed training and if
that very same training will equip them to do God's work.

Another advantage to a short-term model for spiritual counsel is that it reduces the tendency for those being mentored to
become increasingly dependent on their spiritual counselors. Obviously, dependence is not a bad thing. We are all dependent on
other individuals for guidance, information, and assistance in ac-
complishing tasks. But spiritual counselors need to be careful that
they do not foster an overdependence from the one who is receiving soul care. Short-term spiritual counsel may be an aid in preventing unnecessary dependence on a pastor or church leader.
When boundaries are established according to the model presented
in this book, the inclination to overdependence can be greatly
reduced.

A final reason for advocating short-term spiritual counsel is that it decreases the tendency toward endless introspection. Sometimes people can spend so much time focusing on their problems that they end up seeing themselves as powerless victims of life's "bad breaks." But if God is truly at work in the believer's life to make him more like Christ, problems are part of our training in holiness. This does not mean that a spiritual counselor should never explore what has happened in a person's past. But, as we shall see later, such exploration serves as a bridge to uncover faulty worldviews. The goal of spiritual counsel is to bring hurting believers into a vibrant relationship with the living God. Inordinate introspection tends to blind us to God's presence while we focus on our own problems. Spiritual counsel, on the other hand, focuses on God, His grace, and His right to be worshiped, even in the context of personal pain.

ONE PATHWAY TO UNDERSTANDING

In the previous chapter we noted that people have problems because of things that happen to them and because of choices they make in life. We believe that sin is a very real factor behind the problems that people face. But any significant resolution to human problems goes beyond identifying sinful conditions that may exist in people's lives. The goal of providing spiritual counsel will be to help people to respond in a biblically mature manner and to see the presence and power of God that may be evident all about them. But for these goals to occur, the spiritual counselor will need to provide the kind of soul care that answers four very important questions. The pathway to understand people and problems requires us to ask:

- "What will be the extent of my involvement with this person?"
- "What is going on in the person's life?"
- "What new perspective on life with Christ will help the person to change?"

• "How can I help the person to live out this new perspective on life?"

These four questions will enable the caregiver to think about ministry in a constructive way. And the four stages we will discuss in the rest of this chapter will help us to move through the common experiences of confusion that occur when people come to us for help.

Stage 1: The Issue of INVOLVEMENT

James 1:2 teaches that trials come to us in various forms. Not every problem we face is necessarily of the same magnitude or origin. From the perspective of the spiritual counselor, we need to keep in mind that not only are problems different from person to person, but our abilities to handle the problems may differ as well. When we have gone through a specific challenge in life, we find ourselves being able to sympathize with people having similar problems. We might also be able to communicate wisdom to them that we have gained from our own pain (2 Cor. 1:3–4). But this will not be true with every person in our sphere of ministry because we simply have not faced every problem there is to face. Therefore, we have to ask, "What will be the extent of my involvement with this individual?"

There is no simple way to answer this question. A sovereign God sometimes brings people into our lives because He wants us to participate with Him in the work that He is doing. Problems that are initially presented to us may seem impossible to resolve, especially from a human perspective. But God may have other things in mind. Do not be too quick to say, "I'm sorry, but you need to talk with someone else." We might sometimes have to refer to another caregiver in the church or in the community, but we want to get as much information as we can before doing any type of referral. We will have more to say on the subject of referral later in this chapter.

A. Why Will We Be Involved?

As we prepare ourselves to be effective spiritual counselors, we need to think through the issue of why we might get involved in helping people. Again, the answer is different from person to person and minister to minister. Sometimes people come to us through a personal request or because of a particular position that we hold. A woman might serve as a hostess for an adult Sunday school class where her husband is one of the teachers. Each week she greets people warmly and makes them feel at home. A single mother might visit the class and notice that the hostess always makes her feel good about herself. As time passes, the single mother musters up enough courage to ask this older woman for help. Why? Warmth and friendliness mixed with an obvious compassion will draw hurting people to those who seem to have a wisdom that others seek. At the same time, some people will seek out the help of others in the church because of their position, whether it be the pastor, associate pastor, Sunday school teacher, or elder. Those in leadership will frequently be sought out for help because of their public ministry in the church at large.

At other times, people are subtly drawn into other people's problems when crises occur. The family next door has to rush a younger child to the hospital, and you are asked to pick up the two older children at school. You do so with a willing desire to help. But when the mother stops by to pick up her children, she begins to report on the events of the day. The more she talks, the more she reveals other problems that are going on, problems related to marriage, child rearing, and relationships. You ask if there is anything you can do to help. To your surprise the woman arranges to meet with you the next morning. You hadn't planned on such a ministry, but it unfolds in the context of crisis. Eventually you will have to determine the extent of your involvement.

In addition, the spiritual director will want to make some preliminary inquiries about what the person wants from a helping relationship. You can bridge into this information by asking something like:

> I really appreciate you telling me what is going on in your life right now. I would appreciate knowing what else is happening. Tell me what it was that prompted you to come and see me right now.

The question is not designed to send the caregiver on an ego trip. Rather you will want to find out why the person came. Does he just want someone to listen to him? Is he seeking prayer support? Is he expressing frustration over the "bad hand" that life has dealt him? Answers to these types of questions will help to determine the extent of your involvement with the person.

Sometimes we get involved with people and problems because of the need for spiritual restoration. Not everyone who gives spiritual counsel will be involved in the work of restoration, but some obviously will have to undertake this role. We are thinking here of pastors and elders specifically. This is needed when people drift from the faith and from church fellowship because of wrong choices that they have made. Those who are "spiritual" and in positions of authority are to restore them to the faith and the fellowship (Gal. 6:1; James 5:19–20). Acts of restoration are also acts of spiritual direction. Consequently, some in positions of leadership will be called upon to get involved. As the restoration process continues, the caregiver will have to determine the extent of that involvement.

B. How to Limit Involvement

Sometimes caregivers might also choose to limit their involvement. Again, it is important for prospective spiritual counselors to think through the reasons for putting limits on the time they might spend with a person in need. Sometimes this will occur because of continuing confusion and uncertainty. That is, the more that he explores a person's lifestyle and experiences, the more confused the spiritual counselor becomes. However, confusion will always be our experience early in the process as we try to help people. That is why training for both pastors and lay leaders is a necessity.

We might also limit our involvement with people when our training, lack of experience, or the excessive demands of any given case overwhelm us—for example, in the case of people with chemical addictions. They may want help and in some ways could benefit from the help that a mature caregiver can give. But people with chemical addictions need round-the-clock attention, the kind of attention that the average Christian worker cannot give. The same can be said for people struggling with eating disorders and severe forms of depression. The intense demand for care may force some spiritual directors to limit their involvement when the situation is severe.

One other area of limitation has to do with gender issues. When it comes to the ministry of lay leaders especially, we would suggest a policy in which men work with men and women with women. Even pastors should think through the extent to which they will meet with women in the context of soul care. The issue here has nothing to do with competence in helping other people. But since the role of spiritual counselor will often focus on matters of intense emotional pain, pastors would be wise not to get emotionally involved in the pain of a person of the opposite sex. We know of pastors who have a policy to see a woman who is requesting help for only one session. Thereafter, the woman is encouraged to see someone else in the congregation or the community at large. Women who become spiritual counselors will be wise to establish similar guidelines as they develop more and more responsibility for soul care in the congregation. The Bible itself encourages women to minister to women and men to men (Titus 2:1–8), giving us another reason to be strategic about training a number of people to give spiritual counsel.

C. How to Determine One's Involvement

So how does a person prepare for this crucial first stage of involvement? It is one thing to know that limitations to our involvement are appropriate. It is altogether another matter to know when to refer someone to the care of another. How can we make wise decisions about these crucial matters? One of the first things that we can do is to pray. The apostle James encouraged his readers in the midst of trials to ask God for wisdom. It is interesting that the Scriptures do not teach us to ask for a way of escape from the dilemma that we or others are facing. God's Word instructs us to call upon the One who gives insight and wisdom in a generous manner (James 1:5). One form that wisdom will take is that of insight regarding whether to continue helping a spiritually adrift person. And the praying that we do during this involvement stage should be one of continual listening. On one hand we are listening to what people are saying. But we are also listening for the Spirit of God to give us insight into what the person is really saying (1 Thess. 5:17).

Quite often when people come to us for help, we are not prepared for what they are about to tell us. That is why we need to complement our praying by "joining the person where he is." We are not referring primarily to a specific location. Spiritual counsel can sometimes take place over the phone, especially when several miles separate the hurting person and the caregiver. But we join the person when we intentionally give the attention he so desperately needs. We listen. We watch. We show concern both by our willingness to be silent and by the empathy we extend to the individual. And as we join him, we must be careful to put all judgments on hold. This doesn't mean that we will never provide a biblical perspective on a person's thinking or behavior. But in these early hours of extending spiritual counsel we must be careful that we don't interrupt a person's stories with rapid-fire judgments regarding what the person did or did not do. For the person who knows the Word of God, the skill of listening and caring may be one of the most difficult skills to learn.

D. How to Determine if the Person Is Considering Suicide

When people begin to talk about problems, the spiritual counselor may hear what appear to be shocking descriptions of what is currently happening in a person's individual world. The person may even express hopelessness and a desire to escape the current situation in whatever way possible. The wise spiritual counselor will want to ask questions about any "plans" the person might be considering. Even though the first two stages of the process require putting judgments on hold and listening as intently as possible, it is important to find out if suicide is being considered as a possible way of dealing with life pressures. One should never dismiss a person's comments about the possibility of suicide. Bringing up the issue of suicide is not equivalent to putting the thought of suicide into another person's mind. But if you are suspicious about what a person might do, simply ask. The question can be posed something like this:

As I listen to you tell me your story, I must admit that I have some very serious concerns. I am trusting you to be honest with me. Has the thought of suicide ever entered your thinking?

Some people, as discouraged with life as they might be, do not consider taking their own life. But others do. The wise spiritual director will make it a goal to extend hope to the individual who comes for help. In addition, the caregiver will want to ask the person to make a commitment that he or she will not consider suicide as an option in dealing with the current problems. This verbal commitment can be fashioned in the following manner:

> I very much appreciate your telling me how you feel. But the idea of taking your life is not a solution to your problems. I want you to know that I care about you. Even better, God cares about you. In fact, I believe that it is possible for you to learn to cope with the things you are facing right now. What I would like to ask from you is that you will not consider suicide as an option. Will you make that commitment to me right now? In fact, if we agree to continue meeting together, I want you to call me if these thoughts of suicide ever enter your mind in the future. Will you do that?

It is important to note that there are no guarantees that the above inquiry will prevent a suicide attempt. But it is better to ask and seek a commitment from the person than to ignore any hunches you might have about the individual's well-being (Hoff 179).

One other matter needs to be mentioned. When someone acknowledges that he has had suicidal thoughts, should you inform the appropriate authorities? The question is a very sensitive one. We would encourage pastors and their lay spiritual counselors to decide ahead of time how to handle these delicate situations. You may want to reassure the person that what you talk about in your meetings will be held in confidence, but that when issues of suicide are brought up, a trusted pastoral supervisor will also be brought into the caregiving context. When you mention your procedures regarding the acknowledgment of suicide in the involvement stage, you are letting the person know about legitimate guidelines that are being established for the protection of all parties involved. One guidebook on the subject of pastoral care states the following:

> There is no legal duty for pastors, churches, or counselors working under church supervision to assess and intervene effectively to prevent suicide. But in practice, churches should disregard this apparent protection and act as if liability does exist, because they are likely to be sued anyway. . . . The church, then, must intervene effectively with the suicidal person, not so much because of legal duty, but rather to fulfill the call of love and to avoid suit and the massive cost of legal defense. (Ohlschlager and Mosgofian 115–16)

E. How to Clarify Involvement

At this point in the process you may be ready to make a decision in your own mind about whether you will get further involved in the person's life. If you sense that the Holy Spirit is leading you to help this person to get a God-centered perspective on life, you can extend some "hope-filled" words to him. Again you will want to try to see how the person will respond. You might want to say something like the following statement:

> I very much appreciate your openness with me. I sense that you have been experiencing a lot of pain in your life. I don't know what your thoughts are, but I would be willing to meet with you in the next few days to explore what God has to say about the issues you are facing. I want you to know that the road ahead might be a tough one to navigate, but the heavenly Father wants you to know Him even better. Would you be willing to meet with me again so that we can look at your problems from a biblical perspective? I will be sensitive to all that you are facing, but I also would like to help you to see that the Scriptures have a lot to say to give you hope and direction for what you are facing.

Sometimes the person will want to have more time to think about what he will do in the future. Give the person time to make the decision. But encourage him to see that it would be wise to meet again. If he agrees, set a time and place for the next meeting to occur.

We would also suggest that the involvement stage is a good time to give a brief overview as to what will happen in the actual process of spiritual counsel. The person needs to realize that meeting together is not simply a time for pouring out frustrations regarding one's marriage or family situation. That is why we encouraged you earlier to try to find out why the person is coming for assistance in the first place. If the person genuinely wants your assistance in coping with the situation and getting to know God's will for his life, then it is a good time to review what will take place when the meetings do occur. We would suggest that you inform the person regarding three matters: (1) the number of times that you will meet, (2) the length of time the individual meetings will require, and (3) what will occur within the meetings. You will want to explain the process in your own words, but it will sound something like the following:

> Let's try meeting again in two or three days, if that is agreeable with you. We will meet for approximately one hour during each of our meetings. And during those times I will want to ask you some questions. We will not be dwelling on the past, but I would like to discover some of the things that are important to you. Would you be willing to commit to meeting for five or six sessions initially? After those meetings, we will sit down and decide what might happen next. What do you think? Would you be willing to meet with me under those guidelines?

Give the person time to ask questions. And by all means put the information in the above paragraph in your own words. Some caregivers will also have the person sign a statement of consent, a document that provides general guidelines for the meetings that will occur. Again, you will have to be careful in doing so, especially if you want the care that is to be given to be more of an informal ministry. However, pastors may want to protect their ministries from legal action by putting as much of the spiritual-counsel process in writing as they can.

It is wise for church leaders to prepare consent forms that include information about the purpose, length, and obligations relative to the caregiving process. We would discourage churches from charging fees for their helping ministries, but if there are charges for any type of materials being used, this should be stated on the consent form. In addition, this same form should have a very clear statement about confidentiality between the caregiver, the one receiving help, and the one who is providing supervision for the caregiver. After a consent form has been developed it is always wise to have an attorney familiar with church law evaluate the document to make sure it is in compliance with local and state laws. Another document could accompany the consent form that will provide basic information such as the person's name, address, phone number, marital status, and information that tells why the person is seeking help at this time. Examples of these various forms can be found in the writings of Siang-Yang Tan (249–50), Jay Adams (433–44), and Neil Anderson (237–47).

Spiritual counsel is more than being a friend. Many people can fill the important and needed role of listening to people pour out their tales of woe. But a spiritual counselor is concerned with helping people to become more mature in their life with Jesus Christ. That is why asking for the kind of commitments described above is so important. Without such a commitment, our involvement should be limited. We may even want to refer the person to a professional counselor.

Stage 2: The Issue of INVESTIGATION

After answering the question regarding the extent of one's involvement in another person's life, the spiritual counselor needs to focus on the next crucial question. People are usually prompted to come for help because of some stressful matter that has recently occurred in their lives. But usually this "presenting problem" is not at the heart of the matter. Thus the person in the caregiving role must ask, "What is really going on here?" Answering this question means that *investigation* needs to be done. Data need to be collected that will eventually help the spiritual director to guide the person into the will and ways of God.

In the stage of investigation, wise spiritual directors will want to assume a role that is similar to the TV character Columbo. You may remember that Columbo would try to resolve various murder cases, though the TV viewer always knew the culprit behind the crime. But Columbo's success came from collecting what seemed like insignificant data and asking the right questions, questions that led to a clear, reasonable verdict. Spiritual counselors will want to do something similar. They will want to explore where people have been and what kind of thinking governs the things that they do.

A. Investigating with Caution

But what kinds of questions are good questions? What acts of investigation lead to getting the most appropriate data? We begin by reminding the reader of some things that should be avoided. While encouraging people to tell their stories, avoid bombarding them with "machine gun" questions. As much as possible avoid asking questions that begin with the word "why." Most people don't really know "why" they do what they do, so it is futile to ask them. Questions need to be brief and to the point, not overwhelming.

Likewise, as investigation gets under way, do not assume that the process of collecting data can be hurried. As people begin to talk about what has been happening in their lives, the stories will be coupled with expressions of strong emotion. Be careful not to extend false assurances. It is one thing to give hope, namely, that God is present and wants to bring something good out of the person's pain. But false assurances tend to communicate that the problem(s) will go away, and they tend to sound glib or clichéd. We might be tempted to communicate that an unfaithful mate will return or that a child's drug problem will go away. We have no guarantees that such things will occur. But we can tell them that God is present to give strength and wisdom to persevere in life.

Spiritual counselors will also want to be careful not to minimize the problems a person describes. Sometimes caregivers are thinking, *Boy, they think they have problems, but they sure don't have the troubles that the Jones family is facing.* Be careful in thinking such things, and by all means don't say it. Nothing sabotages the helping relationship more than minimizing the pain that someone else is going through. So avoid comparing the problem with that of someone else.

Another common problem that beginning spiritual directors experience is communicating in various ways that they will "take care of the person." We want to avoid "rescuing" people at all costs. When we tell people that they can call us at any time, day or night, or when we imply that we will always be there, we are taking on a role that only God can fill. Ultimately we want the person to learn to be dependent on God and His Word to give guidance. So be careful not to lead the person into a relationship where he or she becomes dependent on you instead of God.

B. Investigating Through Listening

So how do we collect the data that we will ultimately need to give spiritual counsel? We begin by talking less and listening more. We will want to encourage the person to tell his story. A way to begin might sound something like the following:

> I am really glad that we could get together today. When we talked last week, I sensed that you were going through a lot of discomfort. It would be helpful if you could tell me again what has been going on in your life. I would be interested in knowing what has happened since we talked last.

Notice that the above statement is transitional. That is, the one giving spiritual counsel wants to get the person to talk about the most immediate concerns that he has. It doesn't mean that all the data gathering will focus on "current events" alone. But people will tend to talk about what has happened recently. It is fresh in their minds.

Someone might ask, "Should I take notes as I do investigation?" There are different opinions regarding this question. Since many who give spiritual counsel find themselves talking to people in somewhat informal settings, we would suggest that taking notes may not be wise, especially while the person is talking. However, after a session is completed, the spiritual director may want to summarize what was discussed. Since the investigation stage will seek to find how people *feel*, *act*, and *think* in various situations, most of the data will be recalled in order to make the summary report. If you do decide to take notes during the session, ask the person's permission before doing so. If the person seems reluctant, assure him that you are the only one who will have access to the data. Remind him that you will also destroy all of the notes after the two of you stop meeting, unless you have to pass information on to a professional to whom you are referring the person under your care. As a general rule, we would discourage you from taking notes during the actual time of the meeting.

As the person describes the details of any given "presenting problem," try to listen for specific elements. Ask questions about what the person felt when a specific event occurred. Often people will tell about their feelings without being asked to do so. We need to know about feelings because they are like arrows pointing into a person's soul. And it is within the soul, the heart of a person, that the deep issues of life are determined. We need to reflect on a person's feelings to determine what is really important to him. In addition we will want to watch for descriptions of behavior that seem to occur over and over in a person's life. Without interrupting the person's disclosure of his own "story," we will want to ask him what was going on in his thinking. The person may not be able to answer clearly, but a subtle probing will get him to think about what he was telling himself. When we refer to someone's thinking, we are referring to how a person interprets or assesses a given problem. People will often see life as unfair, unjust, or unexpected. What we are saying about the early attempts of investigation is that we should start with the presenting problem and observe the person's feelings, behavior, and assessments (thoughts) with respect to this problem.

C. Investigating: Hearing a Person's Story

As the spiritual counselor learns more about what brought the person to seek help, it will be necessary to explore other areas of life as well. The issue in spiritual counsel is not one particular problem that an individual is facing at a given point in time. In the spirit of Ephesians 4:17–24 we will want to help people to see that old ways of living and thinking are not productive. Spiritual growth toward a God-focused life will mean that we must help people to discover ineffective patterns of living and then guide them in putting off those ineffective patterns so as to embrace the life that God has for each of His children. To get to the God-focused life we must first know what influences the way the person currently views life.

We noted in the preceding chapter that spiritual counsel should not be inordinately focused on what has happened in the past. God Himself is calling us to prepare to live in an eternal kingdom. However, that does not mean that we cannot learn from the events of the past. Part of the investigation process should give attention to what has happened at significant times in a person's life. A helpful way to do this is to ask questions about "primary relationships" and "primary events." *Primary relationships* have to do with those interactions with key people in a person's life who shaped his or her overall worldview. Relationships with parents, siblings, grandparents, friends, and teachers generally have a profound impact on how a person views life. *Primary events* refer to those situations in life that tend to dramatically change the course of one's life or cause significant emotional pain.

A spiritual counselor will want to work at developing questions and transitional statements that naturally lead into a further development of the person's "story line." The conversation might sound something like the following:

You mentioned how awful you felt when your world seemed to come apart last week. I want to hear more about that. But I don't really know a whole lot about you. Tell me a little bit about your family.

As people talk about the key relationships of life, try to build on what has already been said. For instance, if a person reveals something about a primary relationship, build on the story line to learn about primary events.

> It's interesting what you just told me about your father. Did he say those things often to you? Maybe you could give me an example of a time when he told you that you were . . .

Keep in mind that questions and transitional statements are designed to find out what happened in a person's life, how the person was feeling, how he behaved, and how he interpreted what happened. Consequently, as story lines unfold, try to ask questions regarding people and events:

"How did you feel when that happened?"

"What did you do when . . . ?"

"What was going on in your mind when that happened?"

"Tell me what you concluded about life when that occurred."

Your task in giving spiritual counsel is not to ask this exact set of questions, but rather to ask the kinds of questions that fit with your personality and lead to collecting as much data about the person as possible. As information unfolds, the person in the caregiving role will learn about the beliefs and attitudes that motivate people to live as they do. Most of the time, lifestyles will be determined not by biblical guidelines but by personal strategies aimed at keeping one as much as possible from experiencing emotional pain.

D. Investigation Tools

You might be asking at this point, "How many questions do I ask?" There is no exact number of questions a spiritual counselor will want to ask. As a matter of fact, you will not want to think in terms of numbers but in terms of goals. Your goal is to determine the person's worldviews. Once these attitudes about life are uncovered, it will be easier to guide the person to see where they are ineffective and out of touch with the ways of God. So the one who does spiritual counsel will *always* be doing investigation. But certainly the first scheduled meeting should be devoted to getting information from the individual's story line.

Do not neglect asking questions about the person's health and spiritual practices. We will see later in this chapter that any suspicion of health-related problems should initiate referral to a physician. And we will want to be sure to look at primary events and primary relationships through the lenses of spiritual practices as well. That is, we will want to learn about the time of the person's conversion and the story of his growth in Christ, assuming that he has come to faith in Christ. If you are persuaded that the person who has come for help is not a believer, begin to pray silently for an opportunity to present the gospel. In addition, find out what the person's practices have been regarding prayer, Bible study, and church attendance.

At the end of this investigative session, the spiritual director will want to get the person being mentored into the process of taking responsible action. Early on in the process of soul care you may give this individual a simple assignment. Here is where the leading of the Holy Spirit will be important, because assignments will differ with each individual. When you need more information, you might want to give an assignment such as asking the person to write down different things that come to mind about his past. This kind of assignment would help the caregiver to discover more about primary events that have shaped the person's worldview. Or one might ask a person to begin to list the names of people who have had a significant influence in his life, whether positive or negative. Such an assignment will help you to discover more about primary relationships that influence how a person thinks.

A helpful assignment that can be used throughout the process of spiritual counsel is a *daily events journal*. The purpose of the journal is to get the person to monitor his thoughts so that eventually in the power of the Holy Spirit he can take every thought captive. The concept comes initially from those who advocate a paradigm known as cognitive-behavioral counseling. But the process can be helpful for anyone who wants to evaluate what kinds of thoughts really determine our day-to-day actions and attitudes. Ask the person being mentored to take a sheet of paper or a small spiral notebook and write five letters down the left margin. The letters are H-A-F-T-T. Here is what the letters stand for and what should be recorded under each word category.

H—What Happened that was upsetting?
A—How did I Act when this event occurred?
F—What was I Feeling when this event occurred?
T—What was I Telling myself when this occurred?
T—What is the Truth that God wants me to see in this situation?

Have the person who is keeping the journal keep one event recorded per page and to bring the journal with him next week. The person will also need to allow space between each letter to write a response for each one of the questions. During the first week the assignment is given, the spiritual counselor does not need to tell the person what the second "T" means. But in the four or five sessions that follow, instruction can be given to help the person explore the truth of any given situation from the perspective of God's Word. Encouraging the person to get in the habit of keeping a daily events journal can be a helpful process that can be continued even after the spiritual director finishes the mentoring process and encourages the person to get involved in other discipleship activities within the local church. A helpful analogy is to liken the journal process to what happens in a football game. Every game has a "halftime" in which the two teams assess their game plan and make adjustments for the second half. We could tell the person participating in spiritual counsel that he is also engaging in a process of assessment. The only difference is that his journal is called "H-A-F-T-T time." What he learns about earlier "periods" of his life can help him to make adjustments for what God has in store for him in the future.

At the end of the first complete session, try to communicate hope, hope based on the fact that God is at work and wants to do something special in the person's life. Encourage him to be diligent in working through the process. Then be sure to ask the person to join with you as you pray for the individual. This does not mean that the one being mentored has to pray. Some would feel very uncomfortable in doing so, especially during the early sessions as the spiritual counselor and the person being mentored get to know each other. But be sure to pray. In future sessions, prayer might begin and end the sessions.

Finally, set a time when the next session will occur. Depending on what is happening and how stressed a person might be, the spiritual director will probably want to meet again in a week. Time between sessions should not extend beyond two weeks. Your goal has been to investigate what is going on in the person's life and in so doing to build a relationship of trust. Through your observations and interaction you should be seeing some themes that occur frequently over the course of the person's life. These themes are what need to be exposed and surrendered to Jesus Christ for ultimate transformation.

Stage 3: The Issue of IDENTIFICATION

People are often reluctant to reveal too much about themselves. In fact, living in a sinful world and being constantly tempted by fleshly thoughts and desires, people will spend quite a bit of energy in protecting themselves, particularly their images. Yet God is at work to transform us into the image of Jesus Christ. Spiritual counselors will want to cooperate with the Holy Spirit in helping people see the futility of a life lived for personal pleasure and self-protection. That is why it is important once a person comes for help to take the time to develop trust. The initial contact we have with someone during the *involvement* process and well into *investigation* requires that we proceed with caution. Like Columbo we want to get the facts.

By the second and third sessions we hope that rapport and trust have been built. Now it is time to take the facts from primary events and primary relationships to propose what really seems to be going on in the person's life. This third stage is one of *identification*. Again it is important to keep in mind that, like the previous two stages identifying the real issues of a person's life, it will not be a one-time event. The more data that are collected and the more people act on some of the assignments that are given, the more we will be able to discern the thoughts and motivations that influence how they choose to live.

A. Hindrances to Identification

Romans 12:1–2 is a key text in teaching us what God wants to happen in all of our lives. He wants us to put off the ideas and powerful beliefs that have been shaped by the events and relationships of this world and to be transformed by the renewing of our minds. However, our beliefs that we learned in childhood and those that came out of wrong interpretations of life events are not easily discarded. You will remember that we encouraged spiritual counselors to observe feelings and behaviors, not just thoughts. The reason for this is that our beliefs are tied to strong feelings that we have about life. A woman may have been molested or abused by a number of adults while growing up. To simply tell her to love and forgive because the Bible says we should will not work. The reason is that what she believes is coupled with the pain and trauma of what happened in the past.

B. Identification as Partnership

Spiritual counselors will have to take time to discover not only *what is going on* but also *what is keeping the person from participating in a God-focused life.* People who are in emotional/spiritual pain do not always see that what they are doing is *not* working. They live by what they think will *protect* them from further pain. The spiritual director's task is to identify *wrong belief/behavior* patterns and to persuade them to consider embracing *God-focused belief/behavior* patterns.

How can this be done? We return to the need for prayerful action. Spiritual counselors need the wisdom of God to be discerning and courageous with respect to speaking the truth. In addition to praying, it is important to return to the data that have been collected and try to focus on some common themes. Remember that you have been asking people about how they have thought about situations that have occurred in their lives. As individuals report on these things, words and phrases will come up again and again. People will say, "I *wish* that hadn't happened to me." Or, "I *should* have said _____." Or they might say, "I *ought* to tell my boss _____." Watch to see if the person's conversation is filled with "ought's" and "should's." These frequent words and phrases will reveal themes in which the person has a view of life that is not consistent with the will and ways of God. Or the person acts in a way that is not productive as far as living out the will of God.

One helpful way of getting to the truth is to ask the person to make some of his own evaluations of what has happened in the past, or even during a current emotional/spiritual trauma. A good means of inquiry is to say, "Help me to understand what happened when *(a given time or event)* occurred. Was what you *did* very helpful in resolving some of the frustration that you felt?" The spiritual director will want to use this kind of inquiry, especially when a person's behavior is unrighteous or ineffective in getting the kinds of results that he might want. Notice that the focus here is on behavior and feelings again. The goal is to help the person to see that over the long haul his feelings and behaviors have not been as productive as he might have wanted. In fact, you might even ask for a response by saying something like, "It seems to me that what you did wasn't as helpful as you wanted. What do you make of it?"

Soon after exposing some of the ineffective behaviors the person has used, move to identifying the thought patterns that were present in the person's life. Here is where the daily events journal can be very helpful. In fact, if you made this assignment at the end of a previous session, begin the next session in prayer. Follow the prayer with a period of time given to examining the journal. It will be especially helpful if some of the common themes of the *investigation* stage appear again in the daily events journal. As the person talks about what he was thinking with respect to a specific event, follow up with the question, "Do you notice any common thought patterns in these events that you recorded?" Give the person time to evaluate things for himself. As he discovers the faulty thinking that exists, affirm his ability to discern clearly what has been going on.

Follow up with another question: "What do you make of those thoughts? How accurate is that thinking, especially with regard to what you know from God's Word?" Once again, you want the person to make the analysis on his own. The goal at the *identification* stage is to have the one being mentored to see and articulate for himself that past thinking and behavior have been ineffective.

As the spiritual counselor leads the person to a kind of "guided self-discovery," it will be important for the caregiver to pray silently for the Spirit's timing in summarizing some things that have been discovered. This can be done by saying something like the following: "As we have been looking at what is happening and what has happened in your life, it appears that some common things occur frequently in your mind. For instance, you seem to frequently tell yourself that *(whatever the belief pattern might be)*. Notice how you responded to those thoughts by *(describe the behavior)*. Tell me what you think about what I just said." The goal of this line of observation and questioning is to bring the data that have been gathered to some sense of meaning, a general summary of beliefs that seem to govern the way the person believes and behaves.

C. *Identifying with Clarity*

At this point the spiritual counselor can be more directive than at other times in the mentoring process. The more experienced the caregiver becomes, the more he or she can follow summary statements about beliefs with analogies, drawings, or biblical stories that parallel the person's life. For instance, a spiritual counselor might be ministering to someone who is struggling with fear. He might say something like the following:

> Do you remember the story of Gideon in the Old Testament? (Wait for a response.) Gideon was a great warrior, but he was also a man who wrestled with fear, just the way you do. God called him to go and fight against the Midianites. But every time Gideon was challenged to go, he hesitated. He was afraid of what other people would think of him. He was afraid that he wasn't getting the right message from God. He was afraid that he would be outnumbered. He was looking at everything but God. Do you think that you might be doing the same thing in your life?

Even more important, the summary statement of beliefs should be supported as a valid observation by going back to the daily events journal or the description of primary events and relationships to show that a consistent faulty belief system was being practiced. As comparisons are made, the spiritual counselor will want to ask the person if he sees these patterns as well. Actually affirming the truth *identified* on the part of the one being mentored is a very important part of the process.

At the end of this second or third session, the spiritual counselor may want to return to an assignment associated with the daily events journal. Ask the individual to go to the last "T" on the journal pages. Tell him that this "T" stands for "Truth." Then ask him to spend time over the next days between sessions to write "truth statements" for all of the events that he has recorded so far. Then ask him to continue to record events that occur between now and the next session. At the end of each day, ask him to record not only what happened, but also what is the truth about each experience. The person will want to bring the journal next week for further investigation and identification.

Stage 4: The Issue of INITIATION

As more and more data are collected, the spiritual counselor will be feeling more comfortable with what has been discovered. These discoveries will also lead to greater confidence regarding what the caregiver believes is motivating the person who has come for help. In the sessions that follow, greater emphasis should be placed on the Word of God as the source for pursuing a God-focused life. Individuals may have difficulty "putting off" old patterns of living and "putting on" the attitudes and actions of God. But this is what spiritual counsel is all about. Caring for people must go beyond identifying wrong beliefs and behaviors to the point of actually living out the will of God in everyday experiences. Because of the possibilities of resistance, the one who gives spiritual counsel will want to begin to *initiate* action. At this point attention will be given to answering the question, "What action steps does the person need to take to live a God-focused life?" And since the God-focused life is based on living in accordance with God's

Word, truth must be complemented with action.

A. Initiate Realistically

Once again we ask ourselves the question, "How can this be done?" First, it is important to be alert to how people will respond. In many ways it is like the person who has been playing golf for years, but always swinging the club in the wrong way. A professional golfer is hired to help improve the person's game. But every time the golfer tries to take the professional's advice, the new swing feels very uncomfortable. The person might make excuses, but the professional will probably say, "Just keep practicing. Keep trying the new swing until it becomes second nature." The same is true with affirming and acting upon new ways of thinking about life. It will seem uncomfortable at first. But the more it is done, the more it will become part of one's life. So be prepared for expressions of resistance.

People might say, "What if I do this, and it doesn't work?" The way to counter this is to ask, "What do you mean by 'work'? Do you want to do what God wants, or do you want to do only what will make you temporarily comfortable?" People will revert to wanting "quick fixes" to their current problems. Spiritual counselors will need to help them to see that in the long run God honors their obedience. And obedience will lead to maturity (James 1:2–4). Those in pain will also resist making changes by saying, "I can't do this because . . ." They will tell you that they tried something similar in the past and it didn't turn out well. Or they don't want to try something for fear that more pain might occur. Such statements need to be addressed with sensitivity and compassion. However, the spiritual counselor can respond in two ways. First, remind the person that what he has been doing hasn't always worked either. Second, remind him that God is a loving God, not One who wants us to experience a lifetime of pain. Yes, some things may bring short-term discomfort, but God is working a greater good in our lives so that we will become more and more like Jesus Christ. Help the person to keep eternity in view, not just the present difficult circumstances. The apostle Paul reminded the Corinthian believers that "our light and momentary troubles are achieving for us an eternal glory that far outweighs them all" (2 Cor. 4:17). People who participate in spiritual counsel will need to continually be reminded of what is actually true, not what "feels" true. So anticipate the various forms that resistance will take.

B. Initiate with Information

The spiritual director will once more want to go back to what was identified in the previous sessions. It will be important to remind the one being mentored of any faulty ways of thinking, behaving, and feeling that were identified. Return to the daily events journal and have the person identify what he has discovered about God's "truth perspective" regarding his situation. When he has identified the truth accurately, affirm his discoveries. Then ask something like the following: "What do you think you could do to live this new truth out in your life?" Allow for time to ponder answers to this question. If the person is having difficulty coming up with ways to live the truth, paint some possible scenarios. That is, ask "what if" questions. "What do you think you should do if your wife were to respond to your new attempts at loving her by saying that she doesn't trust you?" Make the scenarios realistic and true to the person's lifestyle as much as possible. The more these scenarios are portrayed, the more the person will be able to practice the truth before it is actually needed. The goal is to prepare him to *initiate* action that is appropriate to a new belief system, a belief that is true to the will and ways of God.

As we stated above, the spiritual counselor will want to be more directive in this stage of the process. Some possible between-session assignments in the *initiation* stage will be to provide Scripture passages that can be studied and related to what the person may be facing. John Kruis has put together a very helpful book, *Quick Scripture Reference for Counseling*, that can be used to formulate these kinds of studies. Prior to any of the mentoring sessions the spiritual counselor may want to prepare some simple Bible study questions that focus on specific truths that need to be reinforced. The spiritual counselor's own personal study of the Bible will help in the formulation of these study guides. Encourage the person to reflect on biblical truth as much as possible. Memorizing Scripture can also be of help to a person who is attempting to change from faulty beliefs and behaviors to righteous beliefs and behaviors.

C. Initiate with Clarity

One other matter is very important in the *initiation* stage. Any time you give an assignment to act on biblical truth, make sure the directions are as simple and clear as possible. To ensure that this is happening, ask the person to repeat to you what he is going to do before meeting again for the next session. If he has difficulty explaining what he is to do, return to the action step again. Make sure it is clear. Describe what it would look like in the person's life if it was carried out as assigned. Remember, truth is to be coupled with action. Be sure the one being mentored knows what truth-in-life will look like.

If spiritual counsel is to occur over a five- to six-session time frame, then the *initiation* stage will probably encompass sessions three through five or three through six. The final three or four sessions should be devoted to helping the person to see what truth looks like in life and to actually live it out. And when the person lives in obedience, encourage him often. And by all means, when the person sees the failure of past forms of behavior, do not hesitate to encourage him to repent of wrong attitudes, even confessing to God his sinful beliefs and behaviors. Spiritual counsel may not begin with identifying sinful attitudes, but it may require confession of sin as greater understanding occurs regarding the will and ways of God. But even more, encourage the person to focus on the goodness and greatness of God and the excellence of His ways.

BEFORE AND AFTER CARE

Earlier in this chapter we noted that some problems that people face are beyond the expertise of those who will serve as spiritual directors, whether they be pastors or laypeople. We need to be honest about our own limitations. It is ultimately God who brings about change in a person's life. Spiritual counselors are only instruments in the hands of God's Spirit to support change. That may mean that God uses us, or He may choose to use someone else. As in the lives of those submitting to spiritual counsel, so too must we submit to God's will and allow someone else to help if necessary.

We may have to refer to another when time limitations in the ministry reduce the extent of our *involvement* as pastors and lay leaders. There is also the possibility that one's experiences and training in life are not sufficient for the spiritual/emotional demands that people have. And then there are times when people simply do not change as one tries to move from *investigation* to *identification* and to *initiation*. When progress does not occur, the wise thing may be to refer to someone else.

OK, how do we refer? The best way to do this, in our opinion, is for the church at large to develop a network of caregivers. This would include everyone from the pastoral staff and lay leadership to professionals outside of the local church family. Senior pastors especially will want to find out who is available to provide spiritual counsel within the congregation. At the end of the previous chapter we discussed how referral to other members of the congregation might occur. However, pastoral leaders will also want to know about people in the community who can provide assistance.

Wise pastors will want to take the time to find out what professional counselors believe about the Christian faith before making any kind of referral. It will be necessary to determine their areas of specialization, such as marriage and family counseling, addictions counseling, or other special services. But even more important, find out what they personally believe about caring for people. Do they have views that closely harmonize with the doctrinal positions of the church? What procedures do they employ in caring for people? Do they include counseling philosophies of which you might be skeptical, such as focusing on "repressed memories" of forgotten sexual abuse? How will they cooperate with the local church in caring for individuals referred to them? Likewise, it will be important to find out what fees they require if someone comes under their care. Getting answers to these questions will require some time and effort, but those who are serious about spiritual counsel will find that such information will be extremely helpful in carrying out the church's own program of helping believers mature in Christ.

One final thought: When lay leadership gets involved in providing spiritual counsel as it has been described in this book, it is important that systematic oversight be given. Someone on the pastoral staff, preferably the senior pastor, should meet with lay leaders on a regular basis. Cases should be discussed in confidence and direction given as to how people can respond positively to biblical truth. Regular oversight will encourage lay leaders to take the work of spiritual counsel seriously. It will enable others to know when they can increase their involvement with specific individuals. And it will also help these leaders to know when it is wise to refer to someone else. Spiritual counsel is not about how "we" have helped somebody get beyond his/her pain. It is ultimately about letting the Spirit of God do whatever He chooses to do through each one of us.

— *Putting It Into Practice* —

- *Go back to the investigation stage and review some of the kinds of questions that were presented in that section. Think about how you might phrase each question in your own style and in your own words.*

- *Think of someone who may have casually asked you for help, even if it was nothing more than seeking a listening ear. What were some of the things that frightened you or kept you from wanting to get involved?*

- *What would be some questions you might ask that person if he were to approach you today? Imagine a dialogue that you might have with that person, and pose some questions to him.*

- *Consider starting your own daily events journal. Arrange it according to the pattern described in this chapter. Keep notes in the journal for at least a week. At the end of the week, evaluate your records and see what themes and faulty beliefs have occurred. How would you counter those beliefs with the biblical truth?*

NOTES

Adams, Jay E. *The Christian Counselor's Manual.* Grand Rapids: Zondervan, 1973.

Anderson, Neil T. *The Bondage Breaker.* Eugene, Ore.: Harvest House, 1990.

Crabb, Lawrence J., Jr. *Effective Biblical Counseling: A Model for Helping Caring Christians Become Capable Counselors.* Grand Rapids: Zondervan, 1977.

Hoff, Lee Ann. *People in Crisis: Understanding and Helping.* 3d ed. Redwood City, Calif.: Addison-Wesley, 1989.

Ohlschlager, George W., and Peter T. Mosgofian. *Law for the Christian Counselor.* Dallas: Word, 1992. Vol. 6 of *Contemporary Christian Counseling.*

Oliver, Gary J., Monte Hasz, and Matthew Richburg. *Promoting Change Through Brief Therapy in Christian Counseling.* Wheaton, Ill.: Tyndale, 1997.

Tan, Siang-Yang. *Lay Counseling: Equipping Christians for a Helping Ministry.* Grand Rapids: Zondervan, 1991.

Worthington, Everett L. *When Someone Asks for Help: A Practical Guide for Counseling.* Downers Grove, Ill.: InterVarsity, 1982.

— Chapter 12 —

Spiritual Counsel in the Context of Hopelessness

$\mathcal{J}$im Starr had just finished his sermon on Psalm 22, the third message in a series he titled "Seeing Ourselves in the Psalms." He wanted to show how the Scriptures address the various human emotions that people might be facing in his congregation. Several people had already commented that the series had given them comfort in their own personal struggles. But Jim was not anticipating Paul Turner's comments after Sunday's sermon on hopelessness and despair. He noticed that Paul seemed to hang around the vestibule while others shook the pastor's hand. Paul obviously had something on his mind. After the rest of the congregation had filed out, Paul finally spoke.

"Pastor, I was wondering if I could have a word with you."

Jim moved closer to where Paul was standing and extended his hand to greet his newest member of the deacon board. "What's up, Paul? I hope you're not here to tell me the other deacons have appointed you cochairman of the building committee."

The two men chuckled at the inside joke. Paul had agreed to become a deacon at Faith Community Church, but he had done so reluctantly because he was concerned that with his construction experience others might want him to become the leader of the proposed building plan. Paul had told the pastor that he wasn't ready for that kind of responsibility. Paul spoke rather softly when he said, "Pastor, could we move to your office? I really need to talk to you about some things. And no, it's not about being a deacon."

Jim motioned for Paul to follow him down the hallway. When both men were in the pastor's study, Paul headed for the sofa on the east wall. After slowly sitting down, Paul Turner covered his face with his hands. It took him a while to speak, but then he said, "Pastor, I don't know where to begin. I'm really discouraged. In fact, I had been wanting to talk with you about some things even before you ever approached me about joining the deacon board. Oh, don't worry, I'm not going to tell you about some ugly sin I've committed. I'm just really discouraged with life in general right now."

"What are you talking about, Paul? There's obviously something bothering you. So let's talk. But before we do, let me tell my wife not to wait for me. If you don't mind, I'll ask you to drop me off at my house when we're done. Does that sound OK to you?"

Paul nodded and Jim stepped outside the office to tell his wife and kids to go on without him. When he returned it seemed like Paul was really down about something. His mind was spinning all of a sudden with what he wanted to do in this unannounced call to help. Was this a chance to do spiritual counsel? Was God giving him an opportunity to put some of his new ideas into practice? Over the last several weeks and since attending the seminar on soul care with his friend Tom Parkes, Jim had been thinking through how he would approach people who were in spiritual and emotional pain. As he and Tom interacted they had come up with a fourfold approach, which they called their "Four I's." They agreed that they would think about *involvement, investigation, identification,* and *initiation.*

Jim could tell something rather serious was going on by just looking at Paul's facial expression. But he was already asking himself, "What will be the extent of my involvement with this man who has become a good friend in recent months?"

374

"OK, my friend. Let me close the door." Jim pushed both the door into his secretary's office and his hallway door shut. Then he seated himself in the chair opposite the sofa. "Paul, I sense something is going on in your life right now. Why don't you tell me about it?"

There was silence for what seemed to Jim like an eternity. He still wasn't totally comfortable with his growing role as a caregiver to hurting people. He would rather be preaching right now. But God had obviously ordained this moment, and he wanted to make the most of it. Once more he broke the silence and leaned toward his friend. "How can I be of help to you, Paul?"

Faith Church's newest deacon finally spoke up. "Pastor, I wasn't sure I was going to talk to you, but that sermon was primarily for me. Betsy has been encouraging me for weeks to talk to you, and I've been putting it off. I don't know what it is, but I'm really discouraged. I find myself withdrawing from Betsy and the kids. I guess you noticed that I haven't been coming to Sunday school in the last couple of weeks."

Jim nodded his head to acknowledge that he had missed Paul at some recent church events, the kinds of things where Paul had always seemed to want to participate.

"How long has this been going on, Paul?"

His young deacon thought for a few minutes and then spoke. "I would say for about a month . . . maybe a little longer. And believe me, Pastor, it has nothing to do with being a deacon."

Paul's comment got a grin on both men's faces.

Jim was surprisingly comfortable with the silence that permeated his office. He tried to order his thoughts regarding what he wanted to ask next before he probed too far. "Tell me more," he said. "You mentioned that you haven't been coming to Sunday school. What else has being going on?"

Paul shifted his shoulders back and forth as if to try to think about what else was happening. He reported in a kind of list-type response that he always seemed to be tired, yet he had trouble sleeping; he didn't feel much like eating; he found that he was always second-guessing his thoughts. He told Pastor Jim that he would think about moving ahead with some plan he had formulated, only to tell himself that he wasn't sure that was the right thing to do. He paused for a few seconds and then spoke words that Jim Starr knew were very profound. Paul said, "I just can't seem to do anything right. I have great ideas and then it seems that they burn up right in my face."

"Why do you say 'my plans burn up in my face'?" Jim asked the question rather pointedly, believing that he was on to something.

"Well, my folks seem to think so. They've been tellin' me that for years."

Jim was fast-forwarding his thoughts as he caught a glimpse of Paul's parents in his mind. He knew that Paul Sr. was quick with his personal opinion about people and life in general. Jim didn't think that Paul's father always intended to be harsh with people, but he could only imagine that the senior Mr. Turner could say some pretty harsh things.

"Have they said something to you recently?"

"Oh, I guess it goes back to a discussion we had a few Sundays ago. My dad has never been keen on me striking out on my own and going into business. I told him that I was going to bid on the new high school remodeling project. He told me that I was foolish to even think about that project. Then he went into his typical speech that I could have done better if I would have just stayed in the family business. Then he said I would never get the bid in a thousand years."

Paul's eyes started to well up with tears. He continued. "Pastor, I thought I had really done my homework. I checked everything out—material costs, labor costs, and time needed for completion. I worked on that bid more than any others that I have done in the last year. I was really sure that I had a fair and reasonable bid. And then . . . they gave the bid to a firm over in Murraysville."

Once again, silence seemed to reign in the office. Jim Starr was deeply moved by the pain he saw in his parishioner's life. This was not typical for him. Often he felt frustrated when people showed emotion. It was really a frustration borne out of a feeling of incompetence. But his recent meetings with Tom Parkes were helping him to get a handle on what it meant to truly care for people. He was hoping that the more he met with Tom and the more they practiced their paradigm for spiritual counsel, the more he would be ready to teach these principles to his elders and a few select people in the congregation. But he had to force himself not to think about that for now. Paul Turner needed his attention.

"Paul, is there anything else that has happened recently?"

"Yeah, a lot of things, I guess. Last Friday, Betsy told me that she was thinking about applying for a part-time job at an insurance company here in town. Her sister works there and has been encouraging her to apply for a job. I told her I really wasn't happy with that at all. Pastor, I really don't want Betsy working outside the home, especially while the kids are young. And yet, she told me that with Christmas coming soon, she wants some extra money. I know my business is off a little right now, but I really don't want her going back to work."

Jim made a mental note of what was happening. He had to ask one more question before he would close the session. "Paul, have you had a physical lately? Have you been to a doctor to discuss the way you have been feeling recently?"

Paul Turner shook his head ever so slightly, almost as if to say that he didn't see what that had to do with anything at all.

"I would encourage you to think about getting a checkup. If you need some help seeing a doctor, I recommend Dr. Pointer. He is new to our church, but he's a wonderful Christian. I have been developing a relationship with him regarding medical referrals that I sometimes do. You would do well to have him check things out physically. But be sure to inform him of what you have been going through recently."

Jim Starr tried not to be too obvious about looking at his watch, but it was Sunday afternoon and both men needed to get to their own homes. The pastor was thinking through how he was going to answer this question about the extent of his involvement. He came up with a plan that he sensed must have been Spirit directed.

"Paul, I'm going to give you Dr. Pointer's number. I want to encourage you to tell him some of the things that you have told me. But I would also like to meet with you again. I sense there are some things that are going on in your life that would be good to deal with. I'm not going to try to write off your concerns and obvious pain with a Bible verse and a prayer. But God does want us to grow through our difficulties. I want to be available to help you where I can. So let's try to meet on Wednesday of this week. How's that sound to you?"

Paul nodded his head in agreement.

"What I like to do is meet with people for no more than five times, at least initially. If we could get together either Wednesday afternoon or Wednesday night after prayer meeting, we could explore some of the things you're facing more fully. If it's OK with you, we will meet for about an hour. How does Wednesday sound to you?"

"Sounds great," Paul Turner responded with a soft smile on his face. "Probably after prayer meeting would be best. Betsy can take the car home and maybe you could return my favor and drop me off on your way home, Pastor."

"It's a deal," Jim Starr said, extending his hand to Paul Turner as if they had just signed a contract with each other. "And when you come on Wednesday, I would like you to do something for me. Could you begin to jot down as many things as you can think of that have really gotten you down—caused you to feel hopeless— over the last month? Just write down what comes to mind. We'll start with that on Wednesday night. Now, don't forget, think about calling Dr. Pointer."

Pastor Jim informed his newest spiritual protégé that he wanted to pray for him. After a brief prayer, the two men turned the lights off in the pastor's study and headed for the parking lot. Jim Starr was feeling more and more confident that he might be used of God to guide his parishioner through his sense of hopelessness and on to experiencing real joy in Christ. He pondered the thought that dealing with some of these very real issues of pain could also positively affect Paul's ministry as a husband, father, and deacon. Jim silently prayed that God would turn Paul's bouts with despair into a godly triumph.

INVOLVEMENT WITH DEPRESSED PEOPLE

Few, if any, individuals have gone through life without having some sense of disappointment in life. Feelings of despair can last anywhere from a few minutes to several days or longer. Some people call it depression; others refer to it as the "dark night of the soul." In this chapter we are going to refer to these feelings and perceptions as "hopelessness." For that is exactly what people believe when life becomes overwhelming. They see no way out of their situation. And like Paul Turner in our opening scenario, people might have ideas about how to move on in life, only to second-guess what they are thinking. Hopelessness, or depression as it is commonly identified, is the "common cold" of human spiritual/emotional trials. It is common among Christians and non-Christians alike. However, since God wants us to grow in the grace and knowledge of the Lord Jesus Christ, pastors and lay caregivers must be able to minister to people in their times of disappointment.

The Bible describes several people who experienced times of hopelessness as they lived life this side of eternity. The apostle Paul told of his own experiences when life did not unfold as he had planned (2 Cor. 1:8). Psalm 22 describes the experiences of David, who struggled with the thought that God Himself had turned against him. Whether the feelings are mild or severe, the sensation of hopelessness is common to life. But when people approach prospective spiritual counselors, seeking a formal or informal mentoring relationship, how should these caregivers respond? The best answer is "proceed with caution." Pastor Kirk Johnston confirmed this necessary word of caution when he wrote:

> Many pastors and some Christian counselors apparently still believe that depression is always caused by spiritual/emotional problems. This is unfortunate, because although this is often the case, it isn't necessarily so. Some depression starts with physiological problems. Gary Collins points to a study that indicates that perhaps 40 percent of all depression cases can be linked to physical illness. (143)

Using our model of spiritual counsel as described in the last chapter, we want to describe the way a pastor and lay leader might guide a person through the agony of feeling hopeless.

We begin with the stage of *involvement*. As in every potential mentoring situation, the caregiver must answer the question, "What will be the extent of my involvement?" To answer this question it is important that the one who is asked to give help consider networking with several other key people, especially someone from the medical community. The potential causes behind feelings of despair necessitate this precautionary approach.

Spiritual counselors will want to avoid going it alone when dealing with depressed people because there are so many different kinds of despair that an individual can experience. We will only deal with the most common ones, but the reader will want to begin developing relationships with physicians and counseling professionals to assist in the care of some individuals, especially those who are in a state of hopelessness because of physiological causes.

One form of depression is identified as *bipolar disorder.* It has a physiological cause and may be hereditary. People who manifest bipolar depression often have "highs" and "lows." That is, they will express one of two extreme moods, a feeling of extreme elation or one of extreme depression. Sometimes the individual can experience both moods in a cyclical pattern. The good news is that a bipolar disorder can usually be treated with medication. One can easily see why a need for medication makes networking with other professionals a necessary part of wise spiritual counsel.

A common form of depression for some middle-aged individuals is referred to as *involutional depression.* It often occurs among women between the ages of forty and fifty-five, and among men between the ages of fifty and sixty-five. The onset of involutional depression coincides with what is commonly referred to as "change of life" or midlife crisis. People expressing hopelessness within this category will often appear to be distressed, worried, and even angry. William Backus wrote the following:

This depression can be differentiated from bipolar disorder by the history of no previous episodes. Insomnia, guilt, and anxiety are prominent. Sometimes depressive delusions are prominent. Involutional depression occurs three times more often in females than in males. (144)

Once again, we see that a person trying to give spiritual counsel to someone facing the challenges of this type of despair cannot provide soul care on his or her own. A network of caregivers, including physicians, will serve us well.

When depression or despair is less severe, meaning that normal everyday activities are not disrupted, the condition is sometimes referred to as *dysthymic disorder.* The feelings of hopelessness and sadness may pass away within a matter of hours or a few days. However, Kirk Johnston makes a helpful observation when it comes to caring for people, no matter how severe the depression might be.

It is also true that even if a depression began with spiritual/emotional problems, eventually the depression can become a physical one. This is commonly known as "clinical depression." In this situation the depressed individual needs anti-depressants in order to get well more quickly and to deal with the root causes of depression. (144)

He goes on to clarify matters, however, by noting that medication alone cannot fully cure most depressed people. Direction from God's Word and the acceptance of God's people can go a long way in correcting wrong thinking and wrong behavior. But does this mean that pastors and lay leaders should be suspicious of people's use of medication? Not necessarily. An important word to keep in mind is the word *balance.* We like what one writer has stated regarding the use of medication in caring for depressed people.

It would be a tragedy for a godly pastor or Christ-centered counselor to try helping a person who is physically sick without suggesting some medical attention. On the other hand, for a doctor to think that he or she can cure the whole person with medication is equally tragic. Taking a pill to cure the body is commendable, but taking a pill to cure the soul is deplorable. (Anderson and Baumchen 69)

The wise spiritual counselor will always want to be alert to the severity of depression as he attempts to determine the extent of his involvement with the individual seeking help. The more the person's normal, everyday activities are disrupted, the more one should consider entering into a partnership with other caregivers in the community, especially medical doctors.

In the scenario portrayed in the beginning of this chapter, Pastor Jim Starr was correct in encouraging Paul Turner to seek medical counsel. But let's assume that there are no medical causes behind Paul's feelings of despair. What then? You will recall that Pastor Starr started to ask some very important questions about recent events in Paul's life. Quite frequently, a feeling of hopelessness of the dysthymic kind can occur because of some significant primary event—at least something that is significant to the one who is experiencing the emotional pain. The individual interprets the event as "good" or "bad" and becomes obsessed with the experience and its associated feelings. The spiritual counselor will want to get as much information as possible on these primary events, especially during the involvement process.

In addition, spiritual directors will want to inquire about other matters as well, especially as they relate to the person's overall health. Sometimes new medications that a person may be taking can influence how he feels. You will do well to ask a person under your care if he knows of any possible side effects to the medication. Encourage the person to ask his doctor about any possible side effects. Likewise, it is important to get a handle on how much rest and exercise a person may be getting. All of these factors could be prompting the feelings of hopelessness and despair.

Even though a person's spiritual/emotional problems may have an organic cause, it is still important to investigate a person's spiritual condition. Simply attending church and reading the Bible will not eliminate problems. But spiritual counselors will want to determine if spiritual lethargy has set in. When the normal spiritual routines of life are abandoned, there is usually some cause. A person may have fallen into sin and the guilt is leading to other physical manifestations. Or the individual may be misinterpreting life events to the degree that it affects his spiritual life as well. So find out what is going on spiritually in a troubled person's soul.

As in all contexts of spiritual counsel, involvement should begin on a limited and precautionary basis. It takes time to get medical tests diagnosed, so there may be some time between the point of one feeling depressed and ultimately entering into a mentoring relationship. You will remember that Pastor Jim Starr was intentional about setting up a meeting with Paul Turner, a meeting that was to occur within a few days. Making follow-up appointments does not mean that other appointments will automatically occur. But pastoral care requires that the one who is doing the mentoring will try to ensure as much as possible that the person is getting the help that he needs.

INVESTIGATION WITH PEOPLE WHO ARE DEPRESSED

It should be obvious from what we have stated so far that there are no clear lines of demarcation between the various stages of spiritual counsel. Even though we might be trying to determine the extent of our *involvement*, we still have to do *investigation*. And even while we do *investigation*, we may be trying to *initiate* action that will nurture growth in a person's spiritual life. However, we do need to think in terms of distinct tasks if we are to be effective in this important work of soul care.

While we are doing the work of collecting data, we will almost naturally be drawn to some obvious symptoms. For instance, the way people describe feelings can be indicative of what is going on at the level of the soul. They may talk about feeling "sad" or "blue" all of the time. They may talk about feeling "hurt" or "rejected" when some spoken or unspoken expectation went unfulfilled. Those who engage in soul care will want to remember that expressions of feelings may be symptomatic of faulty ways of interpreting life and life events.

Behavioral symptoms also need to be investigated. By all means watch for nonverbal behavior. What is the person's posture when he begins talking with you? When, if ever, does he change facial expressions? What is his response when subjects are discussed, especially subjects related to the primary individuals who affect the person's life?

People should be asked about their sleeping and work habits. As we noted above with respect to milder forms of depression, people might be able to maintain normal responsibilities. Yet they are likely to express an overall disappointment with their lives. Spiritual counselors will want to get as much data as possible regarding when they started to feel this way and what was happening that led up to these feelings. It will be important to make an assessment of people's lives to see if rejection, anger, and a failure to be honest about their feelings occur as common expressions in their "story lines." You will want to make note of any significant issues related to feelings and behavior. Write them down after your meetings so that you can review them before any future sessions. As we stated in the previous chapter, you do not need to be taking notes while you and the individual under your care are meeting together. Do whatever it takes to continue the process of building a relationship of trust.

IDENTIFICATION AND HOPELESSNESS

What is at the heart of most feelings of hopelessness and despair? The very word *hopelessness* provides us with a strong clue. People are "without hope." They come to the conclusion that there is no valid reason to go on. If we were to monitor their self-talk, they would be saying such things as "It doesn't matter if I act in a certain way. Things are too far gone. I will never be able to recover." Or they might pick up on the evaluations of others, even when those evaluations are wrong, and begin to degrade themselves. They tell themselves such things as "I can't do anything right." "I'll never be happy in this job, and there's nothing else I can do." The negative interpretations of life become the primary criteria for determining if life is "good" or "bad."

Pastor Kirk Johnston states that, at its core, depression is the loss of hope. He described it in the following way:

> Some Christians lose hope of ever being loved again. Others lose hope of ever being gainfully employed. Still others feel that the situation with their rebellious child is hopeless. Some depressed believers do not know why they are depressed, but they feel hopeless about ever feeling better. Whatever the particular reason for the loss of hope, the need for hope is the common denominator among all depressed people. This is why when I begin to counsel a depressed person, I always say up front that he or she will get better, or that things will get better. I always try to give hope. (141)

We concur with Johnston's assessment of core beliefs that need to be changed. One might want to be careful in saying that "you will get better," but we agree that the spiritual counselor does need to aim at giving hope to those who come feeling despairing or extremely disappointed with life.

Notice also in identifying the core beliefs behind these feelings of hopelessness, that general expectations have been shattered. As part of the process of *investigation* and *identification* you will want to explore what surrounded the primary events and primary relationships of life. Identifying some of these key expectations that were not met in the recent past will help you to develop action steps that are built on biblical truth. For instance, Paul Turner started believing certain things that he heard said repeatedly from his father. He also had high expectations that he was going to get a particular bid for his construction business. When disappointments begin to come all at once, it is easy for a person to believe lies about himself. Such deception is part of classic spiritual warfare coming from the world, the flesh, and the devil.

A number of people portrayed in Scripture demonstrated times of hopelessness, and most of those experiences were accompanied by unfulfilled expectations. Take the Old Testament prophet Habakkuk. In the first two chapters of Habakkuk the prophet expressed a strong desire to have God deal with the sin that was so prevalent in Judah. God's response was that He had heard Habakkuk's prayer and was about to send the Babylonians to take God's people into captivity. The prophet complained about God's plans, particularly the concept of God using an evil people to judge evil in Israel. It didn't make sense from Habakkuk's perspective. He was hoping for something different. And when what he had hoped for didn't come, we see a period of frustration and despair entering his soul (Hab. 3:16).

We can observe similar behavior on the part of the prophet Jonah. You will recall how Jonah was called by God to go and preach in Nineveh. But almost as quickly as Jonah got orders from God he attempted to flee and find a safe haven in Tarshish. You are familiar with his story line and how he ended up being thrown overboard, only to be swallowed by a great fish (Jonah 1:17). But why did Jonah flee in the first place? He had other "expectations." He wanted God to judge Nineveh, not redeem it. And even after Jonah was thrust out of the fish and he actually went to Nineveh, he still was not pleased. His preaching ministry got great results, yet Jonah was depressed. He said, "Now, O LORD, take away my life, for it is better for me to die than to live" (Jonah 4:3). God wanted obedience. Jonah wanted Nineveh to be destroyed. And when it didn't happen, the prophet found himself imprisoned in a jail cell of hopelessness.

As you collect data regarding a person's story line, always look for themes that surround the possibility of unfulfilled expectations. You will want to rehearse some of these things with the person under your care, helping him to see what he *wanted* and what he *didn't get*. But start to spoon-feed the person a little hope, showing that even though one expectation was not met, God still wants to do something good in and through him. In fact, you might have him participate in an assignment where he explores the lives of the two prophets cited above. You will want him to reflect on Habakkuk 3 and Jonah 4. But focus the attention on God, His attributes, and His care for people. We want people to acknowledge their own faulty thinking, but we primarily want them to embrace the God-focused life. He is the source of hope in the midst of their very personal despair.

INITIATING HOPE

If you encourage people to start keeping the daily events journal, it will help them to see for themselves what has been occurring and how they have been evaluating those events. That self-evaluation can go a long way in guiding a person to spiritual health. People who are depressed, even those with mild depression, may be reluctant to keep such a record. Their tendency to inactivity and tiredness may temporarily inhibit progress. But encouraging them to write only one or two entries can get them to move in the right direction. The spiritual director may even have to make one or two phone calls between sessions to make sure that the journal is being kept.

In addition to the daily events journal, those involved in spiritual counsel will want to encourage the individual to eat properly and to get sufficient rest and exercise. Even though the person may be reluctant about social interaction, time spent with other people, especially other believers, can be a wonderful source of encouragement. To know that someone else is praying for a person has a way of bolstering that person's feelings.

It will also be important to get the person to return to the Word of God and focus on His work in their lives. Those who give spiritual counsel will want to look for ways to integrate the Word of God into the person's life so that it is more than just hearing a sermon on Sunday mornings.

Spiritual counselors themselves will want to commit to being students of the Word. As you participate in your own Bible study—whether it is a regular Bible reading program, listening to sermons, or personally studying the Scriptures—always read to analyze the text first and then to apply it second. That is, ask probing questions of the passage with regard to the historical background, the meaning of words, and the primary truth the writer was trying to communicate to the original audience. Then meditate on that primary truth and ask the question, "How does this text relate to people and their problems?" If you approach the Word of God with this question in mind, you will discover that you have a lot of material from which to draw.

This same material will also enable you to develop brief homework assignments that you can give to your protégés. Keep in mind, however, that the purpose of such assignments is not to get people to collect information. Instead you want them to see what God is like in relationship to their problems. We have included a sample of a possible worksheet at the end of this chapter. You will want to develop ones that you have studied and developed personally before passing them on to someone else. When you develop and employ such homework assignments, be sure to use them in the very next meeting that you have with the person you are mentoring. If it was worthy of his time and attention, it is worth reviewing in the sessions that follow.

— *Think About It* —

- *Identify some times in your own life when you experienced a sense of hopelessness. Specifically make note of the things that helped you to get beyond your feelings of despair.*
- *Be intentional about listening to casual conversations this week. What are some frequent statements that you hear people saying that could be symptomatic of discouragement and hopelessness in their lives?*
- *What is the truth about God that can be a focus in each of these statements you heard from others?*

"If I'm Saved, Why Am I Depressed?"

(A Homework Assignment in the Practice of Spiritual Counsel)

Most of the questions that follow are related to several key events from the life of Jeremiah. He was a human being like us. He too had times in which he felt depressed. Read each question carefully and record the information in the space provided.

1. Depression is seldom admitted or talked about among Christians. Why do you think that is the case?

2. Please list some of the symptoms and feelings you have experienced that might be classified as depression or hopelessness.

3. Read Jeremiah 1:4–10, 17–19. It is apparent that the sovereign God had a plan for Jeremiah's life, even before he was conceived. God called him to stand for righteousness and promised to enable Jeremiah to do the work. What did God promise to do for him when opposition to his ministry set in?

4. How can a realistic assessment of life's problems and the Lord's resources help you handle discouragement?

5. How did the people from Jeremiah's hometown respond to Jeremiah's message (Jer. 11:18–23)? How could this have contributed to his sense of hopelessness?

6. Why did God require Jeremiah to repent of the attitudes he expressed (Jer. 15:19)?

7. What does Luke 14:28–33 teach you about being realistic about life's challenges?

8. Write out the following passages and refer to them several times during the next several days: Proverbs 15:13; Proverbs 17:22; John 16:33; Philippians 1:6.

NOTES

Anderson, Neil T., and Hal Baumchen. *Finding Hope Again*. Ventura, Calif.: Regal, 1999.

Backus, William. *Telling the Truth to Troubled People*. Minneapolis: Bethany House, 1985.

Johnston, J. Kirk. *When Counseling Is Not Enough: Biblical Answers for Those Who Still Struggle*. Grand Rapids: Discovery House, 1994.

— *Chapter 13* —

Spiritual Counsel in the Context of Fear

$\mathcal{J}$im Starr was surprised when he heard the voice at the other end of the phone line. He had not talked with Gary Jameson in months. They last talked at a denominational meeting in Omaha. Gary and his wife, Mary, had just made a move to the same district where Jim and Kathy Starr had been serving for the last six years. *How strange,* Jim thought to himself. *Here we are serving only an hour or so from each other and we never see the Jamesons that much.* Jim could sense, however, that Gary's call was more than social chitchat.

After the typical greetings and questions about each pastor's ministry experiences, Gary got right to the point, a point that Jim Starr was surprised to hear.

"Jim, I don't know how to ask you this. In fact, I probably should be calling your wife, since she is the one that might be able to help me."

Pastor Starr chuckled. He didn't have to give anyone permission to talk with his wife. He took great pleasure in the fact that Kathy saw ways to minister that he would normally overlook.

"Gary, what's up? How can I help . . . or should I say, how can my wife help?"

"Well, Jim, I am thankful for a lot of things in my life and ministry right now, but I am really concerned about Mary. She really needs someone to talk to. I feel like we're walking on eggshells around our house. My wife seems to be uptight and fearful that things are going to go wrong, just like they did in our last church. I was hoping if Mary and Kathy could get together, maybe my wife would feel a little more at ease with being in ministry."

Jim listened as Pastor Jameson let out a deep sigh. "Gary, I appreciate your sensitivity in calling me first, but I think Kathy would love to get together with Mary. I would encourage your wife to give Kathy a call and set up a time when the four of us can see each other. Tell ya what. Maybe the four of us could get together for dinner over the next few days. Then our wives might want to launch out from there on their own little journey. How's that sound to you?"

The phone conversation didn't last long, but Jim sensed that the Starrs and Jamesons would probably be seeing one another very soon. And sure enough, when Jim Starr walked into his house to get a quick bite for lunch, his wife greeted him with an enthusiastic, "Guess what?" He didn't want to guess. His mind was spinning with the errands he had to do in the afternoon. He also wanted to get in one or two more hours on his sermon for Sunday. But Kathy Starr kept pressing. "Go ahead, guess what happened just about an hour ago?"

"I really don't know, honey. What happened?"

"It has something to do with the class I have been taking with a wonderful pastor and spiritual director."

Jim smiled and suddenly remembered that Kathy was in the training class along with all of his elders and their wives and two other women from the church. He had been telling them and praying for them that people would be coming into their lives for important spiritual guidance. Apparently Kathy was ready to tell him about an answer to his prayers, especially as it related to her.

"OK, tell me about it. Who has God brought into your life?"

"Well, right after I got the kids off to school I was having my devotions. I was praying that God would equip me to be an effective spiritual director. That's what you wanted us to pray, isn't it?" Jim nodded with a smile on his face. "Well, I no more than finished praying and the phone rang. It was Mary Jameson. She seemed a little nervous as we exchanged small talk. She asked if we could go out for dinner with the two of them sometime soon. Then the strangest thing happened. Right after we set a date, she said there was really another reason for getting together. Mary wants to meet with me to talk over some things. She told me she could hardly get through a day without being paralyzed by fear. I guess Gary has been real understanding, but he encouraged her to give me a call."

Jim Starr leaned against the kitchen doorframe with a sly smile on his face. Kathy looked up from fixing his sandwich and said, "Say, did you have anything to do with this?"

"What makes you think that?"

"Well, you're smiling as if you know something I don't know."

"OK, I should tell you that Gary called me early this morning. He did mention that they wanted to get together. But he really wanted to see if you could meet with Mary. I told him to have Mary ask for herself. In fact, I had almost completely forgotten it until you brought it up. By the way, I already knew about the situation. But as you have further conversations with her, I imagine one of the hardest parts will be that you can't really tell me or anyone else details of what she discusses with you, unless it's because you need help in some area. But I guess we will see what happens after our dinner engagement."

"Well, I don't know if it will take that long. Mary and I are getting together on Friday. We're going to meet halfway between our homes. There's a nice little tea room off of Route 14. It should be private enough that we can talk. Jim, all I know is that she seems very fearful and anxious about something. My fear has to do with whether or not I can help. Oops! I meant to say, 'I don't know if I'm ready to be a spiritual director.'"

Can Kathy Starr help? Can people who want to serve Christ be used to help others grow in their relationship with Christ? Absolutely! It may take some understanding of the issues of fear and anxiety. But it is possible to work through the issues that are common to human beings and ultimately disciple them to be the people Christ wants them to be. Individuals like Kathy Starr can be used of the Spirit of God to guide others into emotional and spiritual maturity. Following the model of spiritual counsel described in chapter 11, there are some steps to take that will reduce the fear and apprehension that many caregivers experience and that help them encourage fearful people.

INVOLVEMENT—FEAR SHOWS UP EVERYWHERE

As always, the spiritual counselor will minister to fearful people by answering the question, "What will be the extent of my involvement?" It was stated in earlier chapters that we should always enter into caregiving relationships with a sense of caution. We need to avoid a rush to judgment by trying to discern the causes behind a person's fears. We would do well in all contexts of spiritual counsel to begin by asking if there is even the slightest hint of organic causes behind a person's problems. But if we can safely rule out such physical dysfunctions, we can then move on to helping the person to resolve the conflicts.

It may also be important to try to answer the question, "What will be the settings in which we are drawn into the lives of people trapped by fear and worry?" It is again best to answer the question by noting that we will find ourselves ministering everywhere, in all sorts of situations. Spiritual directors or spiritual counselors are not simply people who serve as pastors and associate staff personnel in local churches. They can be mature believers who serve as elders, deacons, or deaconesses. They may be husbands, wives, or parents. They may be widows or single people. You will find them in corporate offices and along the assembly lines of many factories. Caregivers can be found *everywhere*. And since all people struggle with fear and worry at one time or another, caregivers' services can be sought out in a variety of settings.

For example, marriages can have their anxious moments. A husband and wife might listen to the ministry of God's Word and conclude that it is best for the wife to stay at home and devote time to rearing the children. Yet when the couple decides to act on their beliefs, fear becomes the reality. The husband may not be convinced that they can make it on just one income. Dreams to move to a bigger house might have to be set aside. And then one day over lunch, the husband confides in a Christian colleague, telling him that he doesn't know if his wife should quit her job or not. What a wonderful opportunity to build on an established relationship to engage in spiritual counsel.

A similar setting might unfold in the context of parenting. Christian parents are consistently challenged with rearing children in a postmodern world. Imagine the concern parents would have when they discover that their teenage daughter does not want to go to school. She has been a fairly good student and has been well liked by other children. Now she is two months into her first year of high school. She acknowledges to her mother one morning that the more she studies, the harder her classes seem to become. She has a big test that day and doesn't want to face the possibility of failing. Should a parent avoid caring for a daughter because the emotional pain seems overwhelming? Of course not! It is another wonderful opportunity to do spiritual counsel with a person, especially someone who is filled with fear and anxiety.

And consider the scenario in which Kathy Starr finds herself. Like most pastors' wives she would not categorize herself as a professional. Nevertheless, she got involved because of previous contacts. Casual conversations may have communicated trust and competence to Mary Jameson. Their situations were similar. The challenges they faced were very much the same. Thus one woman feels comfortable in contacting another woman for guidance.

What we want to communicate clearly is that *mature believers can provide the necessary mentoring that is needed to move people from their spiritual/emotional challenges into a growing relationship with Jesus Christ.* However, those who enter into this ministry, whether marriage partners, parents, friends, or pastoral leaders, must remember that fear is not something to be trivialized. What might seem insignificant and irrational to one person can be a major issue of enslavement to someone else. The wise caregiver will get involved with people by avoiding premature judgments, while seeking to build a relationship of trust with the person who is hurting. The ability to communicate warmth and trustworthiness is often used by the Spirit of God to draw one individual to another. But once involvement occurs, investigation must also begin to unfold.

INVESTIGATION—THE NECESSITY OF DIGGING DEEPER INTO FEAR

When people tell us that they are worried, anxious, uptight, or fearful, what do they mean? Books devoted to the subject of fear reveal some very fine distinctions. For the sake of discussion in this chapter, we are going to confine our thinking to the terms *fear* and *anxiety*. They are quite similar, but there may be some slight distinctions between the two. Duncan Buchanan defines fear in this way:

> It is that state of being, be it temporary or permanent, which so fixes on anything which in some way threatens to destroy, or which it is supposed will destroy us, that we cannot avoid being obsessed by it. If that is a working definition of fear, it is at once clear that, by drawing our attention away from God, it is very much the essence of sin. (44)

Kirk Johnston also makes a distinction between fear and anxiety. He observes that with fear there is a sense of uneasiness and tension over something that we know exists. Anxiety, on the other hand, may have this same sense of uneasiness and tension, but one does not know why he or she is feeling that way. However, Johnston goes on to say that even if one makes a subtle distinction between fear and anxiety, resolution of the problem is still a matter of faith (165–66). This is because one's attention is taken off of the living God and placed onto something that does not deserve so much attention. Likewise, we tend to give more power to the object of our concern than it deserves. At the core of any person's fear is an attitude of distress, which itself is caused by a perceived threat to one's well-being.

When we look at life and at the Scriptures, we see that fear expresses itself in two different ways. First, there is what we might refer to as healthy fear, or rational fear. This is the kind of fear that a person learns over time in order to protect oneself from danger. A toddler walks around a room exploring all the new things that might be found. She is attracted to the electrical outlet on the wall and quickly begins to poke around all of the little holes with her fingers. All of a sudden she lets out a scream as parents and grandparents come running. The toddler may return to the electrical outlets for further exploration. But she might also quickly learn that electrical power is something to be feared if not handled properly. She will learn the same thing about heights, some insects, poisonous snakes, and a host of other things.

But learning to have a healthy fear regarding some things in our environment is not the only thing that people need to discover. We all need to have a fear of God. Many times the concept of fearing God is related to the term *reverence*. The assumption is that we are to revere God because of His attributes, especially His mighty power. This is true, but the fear of God is much more than standing in awe of His greatness. Psalm 2:10–12 is a call to the rulers of the earth to "serve the LORD with fear" (v. 11). And what is the basis of this fear? It has to do with the fact that God's Son will one day rule with an iron scepter. He will destroy His enemies like one who is smashing pottery. Reverence is certainly part of the thought behind Psalm 2, but it is also one of standing with a healthy sense of fear before a God who has the power to exercise life and death.

In the same way, Moses warned the people of Israel by calling them to fear the Lord in Deuteronomy 6:13–19. They were specifically warned not to follow other gods, especially the gods of the nations that will surround them. Then Israel's leader told them why fearing the Lord is so essential. If they failed to fear Him alone, they would face destruction as a nation and no longer live in the land He was going to provide for them. They were not called to focus on His great attributes of omnipotence and majesty alone, though such attributes were referred to elsewhere (Josh. 4:20–24). They were to fear God because failure to do so would bring them harm. It is a healthy sense of fear that they were to develop toward God.

It is important for spiritual counselors to know about the fear of God. There will be times when people will need to be called out of their sinful choices to walk in righteousness. They will need to know about God's power and His ability to redeem fallen human beings. But they also need to have a sense of fear regarding God's holiness and justice, lest they face the harsh consequences of sin. Learning how to fear God can be the primary means of overcoming other fears that plague humanity.

And just as there are healthy fears that people can learn over time, we also need to be aware of unhealthy fears. These are the kind that fit in with the definitions we cited above. They are fears that cause distress in our minds and bodies because our thoughts are inordinately focused on things that are getting more attention than they deserve. We want to focus on three kinds of unhealthy fear that people often experience. They seem very, very real, but in reality they are not worthy of the believer's attention and time.

A. Investigating the Fear of Death

One common fear that captures our attention is the fear of death. Consider King David's words in Psalm 55:1–5.

> *Listen to my prayer, O God,*
> *do not ignore my plea;*
> *hear me and answer me.*
> *My thoughts trouble me and I am distraught*
> *at the voice of the enemy,*
> *at the stares of the wicked;*
> *for they bring down suffering upon me*
> *and revile me in their anger.*
> *My heart is in anguish within me;*
> *the terrors of death assail me.*
> *Fear and trembling have beset me;*
> *horror has overwhelmed me.*

David admitted that he was afraid, and the reason for his fear was the pursuit of an enemy that he thought could destroy him. He was afraid of the possibility of death. However, David is not the only one to experience such fears. Hebrews 2:14–15 speaks of the incarnation of Jesus Christ and its relationship to the redemptive plan of God. But the writer observed that all human beings are held in fear of death. It is only faith in Jesus Christ that delivers one from such fear.

When it comes to our fear of death we can experience distress in several forms. We might fear the death of a loved one who is seriously ill. We might fear the possible death of a child we love dearly. We might be afraid of our own ultimate death, or more specifically the actual process of dying. And when death looms before our minds, it becomes an obsession that we cannot easily shake loose.

During the investigation stage of helping fearful people, we will want to find out what it is that has led to faulty beliefs about life and death. Consider the following dialogue between Kathy Starr and her friend Mary Jameson. Even though the dialogue does not have the benefit of facial expressions and a person's tone of voice, we can catch a glimpse of what we might do to discover as much information as possible about a person's fears.

Kathy: Mary, I am so glad that we could get together, just the two of us. I sensed the other day that this is kind of a rough time for you.

Mary: Yes, I have to admit that I haven't been myself. Then again, I'm not sure what it means for me to be myself.

Kathy: Why don't you tell me about it. I would be interested to know what's going on in your life.

Mary: Kathy, I really don't know where to start. There are so many things. My mother, the kids, what Gary is facing at church. It all seems overwhelming to me. [Mary begins to get tears in her eyes. She stops for a few seconds, trying to compose herself. Kathy Starr just listens and says nothing for several seconds.]

Kathy: It seems like there is an awful lot going on. I want you to know that I am here as your friend. I really do care about you, Mary. [Kathy continues the silence for a little while longer.] Maybe you could tell me about your mother. What's going on in your mother's life?

Mary: Oh my . . . I don't know where to start. We moved, as you know, about a year and a half ago to our current church. I will never forget the day I told Mother that we were going to have to leave the old church. She lived just about ten miles from where we lived. She didn't become a member of the church, but we saw one another every week, sometimes two and three times a week. She came to our house and to the church, and we visited her as well. I guess I came to confide in her as a friend, not just as my mother. It was good for her also. Dad had passed away one year before we came to First Community. In fact, we felt it was God's will that we were there so that we could help Mom go through her time of grief and reestablish herself again. [Mary pauses and seems to be reflective even though she says nothing.]

Kathy: Mary, you said, "I will never forget the day I told Mother we were going to have to leave . . ." You sounded like that was a really a difficult day. What was it like?

Mary: Well, it was hard enough for us, but Mother broke down and started to cry. She was visiting our home at the time. She knew that something wasn't right almost immediately when she came in. We had just informed the kids of the upcoming move. When we told my mother, she started to cry, saying, *"You can't. You just can't!"* Then she left the house and drove away. Later that morning she did come back, but it was awful. I felt like I let my mother down. I felt like we were abandoning her. And now this.

Kathy: What do you mean, "And now this"?

Mary: [She begins to cry again. Kathy reaches into her purse for a tissue and hands it to her. Their meeting place is private enough that no one else seems to notice.] Three weeks ago, Gary and I went back to see Mom. We were anxious to get away, especially with some of the pressures Gary has been facing. But we noticed that Mother didn't look very well upon our arrival. After we talked for a short time, I could tell that she wasn't as healthy as I had anticipated. So I asked her if everything was all right. Then she told me that she had gone to her doctor and he ran some tests. One thing led to another, and further tests reveal that she has . . . cancer. We don't know what the future holds, but surgery was necessary. I have made about six trips back home. My sister spends some time there as well, but I am so afraid, Kathy, that I am going to lose my mother. [More tears come to Mary's eyes.]

Kathy: Mary, I am so sorry to hear about your mother. [There is another extended pause in the conversation. Kathy reaches out to touch her friend's hand.] Be assured that Jim and I will be praying, and so will our church, if that's OK.

Mary: Thanks. I really do appreciate it. But what if I lose her? I don't know what I'll do. If we could've stayed close to the area, maybe we could have gotten her to the doctor sooner. And now being so far away, I often wonder if she is getting the care she needs. Oh, Kathy, I don't want to lose my mother. And life is so upside down right now.

Kathy: What are some other things that are going on as well? You say that life is so upside down right now. What do you mean?

No one wants to lose a parent. But notice how Kathy Starr carried out *investigation* in a very subtle manner. She drew her friend out in such a way as to allow her to tell her story. The issue with Mary's mother must have been an important one in Mary's thinking because it was the first thing that she brought up when describing all that was going on. Kathy did several things to build the relationship and to gather data at the same time. But she discovered what many spiritual counselors will also find when dealing with the problem of fear, especially the fear of death. In this case it was the fear that she was going to lose a loved one. At the same time, Mary worried about whether she could have done something to prevent her mother's illness. Her focus appears to be on her inability to control the situation. On top of that, Mary fears that her choices have contributed to her mother's poor health in some way. This fear has become such an obsession in her life that a solution will ultimately come when Mary's thinking is tempered by the truth of God's Word.

B. Investigating the Fear of Failure

A second kind of fear that is common to human beings is the fear of failure. In our more rational moments we can attest to the fact that everyone fails at something. No one is perfect. Yet it is hard to accept failure when it does occur. Moses, God's servant to Israel, was very much concerned with failing, even when he directly heard God's will for his life. Exodus 3 and 4 records the account of God's call for Moses to return to Israel. But Israel's future emancipator first questioned his significance among all the other people of the earth when it came to leading God's people out of bondage (3:11). Then he feared that the people might not recognize the name of the God who had sent him back to Egypt (3:13). Moses also feared that his own people might not accept the account of how God had called him in the first place (4:1). And not to exhaust his options in arguing with God, he pointed out that he was not an eloquent person (4:10). In all of these responses Moses was afraid that he might fail. He had failed in the past when he tried to take things into his own hands (2:11–15). His experience seemed to tell him that he would only fail again if he tried to rescue God's people. The possibility of failing was an insurmountable barrier in the mind of the man who ended up being one of Israel's greatest leaders.

You would do well to go back and examine the dialogue between Moses and God in Exodus 3 and 4. The heavenly Father wants people to see their own helplessness so that they can come to put their confidence and trust in Him. That appears to be the strategy that Yahweh was using with Moses. He would have to face his fears and ultimately return to trust in a God who was both good and powerful. But for any person to get to that point, whether it is Moses or the person across a restaurant table from us, we have to *investigate* to see what's holding the person in bondage.

Follow along in the dialogue between Kathy and Mary and notice what else is keeping one woman in the shackles of fear.

Kathy: Mary, you indicate that some other things are going on as well. Tell me about it.

Mary: Oh, Kathy, I hate to say this, but I really wonder if God has called us into the ministry. Or maybe it's just that Gary shouldn't be a senior pastor. I don't know.

Kathy: Why do you say that?

Mary: Well, ever since we finished seminary—no, ever since we left Gary's first pastorate in Minnesota—it seems that everything goes wrong in the church. We really liked being on the staff at Trinity Chapel. Gary was the adult ed pastor, and people seemed to like us. We got along great with other staff members too. But these last two churches have been quite a challenge.

Kathy: How so?

Mary: Well, our last church didn't want to get involved in community outreach. They didn't want to spend money to fix up the parsonage. They didn't want to hire a youth pastor. Gary had to do everything. When he asked the deacons to do something about water getting into the parsonage basement, they came back and said it would be best if he looked for another church. They told us we just weren't compatible with their congregation. We loved the community and many of the people. But they seemed to buck everything Gary wanted to do. And he wasn't asking for things out of the ordinary when it comes to ministry.

Kathy: So is that how you ended up coming to the church here in Plymouth? How did all of that come about?

Mary: Well, our last church gave us a severance package. We were able to stay in the parsonage for three months, even though Gary wasn't preaching on Sundays. Gary put his name in with the denominational headquarters. He responded to positions listed in magazines. We visited and interviewed with three churches. But they all seemed to be reluctant to call someone who had just been asked to leave his last church. Finally we found out about the ministry here in Plymouth.

Kathy: How long have you been here?

Mary: About a year and a half.

Kathy: Tell me how it's been going. I remember Jim saying that Gary is one of the best preachers in the denomination.

Mary: Yeah, I suppose the people like his preaching. But that might be the only thing that they like.

Kathy: What do you mean?

Mary: Well, the latest thing is that they don't like what Gary has proposed with respect to music.

Kathy: Oh boy! Tell me about it. What pastor hasn't faced "music madness"?

Mary: No, it's more than what goes on in a lot of churches. Gary has been the key in getting several new families into the church. Two of those couples are really talented musically. So Gary asked the deacons if they could use these four people as a worship team. They all agreed. But then some people in the church got upset because we were singing more choruses than hymns. The last several deacon council meetings have seemed to dwell on this issue alone. And Gary is getting some of the blame. Kathy, I don't know if I can go through having to pack up again and move elsewhere.

Kathy: Tell me how you feel when Gary shares these things with you.

Mary: Oh, it's not that he shares everything with me. He doesn't. In fact, he tells me not to worry. But I ask a lot of questions. Sometimes he shares what went on. But it's what other people say when I see them in the grocery store. I am afraid that we are going to get a call any day now from the deacons asking Gary to submit his resignation. With Mom's cancer and the church conflicts, I am afraid that things are only going to get worse.

One of the things many people fear is failure. Mary Jameson is focused on the future and what might happen. But it is so real in her mind that it causes her a great deal of stress. Yet it is in the context of this stress that Kathy Starr, and people like her, can come alongside to give spiritual counsel in times of spiritual/emotional pain.

Notice that Kathy continues to collect data. She allows Mary to reveal her own story line. She would do well to begin to ask at this point about primary relationships and primary events, even though they have already been revealed to some extent. But she is at least getting a picture of how the fear of death and the fear of failure are major issues in Mary's life. And the fear of failure, just as in Moses' case, was based on a past experience that was projected into the future as something that could happen again.

C. Investigating the Fear of People

In addition to the fear of death and the fear of failure, individuals are often enslaved to an accompanying fear of people. Ed Welch gave a very simple description of this kind of distress. He said that we replace God with people. Instead of having a biblically guided fear of God, we end up fearing others. We might also call it "people pleasing" or "peer pressure." At the very root of the problem, individuals are controlled by a fear of what other people might think (14).

The apostle Peter is a classic example of one who was overwhelmed with the fear of people. Luke's account of the arrest and trial of Jesus informs the reader that Peter stood by watching the false accusations hurled at the Savior. While he was warming his hands outside of the high priest's house, a servant girl announced that Peter was one of Jesus' followers, even though he tried to deny it. Three times the same charge was leveled against him. And on all three occasions Peter strongly denied that he knew Jesus. What is interesting is that previously in the same chapter Peter told the Savior that he was willing to go to prison if necessary. Yet Jesus announced that Peter would actually deny Him. Finally the truth was out.

Why did Peter turn away when he had an opportunity to defend the very One he had identified as the Savior of the world? It was because he was afraid of people and what they might think. And he was also afraid of the possibilities of being arrested himself. Peter feared the power of people more than he feared (or trusted) the power of God.

Of all the things that might bring on fear, the fear of people is often one of the most difficult for us to see. We can agree that death is frightening. We might even acknowledge our fear at failing in certain areas of life where we desperately want to succeed. But we don't always see how we are fearful of other people. That is why *investigation* is an important part of the process in spiritual counsel.

But how do we investigate when people are fearful of other people? Follow the forms of fear that Mary Jameson expresses with regard to the people who are part of her life.

Kathy: Mary, I sense that you have some deep concern about what might happen with your mom and with Gary's position in the church. Is there anything else that worries you right now?

Mary: No, I don't think so. I know that the Lord doesn't want me to worry about Gary. And I really do pray for him. I know too that Mom is a believer and that comforts me at times. I just don't want her to have to suffer. I really don't want to lose her.

Kathy: You mentioned learning about your Mom's cancer several weeks ago. You also talked about some of the tensions that are taking place over the music issue in the church. Tell me about anything else that might be going on. Do you get along well with the people in your congregation?

Mary: Oh sure. We have really gotten to know several families well. I have to say they are wonderful people for the most part.

Kathy: "For the most part"? I think I know what you mean. Are there any other issues that are taking place that you would like to talk about?

Mary: Kathy, you really know how to get at the heart of things,

406

don't you? I think you see right through me at times.

Kathy: Am I making you uncomfortable? I don't want to do that. Forgive me.

Mary: [Laughing] No, I'm just kidding, but you seem to be drawing more out of me than what I intended.

Kathy: I need to be honest with you and tell you I have been taking a class that Jim has been teaching at the church. He has given us some good insight into how to ask questions. But I really don't want to make you feel uncomfortable.

Mary: You're not, really. I was just thinking when you asked me about other things. I share this in confidence, you know. [Mary speaks with a softer voice.] I have had a couple of "encounters" with an older woman in the church. Gary and I got to know her family during the candidating process. They are a well-respected family in the church. Her husband is the district school superintendent. Well, I mentioned one day that I was thinking of keeping our daughter out of school for two years to do some homeschooling. I only mentioned it as a thought. Boy, did she ever get on my case. She reminded me in front of four other women that we had a very good school system in our community. There was no need for me to homeschool our daughter, especially since I was the pastor's wife.

Kathy: How did you feel when she said those things?

Mary: [She pauses to collect her thoughts.] I was shocked. I couldn't believe that she was so open and insistent, especially in front of those other women. Then I decided I wouldn't bring it up again. I don't want Gary to become a lightning rod for any more conflict.

Kathy: What are your real feelings about homeschooling?

Mary: I think it's a good thing. Some children can benefit from it more than others. I really think that our daughter could mature a little better if she had one or two years at home with me. But I don't want to risk bringing up conflict with some of the key people in our church.

407

Notice how Mary is reluctant to talk about the issue, at least at first. It is really not an issue primarily about one educational system over another. The real problem has to do with the way Mary thinks about conflict. She is "afraid" that people might turn against her husband. She is fearful that someone she respects might not like her in turn. Mary is facing a fear common to all of us. She is afraid of people. Therefore, it is important for spiritual directors like Kathy Starr to make the person feel comfortable in his or her presence, while at the same time getting the person to talk about feelings and thoughts. There can be no significant change and growth until caregivers investigate what is happening in the person's story line. And when investigation occurs, the caregiver will discover that individuals are primarily afraid of death, failure, and the opinions of other people (Anderson). They may also experience fear of pain or of the future or of other things.

IDENTIFICATION—FROM FEAR TO FAITH

We can never be absolutely certain about the causes behind any given individual's fearful obsessions. But *investigation* will give us enough data, if done well, to help us turn people away from their fear and toward faith in the living Lord Jesus Christ. *Investigation* helps to build a relationship of trust. But *identification* has as its goal to help fearful people to renew a relationship with the One who loves them and is sovereign over all their experiences (Eph. 1:11–12).

How then will *identification* unfold in the context of fear? We return to the matter of building a relationship with those we are mentoring. The reason for emphasizing relationship building is that people do not respond immediately to rational explanations about the inappropriateness of their fears. The ideas they have about certain fearful situations are strongly wedded to emotional reactions they have had to those same fears. Therefore, they tend to change in the context of relationships, a relationship with a wise and compassionate spiritual counselor and a relationship with the Spirit of God.

Remember how Mary Jameson described her situation with

her mother. She told how her mother was so emotionally distraught when Mary and her husband announced that they would be moving to another church. The scene played out in Mary's mind in a vivid way, so that every time she thought about that scene she felt as though she had betrayed her mother. At the same time, every time she thinks about her mother's current health situation she has a tendency to unite past pain with present situations. The result is often irrational thinking about life in general. But to tell Mary that she is not thinking rationally or even biblically will only tend to make her defensive. People like Kathy Starr must become sensitive to these dynamics and build a relationship of trust before spiritual and emotional change can occur.

That leads us to summarize the data from the fearful people with whom we work. As much as possible, spiritual counselors will want to be clear about potential causes behind an individual's obsessive, unhealthy fears. In one sense, as we have already observed, fear is a reality of living in a sinful, fallen world. Genesis 3 describes how Adam and Eve chose to disobey God and live life independently from His will and ways. After they ate of the forbidden fruit, their eyes were opened. Immediately they tried to make garments to cover themselves. And the next response they had was to try to hide from God. In fact they even admitted that they were "afraid" since they were "naked," naked before God with all of their sin.

But fear does not always have to be the result of direct sin. There are times in which people are deceived into believing things that are not true, even though they appear to be true. People make interpretations all the time concerning different events. If those interpretations go unchecked, people can believe what simply is not true. Neil Anderson and Rich Miller describe it in the following way:

> There are two primary ways that such attitudes and beliefs are formed. First, they are assimilated from the environment through prevailing experiences, such as the home you were raised in, the schools you attended, the community you played in, and the church you attended (or didn't attend). Second, they are assimilated

from the environment through traumatic experiences, such as a death or divorce in the family, frightening experiences, and severe traumas such as rape and other violence.

Strongholds are habit patterns of thought that have been burned into our minds over time or by the intensity of traumatic experiences. They are revealed in our personalities and greatly influence how we live and respond to life. For instance, if you see an adult who is afraid to ride an elevator, you can be sure they have had a negative experience that led to this fear. They weren't born with that fear. (35–36)

What is important to make clear is that the person who ends up living in the grips of fear—fear of death, fear of failure, and fear of man, and other fears—usually comes to that place because of sinful choices that were made or because of misguided beliefs about life. Thus the task of the spiritual counselor is to take each person's story line and help that individual to see that he doesn't have to live with unhealthy forms of fear any longer. But to do that we need to help people move from fear to faith.

Two important truths in God's Word will become particularly helpful at this point. The first comes from 1 John 4:18, where the apostle John tells us that "perfect love drives out fear." The "perfect love" that John talks about was described earlier in the chapter when we were told that God loves the believer in a magnificent way. That is, God sent His Son as an atoning sacrifice for our sins. In fact, God took the initiative to love us first and to show that love in the sacrifice of His Son (vv. 10–12). The text also goes on to declare that God's Spirit works in us to confirm His love for us (vv. 13–16). Notice that God is the One who acts in history and time through the redemptive work of Christ. Then He keeps on working in believers to confirm His love through the ministry of the Holy Spirit. Therefore, it is the job of the spiritual director to guide the believer to the wonderful, magnificent, ongoing love of God, because it is God's love that will ultimately drive out fear.

The second thing caregivers will want to do is to guide the fearful person to take comfort in the sovereignty of God. This will undoubtedly be more difficult, but it is crucial if progress in one's spiritual and emotional development is to occur. People will often respond to tragic events in life by saying, "If God is in control, why did He allow this horrible thing to happen?" Or they assume that they are good, at least better than some other people they know, so they wonder why God would allow "bad things" to happen to them. Spiritual counselors must be prepared for these responses.

It is important to keep in mind that we live in a sinful world. Bad things happen because every single aspect of life is permeated with sin. Buildings collapse and kill hundreds of people not only because of bad construction methods but also because in a sinful world things don't work the way we want them to. And when God does intervene He does so as an act of His grace and mercy. He is not obligated to us; we are obligated to worship Him exclusively.

In addition, we forget that God "allows" events, even things that we see as bad, to enter our lives so that we might grow in faith. James 1:2–4 teaches us that trials come so that we might be mature and complete. It is often in the context of difficulty that we can see the goodness and grace of God. If everything were perfect, we would have no need for God. But in a fallen world, God chooses to enter the life of the believer, allowing "bad things" to occur, so that we might grow to become more and more like Jesus Christ (Rom. 8:28–39; Eph. 1:11–12). Therefore, we must also help the person grappling with fear to embrace God's good purposes, even in difficulty, so that he can move beyond fear to faith.

There are procedures spiritual counselors can employ to make sure that *identification* occurs. However, you will want these procedures to fit with your unique personality. Reflect on some of the things Kathy Starr does to guide Mary Jameson toward a life of faith.

Kathy: Mary, I have to say again, my heart goes out to you. You and Gary have really been through a lot in the last several months.

Mary: [Mary nods her head in agreement.] I really wonder if any of this will end. I am so concerned about our future. I get

411

scared, quite frankly. It keeps me awake a lot of nights.

Kathy: Let me ask you something about your mother. You told me about how she responded to your announcement regarding your move. You also told me that you learned of her cancer and felt bad about it.

Mary: Yes, I really do. I sometimes regret that we weren't there with her. Maybe we could have detected things earlier.

Kathy: That's possible, I suppose. But could you have kept her from getting cancer?

Mary: Well . . . no. No, I couldn't have prevented it.

Kathy: Mary, I only ask you that because you really seem to be beating yourself up over something that you had little or no control of.

Mary: Maybe I am. I guess I needed someone to tell me that. But it's hard.

Kathy: And, Mary, you told me that you are concerned about what is going to happen with your mother's health. That is a legitimate concern. You are a wonderful daughter. But who is ultimately in charge of your mother's well-being?

Mary: OK, I know where you are going with that one. You're right again. Yes, God is in control.

Kathy: My friend, this is not a theology quiz, but why do you believe He is in control?

Mary: [Mary's eyes begin to water again, but she also smiles for the first time in a while.] Yes, I know He is in control. We all know Romans 8:28, don't we.

Kathy: You know, Mary, it isn't just Romans 8:28. There is a whole section there where God's love and sovereignty are described. Mary, do you agree that one of the challenges you are facing is that you are having a hard time accepting His love and control in the face of all the pain you are experiencing?

Mary: You're probably right. I guess I needed someone to tell me that too.

Kathy: I want you to know that I am your friend. I want to help you walk through some of these things you are facing right now. Tell me how this sounds to you. How about the two of us getting together every other week for the next two or three months. I would be glad to drive to your house next week. After that you could drive over to our home. What do you think?

Mary: Would you really want to take the time to meet with me?

Kathy: Absolutely!

Mary: Sure. I would really like that.

The session described in this chapter between Mary Jameson and Kathy Starr is obviously abbreviated and describes what might happen in one of the early sessions of spiritual counsel. But notice how Kathy used the information of the *investigation* stage to get her friend to *identify* what is really going on. Mary is letting circumstances blind her to the reality of God's love and sovereignty. Future sessions would want to return to these two important truths. Not everyone will be inclined to accept these truths as quickly as Mary did, but the goal is to build a relationship between the caregiver and the Spirit of God so that *truth* might be identified, truth about oneself and truth about God.

INITIATION—PUTTING FAITH INTO ACTION

Eugene Peterson wrote a book entitled *A Long Obedience in the Same Direction*. We believe the title serves as a good description of what spiritual counsel is all about. It is continually knowing the truth of God's Word and acting upon it. This obedience is a continual aspect of a maturing believer's life. Spiritual counselors are instruments in the hands of the Spirit of God to help people act on faith.

As in the previous chapters we would encourage people caught in the power of fear to keep the daily events journal. They will want to use the H-A-F-T-T acrostic to keep a record of things that have occurred recently in their lives. You may want to return to page 362 to review the actual items that are to be recorded in the journal.

Once the journal is started the spiritual counselor will want to return to it frequently to help the one being mentored to counter fearful thoughts with biblical truth. You may have to help the person identify specific scriptural references that affirm the love of God. You may also have to reassure him that problems are not always an indication of sin but of God's work of maturing a person. James 1:2–8 and Hebrews 12:1–13 can be two helpful passages in dealing with the issue of God's work of sanctification.

There are also some manifestations of fear in which we must unite biblical truth with actual steps of faith. People can become fearful of all sorts of things, such as open spaces or riding in elevators. We must be careful not to force someone to do something that would increase his or her terror. But if the person truly wants to get beyond fear he may have to deal with issues and objects through gradual confrontations. For instance, the person who is afraid of elevators might want to reflect on the object, agreeing that the fear itself has no rational basis. The next step might be to take the person to a building where he would stand outside of the elevator and watch for several minutes as people get on and get off. The person might even watch a friend go to different floors and return to the ground floor. Another step would be to get the person to get on the elevator and ride to just one or two floors. The idea is to get the fearful person to change attitudes and feelings through gradual confrontation with the object of fear. But for this to happen, the friend and spiritual director must be willing to commit to the time and patience that will be necessary for a person to change. It will not happen overnight. But change can occur gradually.

— Think About It —

As we close this chapter we would encourage you to reflect on the following passages of Scripture that deal directly or indirectly with the issue of fear. You will want to keep in mind that truth in the form of God's Word needs to be presented consistently. This is to be followed

— Chapter 14 —

Spiritual Counsel in the Context of Anger

The Coates family had been in Jim Starr's church for the last four years. Randy Coates had agreed to be the AWANA Commander for the previous two years. His wife, Terri, headed up the nursery committee. It was a surprise for Pastor Jim to hear that Randy had a significant problem with anger, a problem that was obviously producing a negative effect on their marriage. Randy seemed so mild mannered, so in control of things. And here was Terri telling Jim Starr that her husband would go into angry tirades that made her very uncomfortable. Jim was doing all he could to concentrate so as to *investigate* the situation as well as he could. This job of being a spiritual director was creating more insight into life than he had originally expected. In fact, he was ever more conscious of the issue of anger becoming more prominent in the culture. Pastor Jim noticed that athletes were expressing their frustration in more violent acts inside and outside of athletic arenas. Drivers seemed more and more willing to display their displeasure with other drivers in shocking acts of revenge. Jim Starr was increasingly less surprised when his own parishioners confessed anger to be a common expression for them.

Later that day Jim finished studying for his sermon on the life of Moses. Wow! He couldn't believe how Moses gave evidence of anger in his life as well. He hurled tablets of stone down on the people of Israel, bringing about major judgment on an idolatrous people. Then in frustration Moses struck the rock that spewed out water for a thirsty nation. He didn't speak to it as God had told him to. He didn't just tap the rock. He struck it twice, showing his contempt for the grumblers who surrounded him. Yes, even Moses was an angry man from time to time.

That evening Faith Church's pastor attended the deacon board meeting, a meeting that he didn't often attend. But this time the deacons wanted him to give some input on the proposed plans for remodeling the nursery. Everything went fine until the discussion got around to the cost of the project. Jim Starr noticed that Rudy Johnson had not said much up to that point. Then like a flash of lightning Rudy snapped at the deacon chairman's comment about how nice this would be for young families coming into the church. "My kids never had the luxury of all these toys and fancy murals on the walls. This is ridiculous spending so much money on fixing up the nursery. Some fresh paint will do just fine." Jim noted that Rudy Johnson wasn't simply giving a suggestion. He was downright angry. He chuckled to himself as he sat pondering the conversations he had been privy to throughout the day. *Why is it that so many people seem to be frustrated and angry about life?* he asked himself.

Jim Starr's musings are certainly apropos. In fact, they are relevant for any person who engages in spiritual counsel. Yes, many people are angry. They manifest their anger in a variety of ways. Some may use words to hurl verbal arrows at those with whom they disagree. Others might use the "silent treatment" to communicate that they don't want to communicate with other individuals, especially those with whom they are angry. And still others will raise their voices and hurl objects close at hand to express extreme displeasure with what is going on in their personal worlds. Some may beat or even kill a spouse. It is an angry world out there, and spiritual counselors will need to know how to navigate it.

So what can those who are committed to caring for the souls of others do to help people grow beyond their enslavement to anger? Following the paradigm we have been discussing throughout the second half of this book, let's look at how it works in the context of anger.

INVOLVEMENT—WHO, ME, ANGRY?

It may seem unusual, but many people who are described by others as angry do not see themselves as angry, at least not initially. They might tell others that they "simply tell it like it is" in the heat of family conflicts. They might even deny their anger by saying, "Just because I raised my voice doesn't mean I'm angry. You don't know what you're talking about." Yet another response appears to be a little more open and honest, even though it is tinged with a hint of denial. The person says, "Yes, I get angry at times, but that's just the way I am. You're going to have to accept it if we're going to live under the same roof."

Anger is perceived as a bad thing, so most people who struggle with the issue will deny it if they can. How is it that spiritual counselors in the local church might end up dealing with people who struggle with bitterness, frustration, and anger? The person will probably not call you and announce, "Say, I have this problem with anger. I was wondering if you could help me get over it?" Instead, anger as a spiritual/emotional problem usually occurs in a mixture of other difficult circumstances. Duncan Buchanan described it this way:

> Most people are not aware of the dark foreboding angers which may well go back to their time in the womb. They know they get depressed, or that they lose their temper, but they are unaware of the forces which produce those feelings. When the feelings become "more than I can cope with," they may well turn to someone for help. (71)

Even though we might question Buchanan's statement about how far back one's anger goes, we agree that anger as a topic of discussion frequently occurs in the context of other painful situations wherein the person has difficulty taking control of his own life.

One of the reasons that people shy away from admitting anger is because of confusion about what anger really is. As we stated earlier in the chapter, some people will try to deny the presence of anger in their lives, usually because they assume it is something bad. Others might admit to its occasional presence, but they really don't want to talk about it. When it comes to spiritual counsel, we have been saying that it is important to be aware of all emotions that occur in a person's life, especially anger. Kirk Johnston made this helpful observation:

> The first purpose for emotions like anger is to help us recognize what we really believe and how we think. Emotions are the windows of our minds and souls. Jonah's anger alerted him to the fact that he did not truly appreciate God's love and mercy (4:2), then God went on to correct his faulty thinking by using a plant and a worm as an object lesson (4:6–11). (176)

The presence of anger is a road sign directing us to go deeper. A person's anger will point to significant core beliefs that that individual uses to interpret life.

All of this means that wise spiritual counselors will want to be aware of all of the ways that anger manifests itself. More specifically we need to be aware that not all anger is bad. For example, a number of times in the Bible God is described as being angry. Romans 1:18 tells us that the wrath of God is being revealed. The apostle Paul states that this wrath is against all the godlessness and wickedness of people who suppress the truth. God is angry with people who reject the revelation of His righteousness.

The Gospels have accounts in which Jesus, the Son of God, expressed anger at people. He was angry with the Jewish religious leaders who were upset because He chose to heal a man on the Sabbath (Mark 3:5–6). And a very dramatic scene in Mark 11:15–19 describes Jesus cleansing the temple area in Jerusalem. He overturned tables and forbad people from carrying merchandise through the temple courts. Although the word *anger* is not used in Mark's gospel, it was obvious that Jesus was angry. Yet in all the accounts of God's wrath, there is no hint of sin occurring. How can this be the case? David Powlison made this helpful observation:

> The crimes that arouse God's wrath are capital crimes: betrayal, rebellion, deceit, blasphemous beliefs. The human heart is treacherous; we desire to believe anything but what is really true about God. The feelings aroused in us when we hear someone described by the word "traitor" give a hint of the reasoning within God's wrath. Human beings were intended to listen to God's life-giving voice and to treat one another with love. ("Anger Part I" 40)

Anger is not always wrong, and sometimes it describes the righteous judgments of God. It is good because it is just (Rom. 11:33–36). It is good because it ultimately disarms the power of sin that stalks the believer (Rom. 5:9). And it is good because God's wrath deals with sins that are committed against the people of God (James 5:1–8).

But it is also possible that human beings can be angry without sinning. The classic text on righteous anger, or "righteous indignation" as it is sometimes called, is Ephesians 4:26–27. Believers are told *not* to sin in their anger. The apostle Paul was stating that there might be a time when one could be angry without sinning. However, the believer must be careful that anger does not drift into sin. Believers are justified in being angry at child abuse, abortion, and war crimes. And there are many other occasions for righteous indignation as well. But in such circumstances the believer must be careful not to take justice into one's own hands to try to resolve the situation. We need to be angry about the things that anger God. However, we need to be careful not to try *to be God* in bringing about a resolution to the injustice.

Oftentimes a person's anger does not fit into this category of righteous indignation. Anger can also be manifested in a sinful manner, and it often is. Anger is not just an emotional response to circumstances that we all face, even though it certainly does have emotional aspects to it. Anger involves the whole person. Powlison had this to say about the comprehensive nature of anger.

That anger is unmistakably physiological lends plausibility to those medicalistic theories that view it as basically physiological, hence something to be soothed through medications. Of course our hormones, blood flow, muscles, and grimaces register anger. But that's not all there is to it. Biblically, the whole person does anger. ("Anger Part I" 45)

He went on to give further evidence that anger involves more than what one might feel when he said:

Anger also consists in thoughts, mental words and pictures, attitudes, judgments. It involves reason, imagination, memory, conscience, every inner faculty. Even if no words or actions come forth, the angry person thinks intensely. ("Anger Part I" 45)

In addition it is important to note that an individual's anger can be active or passive. For instance, one can observe the obvious anger in a person like Potiphar in Genesis 39:19. Joseph was accused of molesting Potiphar's wife. It is said that the Egyptian nobleman "burned with anger." As a result he took steps to put Joseph in prison. His actions reveal an *active* demonstration of anger.

On the other hand, Potiphar's wife appears to portray herself as an innocent victim in the narrative. The biblical record tells how this woman came to Joseph day after day, tempting him to sleep with her (Gen. 39:10). When he refused and tried to flee from her, he left his cloak behind. Potiphar's wife then falsely accused Joseph of trying to "make sport" of her (39:17). Her evil plans were not fulfilled, and as a result she accused Joseph of trying to molest her. Notice that there were no outbursts or wild tantrums on her part. She manipulated life to get what she wanted. We would suggest that her actions demonstrate a passive form of anger.

We will sometimes observe active anger in the father who gets angry with his children because they break a window while playing baseball. He rushes to the scene of the accident and becomes furious at the sight of shattered glass. In response he yells at both of his sons and orders them to go inside. He stops and stares at the neighborhood children, who first watch in amazement and then run off in fear. He doesn't have to say much, but everyone knows that he is angry.

On the other hand, a wife asks her husband when he thinks he will be home that evening from work. He suggests a possible time and picks up his briefcase to leave. She makes a plea to him as he hurries out the door, asking him not to be late. She wants to do some shopping early in the evening before it gets too dark. But the husband gets home an hour later than he announced at the beginning of the day. He is excited because he was able to recruit three new clients and close on a long anticipated deal. He wants to tell his wife all about it. But she says nothing. He asks her what's wrong, and she still says nothing. He suggests that they can celebrate his business successes on the weekend. Nothing! It doesn't take a rocket scientist to know that the wife is angry. Yet she doesn't yell. She doesn't hurl dishes into the sink. She just remains silent. It is a passive form of anger.

Another important aspect of anger is that it can be learned, especially from the people around us. As a child matures and finds life to be frustrating, he or she might learn to express frustration the same way that a parent does, whether it is active or passive anger. Likewise, a person might learn to express anger in a kind of experimental way. One gets frustrated and expresses the frustration by shouting, whether anyone else in the family yells or not. Such a person might also slam doors or throw things. The person discovers that people respond to the way the anger was expressed. So consciously or unconsciously the person does it again the next time frustration occurs.

As we get involved with people to offer soul care, we will observe anger being expressed in a variety of ways. Not all of the expressions will be in the form of righteous indignation. Most of them will be unrighteous expressions of anger that are common to all of us. As we enter into the *involvement* process with people, we will want to remember two important things. First, people will not always be aware of their anger, or at least not aware of the effect their anger has on other people. Second, spiritual directors need to be prepared to stay in control of the caregiving situation, even when the people they are mentoring are out of control. What we mean is that some boundaries may have to be established if one agrees to get involved in helping people.

If anger proves to be an obvious characteristic of one's behavior, the spiritual counselor might have to say, "Listen, I know you feel strongly about some of the things that are happening in your life. But if we are to continue in the process of learning how to live as Christians, I am going to have to ask you not to speak so harshly to the other people in your family." Or the caregiver might say, "I realize you feel strongly about this, but I am not going to agree to help you if you continue to lash out at me the way you are doing." These boundaries are necessary to protect oneself and a person's family members. At the same time, they lay a foundation for getting to the heart of the matter in future sessions.

INVESTIGATION—DIGGING DEEPER INTO ANGER

We have described the kind of awareness a spiritual counselor needs if he or she is to deal effectively with angry people. But why do people experience frustration? Why do people respond by expressing their anger in either active or passive modes? It is not enough to observe that anger exists. Proverbs 20:5 states, "The purposes of a man's heart are deep waters, but a man of understanding draws them out." A wise spiritual counselor will realize that there is more to one's life than observable symptoms. One must begin to probe as to possible worldviews that are not evident at first. These worldviews will often be related to primary relationships and primary events that have been part of a person's ongoing life story.

Consider how story lines might unfold in the kind of setting where Jim Starr does much of his spiritual counsel—the context of pastoral ministry.

Pastor Starr: Terri, you said that you wanted to talk to me about some things that have been going on in your marriage. Why don't you tell me about it?

Terri Coates: Well, I must admit that I feel a little embarrassed about talking about these things. I never imagined that I would be in a situation where I had to talk to any-one, especially my pastor, about my marriage. [Terri starts to cry. Her husband, Randy, squirms in his chair and looks away from her. He has an expression of disgust on his face.]

Pastor: It's OK. Take your time.

Terri: I guess we have been under a lot of tension recently. I'm really scared at the way Randy behaves sometimes. I suppose every couple has their little spats. But I feel like Randy has been expressing his anger in some frightening ways.

Randy: That's your opinion and it's wrong! I get tired of you telling me I get angry and how it scares you. Big deal!

Pastor: Tell you what. I want to hear from both of you. It will be helpful for me to get some perspective on what's going on. So let me lay down one simple rule that will make our time together as productive as possible. The rule is this: One person will tell his or her view of the situation while the other person listens. Both of you will get a chance to re-spond to the other person, but I will decide when the oth-er person can respond. Does that sound fair?

Terri: [Silence at first] Yes, I can agree to that.

Randy: [Even more silence] OK, I'm sorry. I really feel strongly about this issue. But yes, I will listen. However, Pastor, I hope you will hear my side of the story, even though I wasn't the one who made the appointment to be here today.

Pastor: Randy, you can be assured that I'll do my best to hear from both of you. My goal is to help the two of you grow in your relationship with Christ and with each other. [There is a brief pause in the conversation.] OK, since we agree on this basic rule, let's continue. Terri, you were saying that you have some concerns with what's been happening in your marriage.

Terri: Yes, I was saying that I think we have a good marriage. I really want you to know that I love Randy very much. He is under a lot of pressure at work. He's a good husband and a wonderful father. But he gets angry at times and it really scares me the way he responds.

Pastor: Tell me about that. How does he respond?

Terri: Well . . . he really lets us know when he's upset with us or at something that's happened.

Pastor: Can you give me an example? How did Randy express his anger recently?

Terri: Last Monday, just before I called you, Randy came home from work and parked his car next to the one that I drive. I noticed out of the kitchen window that he was walking around the entire car, the one we call the family car. As he was coming inside, I could tell by the look on his face that he was mad. As he walked into the kitchen I didn't get a "Hi, how are you," or anything. He just started yelling. Then he threw his briefcase against the wall and told me he was tired of the way I was taking care of the car. Just then, our son Justin was walking up our driveway bouncing his basketball. Randy saw him and ran outside, yelling at him to not play in the driveway when both cars were sitting there. Justin wasn't even playing basketball. He was just coming home from a neighbor's house. But Randy got all over him. He even took his basketball away from him and threw it behind the garage.

Pastor: Randy, I am going to give you a chance to tell your side of the story. But let me ask Terri one more question. Terri, does this kind of thing happen often?

Terri: It's been happening a lot recently. Randy has always had a short fuse. I knew that he could get upset about things rather easily. But he would always come back and apologize. I really appreciated that quality about him. But yes, he gets angry often.

Pastor: Randy, why don't you tell me what happened last Monday, and then we'll go on from there.

Randy: Pastor, Terri has this thing about perceiving my concerns as expressions of anger. It makes me look like a wild man. I'm not. I simply want my wife and family to have the same values that I have about things.

Pastor: What do you mean by "having the same values that you have"?

Randy: Well, the issue with the car is an important one. You see, I have told Terri at least twenty-five times that when she used the family car to go shopping or when she was taking the kids somewhere to be sure to park away from other cars. Our car is only a few months old. I don't want it to get scratched because of the negligence of other people. But I noticed a scratch on the passenger side door. Terri doesn't seem to care about what the car looks like.

Pastor: Randy, Terri says that you have expressed anger in other situations as well. Do you agree with her or not?

Randy: [Pauses to think about the question.] Yes . . . I will admit that I have been angry. Doesn't everybody get angry at one time or another? I don't think that I'm out of control or that I'm angrier than the next guy.

Pastor: If your children were sitting here in the room with us today, how would they respond? Would they describe you as an angry person?

Randy: I don't know, really. They could probably tell you about times when I've lost my temper. Sure. But I'm not convinced they would say that I'm an angry person.

Pastor: What would be some of those times that you mentioned where they might describe you as being angry?

Randy: Wow . . . that's a tough one. [Pauses to think] OK, probably Justin would talk about what I did with his basketball. Yeah, he would probably mention that one since it was so recent.

Pastor: Help me to understand you a little bit more. Even though you have been active here at Faith Church, I really don't know that much about you other than where you work and some things about your wife and children. Tell me some things about where you grew up and what life was like for you.

Randy: Well . . . I grew up in the western part of the state. My dad was a farmer. We didn't have a lot, but we worked hard. We were God-fearing people. I became a Christian in our little Baptist church. I played basketball in high school and college. I appreciate my parents, my dad especially.

Pastor: Tell me some more about your relationship with your parents. What kind of a relationship did you have with your father?

Randy: I would say that it was a good one. As I said, we lived on a farm and most of our relationship developed around the work that farmers do. I appreciate that I learned how to work from my father.

Pastor: Did the two of you ever disagree on anything? Did you ever have any conflicts?

Randy: No, it just didn't happen in our family. My dad wouldn't tolerate disagreement. My older sister tried that route, and it ended up getting her into a lot of trouble. I did disagree with Dad about things from time to time, but not very often.

Pastor: Like what?

Randy: Well, I thought we should try to expand the farm. It was the only way to make more money as I saw it. Our farm was small, and I was tired of living with little or nothing. My dad didn't mind being small. He said we made enough to live and that was all that really mattered. We argued once about that when I was a teenager. As I said, you didn't argue with Dad about the way he did things.

Pastor: Did your father show much anger in the family?

Randy: Yeah, sometimes. He would get mad if we argued with him. He would get mad if equipment didn't work the way he wanted it to work. But that was about the extent of it. But one thing I promised myself was that I wouldn't stay on that farm the rest of my life. I determined that I was going to make a better living for my family.

Pastor: Randy, tell me how you think you have done in reaching that goal of doing better for your family. How have you done over the years?

Randy: Well, I think I've done well. I guess that is why I want Terri and the kids to take care of the things that I work so hard to provide. I wish they would appreciate the hard work that I put in for their well-being. Terri says that I get mad. I don't see it that way. I see it as being a good steward of what I have. I want my family to have the same view of things.

At this point in Randy's story line we are only getting started. But we are beginning to see that anger has become a serious issue that must be controlled. How can we draw such a conclusion when Randy himself is not convinced that his anger is a serious matter? The primary reason is that it is an important issue to his wife. She shows real concern about what is going on, whether Randy wants to minimize it or not. He admits that his son would also affirm that he has been angry in a very dramatic way. However, *investigation* needs to try to find data that reveal why people like Randy are demonstrating such intense forms of anger.

Randy's expression of anger is not unusual, even though the worldviews behind those expressions might be unique. If we were to study biblical examples of people who demonstrated anger, we would see some common characteristics. For instance, Cain in Genesis 4 brought an offering to the Lord, as did his brother Abel. Abel brought fat portions, while Cain provided some of the fruits that he had apparently grown. God accepted Abel's offering, but not Cain's. As a result, "Cain was very angry, and his face was downcast" (v. 5). Why the anger? Cain had a perception of something that he wanted to have happen, and it did not occur. He wanted his offering to be accepted and honored as much as his brother's was. When it was not, his *expectations* were unfulfilled and he became angry.

Other examples reveal this same pattern. One could look at Naaman (2 Kings 5:11), Ahab (1 Kings 21:4), or Jonah (Jonah 4:1) and see that when a person's expectations are thwarted, anger in its various forms will often be manifested. Likewise, we see anger in Randy Coates's experiences. Notice especially his goal for his own life in contrast with his father's goals. And notice what he wants for his family. This discovery is key to understanding and dealing with anger. Johnston writes:

> Anger is basically the emotion of frustration. When we are angry, it is because someone or something has kept us from accomplishing a personal goal or having something we deeply desire. (179)

If unfulfilled expectations are at the heart of unrighteous angry expressions, what can the spiritual counselor do to get as much data as possible? During the *investigation* stage, consider exploring some of the following areas of a person's life. First, *ask questions of the person to find out where anger most frequently occurs*. People who are angry will express their anger in a variety of settings. But angry expressions will occur most frequently in family settings or in work situations where stress might be higher than normal. Here again is a good opportunity to assign the daily events journal as a way to uncover some of these areas where the emotion is most often expressed. Consider making this kind of an assignment early in the data-gathering process. It will cast light on what might be discussed in future sessions.

Second, *ask questions to find out what a person gets angry about*. You will notice that Pastor Starr gave Randy an opportunity to listen to Terri's description of what brought them to the pastor's office for spiritual counsel. Randy had time to think about how he might respond when it was his turn to talk. But even in his attempts at downplaying the situation he gave some evidence as to why he was angry with his wife. He *perceived* that she did not care as much about the appearance of the car as he did. The wise spiritual director will want to hear about other situations in which a person expressed anger and then follow up with a question like, "Help me to understand why that was important to you. Why was the (*event /experience*) so significant to you that you responded in an angry fashion?" The person's response to several specific

430

events will help the spiritual counselor to piece together information that will point to at least one primary worldview that motivates his actions and expectations.

Third, *ask questions that will reveal how the person expresses his or her anger.* A person might eventually admit that he has been angry and that the anger is a significant part of his life. But people will often speak in generalities. An individual might say, "I get angry a lot." Or he might say, "Sometimes I get angry when things don't go my way." But more information is needed. Keep asking questions that will give you a picture of what the person does when anger occurs. Does he throw things? Does he yell and scream? Does he withdraw? Does he bring harm to himself or others?

These types of questions are important because the person consistently reverts back to the same type of anger-oriented behavior. Yet he does not always see that it really only brings him negative gain. This negative gain can be expressed in a variety of different ways. Glenn Taylor and Rod Wilson refer to two main types of anger expression, *explosion* and *implosion.* Explosive anger is the type of behavior that is more visible and dramatic. It might come in the form of verbal expressions. Sometimes the person can be an "in-your-face" type of individual, using words to intimidate the people who stand in the way of reaching the goals he wants to achieve. Sometimes a person will use information and knowledge to make others feel inferior. Yet the tone of the person's voice makes it clear that the individual communicating the information is very angry.

Implosive anger is more subtle and less likely to be seen as anger by the person who seeks spiritual counsel. Yet it may be the cause behind such symptoms as stomach upset, ulcers, colitis, low-grade infections, and headaches. Implosive anger may also be evident in the person who constantly condemns himself and focuses on his own inadequacies. Implosive anger may also appear in the form of spiritual self-abuse. The person who is rigid and prone to a legalistic lifestyle may also be the individual who is angry with himself or others. Therefore, be sure to encourage the person to tell his story, so that information can be collected about the form of expression anger frequently takes in the person's life (Taylor and Wilson 58–60).

Fourth, *find out the length of time that the anger expresses itself.* Sometimes people will express frustration for only a matter of a few minutes. Other times the individual will be angry for extended periods of time, sometimes for several days. One reason it is important for the spiritual counselor to explore anger's time frame is that it may help him determine if the anger is the result of righteous indignation or unrighteous worldviews. Likewise, some short-term forms of anger can be very explosive, but since the person can move on with other tasks as if nothing is wrong, he might also try to minimize the significance of his anger. Notice the scenario described above where Randy Coates initially tried to minimize his anger. Pastor Starr asked, "If your children were sitting here in the room with us today, how would they respond?" When spiritual counsel exists in the context of marriage, a pastor has the advantage of asking one's mate whether the anger is significant. A spiritual counselor will want to be certain to confront any type of hostility, whether it is of short duration or not.

Fifth, *find out if the person is angry with God.* Most Christians who enter into a mentoring relationship with another person are reluctant to admit that they are angry with God. At the same time, some well-meaning caregivers might even suggest that it is acceptable for someone to be angry with God. The argument usually goes something like this: "God is big enough and mature enough that He isn't going to get upset if you are angry at Him." But the issue isn't whether God is mature enough to handle someone's anger. Of course He is! Spiritual counselors need to explore the possibility of anger toward God so that they can then guide the person toward healthy repentance and an acceptable expression of their anger.

Someone will ask, "Aren't we suppressing someone's anger and causing more problems if we don't allow them to be angry at God?" Here again we need to distinguish between "*admitting* anger at God" and "*being* angry at God." The problem with the latter is that at the core of anger with God is a belief that God is somehow unjust in what He does. And to accuse God of injustice is blasphemous. It is important to have people acknowledge that they are truly angry with God. But we must also be ready to lead them to the Scriptures to see that such attitudes are sinful and must be resolved through repentance. Robert D. Jones put it this way:

> The solution to sinful anger at God lies in continuously repenting of our remaining unbelief and rebellion. We must reject the lies that deny God's goodness, power, and wisdom. We must reaffirm His righteousness, love, sovereignty, and justice. We must repent, knowing that "God opposes the proud, but gives grace to the humble" (James 4:6). (18)

We will explore how we can deal with anger toward God more fully in our suggestions regarding the *initiation* of action. But with respect to *investigation* we need to find out if the person is truly angry with God. Then during the early segments of the *identification* stage, the person should be encouraged to acknowledge such anger, followed by an explanation from Scripture as to why such thinking is nonproductive. This will take some time. You will want to encourage honest expression on one hand without giving the impression that it is acceptable to be angry with the heavenly Father. Obviously we will also want to find out the particulars as to why the person is angry with God.

IDENTIFICATION—HELPING ANGRY PEOPLE SEE THE ERROR OF THEIR WAYS

If one is to take seriously the task of offering spiritual counsel, as opposed to just being a "counselor," it will be important to keep the primary goal in view. This will be true whether we are ministering to people who are angry, fearful, or depressed. And that goal is guiding people to turn from beliefs that are faulty (and often sinful) to worldviews that are focused on the grace of God. This whole process of changing from one perspective to another requires a changing of one's mind. In the context of biblical revelation a change of mind is frequently referred to as "repentance." David Powlison stated:

When you see (or are) a sinfully angry person, voila, the devil's image is displayed. But the devil's hand in anger is no different from his involvement in any other sin. He does not demonize us into sin; he rules us. He tempts and lies in his attempts to control and destroy us. The solution lies not in exorcism from supposed demons of rage, anger, pride, and rebellion; it lies in *repentance* from rage, anger, pride, and rebellion, turning to the Lord of grace. Anger is a moral act, not an indwelling thing, and its solution is a moral act, too. ("Anger Part II" 13)

Yes, the goal is repentance, thinking differently with respect to the expectations we have in life. But how do we bring people to repentance? What steps can we take to expose unrighteous thinking that will lead to a righteous mind-set? It will be different for every situation, since no two individuals are exactly alike. But notice how Pastor Starr attempts to give spiritual counsel to Randy Coates.

Pastor: Randy, I really appreciate you sharing your life so readily with me. I will be honest in telling you that it gives me some helpful insight into some of the challenges you are currently experiencing in your life, especially between you and Terri and you and your children. But let me go back to some things you told me just a short while ago. You mentioned that you wanted to provide for your family in a way that you weren't able to experience when you were growing up. Is that right?

Randy: Yes, but I don't want it to sound like my father was some sort of a vicious man who didn't provide for us. He really did.

Pastor: No, I don't want to say that either. I sense from the way you described your family that you love them very much. They sound like good parents.

Randy: Yeah, they really are.

Pastor: But you did say that you wanted to provide for your children in a way that you didn't experience. Would you agree with me on that?

wife's agenda is just as important as his. In fact, its importance may mean that she can't always control where the car is parked. Bringing a person like Randy to see that his world is not the only world is part of bringing him to repentance. This *identification* and respect of other people's agendas will be hard to accomplish, but it will be crucial to helping a person put off the old sinful life of anger and bitterness and to put on a life of love (Eph. 4:22–32; James 1:19–21).

Likewise, when a person acknowledges his anger at God, the spiritual counselor will want to deal with it respectfully and biblically. To deal with it respectfully is to respect the person's right to express frustrations about what has been happening in life. Every person wants to feel as though he is being heard. At the same time, we need to deal with beliefs and behaviors in a biblical manner. As we said earlier in the chapter, a person can talk about anger and should be encouraged to do so. But at the same time, just as we explore the ineffectiveness of angry behavior, we also need to reveal how anger toward God is not the way of wisdom or righteousness.

Those who offer spiritual counsel need to think through a theology of pain and suffering. All too often in our culture we tend to blame God for broken marriages, failed business dealings, the death of loved ones, and a host of other disappointments that enter our lives. But we fail to see that we live in a fallen world, a world deeply affected by sin. We need to help people see that God is not the cause of our pain. Sin is the ultimate cause, and it corrupts all that we humans attempt to do. Thus we need to help people be angry at sin, not at God. For it is the heavenly Father who will have the ultimate solutions to the things we face. Spiritual directors will want to help people identify the real cause behind the trouble they face, namely, sinful choices in the context of a sinful world.

INITIATION—MOVING FROM WRATH TO WORSHIP

What are some ways we can help people to deal with anger so as to manage it instead of being managed by this intense emotion? There are several steps that people can take. The more you work with individuals who want to grow beyond their anger to be fully devoted followers of Christ, the more you will find creative ways to help them. By all means, help them to confess the sinfulness of angry reactions. One way to do this is to have them actually identify specific times when they have hurt another person by an angry outburst. After they have recorded several such incidents, encourage them to confess the event as an actual sin. You may encourage them to pray, "When I (*event listed*), I hurt (*the person*), and I sinned against You. Thank You for Your grace and forgiveness." Specific acts of repentance can be important first steps in bringing about change.

While encouraging repentance, spiritual counselors will do well to get the person into the Word of God to explore a biblical perspective on anger. We explored some of those texts under the section on *involvement* earlier in this chapter. But it can be helpful to have people look at anger portrayed in the lives of people like David (1 Samuel 25), Ahab (1 Kings 21), and Jonah (Jonah 4). You can also have those under your care look at verses that talk about wrong ways of dealing with it (Eph. 4:26–27; Prov. 17:14; 29:11, 20), followed by texts that deal with proper ways to deal with anger (Rom. 12:19–21; Eph. 4:26, 29, 32; 5:20). These are only representative samples of many texts that could be used. The important thing is to keep people focused on God and His Word.

Help people articulate their values and expectations, even to the point of thinking through ahead of time what they will do if expectations are not met. Help them to actually plan how they might deal with experiences that have been frustrating for them in the past. The instruction might sound something like the following:

Pastor: Randy, you were telling me how frustrating it has been for you to come home and find the car sitting out in the driveway instead of being in the garage. You told me that yelling and ranting hasn't produced any of the results that you really want. You also have heard some of Terri's reasons for not pulling the car in right away.

Randy: Yeah, and I realize that her reasons are legitimate. But it just bugs me when I see the car there in the driveway. I know what you said about my expectations and how the car is a symbol of my achieving my goals. It really isn't, is it?

Pastor: You said so yourself. So, let's think of what you could do that is part of "the righteous life that God desires." What could you do to change from being angry to being calm?

Randy: I guess I could just be calm.

Pastor: But how would you do that? You pull into the driveway and there's the car! What could you do?

Randy: I'm not sure.

Pastor: Have you ever thought about planning to not get angry?

Randy: How could I do that?

Pastor: Here's a suggestion. Take your calendar. There in the appointment section, set a time when you are going to come home. Write down a code phrase like "keep cool." When you see that, say to yourself, "I might very well see the car in the driveway. It might even have a scratch on the passenger's side. But I am not going to get mad. Holy Spirit, help me to be calm and to act in love. Help me to represent You with peaceful words." Randy, I am going to ask you to put that in your calendar right now. Go ahead. Then next week, we are going to see what God does in and through you as you plan to not get angry.

This will only be effective in dealing with anger if the individual is taught to simultaneously trust in the sovereignty and goodness of God. You may want to go back to the last chapter to review some of the information about God's goodness to His people.

With respect to dealing with anger directed toward God, assist people in actually communicating their frustrations in a righteous manner. This is not the same as verbalizing anger toward God. Robert Jones refers to this practice as "holy lamenting."

If anger against God is sin, then how do we deal with our doubts and questions about His providential dealings, especially amid our sufferings? Must we stoically, silently stuff our struggles? Thankfully, God presents another option, the path laid out for us through the lamentation portions of Scripture.

Believers in Christ are sometimes baffled by God's ways, bewildered by His providential dealings and confused by His apparent inconsistencies. Yet Scripture teaches us the art of holy lamenting—learning how to complain in faith—to God about the calamities He sovereignly sends/permits. (18)

Appropriate Scriptures to help people engage in holy lamenting would be Job 1–2, Lamentations, and Psalm 13. The key is to help people express their frustrations and pain without accusing God of being the One who is the cause for such experiences.

The apostle Paul encouraged the Thessalonian Christians to "give thanks in all circumstances" (1 Thess. 5:18). He was not suggesting that they needed to give thanks for everything, but to give thanks in every situation where they found themselves. Paul was referring to a mind-set, a worldview, in which people were focused on what God had done and was doing. Our lives become so busy that we don't always think about worship as a daily activity. But praising God for His sovereignty and His provisions can be a powerful means of getting our attention off of what we want and more onto the person and majesty of God. After all, we were created to be worshipers (1 Pet. 2:9). When we get into a regular routine of praising God and recognizing that He is the source of all good things that we experience, it will be easier to set aside what we think we deserve.

— Think About It —

If we are going to be used by God in mentoring people who struggle with anger, we need to come to grips with our own anger. So do some reflection with respect to your own life. Answer the questions that follow and see what the heavenly Father wants you to do to "bring about the righteous life that God desires."

— Chapter 15 —

Spiritual Counsel in the Context of Guilt

Tad Flossmore was delighted that he and his wife could take Pastor Starr's training class, because it seemed to Tad that an increasing number of students were coming to him with their personal struggles. His work as a high school history teacher equipped him well for working with the young people at Faith Church until a new youth pastor could be hired, but tonight he was tired. As Tad finished setting up the game room, he noticed out of the corner of his eye that someone had come into the room. He finished putting two more chairs in place and then turned around to see who had joined him. Much to his surprise, Billy Guiles was walking his way, hands in pockets and shoulders slouched forward as if he were carrying the world on his shoulders.

"Hey, kiddo, whatcha up to? You're usually one of the last guys to get here on Tuesday nights. Surely you didn't come just to help me set up?" Tad liked joking with Billy, even though the high school senior didn't always seem to make much of a response in turn.

"Mr. Flossmore, I didn't get a chance to talk to you at school today, so I thought maybe I could catch you here at church. I wanted to talk to you if I could."

"Sure. But if you think I'm going to agree with you that the Lakers are going to go all the way this season, you're crazy." Teacher and student laughed together. They had always talked freely about basketball. Billy knew a lot about the game, even though he didn't play on the high school team. But it was obvious that he didn't want to talk about sports. Tad thought to himself, *He sure seems to be down about something. I'd better ease up and not joke so much. I wonder what it is?* His mind started to think about some of the things he was learning in Jim Starr's Spiritual Directors Training Class. Perhaps this was one of those supernaturally arranged appointments that the pastor had so frequently talked about. He silently prayed that he would be a good listener and discern accurately what was going on.

"Billy, you seem a little down. Let's talk." Tad then motioned for Billy to follow him into his nearby office, the one the church had prepared for Tad and any new youth pastor who might come on the scene. Billy didn't need to be told to sit down. He just naturally plopped into the chair near Tad's desk. "So, my friend, what's up?"

Billy sat for a few seconds without saying anything. Finally he spoke, choosing his words ever so carefully. "Mr. Flossmore, I feel like such an idiot. I can't sleep. I don't feel like eating. I doubt if my life is worth much at all. You were right last week in our study time that we reap what we sow. My problem is that I can't do anything about it."

Tad listened and pondered what he had just been hearing. He didn't want to say too much, waiting to see if Billy said anything more. Finally he responded, realizing that he needed to get a lot more *data* to figure out was really going on in Billy Guiles's life. "So tell me what you mean when you say that you are reaping what you sowed. I'm sure glad that you're listening to my talks. But how does it relate to you?"

"Mr. Flossmore, you may know that I have been dating Becky over the last couple of months. She's really a neat girl, but I am really bummed out about where we're at in our relationship. I don't know what to do. That's why I wanted to talk to you."

so in this case he was experiencing a legitimate form of guilt. But he also seemed to experience feelings of shame because of what he heard other people saying about him. In this case the feelings were very much a part of his life, but not legitimate. He felt unworthy and deficient as a human being. In fact, part of the shame he experienced may have been the result of what his girlfriend, Becky, had requested of him. It is certainly noble that she wanted to pursue a life of sexual purity. But for a teenager to ask a date about his past sexual behavior was probably inappropriate in the early stages of their relationship. Tad and others who counsel teenagers in similar circumstances will want to advise their protégés to say something like, "I appreciate your concern for sexual purity; in fact, I admire it and am committed to godly behavior. But at this early stage of our dating relationship, I don't think it's wise for us to talk in detail about sexual issues."

When it comes to getting involved with people who reveal symptoms of guilt, the spiritual counselor will always want to proceed with caution. Quite frankly, symptoms of guilt will usually be associated with other presenting problems. Angry people may be guilt ridden. Hopeless people will often express feelings of guilt. Fearful people will do the same. But because guilt is often legitimate—that is, people have violated the will and ways of God—the spiritual counselor needs to be cautious in discerning what is true and what is false. In fact, as we proceed through the process of spiritual counsel we will use the terms *true guilt* and *false guilt*. The former will refer to those times when one has disobeyed God's Word in some way. The latter term will refer to those occasions when a person feels extremely downcast, but not for legitimate reasons. The key concept to keep in mind with respect to getting involved with people experiencing guilt and shame is that of cautionary discernment.

INVESTIGATION—SYMPTOMS AND SOURCES

Those of us who enter into caregiving ministries with people in distress know that "presenting problems" are not always the real problems. We have also established that the issue of guilt and shame accompanies other spiritual/emotional experiences as well. Therefore, the wise spiritual director will want to get information that helps to clarify the presenting problem. The issue that a person first brings to our attention is only the tip of the iceberg. So we need to search for other issues that will lead us back to the core issues that drive a person's current beliefs and behaviors. We noted in the previous chapter the words of Proverbs 20:5: "The purposes of a man's heart are deep waters, but a man of understanding draws them out." One of the major implications of the verse is that *investigation* is essential to finding out why people are feeling guilty. We must take the time to look at the symptoms. And what we often discover is that symptoms and causes are closely allied when people reveal the primary events and relationships of their lives.

A. Investigating the Symptoms of Guilt

When we look at people experiencing guilt in the Bible, we see several categories of symptoms and causes. For instance, in 2 Samuel 24:10 we see the expression of *self-abasement* and *remorse*. David had authorized a census in Israel for the purpose of finding out how many fighting men actually lived in Israel. Joab, one of David's chief military officers, tried to persuade him not to do it. David overruled his associate's advice and a census was completed. But in the end, David experienced great remorse for what he had done. The reason, according to several Bible scholars, was that David's act was really motivated by pride and an orientation to trust in human power rather than God's power. His guilt was true guilt in the sense that he had violated the will of God to trust in the Almighty alone for deliverance against Israel's enemies.

We have seen similar responses from students who come to a professor, sometimes long after a course has been completed, to confess that they had cheated on an exam. At the time of an exam, some students feel compelled to cheat in order to ensure successful completion of a given course. But after the exam is completed, they feel horrible for what they did. Spiritual counselors will often hear verbal "symptoms" that sound something like this: "I know I was wrong. You probably think I'm a horrible person." The guilt is real and justified, but the symptoms should also cause the spiritual counselor to consider how to deal with the guilt and get the person back on the path to spiritual maturity. This does not mean that we deny the reality of true guilt. But we also need to consider what other motivations might be behind these initial symptoms.

Another accompanying factor associated with feelings of guilt may be that of *disgrace* and *despair.* It may not be that one has personally committed a sin or violated a righteous standard. Nevertheless, the person feels disgrace over what has occurred. We see this in Ezra 9:1–7 and again in Nehemiah 1. Ezra had led a group of Jews from captivity in Babylon and Persia back to the land of Israel. After a time of sacrifice and worship, some people came to Ezra and informed him that some of the people in the land had engaged in evil practices and even married some of the pagans who were also living in the land. Ezra was greatly distressed. He tore his tunic and pulled out his hair. Why? Ezra was guilt ridden over what the people of Israel had done. He had not sinned personally, but those associated with him had.

A similar situation is revealed in Nehemiah 1. It is safe to say that the conditions in Jerusalem were not a direct result of Nehemiah's sinful behavior. God's people had sinned against Yahweh in years past and were paying the consequences right up to Nehemiah's day. While Nehemiah was serving King Artaxerxes in Susa, he received a report about the conditions of Israel's beloved capital. His brothers reported that the people who had survived the exile were in "great trouble and disgrace." They were living in shame. Why? Not because of their own sin, even though they were indirectly associated with Israel's earlier acts of transgression. Nevertheless, these survivors were experiencing a time of great disgrace over their seemingly helpless situation. Sometimes the circumstances surrounding us lead us to feel a sense of guilt or shame.

I (Harry) know of a man who had great dreams of succeeding in the business world. He had spent some time in seminary but came to believe that God truly wanted him to work in the marketplace. Unfortunately the marketplace was not kind to him. He tried to recruit customers one week, only to lose them the next. Cash flow became a real problem. Even though his wife was supportive, he could readily see the strain on her face. One day after a frustrating experience of losing even more customers to competitors, he stopped by my office. It wasn't long until he started to weep. Here was a once confident man working hard to make a good living for his family but feeling as though he had failed. "I just can't keep this up. I seem to fail at every turn. I'm just no good as a salesman." He didn't have to use the words, but he was feeling shame and guilt for the way his life was turning out. Was he violating some moral standard? I am not convinced that sin was the problem. Rather, circumstances had not turned out as he would have liked and shame was the ultimate result. Oh, it is true that his interpretation of events might have led to sin, but outright sin was not the immediate cause. And that is the way with a lot of people. They feel "guilty" because life can be very cruel. They feel as if they don't measure up.

A third common symptom that we discover when *investigating* the existence of guilt and shame is that of *fear* and *terror*. We see this specifically when true guilt is a reality in one's life. By true guilt in this sense we are referring to times when people actually recognize the sinfulness of their own human condition or of disobedient actions that they may have done. The symptoms are very similar to the first situation cited above when King David was conscience-stricken for trusting in military strength over the sovereign protection of God. But Isaiah 6 also illustrates the fear that one experiences in the presence of God. Notice that in the year that King Uzziah died the prophet Isaiah had a vision of God in all of His holiness and purity. Overcome with his own spiritual inadequacies Isaiah cried out, "Woe to me! . . . I am ruined! For I am a man of unclean lips, and I live among a people of unclean lips, and my eyes have seen the King, the LORD Almighty" (Isa. 6:5).

Prior to his embracing justification by faith, Martin Luther was held daily in the clutches of fear and terror. Bruce Shelley said this of the great Protestant reformer:

Luther pushed his body to health-cracking rigors of austerity. He sometimes fasted for three days and slept without a blanket in

the silence to continue without interrupting.] I guess you could say that I didn't always treat the girls with the respect that they deserve. I did some things for which I am really ashamed.

Tad: Would it be true to say that you have had sex with girls in the past?

Billy: [He doesn't look up. He waits again before he answers.] Yeah . . . I really feel bad about those things.

Tad: Billy, I want to talk about that some more and look at why it is important for you to deal with this before the Lord. But you mentioned some other things when you first came into the office. Tell me about your relationship with your father.

Billy: Man, there really isn't anywhere to go with it. I don't have a very good relationship with my dad.

Tad: What do you mean?

Billy: Well, we just don't relate. He gets along really well with my older brother, but not with me. I'm the "loser" in the family. That's what everybody seems to think.

Tad: When you say "everybody," does that mean your mother too? How do the two of you relate?

Billy: No, not my mom. But she doesn't really say much, other than not to worry about what Dad and Joey say. Yet I get so sick and tired of their jokes.

Tad: What kind of jokes?

Billy: It's mostly my brother. He makes fun of the fact that I can't shoot a basketball the way he does. He makes fun of my physique. He comes into my room and makes fun of my music albums and the fact that I like to mess around with my keyboard.

Tad: And what about your father? Does he make fun of you as well?

Billy: It's not that he makes fun of me. It's just that he asks me questions about what I'm going to do with my life. He responds sarcastically when I tell him that I'm thinking about doing something with music. He's told me several times that my goals are a waste of time. He tells me to try to get into sports because that will prepare me for the competition of the real world. Then he shakes his head and walks away. I just wish for once that he would at least listen to the things I want to do.

Tad: Sounds like you would really like a hearing. You have some good ideas but nobody wants to stay around long enough to consider them. Is that how you see it?

Billy: Yeah . . . maybe.

Tad Flossmore is trying to get beyond just discussing real guilt to discover if there are other causes for the feelings of shame and despair in Billy's life. Notice how he does not dismiss the confession of sexual sin but acknowledges that it is serious. But he doesn't rush to deal with that issue alone. Notice also that Tad tries to build a relationship of trust with Billy. He offers hope. He doesn't say that the problem will be solved without any bad consequences. Instead, he commends him for taking steps to deal with the spiritual/emotional issues that are going on in his life. Those who provide spiritual counsel will always want to communicate concern and hope. And when it comes to dealing with people trying to cope with guilt, we need to discover all that may be contributing to the feelings that they express. An exploration of primary relationships will uncover the "deep waters" that Proverbs 20:5 talks about.

IDENTIFICATION AND *INITIATION*—GOING FROM GUILT TO GRACE

Once the symptoms and sources of guilt have been uncovered, the spiritual director will want to guide people through the Scriptures and through accurate biblical thinking to the biblical teachings on grace. Guilt has both a negative and a positive side to it. The positive is that guilt can guide us back to God to appeal to His mercy and find grace to help us in our times of need. The negative side of guilt is that it can also hold people captive and blind them to the spiritually rich life that God wants all of us to enjoy.

Unfortunately Christian leaders can try to capitalize on guilt from either its positive or negative sides. But the Word of God is clear that we are to engage in ministries of reconciliation. That is why the apostle Paul says in 2 Corinthians 5:20–21, "We are therefore Christ's ambassadors, as though God were making his appeal through us. We implore you on Christ's behalf: Be reconciled to God. God made him who had no sin to be sin for us, so that in him we might become the righteousness of God."

So the spiritual counselor must view all mentoring situations as ambassadorial endeavors. We must deal with true guilt by showing people that they have violated the holiness of God and His standards. We must not try to increase their guilt so as to manipulate the person to behave in some way that we think is appropriate. Instead we must represent Christ and biblical truth in trying to resolve it. And God Himself has said that the way of resolution is through the reconciling work of the Savior.

That means that when guilt exists as either *true guilt* or *false guilt* we must guide people back to God's grace in Christ. How do we do that? Let's look first for *true guilt*, the guilt that comes legitimately from violating the moral laws of God. It means that we will *identify* people's source of guilt and then assist them in *initiating* action to apply the grace of God to their lives. At least three steps will help us do this.

A. Initiation Through Teaching

First, we will need to *lovingly teach* people about God's holiness and grace as opposed to coercing them to believe and behave in a certain way. As we noted above, guilt has positive and negative aspects to it. The positive side is that true guilt can be used by God's Spirit to show us that we have offended God's standards, standards that are wise and good. Sinners should feel guilty. Likewise, this same guilt can be used by the Spirit to help us see that there is no way out of our "guiltiness" except the grace of God. His grace enables us to find freedom from sin's guilt and hope in the living Lord Jesus Christ. Think back on your own life when someone has tried to influence you to make a change. What we might call "in-your-face" persuasion doesn't always work. Instead people tend to become defensive.

There is also a negative side to guilt, and that is when God's holiness and grace are never brought into the caregiving equation at all. Some people providing spiritual assistance assume that how people behave is more important than what they believe. So they use guilt to influence a certain kind of behavior. There is a lot of evidence from behavioral research to indicate that people who begin to experience guilt will often resort to further unacceptable behavior. Guilt upon guilt makes them feel that there is no way of escape. So they reason in an irrational manner that it would be better to return to their wrong behavior rather than to pursue a more righteous path. Earl Wilson makes the following observation:

> When people are constantly barraged by guilt-producing statements they become deaf to the motivational aspects and remember only the guilt aspects. There is no evidence that guilt-ridden children are more obedient or more efficient children. More likely, the opposite is true. They get so wrapped up in their feelings of shame and remorse that they fail to follow through on the request made of them. (85)

Scripture must be our primary resource in giving loving teaching about the holiness and grace of God. As we stated earlier, spiritual counsel must be primarily God-focused rather than sin-focused. This does not mean that sin is ignored. By no means! But we want to "direct" people in finding solutions, not give more hurdles to have to get over. We don't want to leave people with a sense that they have to meet a certain level of spiritual growth before they merit our attention or God's grace. And when we focus on God in the caregiving process we come to see that He is a God of grace. We see this clearly in a number of biblical texts. In Titus 2:11–12 the apostle Paul had just concluded telling Titus that he was to give instruction in moral behavior to all the members of the church in Crete. But there was a foundation to those instructions, a very significant starting point. It was the grace of God.

We cannot even approach God's holiness without His grace making us new. Paul put it this way: "For the grace of God that brings salvation has appeared to all men. It teaches us to say 'No' to ungodliness and worldly passions, and to live self-controlled, upright and godly lives in this present age." Paul wanted to appeal to them to live in a certain way. But his aim was not to increase their guilt, but rather to get them to focus on the grace of God. It is the only means of getting people out of the bondage to shame and into the wonderful freedom of life in Christ.

In writing to the Roman Christians Paul again appealed to the grandeur of God's holiness and grace. He rendered weak the argument that says we can go on sinning if we have simply been saved by faith apart from works of the Law. Paul wrote in Romans 5:20–6:4:

> The law was added so that the trespass might increase. But where sin increased, grace increased all the more, so that, just as sin reigned in death, so also grace might reign through righteousness to bring eternal life through Jesus Christ our Lord. What shall we say, then? Shall we go on sinning so that grace may increase? By no means! We died to sin; how can we live in it any longer? Or don't you know that all of us who were baptized into Christ Jesus were baptized into his death? We were therefore buried with him through baptism into death in order that, just as Christ was raised from the dead through the glory of the Father, we too may live a new life.

The apostle was providing spiritual counsel to people who were either ignorant of the grace of God or abusing it. We must do the same. Guilt-ridden people coming to grips with the reality of sin in their lives must be taught that as believers they are brand-new creations. By God's grace they have a brand-new life. We must use Scripture to show the reality of that life and how to live it. The *identification* process must shed a lot of light on this new life in Christ.

B. Initiation Through Encouragement

In addition to providing loving, grace-based teaching, spiritual directors will also want to provide *encouragement* and *exhorta-*

tion. A word of caution needs to introduce this second step. Exhortation does not necessarily mean that we focus on the sin that has been committed. Neither does it refer to getting people to try to change in their own strength. Rather, exhortation has the idea of emphasizing the truth and possible consequences if truth is not embraced. Sometimes exhortation provides a vivid portrayal of what those consequences might be. I (Harry) remember meeting with a man who was separated from his wife and involved in an affair with another woman. At one point in our weekly meetings he was obviously confused about whether to stay in his marriage or not. I showed him what Scripture has to say about the covenant relationship of marriage. He knew what the Word of God says. He had heard it before, and he seemed unmoved. I then went on to tell him what could possibly happen if he pursued a divorce. There was a good chance that his three daughters might not want a relationship with him. There was an even greater possibility that holidays and special family celebrations might be lonelier than he had ever imagined. Was I using guilt? No, the emphasis was not primarily on the sin, even though it was in the background. The focus was on the truth of possible consequences that others had faced in similar circumstances (cf. 2 Sam. 12–18). Encouragement, on the other hand, complements exhortation to give people hope and support as they seek to walk in the Spirit to do God's will. Hebrews 10:24 reminds Christians to encourage one another to persevere in love and good deeds.

And what will we encourage people to do? Once we have taught them about the holiness and grace of God we need to exhort and encourage guilt-ridden people to engage in confession and repentance. Confession is the act of agreeing with God. In Scripture agreeing with God has to do with seeing sin as He sees it. Thus we help people troubled by *true guilt* to agree with God that what they have done is contrary to His will and ways. "Repentance" is that change of mind whereby one begins to turn from self-centered pursuits to live life as God desires. Therefore, confession and repentance mean that we help those we are mentoring to acknowledge their sin and to turn to God. No longer do we see Him as wanting to make us miserable and confine us to our guilt. But we help people to flee to the forgiveness that is in Christ. Spiritual directors like Tad Flossmore will want to help Billy, and those like him, to actually verbalize to God that they have offended His righteous standards. And once confession has occurred, Colossians 1:13–14 can help those experiencing *true guilt* to find encouragement. Paul wrote, "For he has rescued us from the dominion of darkness and brought us into the kingdom of the Son he loves, in whom we have redemption, the forgiveness of sins."

We would again challenge spiritual counselors to care for those they are mentoring by showing tenderness and compassion in the power of the Holy Spirit. We appreciate what Earl Wilson says in this regard:

> I have always been impressed with the ways in which Jesus was able to bring sin into perspective without destroying relationships. When he spoke with the sinful woman at the well he asked questions that got to the issue of her sin. He led her to discover her sin and her need of salvation, but he did not attack her with guilt. (34)

C. Initiating with Restitution

A third approach to *identifying* and *initiating* action in the context of guilt will be to practice *restitution*. "Restitution" is that act where something lost or stolen is returned so that an original situation of good can be reestablished. We usually think of this in material terms where someone returns what he or she has taken from another individual. Zacchaeus made restitution for the things he had done in cheating his Jewish brethren (Luke 19:8–9). But restoration can apply to other areas as well. For instance Jesus made restitution for Adam's sin, thus restoring a lost humanity to a relationship with God (Rom. 5:19).

It seems only logical that if someone has defrauded the honor or respect of another person, that honor should be restored. It might come through a public confession of wrongdoing, assuming that the sin itself was public or has public consequences. Or it might be a one-on-one acknowledgment that wrongdoing has occurred. In the case of the kinds of sinful behavior Billy Guiles acknowledged to his mentor, it only seems appropriate that Billy will be guided to make restitution where he can. That restitution may come in the form of saying something like, "I didn't tell you the truth and I want to ask you to forgive me." Or, "I was unkind and treated you with disrespect. I want to ask you to forgive me." We are aware of the fact that in some situations this kind of restitution may stir up other problems. But when sins have occurred in the recent past, those bearing the guilt of the sins should be directed to make "verbal" restitution where they can and as soon as they can.

Someone may say, "The past is the past. Let it go. Why stir up more trouble?" But restitution is good for the person bearing the *true guilt* of the actions. Gary Collins puts it in these terms:

> But like Zacchaeus, often the forgiven and grateful person is inclined to make things right. In his criticisms of the Roman Catholic confessional, Luther noted that forgiveness from a priest often avoids the penitent person's deepest problem—a broken relationship. If a man publicly criticizes his business partner but goes to a priest or to God to confess the sin, the man may come away knowing that he has been forgiven by God, but the interpersonal tension remains until the critical man takes some action to make restitution to his partner and to work at restoring their relationship. (145)

So we would encourage restitution as a means of acting on the grace that has been received. Such restitution may be verbal or it may be material, as in the case of Zacchaeus. Restitution of material possessions and interpersonal honor can go a long way in helping the guilt-ridden person to mature in his relationship with Christ.

D. Initiating Grace with False Guilt

But what about people who are not experiencing *true guilt* but the kind of strong emotion that comes from what we described earlier as *false guilt?* Here we are thinking of people who endure the shame of growing up in an unhealthy family system. It could include people who have faced the horrible traumas of sexual abuse. Such individuals experience a whole range of emotions; they are angry at people one minute and filled with shame the next. Again we would acknowledge that there are times when anger can lead to sinful actions and thus the experiencing of *true guilt*. But many times these individuals are overwhelmed with shame for what has happened to them. They often wonder what their relationship should be toward people who have hurt them deeply. What about people like Billy Guiles, who apparently faces degrading comments from an older brother and a lack of parental support from his father? It may be that Billy is misinterpreting what his father is trying to do. Caregivers like Tad Flossmore will have to be very careful to not take sides and to get all of the data possible. But how should a spiritual counselor respond when *false guilt* is also part of the picture?

In such situations we would encourage a true believer to pursue God's grace through the practice of forgiving the person who has shamed him. However, this is much easier said than done. That is why it is important to understand and guide people in a biblical manner when it comes to extending forgiveness to others. First, these people need to know what forgiveness is *not*. It is not necessarily forgetting what someone has done to them. Psalm 103:12 is often applied inappropriately at this point. People have been told that since God removes our sins "as far as the east is from the west," believers then should simply forget what others have done to them. But on further reflection we realize that the psalmist is not saying that God doesn't remember our sin anymore. He is God. He is omniscient and knows all things. What the verse is saying is that God has so separated us from the sin He has forgiven that He will not use it against us. It doesn't mean that He doesn't remember what has occurred. Forgiveness is not necessarily forgetting.

Likewise, forgiveness is not tolerating sin or allowing it to continue against us or someone else. Let's say a forty-two-year-old woman in your church comes to you in panic. Unknown to you, her husband has been abusing her for years, and she has recently become afraid that he will kill her or the children. But she tells you her husband has said that if she "submits" to him as she should, he wouldn't have to beat her. She's convinced he's right, and she feels guilty that apparently she has not been submissive enough, but she's terrified of him. She has a hard time believing that her husband is just using Scripture to try to justify his abuse of her. Yet Christians are not instructed to become "doormats" for other people to do with us as they please. Scripture is clear that there are appropriate ways in which people who deliberately bring harm are to be handled (Acts 5:1–11; 1 Cor. 5:1–12; 2 Thess. 3:14–15). One of the reasons that God has established governments is so that they can maintain protection for all citizens and deal with those who bring harm to others (Rom. 13:1–4).

Forgiveness is not tolerating sin or even forgetting what has happened in the past. Harvey and Benner provided a helpful clarification of what it really means to forgive someone:

> To forgive is not necessarily to extend unconditional trust. Genuine forgiveness means that I no longer hold the hurt over the head of the other person. It does not mean that I must assume that I will never again be hurt by them, nor does it mean that I should never take steps to minimize this possibility. (Harvey and Benner, 79)

When we guide someone to forgive we are helping the person to turn the work of justice over to God and His means of making things right. We are refusing to take action on our own in order for justice to be accomplished (1 Sam. 25:32–39; Rom. 12:19). Will this be an easy thing to accomplish? Not at all. Harvey and Benner went on to say:

> There are also difficulties in forgiveness that come from our fears of the process. Some of these fears are closely related to the handling of our anger, so we may have already dealt in part with the resolving of them; for instance the problem of vulnerability to becoming a victim again or the fear that forgiveness means we now have to "feel good about" a person who has done monstrous wrong.

Beyond these there may also be fear of not being able to stick it out. Forgiveness takes time, may consist of repeated acts of fresh beginnings after new disappointments, and we grow tired of difficult relationships. Already exhausted emotionally by the shock of the wrong done you, there may seem to be no energy left for the long haul of forgiving. There's nothing left in me to give you any more, may be your honest feeling. (79)

Spiritual counselors need to be alert to the fact that forgiveness is a process. It will take time to work itself out in the lives of some people. We cannot rush forgiveness through the recitation of a specific prayer or an announcement. This is where we have to return to the grace of God, sometimes again and again, allowing God's Spirit to penetrate the pain that is in a person's heart.

Those who provide spiritual counsel will want to help the offended party to realize that God wants us to be forgiving. We see this in such passages as Matthew 6:14–15 and Ephesians 4:31–32. Believers are to be characterized as people who forgive. It is a practice of one who has new life in Christ. In addition, spiritual counselors will want to help these same people to acknowledge that real pain and hurt have occurred. This is important because some individuals under the guise of spirituality will insist that they weren't hurt, or at least they weren't hurt that badly. We need to help them to acknowledge that something terrible has happened and it is not wrong or unspiritual to admit it.

Exposing people to biblical truth about forgiving others will also mean that we instruct them in the consequences of holding on to bitterness and anger. The apostle Paul warned the Galatian believers that if they kept on being bitter toward one another, it would result in their actually destroying one another (Gal. 5:15). People need to know about the spiritual and physical consequences to an ongoing, unforgiving spirit. Harvey and Benner stated:

> Resentment is a poison that destroys our body, soul, and spirit, and we should, therefore, strive to neutralize this poison with the antidote of forgiveness as soon as we are able. The inability to accept forgiveness is equally destructive. Thus, how vital is our

pastoral ministry of the forgiving grace of God! Forgiveness is an unmerited gift through the sacrificial atonement accomplished by Jesus Christ. It is God's offer of health and wholeness. (28)

One other biblical truth is important to teach people struggling with the shame that has been brought to them by what others have done and said to them. That is, when people come and ask for forgiveness we need to be ready to grant forgiveness. Luke 17:3–4 gives evidence that Jesus wants His followers to be inclined to forgive. In fact, if a person appears a multiple number of times and asks to be forgiven, Christians are to extend forgiveness each time. It is important to add that there should be sincerity in the request of those who come. As we stated earlier in the chapter, forgiveness is to characterize the life of the disciple.

Yet this raises other important matters that spiritual counselors will want to be sensitive to as they minister to people dealing with shame and guilt feelings that have been put upon them by others. What if people never see that their actions have harmed another individual? What if they are confronted and still fail to repent for what they have done? It is a difficult situation that must be carefully informed by biblical teaching. We would suggest that guiding people to live the grace-based life is absolutely essential in the process of spiritual counsel. Forgiveness must be extended when forgiveness is sincerely requested. However, we must be careful in how we encourage people to relate to the unrepentant. John Stott made a helpful observation regarding the passage in Luke 17 cited above:

Although the followers of Jesus never have the right to refuse forgiveness, let alone to take revenge, we are not permitted to cheapen forgiveness by offering it prematurely when there has been no repentance. "If your brother sins," Jesus said, "rebuke him," and only then "if he repents, forgive him" (Luke 17:3). (296)

In situations where people under our caregiving ministries are trying to determine how to relate to people who have hurt them, we would suggest they consider the following:

tain out of a molehill, and I think that there are reasons for concern on my part."

"What are some of your concerns?"

"Well, Bob is so caught up in his business right now that I don't think he has time for me or the kids. And I'm beginning to wonder if he really cares about me anymore." Betsy started to cry. She said nothing and sat with her head down, tears starting to stream down her face. Bob seemed irritated at first and then moved closer to Betsy on the sofa and put his arm around her.

Jim Starr wanted to find out more before he could determine what the extent of his involvement with the Bushes would be. "Betsy, apparently something has triggered your feelings, especially your feelings about Bob not caring for you anymore. What brings you to say that?"

"He's not only busy, but last week when we were talking about him being gone all the time, he got really mad. Then he told me that if I didn't like it I could take the kids and go back and live with my parents. I can't believe he said that. I know that there are some young women working in the company with him, and I wonder if he doesn't have more of an interest in them than in me."

Bob looked at Pastor Starr with a look that indicated that he wanted permission to talk. "Bob, tell me how you are seeing things, especially in light of what Betsy has just said."

"Pastor Jim, I will admit that Betsy has some legitimate issues at times. I really have been very busy of late. I tried to reassure her that I am not interested in anyone else. I love her and the children very much. But she is making a lot more out of this than is really necessary. I have to put in the hours right now or this business isn't really going to go. And when she starts putting demands on me, I get very defensive and want to be alone."

Jim Starr listened as the two revealed different scenarios about their marriage and the conflicts between them that seemed to be more and more frequent. The Bushes have been married for eight years. They live in a nice neighborhood in their community and have two children, a girl and a boy ages five and three. But each one looks at their marriage from different perspectives. Pastor Starr could approach their conflicts from the perspective of teaching communication techniques or time management methods. But is the issue really one of communication? Are the Bushes like most young couples, caught up in the rat race of life and not taking time to smell the roses? Perhaps there is truth to be explored in all of these issues. But at the heart of most marital conflicts is a clash of worldviews. And positive change, if it is to occur at all, will have to take place in each person's soul. So Jim Starr, and spiritual directors like him, will want to deal with issues of the heart, not just outward behavior. How will this happen?

INVOLVEMENT—FIRST READ THE DIRECTIONS

Before children open presents on Christmas morning, some of those toys have to be assembled properly. And if the toys are to work as they were designed, one has to first read the directions. It is the same thing when it comes to the spiritual nurture of marriages. Larry Crabb in his excellent book *The Marriage Builder* made this helpful observation:

> Psychological needs have taken over as the focus of our discussion of roles in marriage. The Bible has been reduced to an optional guidebook as we look for ways to meet our emotional needs. As a result, the value of a plan ("Maybe I should leave my husband" or "I think I'll just not bring it up—it's better than getting into an argument") is measured not in terms of its fidelity to Scripture, but in terms of its perceived effects on people's needs and emotions. The issue of authority is really at stake here. To validate a plan of action by appealing to its potential for meeting needs is to replace the authority of an inerrant Bible with a humanistic value system. (11)

It is for this reason that spiritual counselors in the church need to rehearse afresh what the Bible has to say about marriage.

To understand God's design for marriage we need to also know what it means to be human. Scripture helps us in this task. The opening chapter of the Bible informs us that God Almighty is the Creator of all things. And when it comes to the creation of the heavens and the earth, God looked upon what He made and declared it was good, including the creation of human beings (Gen. 1:31). But why was man created? What did the Creator have in mind when He fashioned human beings as male and female? Several important things need to be affirmed about the creation of human beings and the subsequent establishment of marriage.

First, human beings were uniquely different from the rest of the living things that God had made. They were set apart as being created in the image of God and told to rule over the other living creatures (Gen. 1:26–28). In this regard human beings were created to be God's stewards, His caretakers of the good world that the heavenly Father had fashioned for them. But what does it mean to be "created in His image"? There are a lot of differing opinions on the subject, many of them focusing on something that is "inside of us." But an image-bearer seems to be something that human beings *do*, not just something that we *are*. Edward Welch puts it in these terms:

> When image-bearing is seen as the way we live rather than what we want to get, it leads directly and naturally to the heart of the Scriptures: "faith expressing itself in love" (Gal. 5:6). Image-bearing is expressed in simple acts of obedience, seemingly small obediences that have eternal implications. Imaging is loving God and loving your neighbor. And this is exactly what you should expect. God's glory is manifested in concrete acts of love and justice and we are to mimic God in love and justice. (34)

So to be an image-bearer is to act in a special relationship with God in which we display His glory. We are first and foremost created to be worshipers. Psalm 8 specifically describes our unique position and role as created beings who declare the majesty of God. And as Welch pointed out, we function as worshipers when we act before God in such a way that we declare His glory. We do that as stewards within His creation, and we do it by expressing love for God and for our fellow human beings. Such actions fulfill what Jesus said was the greatest commandment (Matt. 22:34–40). We will see later in this chapter how image-bearers as active worshipers will affect marriage.

Second, marriage is part of God's design for creation. His design includes a covenant relationship. The word *covenant* is very important here because it refers to something that is more than "casual." Rather, it is an agreement between two people that is to be lifelong and carried out in God's very presence (Gen. 2:22–24; Mal. 2:14).

Third, marriage according to God's design is to be an exclusive relationship between a man and a woman. It is the exclusive place where sexual union is to occur. Such restrictions on love and sexuality were designed to bring stability to society at large (1 Cor. 7:3–9; Heb. 13:4).

Fourth, marriage according to God's design was the starting place for the family and the rearing of children. The culture was not designated as the training center. Neither was the church the primary context for nurturing godly children (although the church often needs to train parents in rearing godly children). Marriage and family were to be God's primary training stations (Mal. 2:15; 1 Cor. 7:14; Eph. 6:4).

Fifth, marriage is also designed by God to be carried out as a Spirit-empowered union. We see this specifically in Christian marriages. The Spirit of God is given to believers to effectively carry out our purpose of being worshipers. One way godly husbands are to worship is by loving their wives. And godly wives are to worship showing respect to their husbands through acts of submission (Eph. 5:15–32; 1 Peter 3:1–7).

Sixth, marriage was designed for our earthly existence, not for the life to come (Matt. 22:30). This does not lessen the importance of marriage in any way. In fact, it enhances the fact that we exist to be worshipers, even in the context of marriage, not necessarily to have all of our personal "wants" met by our mates. Meeting needs should occur, but this will not be the primary purpose of marriage.

Why do spiritual counselors need to be reminded of the biblical teaching on marriage? We can so easily be distracted into thinking that "presenting problems" need to be solved. We can focus on communication problems, sexual dysfunction, or conflict resolution. But most marital problems can be ultimately traced back to some violation of God's original design for marriage. What

new home. But I told her that the business would require some travel at first and a lot of hours to get things set up to sell a new product. She told me it was a great idea. But six months into the move and the new job, she started complaining about my work hours. She would complain if I didn't make a special trip home for school events. She would complain because I have had to work some on Saturdays. I thought she was supportive. I get confused and frustrated.

Pastor: When you and Betsy get into arguments, like the one last weekend, how do you feel? What goes on in your mind?

Bob: I feel that I am not a good provider. I feel like she doesn't appreciate what I do or the commitment that I am making to the family so that we can live as best as we can.

Pastor: Tell me what you do when Betsy shares her feelings with you. How do you react?

Bob: Well, I'm ashamed. In fact, I am ashamed that we are even here talking to you tonight. I value your friendship, and I don't like having to talk to you about these things.

Pastor: I want to reassure you that I do not think any less of you for what you're telling me. You are to be commended for valuing your marriage enough to want to work on it. So tell me how you respond.

Bob: I don't respond the way that I should. I tend to get silent. Sometimes I simply try to get out of the house any way that I can. I just don't want to argue with her.

Pastor: Betsy, as you've been listening to Bob's comments, what do you hear him saying about his feelings? Like Bob did a few minutes ago, pretend you're a reporter just describing the facts.

Betsy: I was afraid you were going to ask me to do that. OK . . . well, Bob sometimes interprets me, I mean his wife, as not appreciating what he does. He feels like he isn't always a good provider. . . . Pastor, can I say that Bob is a very good provider, it's just that I want . . .

Pastor: Wait, I just want you to report how he has described his feelings. Are you saying that he sometimes feels as though he doesn't measure up?

Betsy: Yes, I think that is what I heard him saying.

Pastor: Bob, how would you respond? Is she correct?

Bob: Yeah . . . I have to admit that is the case at times.

Pastor: I want to find out some more things, so bear with me as I keep asking some things about your marriage. But it would be helpful if you could both tell me a little bit about your relationship with the Lord these days. Would you say that it is good or in need of some improvement? Bob, why don't you start.

Bob: You really know how to get to a guy, don't you. [Laughter breaks the tension of the moment.] I'm not doing well in that department. I get so busy that I don't take time to pray or read the Scriptures. And I know that I should.

Pastor: Betsy, how about you?

Betsy: Ditto. I know I should be seeking the Lord more than ever, but I don't. I get so discouraged at times that I wonder if He is really working in our marriage. I pray, but I don't see many results.

Pastor: I appreciate you being honest, both of you. I assure you that I am not going to use "Bible talk" to try to cover up issues that are going on. But I think we will want to talk more about this area of your life. So, let me ask some other questions. I want to get as much of a picture of what's going on as I can.

You may have noticed that Pastor Starr focused on the presenting problem and one other incident that Betsy raised. But the important thing to observe is that he also tried to ask probing questions that focused on *feelings, behaviors,* and *thoughts.* This sequence is important, especially when it comes to discovering core beliefs. Sometimes what people say they feel is also an expression of what they are thinking or believing as well. In the dialogue cited above there is still more that can be uncovered. A wise spiritual counselor will want to know what each mate has experienced in the past, specifically the kind of messages (worldviews) they learned growing up. But *investigation* should probe a person's soul with the triad of questions related to *feelings, behaviors,* and *thinking.* This triad should also be followed with a question about the health of a person's spiritual life. Pastor J. Kirk Johnston made an observation about couples with which we would thoroughly agree. He wrote:

> Whenever a couple continues to have serious marital problems, I ask them at some point how their personal relationships with God are. Over the last ten years, without fail, they have admitted that it is not very good. It is hard to say whether a person's relationship with God or one's relationship to one's spouse, goes first, but there is a very definite connection. (235)

We stated earlier that as you ask questions you want to be open to *motivations* and *strategies* that each mate seems to embrace. We believe that people are always motivated to act upon their real worldviews. We use the term *real* because some people will profess certain things, even traditional Christian beliefs, yet their actions betray them. That is why we must be on the lookout for what is really motivating a person to act as he does. Sinful, faulty behaviors are fueled by sinful, faulty beliefs. Spiritual counselors must discover what those motivations really are. Marriage counselor Leslie Vernick stated:

> Information on what they are doing wrong and instruction on what to do right are usually not enough to break long-standing habits of ineffective and hurtful words, actions and attitudes. Instead, you must address problems deeper than conflict resolution and communication techniques. Counselees at odds with each other are also at odds with God. To point them to Christ in these moments, you must shift the agenda of counseling to the motivational themes that fuel their miscommunication and sinful interaction. Otherwise, if you attend only to strengthening a couple's communication, you may inadvertently teach your

counselees how to serve their own sinful hearts more skillfully. (31)

What happens in so many marriages is that each mate is motivated to satisfy one's own desires without enthusiastically considering the needs of a mate. Husbands and wives may want companionship that feeds their desire for wanting recognition or reaffirming that they are OK as human beings. But what they miss is the divine design for human beings and for marriages. We were created to be worshipers who serve God and one another. But in marital conflict the Great Commandment principle of worship and servanthood (Matt. 22:34–40) becomes relegated to an idolatrous motivation for recognition, respect, and attention from the marriage partner. When such motivations are put into operation, the result is usually conflict. We might want a "good marriage" but our motivations to get there are self-centered. We might even do what Bob Bushe talks about and put things in the noble language of "sacrifice for the good of the family." It sounds good, but the results are always spiritually and emotionally unhealthy.

And what strategies do idolatrous motivations usually produce? If we were to probe still further we would discover all kinds of creative ways that marriage partners might employ to get what they want. A word of caution is in order at this point. I (Harry) realize that I am using some rather confrontational words: "selfish," "idolatrous," and "self-centered." This is not to suggest that we should use these words, at least not in the *investigation* stage. Let people come to these conclusions as you take them to the Word of God in the *initiation* stage of the spiritual counsel process. However, it is important for caregivers to realize what is going on in the hearts of human beings.

Strategies quite often take three unhealthy forms (Crabb 30–34). We see glimpses of these ways of dealing with marital distress in the scenario related to the Bushes. One strategy is to so want our goals and motivations met that we simply ignore any desires that our mates might have. In the case of Bob Bushe he would hear his wife's complaints, especially in the form of yelling, and choose to ignore her. It doesn't mean that he won't talk to

something like, "Do you remember when we first started to talk about your marriage and some of the responses you made to (*mate's name*)? In fact, you responded as you did because you felt very strongly about some things. In response to your mate you (*describe the action*)."

- Next, guide the couple, both individually and corporately, to discover for themselves why they acted as they did. A good way to start is to ask them to assess their own behavior and beliefs. The one giving spiritual counsel could say something like this to get the reflective moments started: "You made the statement, 'Sometimes I feel as though I'm not really important to him/her anymore.' I wonder why you said that? I know it had to do with specific things that he/she did. But I wonder if you could describe for me what it is that you really want out of marriage?" Most of the time couples will not have taken the time to think about their motives. Motives are so much a part of everyday activities that people do not take the time to see if they are biblically valid or not. Give them time to reflect on this question even though they might not answer from a biblical perspective initially.

- The next thing a spiritual director will want to try to do is to analyze the core beliefs (idolatrous motivations) that may be driving each spouse. Keep in mind that you will want to present this information in a tentative manner for their consideration. You are not stating in some dogmatic way, "You're having these problems in your marriage simply because you're both selfish." As we have been saying, such assessments might be true, but they will not bring about change. The people being mentored must be prepared to "buy into" what the spiritual counselor is saying.

A better way to expose faulty core beliefs is to say to each person at a time something like: "Would you consider that part of the problem, in fact a major part, might be that you have expectations that can't be met by your husband/wife? You may not say it outright, but you have desires that he/she should meet your needs. Tell me how that strikes you." Give the person a chance to respond. If the person is unconvinced, provide data from his or her story line. You could say something like: "Here is why I am suggesting you have faulty expectations. Remember when (*describe a specific event from the collected data*). I recall that you said you felt (*describe the feeling and belief*). That leads me to think that one of the things that motivates you is this desire to have your husband/wife be the one to meet your needs. And from God's perspective that won't work." The wise spiritual counselor will want to go on to present other incidents that will substantiate that the assessment of faulty core beliefs is valid.

- After discussing core beliefs with the couple, try to guide them to see that both the behaviors and the beliefs they have been practicing are ineffective. You can do this by using the following transitional question to get them to participate in your analysis. You might want to say something like: "Let's think again about some of the things you have been doing in your relationship with each other. What do you think your strategies and your desires have accomplished? Let's use the example when you started yelling at your husband. What did that accomplish?" They might seem embarrassed by answering something they already know to be ineffective, but getting them to agree verbally that a given action was ineffective can be a big step in getting them to try something more righteous.

- You are now at a point where you can go to back to the Word of God to give them instruction on biblical strategies. At this point as a spiritual counselor you can become more directive in what you are saying. Always allow the couple to ask questions. Be sensitive to the fact that they may challenge what you are saying. It is possible that you may have to go back to exploring their motivations and strategies still further. But eventually you will have to let the Spirit of God use the Word of God to bring about change. Therefore, use passages like Ephesians 5:18–33 and 1 Peter 3:1–7 to explore how husbands and wives are to relate to one another. These are not the only passages to use, but they are a good starting point.

Have the husband and wife read the verses that relate to their roles. Then ask a question like this: "How would you evaluate whether or not you are living in this way? On a scale of 1 to 10, 10 being perfect, how would you rate your obedience to this passage?" A follow-up question might be: "Let's assume that you were to become very intentional about obeying this text of Scripture. What would it look like if you were to love your wife as Christ loved the church? Give me some examples." Or you might say to the wife, "Realizing that submission does not mean being a slave, what would it look like if you were submitting in a godly way to your husband?" Their answers then become the means of giving them assignments to carry out before the next meeting. You might encourage the husband to think of additional ways to love his wife and then to carry them out over the next several days. The same can be done with the wife. The goal is to get them to see that when they are intentional about living life from God's perspective they will have a much greater chance of bringing joy to the marriage than they have been doing in the past.

- Before a session like the one we have just been describing is concluded, you might want to ask the couple to join you in praying. Assuming that they have been cooperative in agreeing that their faulty core beliefs are sinful and ineffective, invite them to confess that they have deeply hurt each other in the past. Spiritual directors will want to be very careful not to hurry this important event. Through tears and shame two individuals may be open to expressing their sin toward each other. If so, encourage it to happen. Then invite them to confess their sin to God. But be sure to encourage them to join their confession and repentance with a seeking after God to empower them to be the partners He wants them to be.

Spiritual counsel will generally not be done in one or two sessions. That is why pastors cannot care for the people of their congregations on their own. They will need other spiritually mature people to assist them in providing follow-up and care. And when it comes to follow-up, those who provide soul care will want to help people to put on the garments of righteous behavior (Eph. 4:17–32). This will take time to get rid of old patterns of behavior and to put on new righteous actions. Therefore, the initiation phase that follows the identification of faulty core beliefs (idolatrous motivations) will want to be focused on some specific actions that are supported by Scripture. Let's consider some of those specific actions in the meetings that follow investigation and identification.

First, always follow up with a report about how the couple has been relating since the previous meeting. Review any assignments that have been given. If there has been specific conflict between the husband and wife, help them to explore why it occurred. Quite often you can relate recent situations of distress by showing how one or both of the mates have used the motivations and strategies of the past. Keep showing how these strategies are contrary to what God has planned for them. Specifically show them that being servants to each other and to God has been replaced by more self-centered practices.

Second, take time to teach the couple about the presence and goodness of God. One might think that this is irrelevant to helping couples grow in oneness. However, it is a very important issue because many people are resistant to follow biblical guidelines for living. And the reason they are reluctant to obey is that they have doubts about God's goodness. "If I obey and serve my mate, can I be sure that God will truly care for me?" Crabb put the dilemma in these terms:

> Our failure to readily follow His leading reflects a lack of deep confidence in His goodness. We wonder whether He is merely using us or wants to bless us. The problem with unsteady commitment is not centrally a problem of the *will;* it is rather deficient *belief.* We simply do not believe that the God who tells us to remain committed to our marriage partners is good. If we *knew* He was good, we would sense a deep desire to follow His leading. (116)

through their faith in Christ, Paul went on to reveal his personal prayer for them (Eph. 1:15–18). The apostle wasn't trying to instruct these believers about how to pray. He was revealing something of his own spiritual practices, namely, the practice of prayer. He prayed that God would accomplish His will in these believers. Verse 17 reveals that the inspired apostle wanted them to grow in the intimate knowledge of God.

Paul revealed a similar thought in the prayer that is recorded at the end of Ephesians 3. He desired that believers would come to comprehend the unlimited extent of Christ's love for them (vv. 14–19). But he wanted them to experience this love in what he refers to as their "inner being" (v. 16). The apostle Paul was concerned about soul care.

A similar exhortation is given in Proverbs 4:23. Two images appear in the verse. The first is that of a guard who stands above the gates of the city and keeps an eye out for enemies who might be approaching from a distance. His task is to alert the citizens of danger. The writer of the proverb says that those who follow the living God must also post a similar guard over their hearts. They must take care of their souls. The second line of the proverb gives the reason for posting such a watch. They need to do it because the heart can be the source of spiritual refreshment or spiritual drought. What goes into the soul will eventually come out. And if one's life is to be enriched with a righteous worldview during its earthly journey, the soul must also be nurtured with righteous attitudes.

One Christian worker described his own struggles in the following words:

So here I was, a Christian man, a guy working in Christian service, faced with a growing deadness inside. I was most of the way into the anaconda and joking about it.

For a long time, I was stuck in self-blame and self-pity. How could I let this happen to me? It was my job to be a "spiritual leader"; why had I let the spiritual passion go out of me? Then I'd wonder, how could God let this happen to me? After all, I was doing all the right things. I had biblical ethics and a "successful" ministry. I had the right theology, as far as I knew, so it wasn't that my Christian doctrine was flawed. But impeccable ethics and flawless theology were not enough.

Gradually, I came to see some basic missteps I'd made. Primarily, I had lost my soul to one of the chief rivals of devotion to Christ—that is, service for Him. (Baker 33–34)

Even when we are engaged in the best of endeavors we can neglect what is of greater importance. That is why we must be intentional about spending time with God and getting to know Him through His Word.

Why does this neglect occur? We could place the blame at the feet of a sinful humanity. It would be accurate but too general. There are at least two other common causes that we can do something about. The first has to do with prideful choices that we make. Like our ancestors Adam and Eve, we have come to believe that we can go it alone, even when it comes to spiritual endeavors like preaching, teaching, evangelism, and the care of others. We forget that we only bear fruit in Christian service when we abide in Christ (John 15:4). Christian caregivers can be persuaded that the latest seminar or the most recently published book has the answers to our ministry needs. But such conclusions are symptomatic of prideful choices to live independently from God. It might appear to be a successful approach, but it can be the epitome of deception.

A second cause is closely allied with the first. It is the willingness to succumb to the "hurriedness" of our Western culture. Sometimes we program our days to be filled with one appointment and one task after the other. Some people do it to try to cover other issues that are going on in their lives—a troubled marriage, a wayward teenager, or a fear about growing older. Others might succumb to hurriedness because of thinking that when they are busy they are enhancing their sense of worth. Those of us who have been engaged in pastoral ministry have relished it when people praise us for being so busy. We are encouraged with thoughts that we will certainly not "rust out in service to the Lord." To embrace such thinking is sinful pride. And one of the motives that fuels such thinking is that we determine our personal worth on the basis of being so busy in our service to Christ.

Our neighbors are busy. Our fellow pastors in the denomination are busy. Surely we must be busy too. But the unfortunate result is that in a busy, hurry-up world our souls will suffer.

A COURSE OF ACTION FOR PERSONAL SOUL CARE

Galatians 6:1 has a twofold challenge. On one hand believers, especially those in leadership positions, are to gently restore those who are caught in sin. It is interesting that the apostle specifically teaches that the ministry of restoration is to be gentle, not harsh. But this description is given further explanation in the second challenge. Paul says that those same leaders are to watch themselves or they too may be tempted. His point is that leaders (including spiritual counselors) are never above those to whom they minister. We never come to a point in this life when we can cease from being on guard against sin. The Christian life must be viewed as a rigorous journey and one that takes daily discipline, especially the discipline of self-control. We can count on the fact that God will do His part to sanctify us and empower us to be what He wants us to be. But we also have a responsibility to reverently apply our new life in Christ to the everyday circumstances that we face (Phil. 2:12–13). It doesn't mean that we are trying to be righteous in our own strength. Rather, it means that we are living moment-by-moment as if every situation were a training program held in co-operation with the indwelling Holy Spirit. John Ortberg put it this way:

> Spiritual transformation is not a matter of trying harder, but of training wisely. This is what the apostle Paul means when he encourages his young protégé Timothy to "*train* yourself in godliness." This thought also lies behind his advice to the church at Corinth: "Everyone who competes in the games goes into *strict training*. They do it to get a crown that will not last; but we do it to get a crown that will last forever." (47)

This "training" to which Ortberg refers is sometimes described as the practice of the spiritual disciplines. However, it seems to us that God's training program is more than certain practices that we engage in to harness the work of the flesh in our lives. I (Harry) would prefer to think in terms of the "attitudes and actions of redemptive living." People down through the centuries have engaged in certain activities that later became forms of works righteousness as they compared themselves with others. I believe in the practice of spiritual disciplines, but they need to be preceded by righteous attitudes. That is, the Christian does not participate in specific spiritual disciplines to impress God, but he does so as acts of daily worship, because of what God has done in Jesus Christ. Right attitudes must precede right actions. So let's look to see what some of those attitudes and actions might be.

Redemptive Worship

Often when Christians use the term *worship* they think of church services arranged around a series of hymns, readings, and a sermon that challenges us to live uprightly. But worship is a daily activity. And that activity is to be preceded with a specific attitude, namely, an awareness that God is at work within every believer's life.

For the last several years the city of Chicago has been engaged in a major municipal works program. It is known as the Deep Tunnel Project. "Deep Tunnel" is designed to help with the massive water runoff that occurs every year, sometimes in the summer months after severe rainstorms and again in early spring when snow begins to melt. City engineers are preparing for the future by building a massive tunnel that will help in dealing with these great amounts of water. Yet many people don't even know that the project exists. Work can be going on underground while people on the surface are oblivious to what is happening around them.

Likewise Christians can be unaware of what God is doing. Philippians 2:12–13 calls believers to "work out [their] salvation with fear and trembling." The apostle Paul means that Christians are to live their Christian life in every experience that they face. However, such a command is based on what God is already doing. He is already at work within believers to accomplish His purposes (v. 13).

One of the ways we can engage in "redemptive worship" is to make it a practice to start every day by not only asking God to search our hearts for sin but to look for attitudes of discontent. All too frequently things that happen in our places of employment dishearten us. Or we become discouraged with the fact that we do not have what others have, and this in turn leads to feelings of disappointment. The Bible is very clear that such attitudes are sinful. But they are also indications that we are unappreciative of His grace and His presence in our lives.

Redemptive Patience

Another attitude that precedes any action that we might take as spiritual counselors is what might be referred to as "redemptive patience." Throughout the second half of the book an attempt has been made to give readers some insight into how they might take people from their pain to actually experiencing life from God's perspective. The goals were to go from theories about soul care to actually putting ideas into practice. But there is a danger when we start to talk about specific steps. It is a danger in assuming that just because we have a plan, there will be positive outcomes to the working of that plan. It is almost as if our expectations for change become demands for change. Such attitudes need to be taken captive and replaced with the truth of God's Word (2 Cor. 10:5). That means that we need to engage in "redemptive patience." But what is it?

The apostle Paul reminded young Timothy that he had certain tasks in ministering to the people of God. Timothy was to preach the Word with consistent preparation, whether people responded or not. He was to bring correction, rebuke, and encouragement to those who needed them. But all of these tasks were to be complemented with great patience and careful instruction (2 Tim. 4:2). Change does not happen overnight. In fact, in some situations transformation may not occur at all. And even if it does, God will be the One who has brought it about. Such an attitude is what we mean by "redemptive patience."

Redemptive Friendships

One of the roles that spiritual counselors play is that of friend. We have emphasized throughout that when we care for people in their times of spiritual/emotional trials we need to do the kinds of things that will enable them to trust us. People are inclined to trust others when they see those same people as friends, not just friendly. And yet we often forget that friendship is a two-way street. It is easy for many of us in helping roles to show ourselves to be friends, but it is more difficult for us to receive the benefits of friendship from others. Jerry Bridges wrote:

> The times when we need an extra measure of God's grace are often the times when we are most reluctant to let other people know we need it. This leads to an important principle regarding the ministry of grace. Each of us needs to cultivate a small group of friends with whom we can be transparent and vulnerable. This might be on an individual or small group basis. But we need a few people—including our spouse, if we have one—with whom we feel free to share our failures, hurts, and sorrows. The Puritans used to ask God for one "bosom friend" with whom they could share absolutely everything. That is a good goal for us today. (187)

We would concur. And when it comes to training those who give spiritual counsel, we would do well within the training to encourage the development of long-term friendship with other mature believers.

This whole concept of "redemptive friendships" is portrayed throughout Scripture. One text that speaks to the issue is Romans 12:10–13. The text is not referring to friendship as we might envision it in contemporary culture. But it is talking about how believers are to relate to one another in the body of Christ. The passage on first reflection looks like a series of commands. But it is more than instruction about how believers are to relate to one another. Paul was telling all believers how to mutually support one another. The needs of all the saints, whether leaders or followers, were to be met (v. 13). And even though the New Testament establishes some very distinct leadership roles, there is still a place for mutual edification and accountability through "redemptive relationships" (1 Thess. 5:12–15; Heb. 13:17–21).

Pride will deceive us into thinking that we don't need anyone else. Pride can also take full reign of our rational existence and lead us to conclude that all our opinions and ideas are correct. After all, many people might be helped by our caregiving services. But it is at this point that we need to be extremely careful. We must not forget that the successes we experience aren't ours but God's. For this reason, we must be ready to hear what other people have to say. We don't have a monopoly on the truth. John Ortberg has a very helpful perspective on the matter of *listening* to what others have to say. This listening is a discipline that we need to nurture regularly.

> The ministry of bearing with one another is more than simply tolerating difficult people. It is also learning to hear God speak through them. It is learning to be "for" them. It is learning that the difficult person I have most to deal with is me.
>
> This means that a part of the ministry to which I am called is to free people—repeatedly if necessary—from the little mental prisons to which I consign them. (117)

So be on guard. We pray that God will speak through you. But develop the attitude that God might also speak to you as well through those who come to seek your guidance.

Redemptive Suffering

Another attitude that can be very significant to those who minister to others is what might be called a theology of suffering, or "redemptive suffering." A subtle Western worldview assumes that life should be comfortable, pleasant, and filled with happiness. But Scripture makes no such promise. In fact, many of the New Testament epistles were written against a backdrop of suffering and persecution (James 1:2–4; 1 Peter 1:6). For those early saints, trouble was a way of life. Yet that very same trouble was redemptive in the sense that it cooperates with God's Spirit in transforming us into the image of Christ (Rom. 5:3–5).

So how can we come to embrace "redemptive suffering"? First, we need to learn God's ways. But spiritual directors must especially know God's will and ways as He works out His redemptive program in history and time. The way to do that is to be familiar with God's Word.

In addition, we will want to engage in a life of prayer. This does not mean that God will simply remove all the problems we are facing because we pray. While writing to the Philippian church, the apostle Paul was facing both imprisonment and repercussions from those who were jealous of his ministry. Yet Paul rejoiced in suffering and was confident about the future because of the prayers of the Philippian believers (Phil. 1:18–26). He anticipated that he would be delivered, but "deliverance" did not necessarily mean getting out of prison. Paul anticipated that deliverance could also mean dying and going to heaven. He had an attitude in life that embraced "redemptive suffering." It must be the attitude of every spiritual counselor.

Believers are called upon to encourage one another in times of need (Heb. 10:24–25). My wife and I (Harry) have been part of a church that encourages participation in small groups. One of the groups in our church had a young couple with three little children. In the course of one year both the husband and wife were diagnosed with cancer. You can imagine the strain it placed on the family. But the glorious outcome of their lives was not just that God restored both of them to health, but that their situation brought the entire church family together as never before. In fact, neighbors would ask the couple, "Who are all of these people who keep stopping by with food and childcare?" The couple then had a great opportunity to tell unbelieving neighbors about the Savior who was sustaining them and about their wonderfully supportive church family. This couple has had frequent opportunity to tell their story, which is framed in a healthy biblical view of suffering. Such a view must be part of the lifestyle of spiritual counselors as well.

Redemptive Meditation

The apostle Paul challenged his young disciple Timothy to be a consistent student of the Word of God (2 Tim. 2:15; 3:14–17). In the Old Testament Ezra was acknowledged for his work in helping former exiles to reestablish themselves in the land of Israel. His journey back to the land and his help in encouraging the people were directly associated with his devotion and study of the Law of the Lord (Ezra 7:10). And the psalmist acknowledged that his success in doing battle with sin was a result of knowing and obeying the Word of God (Ps. 119:11–16). The study of the Scriptures is a prominent theme in the sanctifying of God's people.

The temptation we will face as we do spiritual counsel is to get caught up in the busyness of life and neglect study and meditation. We may approach the Scriptures as a kind of first-aid box. It will be used in times of emergency but left unattended when life is comfortable. A better perspective on God's Word is to see it as more of a dining room table prepared by God Himself so that we might feast on His servings. But spiritual directors must always be prepared to serve themselves.

The Word of God is primarily the revelation of God to His elect people, revealing His will and His ways. But it also gives insight into how we are to live with wisdom. Therefore, if we are to help others to live skillfully, we will want to be open to what God has to say about the problems and challenges that human beings face. One way to do this is to probe every passage by asking, "What question (implicit or explicit) is God trying to answer?" We should be open to using whatever resources are made available to us through biblical scholarship in finding the answers to these questions. In addition we will want to seek the Holy Spirit's wisdom in making these answers known to us.

Redemptive Praying

A lifestyle that demonstrates the transforming power of Christ will also be a life devoted to prayer. God-focused spiritual counselors enhance their relationship with the heavenly Father through regular times of communication with Him. Such a life has been demonstrated again and again throughout the pages of Scripture.

In the Old Testament we see men like Nehemiah anticipating that the exiles who were returning from captivity would also be experiencing spiritual renewal. And when reports came to him that things were not well with those who had come back to the land of Israel, Nehemiah immediately turned to God in prayer. It was as automatic for Him to talk to God as it was to the king he served in the citadel of Susa (Neh. 1:1).

We see similar practices in the life of our Lord. He not only prayed consistently, but He also taught His followers to be actively engaged in prayer (Luke 5:16; 11:1–13). In fact, Jesus taught that prayer was so important that His followers should not give up the practice, no matter what might be happening around them (Luke 18:1–8). If prayer was important to the Savior as He ministered to people constantly, it should be important to us as well.

As college professors we often have the opportunity to meet with students who are planning to get married. They radiate an excitement about the plans that they are making and the joy that they have in getting to know each other. However, if there is ever any tension in the relationship, it usually can be traced back to problems in communication. As communication goes, so goes the dynamic of the relationship. It is the same when it comes to a relationship with the heavenly Father. The joy and richness of our new life in Christ is often related to the time we spend in prayer. This does not mean that prayer should be highly formal or shaped according to any specific formula. We pray because we have confidence that He wants us to commune with Him. And we pray because it is part of His will for our lives (1 Thess. 5:17).

So how should we pray as people who will be called upon to minister to others? Perhaps the place to start is to examine in our own lives what poses a hindrance to our praying. Sometimes we are ineffective or disinclined to pray because there is sin in our lives (Ps. 66:18). The obvious way to deal with the problem of known sin is to confess it to God and accept the grace that He has promised to bestow upon us (1 John 1:9). Sometimes prayers can be negated because we go through the motions of communicating with God, yet we follow our praying with doubt. The apostle James teaches us that doubting results in a life of instability (James

1:5–8). Another major barrier to an effective, dynamic prayer life has to do with selfishness. Once again James reminded the first-century saints to whom he wrote that they were having conflicts and unanswered prayers because they were focused only on themselves and what they wanted as individuals. His solution to this problem was to have them humble themselves under the authority of God (James 4:1–10). Another form of self-centeredness can be seen in what Peter told Christian husbands. When they failed to demonstrate love and respect to their wives they risked the possibility of their prayers being unanswered (1 Peter 3:7). The obvious solution is to walk in humility before God and extend grace to other members of the body of Christ, especially our mates.

Once we have identified any hindrances that might exist in our prayer lives, we need to be intentional about "redemptive praying." Just as in the study and meditation of Scripture, we need to set aside time to commune with God. In fact, prayer and Bible study will often go hand in hand. As we sense that God is speaking to us from His Word, it will be natural for us to talk to Him just as if we were talking to a close friend or a spouse. However, we will want to be diligent in setting aside time. We should not be legalistic about it, assuming that mornings are better than evenings or that we have to use a specific formula to get to God. We should come into the presence of God with boldness (Heb. 4:16), but that does not mean that we come irreverently (Heb. 12:28–29). In addition, our praying should not always be presenting what we want from God, but it should also include expressions of thanksgiving for the God who has bestowed His abundant grace upon us (Phil. 4:4–7).

In recent years there has been a renewed interest in the practice of the spiritual disciplines. People have returned to ancient writers to glean wisdom from their pursuit of prayer. Many of these wise sages have suggested praying through the Psalms. The reason for such practices is grounded in the very nature of these Hebrew hymns. Many of them express great depth of emotion, emotions that are common to all men and women. Therefore, when people face particularly "dry" times in their prayer lives, it may be wise for them to pray back the Psalms, which God has preserved for our instruction and fellowship with Himself. Learning prayer as "soul conversation" depends on our willingness to participate in two realities: first, developing an awareness of the depth of our own life experiences; second, establishing a willingness to listen to what God may be trying to say to us out of the depths of His heart.

— *Think About It* —

While riding airplanes from city to city, passengers are given safety procedures at the beginning of every flight. Passengers might be inclined not to pay attention, since we have heard the instructions before. But I always try to remember what is being said even though the words are mostly the same from airline to airline. One specific refrain always gets my attention. It says, "If you are seated next to an exit, you may be called upon to help other passengers who need assistance." Every once in a while I am assigned to one of those exit seats, so I pay closer attention, just in case.

Spiritual counselors will want to be extra alert to what God is saying to them as well. One never knows when the Spirit of God might call upon us to minister in His power and on His behalf. That means that our own souls need to be prepared with the right attitudes and actions. You and I can know step-by-step procedures that will help us to uncover sinful worldviews and faulty strategies for living, but we must also be intimate with the Savior. Consider the questions below and ponder what you can do to be better prepared spiritually to live the God-focused, grace-based life He wants for all of us.

- *Think about the life you have lived over the last six months. Where has pride been most evident?*

- *If discontent is a potential sign of not appreciating the grace of God, where has discontent occurred in your life? What does God want you to do about it?*

514

Bandura, A. *Social Learning Theory.* Englewood Cliffs, N.J.: Prentice-Hall, 1977.

Bandura, A., D. Ross, and A. Ross. "Transmission of Aggression Through Imitation of Aggressive Models." *Journal of Abnormal Psychology* (1961): 63, 575–82.

Baxter, Richard. *The Reformed Pastor.* Carlisle, Pa.: Banner of Truth, 1974.

Beck, A. T., and G. Emory. *Cognitive Therapy of Anxiety and Phobic Disorders.* Philadelphia: Center for Cognitive Therapy, 1979.

Bee, Helen. *The Developing Child.* 8th ed. New York: Longman-Addison Wesley Longman, 1997.

———. *The Growing Child: An Applied Approach.* 2d ed. New York: Longman-Addison Wesley Longman, 1999.

Berkhof, L. *Systematic Theology.* 4th & rev. ed. Grand Rapids: Eerdmans, 1949.

Bernstein, Douglas A., and Peggy W. Nash. *Essentials of Psychology.* Ann. inst. ed. Boston: Houghton Mifflin, 1999.

Bloom, Floyd E. *Brain, Mind, and Behavior.* New York: Freeman, 1988.

Boeree, C. George. *Alfred Adler.* 1997. 1 Oct. 1999 <http://www.ship.edu/~cgboeree/adler.html>.

———. *Carl Rogers.* 1998. 6 Jan. 2000 <http://www.ship.edu/~cgboeree/rogers.html>.

———. *George Kelly.* 1997. 14 Jan. 2000 <http://www.ship.edu/~cgboeree/kelly.html>.

———. *Jean Piaget.* 1999. 14 Jan. 2000 <http://www.ship.edu/~cgboeree/piaget.html>.

———. *Rollo May.* 1998. 5 Jan. 2000 <http://www.ship.edu/~cgboeree/may.html>.

———. *Viktor Frankl.* 1998. 5 Jan. 2000 <http://www.ship.edu/~cgboeree/frankl.html>.

Bordwine, James E. *Sola Scriptura, Sola Gratia, Sola Fide, Solo Christo: An Introductory Study for New Members.* 7 July 1998 <http://www.solochristo.org/sermons/sola.htm>.

Boyd, Jeffrey H. "An Insider's Effort to Blow Up Psychiatry." *Journal of Biblical Counseling* 15.3 (Spring 1997): 21–31.

Bridges, Jerry. *Transforming Grace: Living Confidently in God's Unfailing Love.* Colorado Springs: NavPress, 1991.

Broger, John C. *Self-Confrontation: A Manual for In-Depth Discipleship.* Nashville: Nelson, 1994.

Buchanan, Duncan. *The Counseling of Jesus.* Downers Grove, Ill.: InterVarsity, 1985.

Bulkley, Ed. *Why Christians Can't Trust Psychology.* Eugene, Ore.: Harvest House, 1993.

Cairns, Earle E. *Christianity Through the Centuries.* Rev. ed. Grand Rapids: Zondervan, 1974.

Carter, Les, Paul D. Meier, and Frank B. Minirth. *Good 'N' Angry: How to Handle Your Anger Positively.* Grand Rapids: Baker, 1983.

———. *Why Be Lonely? A Guide to a Meaningful Relationship.* Grand Rapids: Baker, 1982.

Cattell, R. B. *Handbook of Multivariable Experimental Psychology.* Chicago: Rand McNally, 1966.

———. *The Scientific Analysis of Personality.* Chicago: Aldine, 1965.

Collins, Gary. *The Biblical Basis of Christian Counseling for People Helpers.* Colorado Springs: NavPress, 1993.

———. *Christian Counseling: A Comprehensive Guide.* Rev. ed. Dallas: Word, 1988.

———. *How to Be a People-Helper.* Santa Ana, Calif.: Vision, 1976.

Collins, Kenneth J. *Soul Care: Deliverance and Renewal Through the Christian Life.* Wheaton, Ill.: Victor, 1995.

Corey, Gerald. *Theory and Practice of Counseling and Psychotherapy.* 4th ed. Pacific Grove, Calif.: Brooks/Cole, 1991.

Crabb, Lawrence J., Jr. *Connecting: Healing for Ourselves and Our Relationships.* Nashville: Word, 1997.

―――. *Effective Biblical Counseling: A Model for Helping Caring Christians Become Capable Counselors.* Grand Rapids: Zondervan, 1977.

―――. *Finding God.* Grand Rapids: Zondervan, 1993.

―――. *The Marriage Builder: A Blueprint for Couples and Counselors.* Grand Rapids: Zondervan, 1982.

―――. *Understanding People.* Grand Rapids: Zondervan, 1987.

―――. "Where Healing Begins." *Leadership* 18 (Spring 1997): 37–40.

Crabb, Lawrence J., Jr., and Dan Allender. *Encouragement: The Key to Caring.* Grand Rapids: Zondervan, 1984.

Craig, Grace J. *Human Development.* 7th ed. Upper Saddle River, New York: Prentice-Hall, 1996.

―――. *Human Development.* 8th ed. Upper Saddle River, New York: Prentice-Hall, 1999.

Cromartie, Michael. *Freud Analyzed: A Conversation with Paul Vitz.* 1999. 23 Dec. 1999 <http://www.eppc.org/library/articles/cromartie/mcvitz.html>.

Daniels, A. M. "The Promise of the Neurosciences." *British Medical Journal* 317.7174 (19 Dec.–26 Dec. 1998): 18.

Demarest, Bruce A. *General Revelation: Historical Views and Contemporary Issues.* Grand Rapids: Zondervan, 1982.

―――. *Satisfy Your Soul: Restoring the Heart of Christian Spirituality.* Colorado Springs: NavPress, 1999.

Dembski, William A. "Converting Matter into Mind: Alchemy and the Philosopher's Stone in Cognitive Science." *Perspectives on Science & Christian Faith* 42.4 (Dec. 1990): 202–26.

Dobkin, Bruce H. *Brain Matters: Stories of a Neurologist and His Patients.* New York: Crown, 1986.

Dowley, Timothy, ed. *Eerdmans's Handbook to the History of Christianity.* Cons. ed. John H. Y. Briggs, Robert D. Linder, and David F. Wright. Grand Rapids: Eerdmans, 1977.

Ellis, Albert. "Toward a Theory of Personality." *Readings in Current Personality Theories.* Ed. R. J. Corsini. Itasca, Ill.: Reacock, 1978.

Elverud, Amber. *The Essentials of Alfred Adler's Theory of Personality.* 1997. 1 Oct. 1999 <http://www.usd.edu/~aelverud/advcomp/adler.html>.

Engler, Barbara. *Personality Theories: An Introduction.* 5th ed. Boston: Houghton Mifflin, 1999.

Erickson, Millard J. *Christian Theology.* Grand Rapids: Baker, 1990.

Erikson, E. H. *Childhood and Society.* New York: Norton, 1963.

———. *Dimensions of a New Identity.* New York: Norton, 1974.

———. *Gandhi's Truth.* New York: Norton, 1969.

———. *Identity, Youth and Crisis.* New York: Norton, 1968.

———. *Insight and Responsibility.* New York: Norton, 1964.

———. *Life History and the Historical Moment.* New York: Norton, 1975.

———. *Young Man Luther.* New York: Norton, 1958.

Eysenck, H. J., and S. Rachman. *The Cause and Cures for Neurosis.* San Diego: Knapp, 1965.

Faw, Harold W. *Psychology in Christian Perspective: An Analysis of Key Issues.* Grand Rapids: Baker, 1995.

Fosdick, Harry E. *The Modern Use of the Bible.* New York: Macmillan, 1933.

Foster, Timothy. *Called to Counsel.* Nashville: Nelson, 1986.

Frankl, V. *The Doctor and the Soul: From Psychotherapy to Logotherapy.* New York: Souvenir Press, 1969.

———. *Man's Search for Meaning: An Introduction to Logotherapy.* New York: Beacon Press, 1959.

————. *The Unconscious God: Psychotherapy and Theology*. New York: Hodder & Stoughton, 1977.

————. *The Unheard Cry for Meaning*. New York: Simon & Schuster, 1978.

Freud, S. *The Complete Psychological Works: Standard Edition*. Ed. J. Strachey. 24 vols. London: Hogarth Press, 1953.

Gaebelein, Frank E. *The Pattern of God's Truth: The Integration of Faith and Learning*. Chicago: Moody, 1968.

Gallagher, Teresa. *ADD Traits in Famous and Talented People . . . a Scrapbook*. 1997. 5 Feb. 2000 <http://borntoexplore.org/famous.htm>.

Gangel, Kenneth O., and James C. Wilhoit. *The Christian Educator's Handbook on Spiritual Formation*. Wheaton, Ill.: Victor-Scripture Press, 1994.

Ganz, Richard. *Psychobabble: The Failure of Modern Psychology and the Biblical Alternative*. Wheaton, Ill.: Crossway, 1993.

————. *The Secret of Self-Control: What God Wants You to Know About Taking Charge of Your Life*. Wheaton, Ill.: Crossway, 1998.

Glausiusz, Josie. "The Chemistry of Obsession." *Discover* 17.6 (June 1996): 36.

Green, Michael. *Theories of Human Development: A Comparative Approach*. Englewood Cliffs, N.J.: Prentice-Hall, 1989.

Gregory, Richard. "Snapshots from the Decade of the Brain: Brainy Mind." *British Medical Journal* 317.7174 (19 Dec.–26 Dec. 1998): 1693–95.

Guinness, Os, and John Seel, eds. *No God but God: Breaking with the Idols of Our Age*. Chicago: Moody, 1992.

Harlow, J. M. "Recovery from the Passage of an Iron Bar Through the Head." *Journal of the Massachusetts Medical Society* 2 (1868): 327–47.

Harvey, Robert W., and David G. Benner. *Understanding and Facilitating Forgiveness*. Grand Rapids: Baker, 1996.

Heard, Warren J. "Eschatologically Oriented Psychology: A New Paradigm for the Integration of Psychology and Christianity." *God and Culture: Essays in Honor of Carl F. H. Henry.* Grand Rapids: Eerdmans, 1993.

Hindson, Ed, and Howard Eyrich, gen. eds. *Totally Sufficient.* Eugene, Ore.: Harvest House, 1997.

Hinrichs, Bruce. "Brain Research and Folk Psychology." *The Humanist* 57.2 (Mar.–Apr. 1997): 26–31.

Hoff, Lee Ann. *People in Crisis: Understanding and Helping.* 3d ed. Redwood City, Calif.: Addison-Wesley, 1989.

Hurding, Roger F. *The Tree of Healing: Psychological and Biblical Foundations for Counseling and Pastoral Care.* Grand Rapids: Zondervan, 1985.

Jeeves, Malcolm A. *Human Nature at the Millennium: Reflection on the Integration of Psychology and Christianity.* Grand Rapids: Baker, 1997.

Johnston, J. Kirk. *When Counseling Is Not Enough: Biblical Answers for Those Who Still Struggle.* Grand Rapids: Discovery House, 1994.

Jones, D. Gareth. *Our Fragile Brains: A Christian Perspective on Brain Research.* Downers Grove, Ill.: InterVarsity, 1981.

Jones, Robert D. "Anger Against God." *Journal of Biblical Counseling* 14.3 (Spring 1996): 15–20.

Kagan, J. *Galen's Prophecy.* New York: Basic, 1994.

Kegan, R. *The Evolving Self.* Cambridge, Ma.: Harvard Univ., 1982.

Kelly, G. A. *The Psychology of Personal Constructs.* 2 vols. New York: Norton, 1955.

Koessler, John. *God Our Father.* Chicago: Moody, 1999.

Kollar, Charles Allen. *Solution-Focused Pastoral Counseling: An Effective Short-Term Approach for Getting People Back on Track.* Grand Rapids: Zondervan, 1997.

Kraft, Charles H. *Christianity in Culture: A Study in Dynamic Biblical Theologizing in Cross-Cultural Perspective.* Maryknoll, N.Y.: Orbis, 1984.

Kramer, Peter D. *Perspectives: Complex Gifts.* 1996. 23 Dec. 1999 <http://www.cmeinc.com/exclusive/perspectives0396.html>.

Kruis, John G. Quick *Scripture Reference for Counseling.* 2d ed. Grand Rapids: Baker, 1994.

Ladd, George Eldon. *A Theology of the New Testament.* Grand Rapids: Eerdmans, 1982.

LeBar, Lois E., and James E. Plueddemann. *Education That Is Christian: The Classic Bestseller—With Fresh Insights for Today's Families, Churches, and Schools.* Wheaton, Ill.: Victor-Scripture Press, 1989.

MacArthur, John, and Wayne Mack. *Introduction to Biblical Counseling.* Dallas: Word, 1994.

Macaulay, Ranald, and Jerram Barrs. *Being Human: The Nature of Spiritual Experience.* Downers Grove, Ill.: InterVarsity, 1978.

Machen, J. Gresham. *The Christian View of Man.* Edinburgh, Scot.: Banner of Truth-McCorquodale, 1984.

Mack, Wayne A. *A Homework Manual for Biblical Living.* Vol. 1. Phillipsburg, N.J.: Presb. & Ref., 1979.

MacKay, Donald M. *Human Science and Human Dignity.* Downers Grove, Ill.: InterVarsity, 1979.

Maslow, A. *Motivation and Personality.* New York: Harper & Row, 1970.

Matthews, Robert. *Our Leaders Have It in Their Genes, It Seems.* 1999. 20 Apr. 1999 <http://www.smh.com.au/cgi-bin/archive.cgi>.

May, R. *The Courage to Create.* New York: Norton, 1975.

———. *The Cry of Myth.* New York: Norton, 1991.

———. *The Discovery of Being.* New York: Norton, 1983.

———. *Freedom and Destiny.* New York: Norton, 1981.

———. *Love and Will.* New York: Norton, 1969.

————. *Man's Search for Himself.* New York: Norton, 1953.

————. *The Meaning of Anxiety.* New York: Norton, 1977.

————. *Power and Innocence.* New York: Norton, 1972.

————. *Psychology and the Human Dilemma.* New York: Van Norstrand Reinhold, 1967.

McDonald, H. D. *The Christian View of Man.* Westchester, Ill.: Crossway, 1985.

McMinn, Mark. *Christians in the Crossfire.* Newberg, Ore.: Barclay, 1997.

————. *Excellence and Ethics in Counseling Resources for Christian Counseling.* Vol. 30. Dallas: Word, 1991.

————. *Psychology, Theology and Spirituality in Christian Counseling.* Wheaton, Ill.: Tyndale, 1996.

Miller, Patricia H. *Theories of Developmental Psychology.* 3d ed. New York: Freeman, 1993.

Montgomery, Dan. *Beauty in the Stone: How God Sculpts You into the Image of Christ.* Nashville: Nelson, 1996.

Moorehead, Bob. *Counsel Yourself and Others from the Bible.* Sisters, Ore.: Multnomah, 1994.

Murray, H. A. *Exploration in Personality.* Oxford Univ., 1966.

Neisser, Ulric. "Cognitive Psychology." *Grolier Multimedia Encyclopedia Online.* 2000. 27 May 1999 <http://gme.grolier.com/cgi-bin/gme_bp?artbaseid=0066790>.

Newman, Barbara M., and Philip R. Newman. *Development Through Life: A Psychosocial Approach.* 7th ed. Belmont, Calif.: Brooks/Cole, 1999.

Oden, Thomas C. *Pastoral Counsel.* Grand Rapids: Baker, 1987. Vol. 3 of *Classical Pastoral Care.*

O'Driscoll, Kieran, and John Paul Leach. "No Longer Gage: An Iron Bar Through the Head: Early Observations of Personality Change After Injury to the Prefrontal Cortex." *British Medical Journal* 317.7174 (19 Dec.–26 Dec. 1998): 1673–74.

Ogden, Greg. *The New Reformation: Returning the Ministry to the People of God.* Grand Rapids: Zondervan, 1990.

Ohlschlager, George W., and Peter T. Mosgofian. *Law for the Christian Counselor.* Dallas: Word, 1992. Vol. 6 of *Contemporary Christian Counseling.*

Oliver, Gary J. "Sanctification, Theology and the Counseling Process." *Focal Point* 17.4 (Fall 1997): 6–7.

Oliver, Gary J., Monte Hasz, and Matthew Richburg. *Promoting Change Through Brief Therapy in Christian Counseling.* Wheaton, Ill.: Tyndale, 1997.

Olson, G. Keith. *Counseling Teenagers.* Loveland, Colo.: Group, 1984.

Ortberg, John. *The Life You've Always Wanted.* Grand Rapids: Zondervan, 1997.

Pache, Rene. *The Inspiration and Authority of Scripture.* Trans. Helen I. Needham. Chicago: Moody, 1979.

Packer, J. I. *Knowing Man.* Westchester, Ill.: Crossway, 1979. Rpt. of *For Man's Sake.* 1978.

Papert, Seymour. "Time 100: Child Psychology." *Time* 3 March 1999.

Piaget, J. *The Child and Reality.* New York: Basic, 1954.

———. *The Child's Conception of the World.* New York: Harcourt, Brace, 1929.

———. *The Moral Judgement of the Child.* Glencoe, Ill.: Free Press, 1932.

———. *The Origins of Intelligence in Children.* New York: International Univ., 1952.

Personality Styles Research. 23 Apr. 1999 <http://www.insight-learning.com/ researchcolors.htm>.

Pervin, Lawrence. "Personality." *Grolier Multimedia Encyclopedia Online.* 2000. 27 May 1999 <http://gme.grolier.com/cgi-bin/gme_bp?artbaseid=0225130>.

Powlison, David A. "Anger Part I: Understanding Anger." *Journal of Biblical Counseling.* 14.1 (Fall 1995): 40.

———. "Anger Part II: Three Lies About Anger and the Transforming Truth." *Journal of Biblical Counseling* 14.2 (Winter 1996): 12–21.

———. "Competent to Counsel? The History of a Conservative Protestant Anti-Psychiatry Movement." Diss. Univ. of Pennsylvania, 1996.

———. "What Is Biblical Counseling, Anyway?" *Journal of Biblical Counseling* 16.1 (Fall 1997): 2–6.

Reiss, A. J. and Roth, J. A. (Eds.) *Understanding and Preventing Violence.* Washington, D.C.: National Academy Press, 1993.

Restak, Richard M. *The Brain.* New York: Bantam, 1984.

Rogers, C. A. *Client-Centered Therapy: Its Current Practice, Implications and Theory.* Boston: Houghton Mifflin, 1951.

———. *On Becoming a Person: A Therapist's View of Psychotherapy.* Boston: Houghton Mifflin, 1961.

———. *A Way of Being.* Boston: Houghton Mifflin, 1980.

Romeo, Felicia F. *Understanding Anorexia Nervosa.* Springfield, Ill.: C.C. Thomas, 1986.

Rulovo, Ann P., and Jennifer L. Rotondo. "Diamonds in the Rough: Implicit Personality Theories and Views of Partner and Self." *Personality and Social Psychology Bulletin* 24.7 (July 1998): 750–58.

Schuerger, Richard. *Phineas Gage: NeuroHistory.* 1998. 12 Mar. 1999 <http://neuroscience.miningco.com/library/weekly/aa021898.htm?pid=2789&cob=home>.

Scott, Elizabeth. *Anabaptists: Separate by Choice, Marginal by Force.* 1995. 6 July 1998 <http://www.anabaptists.org/history/sepamarg.html>.

Seifert, Kelvin L. *Constructing a Psychology of Teaching and Learning.* Boston: Houghton Mifflin, 1999.

Shelley, Bruce. *Church History in Plain Language.* Dallas: Word, 1982.

Skinner, B. F. *The Behavior of Organisms.* New York: Appleton-Century-Crofts, 1938.

———. *Beyond Freedom and Dignity.* New York: Knopf, 1971.

———. *Contingencies of Reinforcement.* New York: Appleton-Century-Crofts, 1969.

———. *Science and Human Behavior.* New York: Macmillan, 1953.

Stanger, Frank Bateman. *Spiritual Formation in the Local Church.* Grand Rapids: Zondervan, 1989.

Stec, Astrid M., and Douglas A. Bernstein, eds. *Psychology: Fields of Application.* Boston: Houghton Mifflin, 1999.

Stevens, Darryl. *Essentials of Adlerian Theory.* 2000. 1 Oct. 1999 <http://www.montevallo.edu/coe/clf/ceegeepage/community/dtslectures/adler/default.htm>.

Stevens, R. Paul. *Liberating the Laity: Equipping All the Saints for Ministry.* Downers Grove, Ill.: InterVarsity, 1985.

Stott, John R. W. *The Cross of Christ.* Downers Grove, Ill.: InterVarsity, 1986.

Swihart, Judson J., and Gerald C. Richardson. *Counseling in Times of Crisis.* Waco, Tex.: Word, 1987. Vol. 7 of *Resources for Christian Counseling.* Ed. Gary R. Collins.

Talan, Jamie. "Antibiotics for Anorexia?" *Psychology Today* (May–June 1998): 20.

Tan, Siang-Yang. *Lay Counseling: Equipping Christians for a Helping Ministry.* Grand Rapids: Zondervan, 1991.

Taylor, Glenn, and Rod Wilson. *Helping Angry People.* Grand Rapids: Baker, 1997.

Tertullian. *De praescriptione haereticorum.* 24 July 2000 <http://www.tertullian.org/works/de_praescriptione_haereticorum.htm>.

Thomas, Robert L. *I and II Thessalonians.* Grand Rapids: Zondervan, 1978. Vol. 11 of *Expositor's Bible Commentary.* Ed. Frank E. Gaebelein.

Thompson, Richard F. *The Brain: An Introduction to Neuroscience.* New York: Freeman, 1985.

Thornton, Stephen P. *Sigmund Freud.* 1997. 15 July 1999 <http://www.utm.edu/research/iep/f/freud.htm>.

Thurman, Chris. *The Lies We Believe.* Nashville: Nelson, 1989.

———. *The Truths We Must Believe.* Nashville: Nelson, 1991.

Toole, David C. "Divine Ecology and the Apocalypse: A Theological Description of Natural Disasters and the Environmental Crisis." *Theology Today* 55.4 (Jan. 1999): 547–61.

Turner, Jeffrey S., and Donald B. Helms. *Lifespan Development.* 4th ed. Fort Worth: Holt, Rinehart and Winston, 1991.

VanVonderen, Jeff. *Tired of Trying to Measure Up.* Minneapolis: Bethany House, 1989.

Vernick, Leslie. "Getting to the Heart of the Matter in Marriage Counseling." *Journal of Biblical Counseling* 12.3 (Spring 1994): 31–35.

Vitz, P. C. *Psychology as Religion: The Cult of Self-Worship.* 2nd ed. Grand Rapids: Eerdmans, 1994.

Voges, Ken, and Ron Braund. *Understanding How Others Misunderstand You: A Unique and Proven Plan for Strengthening Personal Relationships.* Chicago: Moody, 1990.

Ward, Waylon O. *The Bible in Counseling.* Chicago: Moody, 1977.

Watson, John B. *Behaviorism.* New York: Norton, 1930.

Weiten, Wayne. *Psychology: Themes and Variations.* 3rd ed. Pacific Grove, Calif.: Brooks/Cole, 1995.

Weitzenfeld, Julian. "History of Psychology." *Grolier Multimedia Encyclopedia Online.* 2000. 27 May 1999 <http://gme.grolier.com/cgi-bin/gme_bp?artbaseid=0237885>.

Welch, Edward T. *When People Are Big and God Is Small.* Phillipsburg, N.J.: Presb. & Ref., 1997.

———. "Who Are We? Needs, Longings and the Image of God in Man." *Journal of Biblical Counseling* 13.1 (Fall 1994): 25–38.

Wilhelmsen, Sonja, Stein Inge Asmul, and Oyvind Meistad. *CSCL— A Brief Overview and Interesting Links for Further Study*. 1998. 24 Jan. 2000 <http://www.uib.no/people/sinis/CSCL/web_struktur-834.htm>.

Wilson, Earl D. *Counseling and Guilt*. Waco, Tex.: Word, 1987. Vol. 8 of *Resources for Christian Counseling*.

Wolf, Ernest S. "Psychoanalysis." *Grolier Multimedia Encyclopedia Online*. 2000. 27 May 1999 <http://gme.grolier.com/cgi-bin/gme_bp?artbaseid=0237820>.

Wolfe, Pat, and Ron Brandt. "What Do We Know from Brain Research?" *Educational Leadership* 56.3 (Nov. 1998): 8–13.

Worthington, Everett L. *When Someone Asks for Help: A Practical Guide for Counseling*. Downers Grove, Ill.: InterVarsity, 1982.

*I*NDEX

monism, 73–79
  semi-materialistic monism, 77–79
  spiritual monism, 74–75
  trichotomist view, 69–71
constructivist view. *See* cognitive paradigm of personality
Copply, Jean, 127, 132–33
core beliefs. *See* motivations
cosmos (the world), 95
Costa, Paul T., 154, 164
counseling. *See also* spiritual counsel
  Bible-and approach, 46–47, 50
  Bible-only approach, 44–46, 50
  Bible-over approach, 47–50
  client/counselor relationship, 68, 276–77
  complexity, 84, 117
  resistance to, 278
  and Scripture, 44–50, 85
  techniques, 284–85
courage, 244
covenant, marriage, 478
Covey, Stephen, 43
Crabb, Larry
  on God's goodness, 494
  on guilt, 456–57
  on human will, 321–22
  on marriage, 476, 486
  seven-stage counseling process, 341–42
  on shepherding (lay counseling), 306, 328
  on significance, 496
creation, 57–58, 64–66
creative values, 239
creativity, 66, 244, 247
crisis events, 316–18. *See also* suffering/struggles
Cromartie, Michael, 208
culture and society, 232
curiosity, 255–56

value, human. *See* worth

values

 developing new, 244

 hidden, 325–26

 loss of traditional, 243

Van Til, Cornelius, 26

VanVonderen, Jeff, 449

Vernick, Leslie, 485–86

vicarious reinforcement, 174

Viennese Analytic Society, 271

violence in media, 170, 177

Vitz, Paul, 208, 248

volition, 67, 237, 275, 321–22

Walden Two (Skinner), 171

Washington, George, 133

water, 79–80

Watson, John B., 145, 167–68, 171

weaker brother principle, 51

Weiten, Wayne, 154

Welch, Edward T., 72, 405, 477

Wernicke, Carl, 159

will, human. *See* volition

Wilson, Earl, 462, 465

Wilson, Rod, 431

Wood, Kerry, 106–7

Word of God. *See* Scripture

world (cosmos), 95

worldview, 88–94, 479

worshipers

 created to be, 477

 marriage partners as, 486, 487

 redemptive worship, 506–7

worth, 61–62, 178–79, 218–19

Worthington, Everett, 341

Y2K bug, national response to, 228